Classical Rhetoric and Its Christian and Secular Tradition from Ancient to Modern Times

Classical Rhetoric and Its Christian and Secular Tradition from Ancient to Modern Times

by George A. Kennedy

The University of North Carolina Press

Chapel Hill

© 1980 The University of North Carolina Press
All rights reserved
Manufactured in the United States of America
ISBN 0-8078-1401-6

Cloth Edition ISBN 0-8078-1401-6
Paperback Edition ISBN 0-8078-4058-0
Library of Congress Catalog Card Number 79-9295

Library of Congress Cataloging in Publication Data

Kennedy, George Alexander, 1928–
Classical rhetoric and its Christian and secular
tradition from ancient to modern times.

Bibliography: p.
Includes index.
1. Rhetoric—History. I. Title.
PN183.K4   808   79-9295
ISBN 0-8078-1401-6
ISBN 0-8078-4058-0 pbk.

TO MARY LEE KENNEDY
*On the approach of our twenty-fifth
wedding anniversary*

4-22-80

Contents

CONTENTS

CONTENTS

Preface

This book is intended to be a short introduction to a vast subject, the history of man's effort to accomplish his purposes by speech. That history as a whole cannot yet be written; the part of it which can be best known is the theory of rhetoric which emerged in Greek and Roman times and was studied, commented upon, or reinterpreted down to our own age. Even the history of this tradition must be viewed as a preliminary statement, for many aspects of it have not been thoroughly explored. For the medieval and renaissance periods in particular we do not have adequate texts, to say nothing of evaluation. But progress is being made and in another decade it may be possible for me or someone else to rewrite this book with greater accuracy.

The audience I envision is primarily made up of English-speaking students and nonspecialists in the classics who are interested in discourse in a variety of ways, including religious discourse, and do not have the special tools to study it in works now available or who wish to go beyond the limits of their special training. I have deliberately avoided much of the apparatus of scholarship which appears in my earlier books on rhetoric, but have given reference to fuller discussions and where available have identified English translations of the works here discussed. This book could thus be used as a text for the study of the history of rhetoric if accompanied by reading of the major writers of each period.

I am very much indebted to Fr. John W. O'Malley of the University of Detroit and Dr. H. Kenneth Snipes of The University of North Carolina at Chapel Hill for their comments and suggestions about portions of the manuscript; also to George S. Angell and Paul J. Korczak of The University of North Carolina at Chapel Hill and to Nancy J. Honeycutt, Juanita Mason, and Erline Nipper of the classics department staff; and finally to Lewis Bateman and Laura S. Oaks of The University of North Carolina Press and two anonymous readers for the Press.

Chapel Hill
5 February 1979

Classical Rhetoric and Its Christian and Secular Tradition from Ancient to Modern Times

The lyvelie pithhe of Platoes witte and Aristots ingeine,
The pleasant vayne of Cicero, and of Quintiliane
The judgment highe, here thou maiest see: therefor if thou be wise,
No farther seeke but in this booke thy self doe exercise.

Roland M'Kilwein,
The Logike of the Most Excellent Philosopher,
P. Ramus Martyr

Chapter 1
Traditional and
Conceptual Rhetoric

Classical rhetoric is superficially very easy to describe. It is that theory of discourse developed by Greeks and Romans of the classical period, applied both in oratory and in literary genres, and taught in schools in antiquity, in the Greek and western Middle Ages, and throughout the Renaissance and early modern period. Problems emerge, however, as soon as an effort is made to define the characteristic contents of this theory. How does it differ from universal or natural rhetoric anywhere else in the world? At what point in history, if ever, does the rhetoric taught in western schools cease to be "classical" and begin to be predominantly some other, postclassical or modern rhetoric? Is this rhetoric an intellectual faculty, a science of persuasion, an art of speaking well, or a means of literary composition? The most famous discussion of rhetoric in Greek is surely that by Aristotle, but it was just as surely not rhetoric as described by Aristotle that was taught in schools for the next two thousand years. The most influential discussions of rhetoric written in antiquity are doubtless those by Cicero, but there is very little in Ciceronian rhetoric which is original with Cicero, and as great as his influence was in the West, he was almost totally unknown in the Greek-speaking East. A definition of classical rhetoric that excludes Aristotle or excludes Cicero or excludes Byzantium is not a very satisfactory definition. This book as a whole is an attempt to define classical rhetoric and its tradition by examining the various strands of thought which are woven together in different ways at different times. Though these strands are sometimes reduced to slender threads, they do not totally ravel out of the fabric.

Certain questions repeatedly occur in the study of the classical tradition in rhetoric and help to define its nature. Among them are: What is the relationship of the art or discipline called rhetoric to the art or discipline called dialectic, the art of reasoning? What is the relationship of rhetoric to oral speech in contrast to writing? What relative weight of importance at difference stages in the history of classical rhetoric is given to each of the factors in the speech act—the speaker, the speech itself, and the audience? What is the relationship of classical rhetoric to political and legal institutions? To poetics and literary history? To religion, in particular to Christianity and the Judeo-Christian rhetorical tradition?

Rhetoric is a form of communication. The author of a communication has some kind of purpose, and rhetoric certainly includes the ways by which he seeks to accomplish that purpose. The ancient world commonly thought of this purpose as persuasion, but meant by that something much looser and more inclusive than persuasion as understood by a modern social scientist. Purposes cover a whole spectrum from converting hearers to a view opposed to that they previously held, to implanting a conviction not otherwise considered, to the deepening of belief in a view already favorably entertained, to a demonstration of the cleverness of the author, to teaching or exposition. In practice almost every communication is rhetorical in that it uses some device to try to affect the thought, actions, or emotions of an audience, but the degree of rhetoric varies enormously. The white pages of the telephone directory are relatively nonrhetorical. Their one common artistic technique is alphabetization, and except for occasional flashes of bold type their author does not seek to influence a reader to call one number rather than another. The yellow pages are distinctly more rhetorical, seeking to make an effect upon the audience and using a variety of devices of emphasis to do so.

Certain definitions may help us trace the threads of classical rhetoric. One of these is the concept of "primary" rhetoric, in both the logical and the historical sense. Primary rhetoric is the conception of rhetoric as held by the Greeks when the art was, as they put it, "invented" in the fifth century B.C. Rhetoric was "primarily" an art of persuasion; it was primarily used in civic life; it was primarily oral. Primary rhetoric involves an act of enunciation on a specific occasion; in itself it has no text, though subsequently an enunciation can be treated as a text. The primacy of primary rhetoric is a fundamental fact in the classical tradition: throughout the Roman Empire, whatever was the real situation of their students, teachers of rhetoric took as their nominal goal the training of persuasive public speakers; even in the early Middle Ages when there was reduced practical opportunity to exercise civic rhetoric, the definition and content of rhetoric as set forth by Isidore and Alcuin, for example, show the same civic bent; the revival of classical rhetoric in renaissance Italy is foreshadowed by the renewed need for civic rhetoric in the cities of the twelfth and thirteenth centuries; and the great period of neoclassical rhetoric is the time when public speaking emerges as a major force in France, England, and America, both in church and in state.

"Secondary" rhetoric, on the other hand, is the apparatus of rhetorical techniques clustering around discourse or art forms when those techniques are not being used for their primary oral purpose. In secondary rhetoric the speech act is not of central importance; that role is taken over by the text. The most frequent manifestations of secondary rhetoric are commonplaces, figures of speech and thought, and tropes in elaborate writing. Much literature, art, and informal discourse is decorated by secondary rhetoric, which may be a mannerism of the historical period in which it is composed. Secondary rhetoric contributes to the purpose of the speaker or writer, but indirectly or at a secondary level. It may demonstrate the author's education, eloquence, or skill, and it often makes him more acceptable to his audience. Forms of etiquette are largely made up of secondary rhetoric. Secondary rhetoric is also used to secure varying patterns of emphasis on the surface of a communication, relieving the tedium of the audience and helping to point to what is most important in the communication. It is thus not insignificant rhetorically. This is especially true in the case of mystical or highly poetic expression, where noncognitive goals are sought by patterns of style or associations of images (for example, in the *Confessions* of Saint Augustine).

It has been a persistent characteristic of classical rhetoric, in almost every phase of its ancient and modern history, to move from primary into secondary forms. For this phenomenon the Italian term *letteraturizzazione* is convenient shorthand.[1] *Letteraturizzazione* is the tendency of rhetoric to shift its focus from persuasion to narration, from civic to personal contexts, and from discourse to literature, including poetry. Such slippage can be observed in the Hellenistic period, in the Roman Empire, in medieval France, and in the sixteenth and eighteenth centuries throughout Europe. The primary reason for the *letteraturizzazione* of rhetoric is probably the place given rhetoric in education and the recurring tendency to teach it by rote to young children rather than to make it a more intellectually demanding advanced discipline, but the development is of course directly influenced by the opportunities, or lack of opportunities, open to primary rhetoric throughout history.

There is also a secondary rhetoric in arts other than literature. In antiquity the analogy between rhetoric and painting or sculpture was repeatedly noticed, by Aristotle, Cicero, and Quintilian among others, and the analogy to architecture is occasionally mentioned as well. Writers on the arts sometimes borrow terminology from rhetoric. In the Renaissance and later, treatises on music, painting, and other arts were often based on the structure and categories of classical rhetoric.

All arts, including the arts of discourse, employ techniques to accomplish their purposes. The author may know how to use these techniques, but he may never have taken thought to define them, catalogue them, or conceptualize them. That is, he may be unable to state general concepts describing what he does when speaking, even though he may be a good speaker. One of the most remarkable features of the classical period in Greece is the conscious conceptualization of human faculties, including grammar, rhetoric, logic, and poetics. Conceptualization of great art is, however, always partial and incomplete, and great artists go beyond anything which can be analyzed in the critical systems of their own times. Virgil, Augustine, Dante, Shakespeare, and Racine, for example, were all acquainted with systems of rhetoric, but analysis of their creations in terms of the rhetorical theory of their times will do only partial justice to their total achievement. Literary criticism is a form of rhetoric which attempts to describe techniques available to artists, or used by artists in the past, to fulfill their purposes. It is itself a creative art in that it must constantly seek to conceptualize achievements which burst the limits of rhetoric as known heretofore.

Traditional or natural rhetoric occurs in all societies. It is best observed in traditional societies which have felt little or no direct influence from western civilization or in records of speech before the advent of conscious conceptualization. The subject of traditional rhetoric has been rather little studied by rhetoricians, though anthropologists have collected a considerable amount of information in their study of social or political structures and functions in various societies. Oratory is an important avenue to power, for example, among the Maori, the aboriginal inhabitants of New Zealand, who in practice seem to expect good speech to show qualities of creativity, erudition, appropriateness, and dramatic power, though they have not conceptualized these requirements into "virtues" or "characters" of style as did Greek rhetoricians.[2] In Tikopia in the Solomon Islands various words are used for different kinds of speech-making: *oriori* is to make formal address of praise and thanks; *fono* is to address a formal assembly, either to announce a decision or to give advice on a particular topic.[3] Each of these forms has conventions which are well understood in the society but have not been conceptualized except by the visiting anthropologists who have studied them. The conventions could be restated as categories and rules for epideictic and deliberative oratory. In Tengahpadang on Bali public address generally shows four main parts: in the first the speaker indicates his lack of knowledge or fitness to speak; in the second he states what is commonly known and accepted under discussion; in the third he advances his own opinion; in the fourth he "surrenders to the banjar," or indicates his willingness to follow what the assembly decides.[4] A Balinese orator is ideally brave, refined, sweet-speaking, and able to captivate an audience. All of these qualities could be conceptualized or restated as categories of a rhetorical system, and many are not dissimilar to categories of Greek rhetoric.

Although not conceptualized, most traditional rhetoric is conscious rhetoric. The speaker knows what he wants to say and he is aware of topics, formulae, or patterns of discourse, but he would not be able to give a systematic description of his method, at least not without considerable thought and prompting. In the *Apology* (21e), Plato makes Socrates ridicule the inability of fifth-century Athenian politicians and poets to describe what they were nevertheless often able to do well.

Conceptualization of rhetoric takes place in varying degrees in advanced societies depending on the practical need for it, the extent to which the society is introspective, and the rhetorical values which the society holds. Some consciousness of rhetorical method is evident in ancient India, for example, in the sixth century B.C. in the Buddha's advice to his followers about preaching, and a group of treatises on poetics in Sanskrit deals with what has here been called secondary rhetoric.[5] Even greater interest in rhetorical methods can be found in ancient China, as may be seen, for example, in some writings by and about Confucius in the sixth and fifth centuries B.C. and in the treatise *Difficulties in the Way of Persuasion* by Han Fei Tzu, composed in the third century B.C.[6] Neither in India nor in China, however, did rhetoric become a separate discipline with a fully developed theory, its own logical structure, and a corpus of pragmatic handbooks. Such a degree of conceptualization is apparently found only in the Greco-Roman world, where it begins to appear coincident with the rise of Greek philosophy and other forms of conceptualization in the fifth and fourth centuries B.C. Direct connexion between the tendency toward conceptualization of rhetoric in India, China, and Greece is unlikely, even though the developments are roughly contemporary. On the other hand, most subsequent rhetoric all over the world has been influenced by Greek ideas on the subject. This influence exists in two forms: the oratory of traditional societies has been subtly influenced by western conventions since the first contacts with Europeans, and the description of systems of traditional rhetoric has been influenced by categories of Greek rhetoric. A good example of the latter is the description of Chinese rhetoric made by Jean-Baptiste DuHalde in the early eighteenth century on the basis of reports by Jesuit missionaries.[7]

Conceptualized rhetoric may be induced or deduced. It is induced if the system is described objectively on the basis of a traditional practice. At least in theory a modern anthropologist could do this with a traditional rhetoric which has been little contaminated by western traditions. Conceptualized rhetoric is deduced when certain principles are accepted by a theorist and made the basis of a logical system of rhetorical rules. The principles may come from another system of rhetoric, or they may be philosophical or psychological assumptions made by the conceptualizer. One of the first problems facing the historian of rhetoric in Greece is whether the conceptualization which occurred there was inductive or deductive. Corax and Tisias, who are discussed in the next chapter, are traditionally described as "inventors" of rhetoric. "Invent" (from Latin *invenire*) literally means "to discover or find out," and only secondarily comes to mean "create," and much the same is true of the Greek word *heuriskein*. Greek rhetorical practice to some extent represents a continuum from the Homeric poems through the time of conceptualization, but the founders of conceptualized rhetoric in Greece were also doctrinaire. They clung to certain rational principles which cannot with confidence be illustrated from the tradition or are at least not much earlier than their own times. The most important of these doctrines is argument from probability. It seems likely that Corax and Tisias and certain Greek sophists apprehended the utility of argument from probability, even though it had as yet been little used in practical oratory, and made it the basis of a deductive rhetoric. Later writers on classical rhetoric sometimes referred to this action as though induced from trial-and-error experiment, but that conclusion was an assumption on their part without evidence.[8]

It should, in theory, be possible to generate a new rhetoric like a new language or a new algebra, and some modern rhetoricians seek to do so. There are obvious limits to this, however, and there may well exist a basic or "deep" human rhetoric, universal to mankind, defined by man's abilities to make certain sounds, symbols, and motions and by the nature of his brain. One of the objectives of the historical study of rhetoric is to come to an understanding of the common ground of rhetorics and to see what may be universal and what may be historical accident. There certainly exists a variety of historical manifestations of rhetoric, more or less defined by other values and functions of culture and more or less influenced by earlier historical rhetorics.

In an attempt to define the nature of rhetoric and its historical manifestations we are fortunate in having on record descriptions of the circumstances and contents of speeches that were composed before the conceptualization of rhetoric. Such records exist in India and China, and in the West are represented in their most remarkable form by the Homeric poems in Greece and by the Old Testament. It is true, of course, that neither of these works is a verbatim account of what was said by orators. What matters for our purposes, however, is that the statement of the tradition, the version of the text which we have, in each case with minor variations, antedates the conceptualization of rhetoric in the eastern Mediterranean. The *Iliad* and *Odyssey* arc the written versions of an oral epic tradition which developed between 1250 B.C., which is the approximate archeological date of the fall of Troy, and about 750 B.C., when the Phoenician alphabet was introduced into Greece and the epics written down in substantially the form we have. At the very latest the poems thus represent a picture of rhetoric two hundred years earlier than its conceptualization in Greece. The Old Testament books in substantially their present form represent a time span of composition roughly from the eighth to the fifth century B.C. The arrangement here adopted will be to consider Homeric rhetoric as the basis of the rhetorical traditions of Greece and then in chapter 7 to return to Old Testament rhetoric and the tradition which it developed.

Homeric Rhetoric

The world of the Homeric poems is an oral society. It has its own oral literature, the songs of bards on heroic or mythological subjects. How such a literature can be created and transmitted is now reasonably well understood from modern study of the oral poets of Yugoslavia and other areas.[9] Bards do not memorize songs, but recreate them on each delivery from common elements—the structure of folktales; themes or incidents useful in the telling of many stories, such as festivals, banquets, duels, or journeys, adapted to the needs of the particular occasion; and formulae or verbatim repetitions consisting of whole passages, single lines, phrases, or combinations of words useful as building blocks in the narrative. A bard learns his craft by listening to other bards, trying to imitate them, and building up a reservoir of structures, themes, and formulae. In the singing of a really successful bard there is also an element which neither he nor his audience can explain, his "inspiration." The successful bard does not call on a rational understanding of his art: he feels a god singing to him. This is not a literary fiction. Some modern scholars believe that until the end of the second millenium the human brain had not achieved spatial consciousness as we know it, that one hemisphere "spoke" to the individual without his understanding it; it was literally heard as the voice of a god. Vestiges of this phenomenon are said to survive in inspired poetry, oracles, and schizophrenia.[10]

In Homeric society and other traditional societies the world over, and to a degree also in more complex society, public speaking is learned the same way. The would-be orator listens to speakers and acquires a sense of oratorical conventions and of what is effective. He does not work out a theory, but he imitates, and sometimes succeeds. He builds up a technique of organizing the subject and a collection of examples, of stock phrases, of themes. The Homeric orator is always understood as speaking extempore, and when he is at his best he has a gift of speech, an inspiration from the gods, which is something more than his own understanding. To a limited extent this phenomenon continues throughout the history of great oratory.

Achilles, the hero of the *Iliad*, was taught by Phoenix to be a speaker of words and a doer of deeds (*Iliad* 9.443). These are the two great areas of distinction for the Homeric hero, and Achilles and Odysseus excel at both. Because the Homeric poems were the textbook out of which the Greeks, and later the Romans, learned to read, and were venerated almost as the bibles of the culture, the attitude toward speech in the *Iliad* strongly influenced the conception of the orator in Greco-Roman civilization. The classical orator is usually heroic; he puts the stamp of his personality on his speech, he imposes his will on others. In contrast, the role of the speaker is much less emphasized in the rhetoric of India or China, where harmony rather than victory is often the goal. The classical orator is a fighter in a lonely contest.

Unlike Achilles, Telemachus, the son of Odysseus, has been left at home, and in the opening books of the *Odyssey* he is faced with the difficult situation of how to deal with the suitors besetting his mother. He has had no model or critic in oratory. In the second book of the *Odyssey* he does succeed in summoning an assembly of the men of Ithaca, before whom he presents his complaints, but he lacks adequate authority to prevail, even though Athene gives him a physical charisma beyond his years. The Homeric orator must have authority. This only partly comes from his position in society by birth; it is an authority which he himself must bolster by what he has done, by how he carries himself, by what sanctions he can bring to support his words. Because personality is important, different styles of delivery can be expected. Menelaus spoke rapidly, clearly, and simply, while Odysseus burst out in a veritable storm of oratory (*Iliad* 3.212–224). Nestor, oldest of the orators, was garrulous, but his words were like honey (*Iliad* 1.247–

252). Such differences become important in defining the characters of style and delivery in classical rhetoric.

Classical rhetoricians later became interested in defining the categories of oratory: When are speeches employed and how do they differ with their different functions? The Homeric poems do not reveal any sense of different kinds of oratory or any sign that, as in some traditional societies, different dialects were regarded as appropriate for different settings, but oratory was certainly used on a variety of occasions. Many of the occasions for speech in the Homeric poems are personal encounters, more appropriate for conversation than for oratory, but when Odysseus is asked in the *Odyssey* to tell who he is, he regularly replies with an extended formal speech—and regularly the contents are totally fictitious. This tendency to arrange ideas into speeches was another permanent influence of the Homeric poems on the classical period, when formal oratory was an established part of history, drama, and many forms of poetry. In addition to casual encounters, oratory in Homer is engendered by formal occasions: meetings of the council of leaders of the army; meetings of the assembly of the soldiers, or of citizens of cities in the *Odyssey*; embassies, both official such as that to Achilles in *Iliad*, Book 9, or unofficial as in Book 24. Some speeches in council, in assembly, or on embassies are declarative, in which a person with some power or authority simply announces what he is going to do—for example, Agamemnon's announcement to the council in Book 2 of the *Iliad* that he will test the army. The only trial in the Homeric poems is that carved on the shield of Achilles described in Book 18 of the *Iliad*, but some speeches are in fact calls for justice and resemble judicial occasions, as, for example, the debate between Agamemnon and Achilles in the first book of the *Iliad* or Telemachus' complaints in the second book of the *Odyssey*. There are also some speeches which anticipate the occasions of later epideictic oratory, such as the various speeches of lament for Hector in the eighteenth and twenty-fourth books of the *Iliad* and Achilles' speech of consolation to Priam in the *Iliad*, Book 24 (599–620).

The ninth book of the *Iliad* contains perhaps the finest set of speeches in the poem and is interesting for study because it shows the difference in technique of three different orators and the reply of Achilles to each. Some of the techniques employed anticipate categories of classical rhetoric. The occasion is the embassy sent by the Greek army with the consent of Agamemnon to try to persuade Achilles to return to battle. There are three ambassadors, Odysseus, Phoenix, and Ajax, chosen for their potential influence on Achilles. He acknowledges (9.204) that they are the men he loves most.

Odysseus speaks first, and his address is the most carefully organized in the group. It falls into five parts. First he addresses Achilles and expresses thanks for his hospitality (225–228), intending thus to establish a cordial tone. This corresponds to the proemium, or introduction, of a classical oration, which seeks the attention and goodwill of the audience. Second, he states his proposition (228–231): the ships will be destroyed unless Achilles returns to help the Greeks. The sudden contrast between the pleasant setting beside the campfire and the realities of the military situation is a startling note. Odysseus may be thought to exaggerate the danger slightly, for his own purposes, but only slightly. In any event his picture of the situation is direct, clear, and brief. He then moves on to a third part, a narrative of how the situation developed (232–246). This too is clear and rapid, and predominance is given to Achilles' rival Hector. At the end of the narrative Hector's threat to the ships is amplified in three clauses (*tricolon* in the terminology of classical rhetoric): "to shear the uttermost horns from the ships' sterns," "to light the ships themselves with ravening fire," and "to cut down the Achaeans themselves as they stir from the smoke beside them."[11] The clauses are arranged in a "climax" both in meaning and in length; in the Greek there are four words plus four words plus seven words. The fourth part of Odysseus' speech is his command "Up!" (247–248). Finally comes the proof, the reasons why Achilles should return to battle (249–306). There are five reasons given. The first is ethical: he will regret it later if he fails to help the Greeks. The second might be called authoritative: Achilles' father, so Odysseus says, had advised him to control his anger and avoid quarrels. The father's words are directly quoted as though he were speaking. This is a dramatic device which is given development in classical rhetoric as the figure *prosopopoeia*. The third reason is what Aristotle would call "nonartistic": that is, it is not an idea originating in the speaker's art, but a list of specific inducements offered by Agamemnon to Achilles if he will come back. Some of these are available immediately, including seven tripods, ten talents of gold, etc., along with restoration of the girl Briseis, whom Agamemnon claims not to have touched. Other inducements are promises of prizes when Troy will have been taken, including twenty Trojan women and Agamemnon's daughter as wife. These two lists are the largest element in the speech. The fourth reason that Achilles should return is his pity for the Achaeans and the glory he will gain from them if he does. Such an appeal to emotions could be described by the rhetorical term *pathos*. The final reason is also emotional: the present circumstances offer Achilles a chance to kill Hector, who now boasts that no one is his equal.

Odysseus' argumentation is based on an attempt to identify the interests of Achilles with those of the Greeks. The emotionalism is rather obvious, especially his mention of Achilles' father, and the psychological devices are rather flagrant, particularly his waving the red flag of Hector's vaunting victory in Achilles' face at the end. Odysseus' remarks in fact prove counterproductive.

In contrast to Odysseus' formal and carefully ordered speech, Achilles' reply is personal and rather digressive, though it has some structural framework beneath the surface. After a polite introductory apology at being so negative, his remarks fall into three groups: his view of the situation, his reaction to the specific offers of Agamemnon, and his advice to the ambassadors. His general reaction is that fighting gets one nowhere: "A man dies still if he has done nothing, as one who has done much" (318). Such general statements become a regular part of classical rhetoric under the label "maxims," or *sententiae*. He introduces a simile, comparing himself to a mother bird (323). He is ironic: "Let Agamemnon sleep with Briseis and enjoy himself" (336–337). Lines repeatedly begin with the same words (a device technically known as *anaphora*): "not even" or "not even if." As for Hector, he has shown his fear of Achilles. Achilles will now fight him no more and plans to sail home the next morning. This threat has not previously been mentioned and results apparently from Odysseus' reference to Hector at the end of his speech. Achilles takes a more extreme position in defense than he would have otherwise, for under the force of the following discourses he will gradually retreat from what he says here.

In the next part of his speech Achilles proceeds to reject Agamemnon's offers in detail. The character (*ethos*) of Agamemnon, which he regards as evil, is to him a more important factor than the emotional appeals which have been made. His own character, even personality, emerges clearly: he is moody, sensitive, offended, but idealistic and principled in his way. If Odysseus' appeal can be called generally "pathetical," Achilles' response is generally "ethical," that is, based on the *ethos* of himself and Agamemnon. He makes no mention of his father, but does cite the tragic choice offered him by his mother: a short life made glorious by victory at Troy, or an inglorious return to a long life at home. The last part of Achilles' speech is his advice to the ambassadors (421–429). They should go back to the Greek camp and find some other solution to the problem. Let Phoenix stay with Achilles and decide if he wants to go home with him to Greece.

Phoenix then takes up the appeal to Achilles with a long and very personal speech. His remarks have two special features. The first is an extended account of his own early life and his relationship to Achilles. Its object is to establish Phoenix in the role and with the authority of a parent to Achilles. "It was you," he says, "godlike Achilles, I made my own child, so that some day you might keep hard affliction from me. Then, Achilles, beat down your great anger . . ." (494–496). The second feature of Phoenix' speech is the story of Meleager (529–599), which provides a parallel to Achilles' situation: what happens to a hero who withdraws from his duty? This is analogous to the use of "examples" by later orators. At the end Phoenix briefly sums up his main points: come back now to aid the Greeks. You will get gifts and honor. If you wait you will eventually have to come, but without gifts and honor.

Achilles' reply to Phoenix is brief: I have enough honor; it does not become you to take Agamemnon's side; stay and share my life. But Achilles is not unaffected by Phoenix' appeal, and the latter's speech is not counterproductive in the way Odysseus' was. Achilles no longer says that he will leave in the morning. Rather, he will decide in the morning whether or not to leave. It is difficult of course to say specifically what the poet intends to have produced this change of heart, but the general nature of Phoenix' speech would suggest that Achilles has been touched by their personal relationship. He finds it harder to say no to Phoenix, and he may have been impressed by the example of Meleager.

The third ambassador is Ajax, who throughout the *Iliad* is presented as a blunt soldier. His short speech here does not begin by addressing Achilles. Instead, he turns aside (*apostrophe*) to speak to Odysseus, saying essentially "let's go home—we are wasting our time." But he obviously intends Achilles to hear and easily slips into the second person referring to Achilles (636), reminds him of the inducements offered to him, and concludes with a protestation of love and honor from Achilles' friends. This personal appeal, added to Phoenix', has effect on Achilles. He further retreats from his declared intention to go home and tells Ajax that though his anger at Agamemnon remains strong, he will stay in the Troad, and if Hector breaks through to his own camp, he will fight him.

Much can be learned about classical rhetoric from the ninth book of the *Iliad*. Many devices of invention, arrangement, and style were clearly in use long before they were conceptualized and named. Although attempts to use evidence and to develop a logical argument are present, it seems clear that there is a distinct difference between this traditional rhetoric and what later constitutes logic and dialectic. The role of ethos, or character, is particularly strong and results in quite different presentations by the three orators. Individually the speeches show a sense of structure, and as a group there are balances between the speeches: Phoenix and Achilles in the center, framed by Odysseus and Ajax.[12] Classical literature, including Greek oratory, has a predilection for balance, symmetry, and framing.

A convenient way to define differences between different forms of rhetoric is to ask which of the three elements of the act of communication—speaker, speech, or audience—is most dominant.[13] Considering the fact that techniques are not yet conceptualized, the oratory in Homer is a remarkable balance of the three elements. Each of the three orators gives effective expression of his personality and is clearly very conscious of the role he is playing. Each speech has a unity and represents vocalization of a technique. Each is adapted to the personality and role of Achilles. This natural balance will sometimes be disturbed by future theorists of rhetoric.

And yet the ninth book of the *Iliad* is a picture of the failure of formal rhetoric in dealing with a highly personal situation. Arguments based on practical expediencies are not persuasive, and the attempt to awaken passions is here counterproductive. Personal loyalty and friendship are what make the greatest impression. In the first work of European literature we are brought face to face with some of the limitations of rhetoric.

The rhetoric we have been studying in the ninth book of the *Iliad* is primary rhetoric, though expressed in a literary work and thus given a text. As a neoclassical critic might say, the poet is imitating nature and nature includes speech. Nevertheless, the fact that rhetoric plays such an important role in the earliest work of European literature is an important influence on the later tendency to equate rhetoric with literary devices. Poets through the centuries have imitated Homer's techniques, and not always in such clearly oratorical situations.

The Conceptualization of Rhetoric

The collapse of the civilization pictured in the *Iliad* was followed by what is called the dark ages in Greece. Out of this a new "classical" age began to emerge in the eighth century B.C. with the development of the city state as we know it, the adoption of the Phoenician alphabet, including the Greek invention of vowels, and such cultural phenomena as the Olympic games and written texts of the *Iliad* and *Odyssey*. These were the harbingers of many remarkable developments, especially during the sixth, fifth, and fourth centuries: democratic government in Athens, new literary forms like tragedy and comedy, Doric and Ionic architecture, sculpture and painting with emphasis on the human form, and the conceptualization of grammar, rhetoric, logical reasoning, ethics, politics, medicine, physics, and metaphysics. That is, these subjects began to emerge into the Greek consciousness as distinct entities; they began to be defined, to develop a terminology, to be taught, and to take shape as disciplines.

An explanation for this unprecedented advance in human self-consciousness in Greece at this time is not easily known or stated, and will not be attempted here. The causes inhere in the unusual geographical, religious, and intellectual situation of the Greeks in these centuries, both among themselves and in relation to their Near Eastern neighbors. The process was characterized by an interest in giving an account of why things are as they are, by an attempt to make generalizations, and by what amounted to an obsession with the relationship of the one and the many, or the particular and the universal, seen not only in philosophy, but in art. Rhetoric, like other areas of humanistic consciousness, contains forces moving in two directions, towards general statements of rules applicable in all situations, and towards a breaking down of universals into categories and subcategories which better define the particular.

Out of the experience of conceptualization in fifth-century Greece there emerged three views of rhetoric which are continuing strands in the tradition of rhetoric throughout the history of western Europe. The first and most conceptualized of these strands may be called "technical" rhetoric in that it is the rhetorical theory of the *technai*, or handbooks of rhetoric. Technical rhetoric grew directly out of the needs of the democracies in Sicily and Greece, especially at Athens, and it always remained primarily concerned with civil questions. Of the three factors in the speech situation identified by Aristotle (*Rhetoric* 1.3.1358a38)—speaker, speech, and audience—technical rhetoric concentrates on the speech at the expense of the other two. It is highly pragmatic; it shows how to present a subject efficiently and successfully but makes no attempt to judge the morality of the speaker or his effect on an audience. The characteristic definition of rhetoric in this technical tradition is "the art of persuasion." Technical rhetoric of the fifth and fourth centuries is the direct ancestor of manuals such as Cicero's *De Inventione* and the *Rhetorica ad Herennium*. Its focus on public life, and especially on the law courts, made it attractive to the Romans, who transmitted it in turn to the western Middle Ages and thus to later times. Technical rhetoric repeatedly experiences *letteraturizzazione* and is often reduced to guides to composition and style.

The second strand, also a development of the fifth century B.C., is "sophistic" rhetoric, the rhetoric of great sophists like Gorgias, carried to full development by Isocrates in the fourth century, revived in the Second Sophistic of Roman times, and converted to Christianity by preachers like Gregory of Nazianzus in the fourth century of our era.

Sophistic rhetoric is a stronger strand in the Byzantine or Greek medieval tradition than in the West, but it reemerges as a powerful force in the Renaissance. It emphasizes the speaker, rather than the speech or audience, and is responsible for pictures of an ideal orator leading society to noble fulfillment of national ideals. It is often ceremonial and cultural, rather than active and civic, and though moral in tone, tends not to press for difficult decisions or immediate action. Sophistic rhetoric is a natural spawning ground for amplification, elaborate conceits, and stylistic refinement, and thus is often criticized, but it has positive qualities which have ensured its survival. Like technical rhetoric, the sophistic strand often experiences *letteraturizzazione,* seen in large-scale written works in oratorical form. Some of these may have functioned as primary rhetoric at the time of original conception, but were polished and published as works of literature to be read and enjoyed for their eloquence by subsequent readers. The tradition of literary oratory from Isocrates and Demosthenes to Edmund Burke and later has been the most evident product of classical rhetoric; it has given concrete reality to the theory of classical rhetoric and served as a continual model for the development of secondary rhetoric in other literary genres.

The third strand begins with Socrates' objections to technical and sophistic rhetoric and may be called "philosophical" rhetoric. It tends to deemphasize the speaker and to stress the validity of his message and the nature of his effect on an audience. Furthermore, it classifies speeches on the basis of the audience, whether they are only spectators or are judges of past or future events. Philosophical rhetoric has close ties with dialectic or logic, and sometimes with psychology; its natural topic is deliberation about the best interests of the audience. Deliberative oratory, Aristotle declares (*Rhetoric* 1.1.1354b25), is the noblest and most public form. The emphasis in philosophical rhetoric on what hearers should believe and should do parallels the rhetoric of religious movements like Judaism and Christianity. Philosophical rhetoric exercised some influence on subsequent classical rhetorical theory, but its principles were often diluted or distorted, just as deliberative oratory was often a victim of political intimidation, and its strand at times is difficult to find in the fabric of rhetorical history. In the Middle Ages the chief manifestation of philosophical rhetoric is in dialectic, and in the Renaissance the philosophical view of rhetoric inspires the transfer of invention from rhetoric to dialectic, but the purer strain reappears in Francis Bacon and Fénelon in the seventeenth century.

We may now turn to consider the early history of each of these three strands of rhetoric.

Chapter 2
Technical Rhetoric

Although the wider causes of the conceptualization of rhetoric in Greece are difficult to define precisely, the specific practical influence which produced the first attempt at statement of a theory of rhetoric is clear. That influence is democracy, and particularly the establishment of democratic lawcourts with large juries chosen by lot.

Democracy in Athens was the result of a series of political changes over a period of more than two hundred years: limitation of the length of term of rulers, their election to office, establishment of an elected council, extension of the right to vote and eligibility to office to poorer classes of citizens, increasing use of the lot rather than of voting in the choice of officials, and provisions for trial before large, democratically chosen juries with power to determine both law and fact. The minimum size of an Athenian jury of this sort was 201 members, and the procedure in court consisted primarily of a speech by the plaintiff and a reply by the defendant, each in the form of a continuous address to the jury. During the century and a half from Solon to Pericles Athenian citizens had more and more opportunity and need to speak in council, in the assembly of all the citizens, and in lawcourts, but they had time to develop these skills by observation, imitation, and experimentation, and no crisis in education seems to have occurred. In Syracuse in Sicily, on the other hand, democracy on the Athenian pattern was introduced suddenly in 467 B.C. Citizens found themselves involved in litigation over the ownership of property or other matters and forced to take up their own cases before the courts. Nowhere in Greece did the profession of lawyer, advocate, or patron at the bar exist. Need to speak in the democratic Syracusan assembly was less pressing, but opportunities for political leadership came to involve the skill of public speaking in a way not previously evident. A few clever Sicilians developed simple techniques (Greek *techne* means "art") for effective presentation and argumentation in the law courts and taught these to others for a price. According to later tradition, the two leading teachers were Corax, whose name means "crow," which invited various puns, and a slightly younger, better known teacher, perhaps Corax' pupil, named Tisias.[1]

The art of Corax and Tisias, originally taught orally, was at some point written down in notes (*hypomnemata*), either by the two teachers themselves or by those they taught, and copies were made and sold. These writings were known as "Arts" (*technai*) since they contained the art or technique of effective discourse. Copies reached Athens and various people there also undertook to teach the art and to publish "Arts." By the end of the fifth century a handbook literature existed to which anyone could turn to secure basic principles of public speaking. Coincidentally, the standards of public address in the assembly and lawcourts in Athens, Syracuse, and the other democracies improved. A speaker who did not know the conventions was increasingly at a loss, and the sophistication of the assembly and the juries was considerable. Indeed, by the end of the fifth century the Athenian lawcourts had become one of the principal forms of entertainment in the city, and service on juries was popular not only because it provided a day's pay for poorer citizens but because it offered an opportunity to hear the clever and eloquent pleas of litigants. Aristophanes' comedy *The Wasps* (produced 422 B.C.) utilizes the situation for comic effect.

The development of handbooks continued in the fourth century and eventually produced the corpus of classical rhetoric to be described in chapter 5. Some material from the earliest tradition is included in Aristotle's *Rhetoric*, and more can be found in Anaximenes' *Rhetoric to Alexander*, dating from the late fourth century B.C. Equally important, sometime in the third quarter of the fourth century Aristotle put together his *Synagoge Technon*, or *Collection of the Arts*, a summary of the content of the various handbooks then in existence. This has not survived, but together with a few references in Plato it is the basis of our knowledge of the teaching of early rhetoricians like Corax, Tisias, and Theodorus, for it was repeatedly quoted by later writers.[2] The existence of Aristotle's summary seems to have rendered the survival of the original handbooks superfluous. They ceased to be copied and preserved, and save for the work of Anaximenes, which comes at the end of the tradition and was misrepresented by a later editor as a work of Aristotle, none survives.

The best picture of the contents of these early "Arts," or technical handbooks, is to be found in Plato's dialogue *Phaedrus*, written in the second quarter of the fourth century when they still existed and were widely studied. In discussing the nature of rhetoric Phaedrus reminds Socrates that there are books on the subject, and Socrates surveys their contents (266–267d). He says that they indicate that a speaker should begin with a *proemium*, or introduction, and should then continue with a *diegesis*, or narrative, followed by witnesses, evidence, and probabilities. Theodorus of Byzantium was one of the writers of handbooks, and Socrates says he called this part of a speech the *pistis* and *epipistis*, or proof and supplementary proof. Then there is advice about how to handle a refutation and supplementary refutation, both in accusation and in defense. Socrates ironically claims that Tisias and Gorgias showed how much more important probabilities were than facts and could make small things great, great things small, new things old, old things new, and discuss anything for any length. Such amplification suggests matters of style, and Socrates goes on to note categories of diction identified in handbooks by Polus, Licymnius, and Protagoras. Included are proper words, figurative words, poetic words, and devices for securing pathos which were discussed by Thrasymachus. Finally we are told that a speech is supposed to have an *epilogos*, or conclusion, in which there is a recapitulation of the argument.

From this account certain observations can be drawn which are confirmed by other evidence. First, the handbooks were intended, at least primarily, as preparation for speeches in courts of law, even though some who wrote handbooks may also have been interested in deliberative oratory and many of the techniques they mention could be applied to speeches in the assembly. Second, a major consideration in the handbooks, and apparently the basis of their organization, was the structure of judicial oratory: introduction, narration, proof, refutation, and conclusion. Third, at least some of the handbooks included discussions of style, specifically of the various kinds of diction available to the orator and the forms of linguistic ornamentation which he could use. As we will see in the next chapter, this development was probably a result of the influence of the sophists. The addition of style to technical rhetoric is of great importance, for in later antiquity, in the Middle Ages, and in the Renaissance, the subject of style and especially the ornaments of style was often regarded as the heart of rhetoric. Fourth, though not least in importance, argument from probability was the basis of proof as presented in the handbooks. Tisias is one of the writers to whom this theory is attributed, and he is in fact the earliest of any of the rhetoricians mentioned by Plato in this passage.

What Tisias had to say about argument from probability is suggested a few pages later in the *Phaedrus* (273a–c). Socrates says that by *eikos*, or probability, Tisias meant that which seems true to the multitude, and he quotes the following example:

If a weak and brave man, having beaten up a strong and cowardly man, is brought into court, neither must tell the truth. The coward must claim that he was not beaten by a single brave man: i.e., he must claim to have been attacked by two or more, whereas the other must refute this, insisting that the two of them were alone, in order to use the argument "how could a little one like me have attacked a big one like him?" (273b4–c1)

There is in argument from probability, therefore, a possibility of using probabilities on either side of the case. Far from discrediting the technique as immoral, this seems to have recommended it to the Greeks of the fifth century, who delighted in such subtleties of argument and in the demonstration that one probability was more probable than another probability. Conversely, they deeply distrusted direct evidence in both criminal and civil cases because of a knowledge that it could be faked or bribed. Now of course most oratory deals with matters of probability, not certainty, and most evidence is in the realm of the probable, not the scientifically demonstrable; but later orators usually prefer to construct a complex fabric of argumentation in which probable conclusions are drawn on the basis of more or less hard evidence, using the personality of those involved and their motivations as important factors. Fifth-century orators as we know them, and to some extent the argumentation seen in fifth-century dramatic and historical writing, make much less use of the specific character or personality of those involved and prefer to rest on the probability of basic human action: What would anybody have believed or done under the circumstances?

Another aspect of rhetoric which is even more lacking from the handbooks so far as we can judge and almost totally foreign to fifth-century argumentation is appeal to authority or the attempt of an orator to speak as an authority figure, though both are highly characteristic of preconceptual rhetoric, not only in other cultures like Israel and Rome, but even in Greece. Such use of authority was not only uncongenial to fifth-century democratic ideas, but in practice most fifth-century orators in the lawcourts—unlike Cicero—had no particular personal authority to invoke, for any Athenian male was expected to conduct his own business and that of his family. The result is that of the three chief operative factors in a speech act—speaker, speech, and audience—fifth century judicial rhetoric centers almost all its attention on the speech.

Technical rhetoric, or the rhetoric of the handbooks, constitutes a major force in the history of rhetoric. It is generally easy to distinguish from other strands of classical rhetoric because of its emphasis on judicial oratory, on the parts of an oration as given in a court of law, and on techniques which will lead to success or devices which will ornament the contexts. Writers of such handbooks usually do not regard it as part of their task to tell an orator what cases he should or should not undertake or what should be the limits of his appeal to an audience; they do undertake to tell him how to present any case as effectively as possible. It is often easy to recognize their characteristically prescriptive language: "you should. . . ." The previous two sentences need the words "usually" and "often" since there are works like Cicero's *Orator* or Quintilian's *Institutio Oratoria* which integrate handbook material with other forms of rhetorical theory, sophistic or philosophical. Even Aristotle, as we shall see, occasionally uses prescriptive language and draws on the handbooks, especially in the second half of the third book of the *Rhetoric*, which discusses the parts of orations, but also in discussions of the contents of all three forms of oratory in Books 1 and 2. Aristotle was writing lectures on rhetoric for students in his philosophical school and laying out the subject systematically as a discipline, but his inquiring mind tended to draw everything he found into a unified picture, and this included the rhetoric he found in handbooks. Some sophists in the fifth and fourth centuries also wrote handbooks, presumably going beyond the immediate needs of speakers in lawcourts, as Aristotle does. It is the influence of sophists and philosophers which tended to expand the content of the handbook to include style and eventually other subjects.

This larger view of the subject is evident in our only surviving handbook from the fourth century B.C., the *Rhetoric to Alexander*.[3] Probably originally the work of Anaximenes of Lampsacus (ca. 380–320 B.C.), it has an introductory letter purporting to be by Aristotle, who is sending the treatise to Alexander the Great. This may well be a later addition, and the treatise may have suffered other changes as well. It shows the influence of Aristotle's conception of three kinds of rhetoric, but treats oratory as falling into seven species: exhortation and dissuasion; encomium and vituperation; prosecution and defense; and examination, which includes the questioning of an opponent. These are discussed in chapters 2 through 5. The author then treats at length (chapters 6 through 28) matters common to all species, which include common topics, amplification, proofs, anticipation of the other speaker, irony, choice and arrangement of words, and a few devices of style. What he has to say about proof includes argument from probability. Finally the parts of the oration are taken up in terms of the seven species of oratory (chapters 29–37), with a miscellaneous chapter at the end, partly spurious.

The structure of the *Rhetoric to Alexander* is not entirely satisfactory, and the question how to integrate discussion of the parts of rhetoric (invention, style, and others to be added) with the kinds of oratory and the parts of the oration remained a problem for handbook writers throughout antiquity. The problem was compounded by the development of *stasis* theory by Hermagoras in the second century B.C. Various solutions were found, but the parts of the oration, which we saw in the *Phaedrus* to be the fundamental structure of the earliest handbooks, remained a very important element. In the fullest ancient treatise on rhetoric, Quintilian's *Institutio Oratoria*, most material relating to the content and argument of a speech, including ethos and pathos, is inserted into a discussion of the eight parts of a judicial oration that runs from Books 4 through 6, treating in order proemium (or in Latin *exordium*), narration, digression, proposition, partition, proof, refutation, and conclusion (in Latin *peroratio*).

Technical rhetoric came into existence under the conditions of the Greek city-states where all citizens were deemed equal and were expected to be able to speak on their own behalf. In origin it is associated with freedom of speech and with amateurism, first in the law-courts, but also in democratic political assemblies. Freedom of speech on political issues received major setbacks with the defeat of the Greek states by Macedon in 338 B.C. and with the establishment of the Roman empire by Augustus after the battle of Actium in 31 B.C., though to some extent it survived in courts of law throughout the Roman period. Amateurism survived in local courts in Greece until the time of the Roman empire; in Rome, however, the patron-client system was already in existence before the Romans became aware of Greek rhetoric around 200 B.C., and oratory in Rome, in the lawcourts, the senate, and assemblies, was practiced chiefly by a relatively small number of professional orators, highly conscious of techniques and of their own roles.

Despite these restrictions on the use of rhetoric, technical rhetoric not only survived throughout the Roman period, but was made the subject of enormous elaboration in detail. The reason for this is primarily the role it came to play in what may roughly be called secondary education. Both in Greece and in Rome formal education was largely devoted to the verbal arts, first to grammar, and then from the age of twelve or thirteen to seventeen on, to the study of rhetoric and to exercises in rhetorical composition and delivery. These exercises, especially in the Roman schools, took the form of speeches in imaginary trials, and the whole system of technical rhetoric functioned as theoretical training for the exercises. The system tended to encourage a high degree of verbal sophistication, but often put a premium on artificial concepts and bizarre imagination. It created a feeling of frustration when individuals left school and found little opportunity to use their skills, and it helped make Latin literature of the empire among the most striking manifestations of artificial secondary rhetoric.

In late antiquity and the early Middle Ages the theory of technical rhetoric is summarized in the influential works of Martianus Capella, Cassiodorus, and Isidore of Seville, which together with Cicero's technical treatise *De Inventione* and the *Rhetorica ad Herennium* are the main sources for the teaching of rhetoric throughout the western Middle Ages. In Byzantium the technical treatises of Hermogenes played a similar role and were the subject of numerous vast commentaries throughout the medieval period. Technical handbooks on classical rhetoric, often adapted for very elementary students and treating either rhetoric as a whole or only the ornaments of style, are common in the later Middle Ages, the Renaissance, and the neoclassical period. Lectures on rhetoric in universities, including those in early American colleges, were an adaptation of the technical tradition. At first lectures usually took the form of commentaries on an authoritative text of Cicero, or later Quintilian or even Aristotle, but eventually professors began to restate classical theory in their own words and to refer students to the classics for additional studies. Some of these courses of lectures were then published and used by students elsewhere as texts, as happened in the case of Hugh Blair's lectures, based in large part on Quintilian, which were delivered at the University of Edinburgh over two decades, published in 1783 as *Lectures on Rhetoric and Belles Lettres*, and thereafter widely studied throughout the English-speaking world.

The paradox of technical rhetoric is that throughout the Middle Ages, both Greek and Latin, it remained theoretically concerned with addressing a jury in a court of law, even though such juries passed out of existence and judicial rhetoric had considerably reduced uses for around fifteen hundred years. The areas of greatest rhetorical expression in the Middle Ages and Renaissance were in preaching, in the writing of letters, in panegyric, and in religious disputation, which are fields for deliberative and epideictic rhetoric. Technical handbooks were eventually developed in most of these areas, but were slow in coming, and the traditional exposition of judicial rhetoric long held the central field. By the seventeenth and eighteenth centuries, however, preaching had become the major oratorical form as discussed in lectures on rhetoric before university classes.

Chapter 3
Sophistic Rhetoric

Technical handbooks were the most fully conceptualized expression of rhetoric available in the fifth century B.C. and are the direct ancestors of much of the writing on rhetoric in classical and later times. Handbooks, however, were not the only source of skill for one who wished to learn public speaking and argumentation. The older tradition of imitating a successful orator, with little or no conscious conceptualization of the techniques involved, continued to be followed and became the characteristic form of rhetorical study in what may be loosely called the "schools" of the sophists.

The word *sophist* is derived from the adjective *sophos*, meaning "wise," and might be translated "craftsman." In the fifth century Protagoras and others used it of themselves and others as members of a particular profession. Sophists were self-appointed professors of how to succeed in the civic life of the Greek states. Most were not themselves Athenians, but the young men of Athens constituted their chief clientele. They taught primarily by public or private declamation of speeches which presented in striking form their ideas and their techniques of proof. Some of the leading sophists, Protagoras for example, may rightly be thought of as philosophers who developed ideas and published treatises on what we might call epistemology, anthropology, linguistics, and almost anything involving human life and belief. Others were little more than teachers of devices of argument or emphasis. The crucial issue in their exposition was often the antithesis between what the Greeks called *physis*, or nature (i.e., that which is objectively true), and *nomos*, which means "law," but which included all man-made institutions and conventions. Their vigorous presentation of paradoxes and controversial moral views illustrated the potential of rhetoric for social change and also for amoral self-aggrandizement. A kind of intoxication with the unlimited power of the word spread out from Athens to excite and sometimes to alarm the Greek world.

Exactly what went on in the schools of the sophists is not well known, but a central activity was certainly listening to the sophist speak or reading versions of his speeches, followed by the memorization or imitation of these works as models. Some of these models were of a sort useful for a person expecting to speak in a court of law; others, as we will see, were of a more ambitious and colorful nature. The earliest example of the former type and the best illustration of how judicial oratory could be learned from sophistic specimen speeches are the *Tetralogies* of Antiphon.

Antiphon

Antiphon, the presumed author of these speeches, is probably the oligarchic politician of that name who was executed as a result of the failure of the revolution of 411 B.C. in Athens. If so, he is also the author of three surviving speeches written for clients to deliver in murder trials in Athens and perhaps also the person known as Antiphon the Sophist, author of a treatise entitled *On Truth*.[1] The *Tetralogies* are three sets of four speeches, two for the prosecution and two for the defense in each case, in imaginary trials under Athenian homicide laws. They were composed in the third quarter of the fifth century and are clearly intended to serve as models of effective techniques of judicial oratory.

The situation imagined in the first *Tetralogy* is as follows. A man has been killed in a lonely spot. The slave accompanying him was also attacked and has died, but not without stating that the defendant was the murderer. None of the characters in the *Tetralogies* are given any names. The trial in a case like this would be held before the Areopagus, an ancient council with judicial powers made up of all former archons; it is difficult to estimate the number who would have served in the Areopagus, but it might well be a hundred or more. Since there was no public prosecutor in Athens, criminal actions were brought by anyone who felt injured. In murder trials this was usually a close relative of the deceased. In this case the prosecutor claims to be concerned about the religious pollution which will infect the city if a murderer is allowed to go free. The prosecutor opens his speech as follows:

Whatever actions result from plots by ordinary citizens are not difficult to prove, but if people of considerable ability are the perpetrators, experienced in the business, and at a time of life when they are at the peak of their mental powers, they are difficult to discover and convict. Through the greatness of the risk, they pay much attention to the safety of their schemes, and they take no action until they have provided against every suspicion. Knowing this, it is necessary for you [the jury] to put great trust in any probability you perceive. . . .

It is unlikely that muggers killed the man, for no one who ran the risk of his life would have abandoned the object of his robbery when he had it in his hands. Yet the victims were found with all their property [literally, "their cloaks"] intact. Nor did someone kill them in a drunken frenzy, for we would have information from fellow drinkers. Nor did the murder result from an argument, for they wouldn't have been arguing in the middle of the night in a deserted spot. Nor did the murderer kill the victim in mistake for somebody else, for he would not have killed both him and his slave. Since these possibilities are dismissed, the fact of the death points to the man having died as a result of premeditation. And who is more likely to have set upon him than one who had already suffered great wrongs at his hands and was expecting to suffer still more? That man is the defendant. (4–5)

The orator continues his development of probabilities, then adds the evidence of the slave as corroboration of them, and finally summarizes what he has said and stresses the importance of removing the pollution from the city. Greek judicial speeches were sometimes rather short, but this model, not having much material to amplify, is especially short. In particular, a real speech would have included a narration; here we have only proemium, proof from probabilities, evidence, and epilogue.

In the second speech in the same *Tetralogy* it is interesting to see how the defendant deals with the argument we have just quoted. Under Athenian law he is required to defend himself, and he responds that

it is not unlikely, as they say, but likely that a person wandering around in the middle of the night should be killed for his property. That he was not robbed is a sign of nothing. But if the assailants had not yet stripped him, but left in fear of somebody who was coming, they were sensible and not at all mad to prefer safety to profit. (5)

He goes on to suggest other motives for the murder, and he dismisses the evidence of the slave on the ground that in terror for his life he was not likely to have recognized the murderer and in his dying state was more than likely to have agreed with anything to please his master's family. The speaker points out that the evidence of slaves is distrusted under Athenian law: usually evidence against the master could be accepted in a court only if taken under torture.

Argumentation in the other *Tetralogies* is similar and the practice of Antiphon in the three surviving speeches written for participants in actual cases is basically along the same lines. Even the fragments of his speech on his own defense for treason indicate that he argued there that it was unlikely he would have plotted to overthrow the government for his own advantage.

The *Tetralogies* of Antiphon are examples of a form of rhetorical instruction which flourished in Athens. In the case of argument from probability as seen in the *Tetralogies* we know that the technique had been conceptualized in the fifth-century handbooks. In the case of some other techniques of argument and devices of style, we do not know how specific the conceptualization was, whether the teacher simply gave examples of effective treatment which his students memorized or imitated, or whether he accompanied his model speeches with critical remarks as a modern teacher would be apt to do. In the opening pages of Plato's *Phaedrus* we find Phaedrus studying a speech by Lysias; impressed with it on first hearing, he has made Lysias repeat it several times, borrowed the manuscript, and is now learning it by heart (*Phaedrus* 228a–b). It is obvious in this case that there has been no discussion of the technique of the speech until Phaedrus encounters Socrates, but it is not clear whether Lysias is in any sense a teacher of rhetoric. His intent may have been only to give a virtuoso performance. Otherwise, evidence against conceptualization on the part of the sophists would include the passage from Plato's *Apology* (21c) referred to earlier, Aristotle's complaint in his treatise *On Sophistical Refutations* (183b–184a) that the pragmatic method of Gorgias consisted only of furnishing speeches to be memorized by students, much as if one tried to teach shoemaking by giving the student a collection of shoes, and finally the practice of later Greek sophists, which put emphasis on declamation by teacher and student, rather than on theory and analysis. On the other hand, conceptualization was an important factor in some sophists' teaching; Protagoras, for example, sought to understand categories of syntax and grammatical gender.

Students of the sophists did not necessarily memorize and reproduce only whole speeches. Just as the composition of oral poetry and the oratory in it was built up with blocks of memorized material adapted to a variety of situations, so sophistic oratory was to a considerable extent a pastiche, or piecing together of commonplaces, long or short. Some of these commonplaces even appear in actual judicial speeches given in Athens, especially in the introductions and in treatment of stock questions such as the reliability of evidence taken under torture. We have a collection of introductions, or *proemia*, by Demosthenes, which he and others drew on as needed, and the discussion of style, amplification, and emotional appeal in the account of the handbooks in the *Phaedrus* seems to suggest that some of these included collections of material made by a sophist whose students could then incorporate it in their speeches at will. In the fragmentary speech *Against the Sophists* (12–13) Isocrates compares the teaching of rhetoric by some sophists to teaching the alphabet. The student memorized passages as he would letters and made up a speech out of these elements as he would words out of letters. Except, says Isocrates, that the sophists neither knew nor could teach their students how to combine the passages in a useful or appropriate way, for composition is a creative process and not something with definite rules, like spelling. The use of commonplaces of the sophistic type (to be distinguished from topics of dialectic) remains characteristic of sophistic oratory and of some secondary rhetoric as well. In the Middle Ages handbooks of letter-writing often contained formulae, such as openings and closes, which the student could insert into a letter, and a whole series of formulary rhetorics existed in the Renaissance. A modern successor is the collection of anecdotes and after-dinner stories for the use of speakers.

Gorgias

Among the sophists the one most famous in the history of rhetoric is Gorgias, whose long life stretched from sometime around 480 to around 375 B.C.[2] Gorgias was a native of Leontini in Sicily, near Syracuse. He is supposed to have been a student of the philosopher Empedocles and may well have known Corax or Tisias. In 427 he was sent by his native city as an ambassador to Athens, where his remarkable oratorical style became a fad. Although the devices which he used were largely drawn from Greek poetry and could individually be found in Attic Greek (the language of Athens) before his arrival, he exploited them to an unprecedented degree. On Gorgias' lips oratory became a tintinnabulation of rhyming words and echoing rhythms. Antithetical structure, which is native to Greek syntax, became an obsession. Clauses were constructed with persistent parallelism and attention to corresponding length, even down to equalizing the number of syllables in each. This is difficult to convey in English with full effect, but the following rendering of Gorgias' description of Helen of Troy might suggest something of the style:

Born from such stock, she had godlike beauty, which taking and not mistaking, she kept. In many did she work much desire for her love, and her one body was the cause of bringing together many bodies of men thinking great thoughts for great goals, of whom some had greatness of wealth, some the glory of ancient nobility, some the vigor of personal agility, some command of acquired knowledge. And all came because of a passion which loved to conquer and a love of honor which was unconquered. . . . (4)

This is called the Gorgianic style. The particular devices on which it is based were among the first to be noted in handbooks, perhaps by Gorgias' students, and are called *schemata* in Greek, or *figurae* in Latin, English "schemes" or "figures." Accounts of the figures are already found in fourth-century rhetorical treatises.[3] Gorgianic figures continued to be treated as a group by later writers and were often regarded as somewhat gauche. In Gorgias' own time they were imitated widely, by Thucydides the historian, Lysias the orator, and Isocrates, for example, but with greater restraint than their originator showed. Gorgias borrowed the figures from poetry, where all of them can be found before his time, though usually not in the same density. This is the period of the first development of artistic prose in Greek, and it is not surprising that poetry would furnish models for style.

What was the point of the Gorgianic figures and why did Gorgias use them? To attract attention to himself as a teacher of speech? Or do they imply some more profound theory of speech? Jacqueline de Romilly has argued that Gorgias saw magic in speech, the same kind of magic which appeared in religious poetry or in the healing incantations of prerational medicine men.[4] In support of this view she cites a passage in Gorgias' *Encomium of Helen* (8–14) where he speaks of the power of speech: "By means of the finest and most invisible body it effects the divinest works: it can stop fear and banish grief and create joy and nurture pity." The Gorgianic figures should be viewed as the specific devices by which Gorgias sought to work his magic. They are the techniques which stir the passions or obsess the mind and draw on the listener to unconscious agreement with the speaker. The view of Gorgias as a "magician" seems supported by the general reaction to him in antiquity. He was regularly presented as a rhetorician, not a philosopher. In Plato he seems quite incapable of conceptualization or analysis of what he does, and the quotations or references to him in ancient writers are largely to speeches.

A number of modern scholars, however, have thought that Gorgias was a serious philosopher, interested in ontology and epistemology and influenced by the Pythagoreans and Empedocles.[5] Gorgias shares with the philosophers an interest in opposites and a fondness for antithesis. More important, his treatise *On the Nonexistent, or On Nature*, which survives in outline form, can be approached as a serious effort at logical argument. Here Gorgias maintains that nothing exists, that even if anything does exist it is inapprehensible by man, and even if it were apprehensible it would be impossible to communicate. The argument is supported through the identification and elimination of alternative possibilities. Such a view is not only a clever paradox and example of technique, but also, it is argued, a statement of philosophy. In consequence, since the truth cannot be known rationally, the function of an orator is not logical demonstration so much as emotional presentation which will stir the audience's will to believe. Thus for Gorgias the power of persuasion involves deceiving "the emotional and mental state of listeners by artificially stimulating sensory reactions through words." [6]

The philosophical approach to Gorgias, valuable as it is in relating him to other intellectual developments of the fifth century, probably exaggerates his intellectual sophistication and credits him with an uncharacteristic power of conceptualization. Gorgias imitated what he found in the philosophers as he did what he found in the poets, not as reflections of a theory of knowledge, but as a technique of speech. It is not clear that he cared about its philosophical implications. What is important in him, and what remains characteristic of the sophistic strand in rhetoric, is his sense of the power of the orator to accomplish whatever he wishes, to make great things small, small things great, and even the worse seem the better cause. This technique Gorgias illustrated and taught to others through furnishing them models for imitation.

Isocrates

The various trends and influences of Greek sophistic rhetoric are brought together and further developed in the work of Isocrates (436–338 B.C.).[7] Isocrates made rhetoric the permanent basis of the educational system of the Greek and the Roman world and thus of many later centuries as well, and he made oratory a literary form. Although Isocrates was in the outer fringes of the Socratic circle and shows the influence of Socrates, his thought did not move in the dialectical and metaphysical direction of Plato's. Having lost his family wealth in the Peloponnesian War, he subsisted for awhile as a logographer, or writer of speeches for others to deliver, but about 393 or 392, several years before Plato founded the Academy, he opened a school for advanced students to deepen their liberal education and prepare themselves for careers of leadership in various cities of the Greek world. Among the most famous to study with him were Nicocles, son of the king of Cyprus, and Timotheus, the most important Athenian general of the second quarter of the fourth century. Isocrates' school was a development of the "schools" of the sophists, but unlike other sophists he did not travel around: he required students to come to him and to stay for an extended period of time. This gave his school a stability which the demonstrations of other sophists lacked. To judge from what he says in *Antidosis* (287–290), he also took a personal interest in the students and their development in self-discipline, which as far as we know other sophists did not do. Finally, his school had clearly stated goals and a consistent curriculum which he maintained for over fifty years.

Basic acquaintance with Isocrates' goals and methods can be gained from reading three of his speeches, *Against the Sophists, Panegyricus,* and *Antidosis,* though a full understanding of his career, his significance to his contemporaries, and his political ideas would involve extensive reading in his other works.[8] *Against the Sophists* is a program-speech composed and published by Isocrates soon after opening his school. He never delivered any of his speeches in public, though he did read them to his students and invite their criticism. *Against the Sophists* is primarily intended to differentiate his own school from that of other sophists, both those who taught tricks of argumentation and those who taught public speaking through model speeches and commonplaces. His own views are that one must start with native ability, which training can sharpen, but not create. There are in fact three elements in successful oratory—and these remain permanent features of classical rhetorical theory—nature, training, and practice. It is the function of the teacher to explain the principles of rhetoric and also to set an example of oratory on which the students can pattern themselves. Isocrates calls this training "philosophy" or pursuit of wisdom, by which he means chiefly a practical wisdom useful to men. A very important factor in it, in his judgment, is moral character; that cannot be taught, he says, but the study of speech and of politics can help to encourage and train moral consciousness. Unfortunately, the extant text of the speech ends at this point.

To continue consideration of Isocrates' ideas on education it is necessary to turn to the *Antidosis,* a long speech which he published about 353 B.C. to justify his life's work and to answer mounting criticism of himself. It takes the form of a judicial defense in an antidosis trial, a trial in which the defendant is challenged to undertake an expensive public service or else exchange property with another citizen who has been assigned the obligation to pay for the service in question. The Athenians expected wealthy individuals to pay for dramatic productions, the construction of warships, and other public needs, but allowed them to challenge somebody else and attempt to prove that that person was better able to bear the expense. Here the claim is imagined that Isocrates has made great sums from his school, but the charge is extended into one of corrupting the young by teaching them to speak and thus to gain an advantage in contests contrary to justice. Isocrates means his readers to think of the charges made against Socrates forty-odd years before and presents himself throughout the speech as a Socrates-like figure.

The *Antidosis* is exceedingly wordy and becomes rather tiresome, though it is interesting to see how Isocrates introduces passages from three of his earlier speeches as "witnesses" on his behalf, as well as naming his leading students and discussing in considerable detail the activities of one of them, Timotheus. He denies (32–43) that he has been active in the courts or that he has taught techniques of judicial oratory, and he claims (67) that all his writings have tended toward virtue and justice. In the later part of the speech he turns to the question of the arts and his method of instruction and takes up some of the matters touched on in his speech *Against the Sophists*. Arts are divided into that of the mind and that of the body (180–185): the former is philosophy, which teaches forms of discourse; the latter is gymnastic, which teaches postures of the body. Each is an *antistrophos*, or counterpart, of the other (182). (This concept will be of interest in contrast to remarks by Plato and Aristotle on the relationship of the arts.) Isocrates glorifies the art of discourse (253–257) in a passage he borrows from his *Nicocles* (5–9); he warns against the moral and intellectual dangers of dialectic and abstruse philosophy, and he elaborates his conception of how the study and practice of speech can improve men. The argument is that the truly ambitious orator, the kind trained in Isocrates' school, will first of all choose as his subject only great themes for the good of man. Second, he will select examples to prove his points from the noble actions of great men. In doing so he will accustom himself to contemplate virtue and will feel its influence, not only in the planning of a particular speech, but throughout his life, "so that eloquence and wisdom will become the possession of those who are philosophically and honorably disposed toward speech" (277).

It should be remembered that by the time Isocrates wrote these words Plato, who was to some extent his rival as an educator, had published the *Gorgias* and the *Phaedrus* and had developed his morally austere view of rhetoric, which we will consider in the next chapter. Isocrates' response is in terms not of rhetoric, but of the orator. Rhetoric as a system is presumably neither good nor bad; only men are good and bad, and Isocrates would start with a young man who is good, developing that potential for goodness by the contemplation of great models. This view of the orator is a permanent feature of classical rhetoric, most developed in the ensuing centuries by Cicero and Quintilian, who claim that only a good man can be a good orator. The need to answer the moral objections against rhetoric as practiced by sophists and demagogues in Athens is probably the second great influence in the development of the concept of the classical orator, the first having been the model of the heroic orator of the Homeric poems.

Isocrates says (295–296) that Athens is the school of orators and teachers of rhetoric, and that the reason for this is that Athens holds out the greatest prizes to their ability, offers the largest number and greatest variety of opportunities, provides the most practical opportunities to speak, and has the best of the Greek dialects as its native speech; thus it is not unjust that all great speakers should be pupils of Athens. The view is tenable in terms of the role that Athenian democracy and intellectual history played in the development of rhetoric and eloquence.

It would be interesting to know more details about the actual curriculum of Isocrates' school and his conceptualization of rhetoric therein. Some features may be surmised on the basis of his practice and fragmentary information preserved elsewhere. He probably took over the teachings of predecessors about the structure of oratory and about argument from probability. His own technical contributions came primarily in the area of style; imitation of this style, rather than technical study, was probably the main occupation of his students. Seeking a medium for the expression of his noble, if somewhat bland ideas, he developed an extraordinarily smooth prose. The diction is pure, unusual or poetic words being generally avoided. Taking advantage of the fact that he is writing and not speaking, Isocrates weaves these words together into very long periodic sentences. Antithesis, *isocolon*, causal and result clauses, and an inclination not only to make a positive statement but to deny its contrary, keep the thought remarkably clear. Isocrates is one of the easiest writers to read in Greek, despite the long sentences, because he never leaves anything unsaid and never makes abrupt jumps of thought. Symbolic of his concern for smoothness is his obsession with avoiding *hiatus*, or the clash of sound that results from juxtaposing words ending and beginning with vowels. These stylistic features were permanently influential on Greek prose, though as was the case with Gorgianic figures they are not carried to such extremes by Isocrates' successors.

Also permanently influential was the creation of a rhetorical school. Successors flourished not only in Athens but through the Hellenistic cities in the coming centuries, and the institution was eventually exported to Rome, survived in Byzantium, and reappeared in renaissance Italy. Before Isocrates' time education in Greece had little structure. After his time a regular pattern evolved consisting of roughly seven years of instruction in a primary or grammar school, followed by several years studying rhetorical theory and practicing the composition of speeches with a rhetorician. Beyond that might come advanced study in rhetoric or in philosophy. In late antiquity and the Middle Ages this system develops into the *trivium*—grammar, rhetoric, and dialectic. Although Greek and Roman students learned some arithmetic and geometry at the elementary level, and picked up a fair amount of mythology, religion, geography, history, and politics incidentally in their reading, and though Greek students, but not Romans, regularly studied music and gymnastics, ancient education was fundamentally literary and rhetorical. Isocrates' view that this was the basis of leadership in a city made it the study par excellence of the free man, and thus the primary "liberal" art.

Isocrates' greatest speech is the *Panegyricus*, published about 380 B.C., relatively early in his career as a teacher. A number of later speeches, such as the *Areopagiticus* or the *Panathenaicus*, resemble it, but are less successful. The *Panegyricus* is the finest and most carefully executed example of Isocrates' prose style as just discussed; it has greater unity of theme, structure, and even imagery than any of his other speeches, and it well illustrates his goal of dealing with only the greatest issues and illustrating them with the noblest actions. The argument is that all Greeks should unite against the barbarians and that the leadership in such a union belongs morally and historically to Athens. Gorgias and Lysias had spoken on panhellenism at Olympia earlier, and Isocrates here imagines himself doing the same. The unity of Greek culture and Greek traditions remained for centuries a rallying cry which was effectively used by orators and kept Hellenism alive until the end of the Roman Empire. Among the proofs of Athens' greatness Isocrates cites the role there of "philosophy" as he understands it, and more particularly of speech, in a splendid period (47–50), a translation of which appears in the diagram on p. 36. The translation attempts to show how some of the Gorgianic figures are utilized. There is a pervasive antithesis or balancing of concepts, two or more clauses or phrases are often given approximately the same shape and length, and in the original there is a considerable amount of similarity of sound at the beginning or end of sense units. In the translation some of these sound effects are identified by italics. The rhythm of the concluding words in Greek is that of the end of a line of heroic verse: dactyl plus spondee.

A final contribution of Isocrates to rhetorical tradition should not be overlooked. It is that he is the first major "orator" who did not deliver his speeches orally. They were carefully edited, polished, and published in written (but of course not printed) form. By his action speech was converted into literature, another influence toward the *letteraturizzazione* of rhetoric.

Love of wisdom, then,
    which has helped us *to discover*
        and helped *to establish* all that makes Athens great,
    which *has educated* us *for practical affairs*
        and made gentle our relations *with each other*,
    which *has distinguished* misfortunes of ignorance
            from those of necessity
        and *taught* us to guard against the former
            and bear up against the latter,
[this love of wisdom] OUR CITY *made manifest*
        and honored Speech,
            which all *desire*
                and *envy* those who know,
    recognizing, on the one hand
        that this is the natural feature distinguishing us from all animals
        and that through the advantage it gives us we excel them in all other things,
    and seeing, on the other hand,
        that in other areas fortune is troublesome
            so that in those areas the wise fail
                and the ignorant succeed,
    and that there is no share of noble and artistic speech to the wicked,
        but *it is* the product of a well-knowing soul,
    and that the wise and those seemingly unlearned most *differ* from each other in this
    and that those *educated* liberally, right from the start, are not *recognized*
                by courage and wealth and such benefits,
            but most by what has been said,
    and that those who *use* speech well are not only *powerful* in their own cities,
                but also honored among other men;
            and
to such an extent has OUR CITY outstripped the rest of mankind in wisdom and speech
    that her students have become the teachers of others,
    and she has made the name of the Hellenes seem no longer that of a people,
                but that of an intelligence,
    and that those rather are called Greeks
                who share our education
                than those who share our blood.

Declamation

The sophistic rhetoric of the fifth and fourth centuries B.C. is an important strand in subsequent classical rhetoric.[9] Cicero (*De Inventione* 2.8) and Quintilian (3.1.14) speak of two traditions, the Isocratean, which is the sophistic form, and the Aristotelian, or philosophical, though Cicero indicates that both have come together in the kind of handbook of technical rhetoric which he is composing. During the Hellenistic period, from the late fourth to the late first century B.C., the term sophist is often used to mean a professional teacher of rhetoric, such as those who flourished in most Greek cities. An early example is the orator Aeschines, who went into exile after being defeated by Demosthenes in the trial of Ctesiphon in 330 B.C. and taught rhetoric on the island of Rhodes.

The characteristic rhetorical form of Hellenistic and later rhetorical schools is the *melete*, or practice exercise. A theme is proposed by the teacher, and the student of rhetoric composes and delivers a speech on that theme. Themes were sometimes "theses" like those also practiced in the philosophical schools, in which the student would attack or defend a statement such as "it is right to kill a tyrant"; or they might be "hypotheses," which are theses with specific names introduced, such as the statement "Harmodius and Aristogeiton were right to kill the tyrant Hipparchus." Such subjects of course could be treated in the form of a mock trial, and they became the ancestor of the *controversiae*, or judicial exercises in declamation of the Roman rhetorical schools, best known from the writings of Seneca the Elder. Quintilian (2.4.41) says that the use of fictitious cases in imitation of the lawcourts began in the time of Demetrius of Phaleron, who ruled Athens from 317 to 307 B.C.

The practice of declamation continued in the East through the Byzantine period. In the West it largely died out in the early Middle Ages, or was absorbed into dialectic, but it reappeared in late medieval and renaissance schools and was introduced into America in the seventeenth century. Most American colleges of the early nineteenth century still provided for declamation in the formal curriculum and at commencement, as well as through the programs of debating societies.

The Second Sophistic

In the first century after Christ a movement appeared which was given the name "Second Sophistic" by the sophist Philostratus, who wrote a history of it up to around A.D. 200.[10] Philostratus distinguishes two kinds of sophist: the pure sophist and the philosophical sophist. The pure sophists were teachers of rhetoric who taught their students some theory, but from Philostratus' account and other sources their emphasis seems clearly to have been on declamation, sometimes of judicial themes, but also of historical and deliberative themes, which are found in Latin under the title *suasoriae*. The pure sophist's own declamation before his class was the chief form of instruction. In a typical case he imagines himself in some situation in classical Greek history and composes an appropriate speech for the situation. He might, for example, reply to an extant harangue of Demosthenes or he might even try to outdo a speech of Demosthenes by composing one on the same subject and in Demosthenes' style.

The other kind of sophist according to Philostratus is the philosophical sophist, who uses oratory to expound his views on political, moral, or aesthetic subjects. Dio Chrysostom (ca. A.D. 40–115) is an early example of the type. These sophists usually also taught declamation, but they became famous orators and often served as ambassadors of their native cities or spoke on civic occasions, and like the earlier sophists they traveled widely, giving demonstrations of their art. In the second century of the Christian era this art form became extraordinarily popular as a form of public entertainment and some sophists became very rich, but they also performed an important cultural function. The commonest themes of the great sophists of the empire were the cultural values of Greek civilization and their manifestation in the Roman Empire. The sophists were like fashionable preachers who encouraged belief in inherited values of religion and morality in the most polished and elegant form, and they contributed significantly to the stability of a society whose major goal was preservation of the status quo in the face of barbarian attack and new religious movements. The most famous of the second-century sophists were Aelius Aristides and Herodes Atticus.[11] Sophists existed throughout the third century, but wars and economic crises made life as difficult for them as for others. In the fourth century, with more stable conditions, there is another flowering of influential sophists: Libanius in Antioch, Themistius in Constantinople, Himerius in Athens, and the emperor Julian the Apostate. Although most of these sophists actually delivered speeches, like Isocrates they also wrote down, edited, and published their greatest efforts as works of literature. An interesting feature of the Second Sophistic is the reappearance in it of the magical element celebrated by Gorgias. This is most evident in Aristides.[12]

Sophistry thus filled an intellectual, emotional, and ceremonial role in antiquity. In particular, the orations of the Second Sophistic fall into a number of formal genres, each with a technical name and certain conventions of structure and content. These include *panegyric*, which is technically a speech at a festival, *gamelion*, or speech at a marriage, *genethliac*, or speech on a birthday, *prosphonetic*, or address to a ruler, and *epitaphios*, or funeral oration. The forms are discussed in a handbook by a rhetorician named Menander, who lived in the third century.[13] They have in common the topic of praise or blame and are thus subdivisions of what Aristotle had called epideictic oratory, but it is not desirable to equate sophistic oratory with epideictic. Sophistic declamation was often in judicial and deliberative forms and even the display speeches of the great sophists are sometimes deliberative in form or intent. We will return to the problem of classification in the next chapter.

The Second Sophistic was primarily a Greek movement, but it was imitated by Romans, and Latin encomia of Roman emperors have survived in considerable numbers, beginning with the *Panegyric* of Trajan by Pliny the Younger. Sophistry was also pagan in origin, and it was often criticized by Christians because of its celebration of the beauties of pagan mythology or because of the emphasis it gave to style, ornament, and the cleverness of the orator. But the Second Sophistic in fact influenced Christianity as early as the second century. In the fourth century, when Christianity had become the official religion of the empire, both the emperors and the orators who celebrated their virtues were usually Christians, and a Christian sophistry was created by Fathers of the Church like Gregory of Nazianzus in the form of panegyrical sermons for the great feasts of the Christian year or for funerals. Gregory and Basil the Great, both trained in the schools of sophists, are their artistic equals in oratory. This tradition of Christian sophistry remains strong throughout the Byzantine period in the East. It can be found in the western Middle Ages as well, but in a more subdued form, and it was embraced with enthusiasm by the humanists of the Renaissance both as a way of ingratiating an orator or writer with the rich or powerful and for the sheer joy of unrestrained artistic expression. French ecclesiastical oratory of the seventeenth century, especially its funeral eulogies, is part of the sophistic tradition, and so is the American Memorial Day or Fourth of July oration.

Sophistry has a bad name with many critics. Plato's objections to the relativism of early sophists began this attitude and the distaste of austere Christians for meretricious ornament perpetuated it. There is an empty verbosity and self-indulgence evident in the vast orations of Isocrates and Aelius Aristides, for all their impeccable standards of language and expression. But sophistry, like rhetoric itself, is not necessarily depraved, decadent, or in poor taste. It is that natural aspect of rhetoric which emphasizes the role of the speaker and the process of learning to speak or to write primarily by imitation of models. Imitation is a subject to which we will return in the discussion of literary rhetoric. Sophistry is also one place within the rhetorical system where allowance is made for genius and inspiration, something which technical handbooks cannot create. In this sense the great critical work of the sophistic movement is the treatise *On Sublimity*, attributed to Longinus and written on the eve of the development of the Second Sophistic. The rediscovery of "Longinus" in the Renaissance was to have important implications for neoclassical rhetoric.

If sophists have sometimes liked to shock or indulge conceits, it should be remembered that most sophists have believed that the orator should be a good man, and their most consistent theme has not been how to make the worse seem the better cause, but celebration of enlightened government, the love of the gods, the beauty of classical cities, the values of friendship, the meaning of patriotism, the triumph of reason, and the artistry of speech.

Chapter 4
Philosophical Rhetoric

There is little distrust of rhetoric in traditional societies, and this seems to have been the case in Greece before conceptualization, but the creation of rhetorical handbooks and the claims of sophists to teach rhetoric made the art vulnerable to criticism. Bold claims about the role of the orator and the power of speech replaced tacit assumptions about aristocratic leaders, and rhetoric could now be learned by anyone interested. Intimately involved with democracy, it awakened the hostility of oligarchs. Because of its newness, it tended to overdo experiments in argument and style. Not only did it easily seem vulgar or tasteless, it could seem to treat the truth with indifference and to make the worse seem the better cause. Reaction was predictable, and that reaction produced what may conveniently be termed "philosophical" rhetoric, the view of rhetoric expounded by Socrates, Plato, and Aristotle.

Socrates (469–399 B.C.) resembled the sophists superficially. He had little interest in physics or astronomy as studied by earlier philosophers and was deeply concerned with human life and human judgment, as were Protagoras and the more philosophical sophists. Like them, he contributed to conceptualization; like them he taught orally, was interested in words, and showed a fondness for paradox. He is distinguished from the sophists by a preference for the question-and-answer method of dialectic rather than lectures or speeches to expound his views; by a rejection of the claims of *nomos*, or convention, as the basis of thought and action; by the fact that he did not accept fees from his followers; and most of all perhaps by his rejection of the rhetorical and assertive role of a sophist. In addition he believed that little good had been accomplished by the debates of the Athenian democracy and doubted that justice was being achieved by the rhetoric of the lawcourts. At least so it would seem, for in common with several other great teachers of antiquity, Socrates left no writings expounding his views. We know him only from the reports of his followers or the reactions of his critics.

By far the most important of these followers is Plato (ca. 429–347 B.C.), who took up many of Socrates' views and developed them over a period of fifty years in a series of dialogues, most of which are represented as Socrates' conversations. What is often called the "Socratic question" is the problem of the extent to which these dialogues represent actual views of Socrates and the extent to which they are vehicles for Plato's own philosophical speculations. The commonest view today is that the historical Socrates stressed the need to examine assumptions and make definitions and that though the seeds of many Platonic doctrines such as the "forms," recollection, and imitation were perhaps implicit in Socrates' interests, Plato felt free to develop his own beliefs, retaining Socrates as a dramatic figure in the exposition.[1] If this is the case, the earlier Platonic writings are likely to be more Socratic than the later ones.

Plato is the greatest Greek prose writer, a master of structure, characterization, and style, as well as one of the greatest thinkers of all time. He is a consummate rhetorician and a literary artist of so many dimensions that any analysis of his work is likely to fall far short of appreciating its full meaning. No dialogue of Plato is untouched by rhetoric—the *Republic*, the *Symposium*, and the *Menexenus* in particular contain interesting applications of the art—but the *Apology* provides the best example of the Socratic orator, and the *Gorgias* and the *Phaedrus* most specifically discuss the nature of rhetoric, so that the discussion here can be limited to these three works.

The *Apology*

The *Apology* is Plato's after-the-fact version of a speech for Socrates at the trial in 399 B.C. which led to his conviction on charges of atheism and corrupting the young and to his eventual execution.[2] A majority of critics have preferred to think that it was composed in the first year or two after the trial, which Plato attended (*Apology* 38b6),[3] but it is possible that the work was written sometime around 390 B.C. in reply to the publication of the *Accusation against Socrates* (now lost) by Polycrates. In any event the *Apology* is one of the earliest works of Plato and is thus one of the closest in time and thought to the actual Socrates. If Socrates did not say what is here attributed to him, the discourse is at least something which, within ten years of his death, he was regarded as capable of having said.

The opening lines of the *Apology* make clear the premise on which philosophical rhetoric is developed, but also the ambivalence of the philosophical orator in regard to conventional rhetoric. Socrates is represented as trying to counteract a warning by the prosecution that the jury should beware of him as a clever speaker. He says that he will soon reveal how lacking in cleverness he is, "unless they label clever one who speaks the truth" (17b4–5). He goes on to say that he will tell the whole truth, that there will be no flowery language, that he is confident in the justice of his cause, that he will speak in his usual way, without affectation, and that since he has never been in court before, the jury should excuse his inexperience and consider only whether he says what is just or not, "for this is the excellence of a juryman, and of an orator it is to speak the truth" (18a5–6). This is a vignette of the philosophical orator consistent with what is pictured elsewhere. As it happens, however, it is also largely consistent with the conventional claims of a litigant in a Greek court of law as seen in the introductions of judicial speeches—for example, in Antiphon's speech *On the Murder of Herodes* (103). Similarly, at the end of his defense (34c–d) Socrates rejects the kind of emotional appeal by relatives and friends which was commonly introduced into the epilogue of a Greek judicial speech, but even in doing so he manages to include pathetic reference to his three sons, two of them still children. The reason given by Socrates for including the reference here is to prevent resentment by a juryman who might think Socrates arrogant; but in a perfectly philosophical speech all this would be irrelevant.

What intervenes between proemium and epilogue in Socrates' speech falls into three main parts: a statement of the case, which is Socrates' denial of the charges (19a–20d); an explanation of the prejudice which has arisen against him over a period of many years (20d–24b); and finally, refutation of the specific charges made against him now. The second of these parts constitutes a narration, since the technique followed is a very candid and vivid narrative of Socrates' way of life in Athens and his encounters with others. The technique in the refutation, by contrast, is basically dialectical. Meletus is interrogated in a way characteristic of Socrates in Plato's other writings, and his claims that Socrates has misled the youths and is an atheist are reduced to absurdities. Although the terminology of argument from probability is not paraded, Socrates in fact claims that it is improbable that he would intentionally have an evil influence in the city in which he lives (25d–26a) and that it is improbable that anyone would believe in supernatural activities, as Meletus admits Socrates does, and not also believe in supernatural beings (27b–e). Socrates then returns to the topics of the hostility to himself and his situation before the court and introduces an excursus in which he reveals his philosophy of life and explains why he cannot abandon it now, even to save himself from death (28a–34b). From the point of view of the legal charges this excursus is a digression (*parekbasis*), but a digression in support of a deeper understanding of the ethical situation. Such "relevant" digressions are highly characteristic of classical oratory. Antiphon's speech *On the Murder of Herodes* has one (64–73), and the "ethical digression" in particular is a feature of the greatest speeches of Aeschines, Demosthenes, Lycurgus, and especially Cicero.

Plato's *Apology* consists of three speeches. The first, which we have been considering, is Socrates' defense. The jurors then cast their ballots and found him guilty, probably by a vote of 280 to 221 (36a–b). Since the law provided no specific penalty, each side next made a proposal about what punishment Socrates should be given. The prosecution proposed death. Socrates would probably have escaped death if he had proposed exile instead, but he regarded that as a betrayal of his philosophy of life and finally proposed a fine. The second speech in the *Apology*, Socrates' discussion of the proposals for punishment, contains a passage relevant to Plato's later picture of philosophical rhetoric (36b–c). Socrates refers to his rejection of ordinary political life in the city, with its assemblies and meetings, and his choice instead to address citizens on an individual basis, "trying to persuade each of you not to have a greater concern for anything you have than for yourselves, that each of you may be the best and wisest person possible, nor to consider the affairs of the city in preference to the well-being of the city itself" (36c5–9). Socrates has thus been engaged in what we have called rhetoric, but on a one-to-one basis and not in oratory to the masses.

The jury then voted on the two proposals and chose death by 360 to 141, some of the jurymen who had earlier voted for acquittal having been antagonized by Socrates' intransigent attitude. Before being taken off to prison—the actual building has now been identified in the excavations near the Athenian *agora*—Socrates is presented as delivering his thoughts on death, which make up a third speech in the *Apology*. Among other things he says:

Perhaps, gentlemen of the jury, you think that I have been convicted because of a lack of the kind of words by which I would have persuaded you if I had thought it right to do and say everything so as to escape the charge. Far from it. I have been convicted by a lack of daring and shamelessness and of wanting to say to you the kinds of things which you most like to hear: you would have liked me to wail and carry on and do and say lots of things unworthy of me in my own judgment. This is what others have accustomed you to hear. But during the trial I didn't think I should do anything slavish and I have no regrets now at the nature of my defense; indeed, I much prefer to die after a defense like this than to live after another kind of defense. Neither in court nor in battle should I, nor anyone else, fight in order to avoid death at any cost. . . . Avoiding death, gentlemen, is probably not very difficult; it is much more difficult to avoid doing wrong. . . . Now having been condemned to death I leave you, but my opponents leave having been convicted by the Truth of wickedness and injustice. I stick with my punishment and they can have theirs. (38d–39b)

It should be noted that Socrates blames orators and not jurors or others for the vitiated form of rhetoric which so widely prevails. Jurors are easily satisfied by hearing what they want to hear, and this form of flattery works on the weaker aspect of human nature, but the orator who uses such flattery is demeaning himself and destroying justice in the state of which he is a part.

Plato's *Gorgias*

The *Gorgias* is one of the earlier dialogues and was probably written soon after Plato's visit to Sicily in 387 B.C.[4] It is a dramatic presentation of a discussion between Socrates, Gorgias, Polus, and Callicles imagined to have taken place in Athens in the late fifth century. Although the interlocutors in most of Plato's dialogues were dead by the time he portrayed them, Gorgias was still alive in the 380s and is reported by Athenaeus (9.505d) to have remarked "How well Plato knows how to satirize!"

The dialogue has three main parts. The first is a conversation between Socrates and Gorgias that is concerned with the definition of rhetoric; in the second part, the conversation between Socrates and Gorgias' follower Polus, the focus shifts to the question whether it is better to do or to suffer wrong, and thus how rhetoric should be used; in the third part, the conversation with Callicles, the still broader topic of how one should live is the context in which rhetoric is given treatment. Dramatically the dialogue as a whole is a confrontation between the dialectician Socrates and three rhetoricians, each in turn more sophistic and further removed from sympathy with Socrates. Polarization thus increases as the dialogue progresses. Socrates seeks to carry on the discussion as dialectic; that is, he asks questions to which the respondent can be expected to know an answer. From argument based on the answer he then can lead his opponent, and the audience in general, along a path to greater understanding. As in other dialogues, for example *Meno*, false knowledge must be destroyed or refuted before a better hypothesis can be advanced and tested. This process can then lead to what Plato calls "true opinion" and at its best to philosophical knowledge.

Dialectic is a faculty of discovering available arguments to answer proposed questions, and in Plato it is the only acceptable form of philosophical reasoning. It follows a method of division of the question and definition of the factors involved, testing hypotheses as they are advanced. In theory the leader of the discussion does not know, at least not with any certainty, what the conclusion will be (see, for example, the words of Socrates in *Republic* 3.394d8–9), but the Platonic Socrates certainly has predilections, and his hypotheses often work out with a feeling of inevitability. Plato would say that this is because new truth is not discovered, but rather old truth is recollected: we all existed before birth and we know much more than we can immediately remember.

In contrast to dialectic, rhetoric involves a preselected arbitrary conclusion: that a defendant is guilty or that the assembly should follow a particular policy or that a certain proposition is feasible. The orator chooses those arguments which prove or seem to prove the conclusion to which he is committed, whether or not it is true. Plato had little confidence in the democratic process, partly as a result of having witnessed the worst excesses of the late fifth century B.C., and he was unwilling to consider debate in the assembly or the speeches of litigants before a court as potentially a larger-scale form of dialectic in which conflicting hypotheses are tried before an audience and justice or wise policy determined by clarification and compromise. (Demosthenes and other Greek orators, in contrast, saw clearly the strength of debate and the dynamics contained within it.) On the other hand, Plato does seem to recognize that there are situations in which dialectic will not work and where recourse to rhetoric may be the only alternative. This happens in the *Gorgias* (505b–509c) when Callicles becomes so angry that for a while he will not continue the conversation and Socrates is forced to expound some of his argument in a continuous speech.

In the following discussion of the *Gorgias* many philosophically important features of the dialogue are ignored; the objective here is to state as clearly and simply as possible what the dialogue has to say about rhetoric.

Socrates asks Gorgias what art he knows and what he should be called (449a3). Gorgias replies that he knows rhetoric and should be called a *rhetor*, a word which in classical Greek ordinarily means "orator," but here is specifically extended to mean one who knows how to teach rhetoric to others.[5] Socrates then, following his method of definition and division, asks what class of objects is included in the knowledge which constitutes rhetoric (449d8–9). Gorgias replies knowledge about words. Socrates next wants to know what kind of words: for example, does it include knowledge of words which explain to the ill how they can get well? Gorgias says that it does not. If this were the report of an actual discussion between Socrates and Gorgias, we should label Gorgias' answer a tactical mistake. As he appears in the dialogue he has not clearly conceptualized what rhetoric is, but his general view is that rhetoric is an art or faculty which can take any subject matter and present it persuasively. Somewhat later (456b) he describes how he himself has accompanied his brother, a physician, on his rounds and used rhetoric for the very purposes about which Socrates here asks.

Gorgias' dialectical position would be stronger throughout if he had been able to compare rhetoric to logic or dialectic and other arts which cut across the disciplines, but it is likely that this was not clearly stated before the time of Aristotle. The Platonic Socrates has no interest in helping Gorgias to such a definition because it runs counter to his philosophical views. Since knowledge in Socrates' view is something grounded in nature and not in convention, only those arts built on knowledge have any validity. The verbal faculty which fulfills that requirement most generally is dialectic, though the *Gorgias* eventually isolates a small valid function for rhetoric in the scheme of things.

Under Socrates' questioning, Gorgias explains that he understands rhetoric to be an art productive of persuasion by means of words and that its sphere is the lawcourts, the council, the assembly, and other public meetings (452e). To this he is subsequently forced to add that it deals with justice and injustice (454b7) and that it is the kind of persuasion which produces belief, not knowledge (454e8). The last point again would have been a mistake in a real debate: the orator deals with both knowledge and belief, depending on the evidence available or the nature of the subject. It subsequently emerges that Gorgias has a low estimate of knowledge (459c), which is consistent with the views of the real Gorgias as expounded in the treatise *On the Nonexistent, or On Nature*. He rather casually asserts (460a) that if one of his students lacks knowledge of a subject he will teach it to him. Conversely, Socrates' very high opinion of knowledge leads him to what may be called the fallacy of the expert, in which the generally educated citizen is seen to be incapable of making any determination of public policy. Socrates unrealistically distinguishes the expert and the orator. He says, for example, in his ironic way, that if the city is considering building a wall, the rhetorician will keep silent and the master builder will give advice (455b). Gorgias fails to take this up and to point out the existence in one and the same human being of a rhetorical function and the knowledge of a builder. Plato portrays Gorgias as very enthusiastic about rhetoric and more interested in making claims for its greatness than in understanding its nature, which may well be true historically, but he does allow him one good speech (456a7–457c3) in which he distinguishes clearly between rhetoric as an amoral force and the morality of the orator. It is not fair, in Gorgias' view, to blame the teacher of rhetoric if a pupil makes an unjust use of the art he has learned. The speaker must bear moral responsibility for what he says.

Socrates is not very satisfied with the direction the conversation has begun to take and asks Gorgias if he can make anyone into a rhetorician. Gorgias says yes but rather gratuitously points out that the orator's ability will be evident "in a crowd" (459a3). Socrates then asks if that does not in fact mean "among the ignorant," and Gorgias says yes. The functional role of rhetoric is once again obscured because of Socrates' insistence on the necessity of knowledge. Rhetoric, he claims, has no need of facts and is a tool of persuasion which makes the unknowing seem to know more than the knowing (459b8–c2). This is then applied specifically to knowledge of justice and injustice. Socrates asserts that since it has been agreed that rhetoric deals with justice, it is inconsistent to say that the orator might use rhetoric for unjust purposes (460e5–461b2). This is an application of the general Socratic paradox that if a person knows what is good he will do it. Thus if an orator knows what is just he will not seek to persuade what is unjust.

At this point Polus breaks in with some irritation, claiming that Gorgias has been too polite to Socrates and has been embarrassed to insist that he had a knowledge of justice and other subjects and could teach this to his students as they needed it. Polus tries to take the lead in the dialectical process and sets out to grill Socrates on his personal views of rhetoric. The attempt leads to the celebrated comparison of rhetoric and the art of cooking (462b–466a). The passage is intended to startle and amuse; it is somewhat tongue-in-cheek in tone and is provoked by the brash personality of Polus, whose name means "the colt." Socrates would not have expounded the image to Gorgias, at least not in these terms. On the other hand, the comparison, like other images in Plato, is seriously intended as a way of getting at the truth and vividly presents Socrates' deepest feelings about rhetoric.

Rhetoric, Socrates says, is not *techne* in any true sense; that is, it is not based on knowledge and rule, but is *empeiria*, a matter of experience, a facility gained from trial and error, or *tribe*, a knack, an empirically acquired cleverness at something. Three other *empeiriai* in this sense are sophistic argument (which is the acquired skill of seeming to prove an argument by verbal trickery), cosmetics (which is the skill to make the flesh look young and healthy by application of paints and powders), and cookery (which is the skill of producing pleasure through food). These four *empeiriai* are forms of flattery (*kolakeia*) and images or reflections (*eidola*) of four true arts. The true arts are divided into two groups: those which work upon the soul, or politics, and those working on the body, which have no collective name in Greek, but might be labeled physical culture in English. Politics in turn is subdivided into two parts, the art of making laws, or legislation, and the art of administering justice. Similarly, physical culture is divided into two parts, gymnastics, or the art of training the body, and medicine, or the art of curing bodily illness. These constitute a proportion: as legislation is to the administration of justice, gymnastics is to medicine. The first member of each pair is normative and looks toward the future; the second is corrective, setting right what has gone wrong in the past. Plato describes each (464b8) as the *antistrophos*, or counterpart, of the other, a term we have seen in Isocrates, who may have been influenced by this passage.

THE TRUE ARTS

Of the Soul: Politics		*Of the Body: Physical Culture*	
Legislation	Justice	Gymnastics	Medicine
(Normative)	(Corrective)	(Normative)	(Corrective)

FORMS OF FLATTERY

Of the Soul		*Of the Body*	
Sophistic	Rhetoric	Cosmetics	Cookery
(Normative)	(Corrective)	(Normative)	(Corrective)

In Plato's version, set against the four true arts are the "arts" of flattery, also involving soul and body. The two knacks of flattery of the soul are sophistic, which Socrates arbitrarily defines as a sham form of inducing belief in some fake principles or norms for conduct or action, and rhetoric, which is a sham form of persuading an audience by flattery that something is just. The former, being normative, can be compared with legislation; the latter, a corrective technique, with the administration of justice. The two arts of flattery of the body are cosmetics, corresponding to gymnastics, which makes the body seem to be healthy and strong when it is not, and cookery, which corresponds to medicine and tries to correct weakness or illness by pleasurable feelings of well-being. The true arts are always based on knowledge and aim at the good; the sham arts or flatteries are based on experience and aim at producing pleasure. The diagram above outlines the relationships and may help to make clear how the arts as viewed by Plato are counterparts to each other, a concept also important for Aristotle's description of rhetoric as the antistrophe to dialectic.

The long discussion which follows (466b–479e) takes its start from the sophistic theme of the power of the orator in the community and leads to Socrates' conclusions that it is more wretched to do than to suffer injustice and that a person who is not punished for crimes is more wretched than one who is. Under those circumstances, Socrates asks (480a2), what great use is there for rhetoric? If a person really has done wrong he will only make himself more miserable if he uses rhetoric to defend himself. It would be better for him to use techniques of rhetoric to make his crimes clear and thus to rid himself of injustice (480d)! (The greatest literary example of this form of self-deprecatory rhetoric is perhaps Augustine's *Confessions*.) Socrates also suggests using rhetoric to prevent an enemy from being punished, thus forcing him to languish in the wretchedness of injustice (480e–481b).

The third and longest part of the *Gorgias* is the conversation with Callicles, who is the most violent of the three interlocutors. He expounds his views of nature and convention (482d5–6), makes fun of philosophy as childish inanity, cites the authority of Homer for the importance of speech, and regards speech as an important way for a man to defend himself (486a–c). In general Callicles admires drive, energy, acquisitiveness, hardheadedness, lack of concern for others, self-confidence, the attainment of luxuries, and above all, success. He is an ambitious Athenian of the fifth century and would also have been at home in the cities of the Renaissance. Rhetoric is important to him. Socrates by contrast admires justice, philosophy, restraint, self-examination, and simplicity. Rhetoric is not an acceptable way to attain his goals, at least not in its common forms. Of course Socrates does have a "rhetoric" of his own; he attains his purposes by valid argument, but also by irony, by subtly appealing to the better instincts in men, and elsewhere sometimes by a mystical pathos.

In the course of the discussion Socrates asks Callicles if there are not forms of flattery which aim at pleasure without consideration of what is better or worse (501b5). Callicles is already incredulous about the entire discussion, but he admits there are such forms and also that it is possible to play upon the souls of not just one or two, but many people at the same time. This leads to consideration of poetry, which Socrates describes as a rhetorical public address, "Or don't poets seem to you to use rhetoric in their plays?" (502d2–3). Since public address is a form of flattery, it is not very admirable in Socrates' view, but Callicles observes that some orators speak with a concern for the citizens (503a3), and Socrates almost unexpectedly agrees. There is, he says, the rhetoric of flattery and shameless address to the public, but there is another kind of rhetoric too, "and this other is beautiful, making provision that the souls of citizens will be the best possible, striving to say what is best, whether this is more pleasant or more unpleasant to the audience. But you have never seen this rhetoric. Or if you are able to name any such orator, why have you not told me who he is?" (503a7–b3). This orator will be a good man; he will speak nothing at random; he will always keep his mind on his purpose (503d–e).

Will not that orator, artist and good man that he is, look to justice and temperance? And will he not apply his words to the souls of those to whom he speaks, and his actions too, and whether he gives something to someone or takes something away from someone, will he not do it with his mind always on this purpose: how justice may come into being in the souls of his citizens and how injustice may be removed, and how temperance may be engendered and intemperance be removed, and every other virtue be brought in and vice depart? (504d5–e3)

This is the primary statement of the true or philosophical rhetoric found in the *Gorgias*. It represents a considerable advance over the description of rhetoric as flattery in the conversation with Polus and even over the acceptance of a kind of rhetoric by which the repentant sinner may lay open his sins.

In answer to Socrates' inquiry as to whether there have been any good orators Callicles suggests Themistocles, Cimon, Miltiades, and Pericles (503c1–2), all statesmen of the fifth-century Athenian democracy. Socrates does not reply at the time, but he later (515c–517a) takes up the topic and concludes that there has not been a single good politician in the state of Athens. The test he imposes is whether the statesman made the citizens better than they were when he entered office, and all are rejected because of the way the people turned against them. But the statesman must not fear death, and the final pages of the dialogue present the myth of Minos, Rhadamanthus, and Aeacus, judges of the underworld.

The conclusion of the *Gorgias* is that one must study to be good. The bad must be punished; flattery of all sorts should be avoided; and rhetoric, like other things, must only be used for the sake of justice (527c3–4). The work may be viewed as a preliminary statement which needs considerable development before being accepted. Its main strength is the insistence on knowledge as the true basis of valid communication. Its main logical flaw is Socrates' unwillingness to separate those arts like politics which have a specific subject matter from those like rhetoric which are reasoning faculties applicable to all subjects. The need for the orator to be a good man was recognized also by Isocrates and the more responsible sophists, but their separation of the rhetorical function from other qualities in an individual, logical as it is, did indeed run the risk of tolerating evil. Plato's integration of the intellectual, moral, and rhetorical qualities of the orator into the whole man avoids that risk, but at the cost of practical effectiveness. Socrates was executed on a charge of which he was innocent, whereas rhetoric perhaps could have secured his escape at the cost of some flattery of the jury. Philosophical rhetoric is thus an ideal, beyond the possibilities of the Greek city. Plato's recognition of this fact is shown in the *Republic*, which takes up many of the moral concepts of the *Gorgias*, but it proves necessary in the later dialogue to construct an ideal state in order to discover justice. The *Republic* also has much to say about the proper forms and functions of poetry, which turns out to be very similar to philosophical rhetoric. But it has little to say about rhetoric in the narrow sense, for which we must turn instead to the *Phaedrus*.

The *Phaedrus*

The *Phaedrus* is one of the middle group of Platonic dialogues, as is the *Republic*, and it was composed ten or fifteen years after the *Gorgias*.[6] The exact date cannot be determined, nor can we even say with certainty whether it followed or preceded the *Republic*. It is tempting to see a relationship between the development of views on rhetoric in Plato's Academy and the works emanating from Isocrates' school, in which case a probable sequence could be drawn beginning with Isocrates' *Against the Sophists*, followed by Plato's *Gorgias*, then Isocrates' *Helen*, followed by Plato's *Phaedrus*, Isocrates' *Antidosis*, and early works of Aristotle in the Academy. Aristotle is said to have begun his teaching of rhetoric with the remark that it was shameful to keep silent and allow Isocrates to teach (Cicero, *De Oratore* 3.141). This sequence would put the *Phaedrus* in the late 370s or early 360s, but it must be regarded only as a hypothesis and should not be used as the sole basis of dating or interpretation of the works involved.

The *Phaedrus* is among the most complex of Plato's dialogues in a literary sense. Although the view of rhetoric which emerges from it is relatively clear, that subject is subtly connected with the theme of love and complicated by the question of the relative value of the spoken and the written word. Here Plato goes significantly beyond the suggestions of the *Gorgias* about the positive role of rhetoric; he lays the foundation for basic features of Aristotle's *Rhetoric*, and he integrates rhetoric into his other philosophical ideas in a way not attempted elsewhere.

The tone of the dialogue is vastly different from the *Gorgias* from the outset. Instead of a conversation with three sophists with whom Socrates is personally at odds we find here a conversation with a young man to whom Socrates is strongly attracted and who responds to him warmly. Indeed, the first half of the dialogue has a pervasive erotic tone. Not only is the subject of homosexual love discussed, but the dialogue is set in an almost voluptuous vale of rustic beauty, unique in Plato, and were anyone other than Socrates involved it would not be difficult to imagine the scene developing into a physical intimacy. Homosexual love was an acceptable convention in many parts of fifth century Athenian society, especially in the aristocratic group associated with Socrates. Historically this is certainly to be associated with the very suppressed role of women in Greece, which precluded their being either intellectual or social companions of men; heterosexual relationships were often thought of as limited to biological reproduction, whereas the relationship between males was capable of idealization into a union of two immortal and similar souls. Phaedrus entices Socrates, partially seduces him to the pleasures of sophistic rhetoric, and even threatens rape (236c8–d1). Socrates flirts with him in turn, but in the course of the dialogue converts the relationship into a higher level of philosophical, or what has come to be called Platonic, love.

The dialogue falls into two parts. The first part is largely made up of three speeches. Phaedrus has attended an exhibition by Lysias in which that orator, known to us chiefly as the writer of speeches for clients in the lawcourts, argued that an imaginary young man should accept the attentions of another who does not love him but is physically attracted to him. The result would be a pleasant relationship in which neither would be emotionally hurt. Phaedrus is much impressed with the cleverness of the paradox and has secured a copy of the speech to memorize. He is prevailed upon to read it to Socrates. We do not know whether this speech is an actual work by Lysias or whether it is a creation of Plato in the style of erotic sophistry. The latter is perhaps likely considering the custom of historians and others of inserting in their works speeches which they themselves composed. Plato clearly delighted in imitating the style of sophists such as Protagoras or Gorgias and may have tried his hand with that of Lysias, whom he knew personally.

The speech is erotically exciting to both Phaedrus and Socrates, but of course it represents the antithesis of Socrates' view of what rhetoric should be. It is deceitful and untrue; if successful it will adversely affect the soul of the one addressed, and it is thus philosophically immoral. Socrates does not begin with that objection, however; what he finds wanting in the speech is its method, for it is repetitive and lacks structure. He is thus led to compose a better speech on the same theme, but he veils his head to avoid the embarrassment of catching Phaedrus' eye, and he makes one small change in the situation: he imagines the speaker as secretly in love with the boy he is addressing; pretending not to love him is a ploy to secure his attention (237b4). Socrates' speech is characterized by a definition of love, lacking in Lysias' version, and by a logical division of the subject, but many of the arguments are necessarily similar to those in the first speech.

After speaking, Socrates prepares to leave before he is led into doing anything more immoral (242a1–2). As he is about to cross the stream on the way home, and thus to escape from the incident, the divine voice which speaks to his conscience comes to him. He turns back and confesses to Phaedrus that his speech has been dreadful, for it represents love as an evil whereas love is in fact divine. A recantation is necessary, for the boy should accept the love of a true lover. "Where is that boy to whom I was speaking?" he says. "Here he is, very close beside you, whenever you want him," replies Phaedrus (243e).

Socrates' second speech is to be taken as an example of "true" rhetoric. Love may be a form of madness, but madness is not necessarily an evil. Beneficent madness has at least four forms: the inspiration of prophets like the prophetess of Apollo at Delphi, rites of purification such as those of Dionysus, poetic inspiration from the Muses, and the madness of love. To understand the last we must understand the soul, which Socrates describes mythically in terms of a charioteer and two winged horses. One horse is spiritual and noble, one physical and evil. It is natural for the soul to rise, and in the intervals between its lives on earth the soul rises up through the heavens to a glimpse of the reality of beauty and truth. When the soul is born in a human being it loses much of this vision, but it continues to be drawn to beauty, and when it sees beauty in a boy it is moved to love. The great danger is that the vicious horse of physical passion will pull the two lovers down to sordid hedonism, but if the better element can prevail, the two lovers can mount to a philosophical and orderly life which is the greatest experience for man. Socrates' speech is vibrant with a mystical intensity and a beauty of image which inspires Phaedrus, and has inspired readers for twenty-five hundred years. The tone of the dialogue is thus transferred from the sensual cleverness of the sophists to the vision of the philosopher.

Socrates' second speech is not specifically foreshadowed by the description of good rhetoric in the *Gorgias*, in the sense that the latter was limited chiefly to judicial or public deliberation, but it is consistent with the standards foreseen in the *Gorgias*, reflecting the need to address the soul of the hearer, to make that soul better, and to move it toward temperance and virtue. This is largely accomplished not by dialectic, for all Socrates' definitions and divisions, but by the ethical force of the speaker and by the emotional impact of the myth. Such a use of myth is an important part of Plato's own rhetoric in many dialogues, the most famous example being the somewhat similar myth of Er at the end of the *Republic*.

The first half of the *Phaedrus* is a drama of the rhetorical encounter between good and evil on the field of love. The speech of Lysias is an initial victory for evil; the first speech of Socrates is a more significant victory for evil in that it is not merely sophistic cleverness which triumphs, but a use of the dialectic of definition and division for evil purposes. The situation is then dramatically turned around by intervention of the divine voice which leads to the delivery of a second speech by Socrates and the persuasive victory of the true and philosophical rhetoric. This sudden inspiration is interesting historically, since outside of Platonism the other great field for philosophical rhetoric is that of religion, especially Christianity, and there too the impulse to valid rhetoric is often represented as dependent on the act of God in warming the heart so that truth can be revealed, as we shall see in chapter 7. Within the classical tradition in rhetoric this supernatural feature is generally lacking. Its chief classical counterpart in the composition of noble oratory is a living sense of tradition, seen in Isocrates' philosophy of Hellenism, shared also by orators of the Second Sophistic, and in the patriotism of Demosthenes or of Cicero. These traditions furnish the orator with an outside test of the consistency and value of his ideas in the way that philosophy did to Plato and religion to the Christian orator.

The first half of the *Phaedrus* illustrates forms of rhetoric and utilizes examples of sophistic oratory and the tradition of composition by imitation, which we have seen extending from the Homeric poems down to the fifth century. The second half of the *Phaedrus* conceptualizes the ingredients of oratory and standards for speaking and appropriately considers the contents of the rhetorical handbooks of the time.

The first subject mentioned is that of writing speeches (257c–258e). Lysias is a speech writer. Is that disgraceful? Not necessarily, Socrates says; disgrace comes from speaking or writing badly. A more important question is how we are able to distinguish these qualities. A brief digression (258e–259d) then reminds us of the physical setting of the dialogue and of the Muses who combine attention to heavenly things with an interest in human discourse, thus symbolizing philosophical rhetoric.

The question of the standards of good speech is then discussed at some length (259d–274b). This discussion first raises briefly the matter of the orator's knowledge (259d–261a). Can he be content with what *seems* to be true? Does he need to know the good and the beautiful or only what *seems* good and beautiful? It is quickly agreed that knowledge is required, and the subject is put aside for the moment in favor of a second question: granted that the orator needs knowledge, is that adequate for him or is rhetoric an art and if so what does it include?

Socrates gives a preliminary definition of the rhetorical art as "a kind of leading the soul by means of words, not only in lawcourts and public assemblies." Socrates' two speeches in the first half of the dialogue and his view of the relationships of the speaker to the hearer's soul certainly indicate that a one-to-one relationship can be as rhetorical as a public address. Even though private applications can be found in all periods and all literary forms (for instance, the epistle eventually emerges as a specific manifestation of private rhetoric), classical rhetorical theory consistently limited the scope of formal rhetoric to public speaking. It is regrettable that Plato's suggestions of a wider application were not taken up by Aristotle, since the result might well have been greater attention to the nature of the rhetorical act and less to the conventions of forms of public address. Socrates here points out that debate can occur in a public assembly, but also between two individuals, and he describes the art involved as one by which a person can make everything similar to everything or refute another speaker who seeks to do so. Similarities or dissimilarities are often matters of very small differences, and the conclusion is, therefore, that the orator needs knowledge adequate to make such distinctions. Particularly he must be able to make definitions (as Socrates did in his speeches) and to divide the subject into logical categories (263b6–9). Lysias' speech illustrates the failure to do this and also the failure to order the material and create unity of related parts: "It is necessary for every speech to cohere like a living thing having its own body so that nothing is lacking in head nor foot, but to have a middle and extremities suitable to each other, sketched as part of a whole" (264c6–9).

This is probably the most influential single critical statement in Plato, reflected for example in Aristotle's requirement that tragedy have a beginning, middle, and end, and important for the development of the critical method of the Neoplatonists of late antiquity, who insisted on approaching the Platonic dialogues and other major works of literature as absolutely consistent wholes. The idea was partially anticipated in the *Gorgias* (505d1–2), where Socrates does not want to break off the argument "without a head," that is without a proper conclusion. These abilities to structure the argument and achieve a unity are restated by Socrates as two contrasting faculties: that of bringing widely scattered material together into a single "idea," and that of dividing material into species on the basis of its natural articulation (265d–e). Those who can do this, he says (266c1), he has been accustomed to call "dialecticians," but he does not insist on that word. That is, a true "rhetorician" would do something similar and there is little logical difference between dialectic, or the discovery of truth, and rhetoric, or the persuasive exposition of truth. Both have the same logical structure.

The subject then turns to a consideration of existing rhetorical handbooks to see what features of rhetoric they omit. The handbooks turn out to be devoted, as we saw in chapter 2, to the parts of the judicial oration, to types of diction, and to lists of commonplaces. Phaedrus is quickly led to see that they fail to provide an understanding of when it is appropriate to use these materials. Their authors are dealing only with preliminaries; they lack the dialectic necessary to understand rhetoric; and they leave it up to their students to achieve organization and unity in speech (269b–c). Oratorical ability, like everything else, is a combined result of nature, knowledge, and practice (269d), as Isocrates and most ancient rhetoricians would agree. For great oratory one additional requirement looms large, a loftiness of mind striving always for perfection (270a). This comes from philosophy and in particular involves a knowledge of the soul:

It is clear then that Thrasymachus and anyone else who seriously publishes an art of rhetoric will first, with all possible accuracy, describe and make us see the soul, whether it is one thing and uniform or multiple like the nature of the body. . . . And secondly he will describe what the soul does to what other thing or has done to it by something else, in accordance with its nature. . . . And third, arranging in order the kinds of speeches and the kinds of souls and their various states, he will describe all the causes of change in the soul, fitting each kind of speech to each state and teaching what soul is necessarily persuaded by what speech through what cause and what is unpersuaded. (271a4–b5)

This is the outline of what Plato conceives to be a true art of rhetoric. Although Socrates restates the art in slightly fuller terms (271c10–272b4), Plato never worked out the outline in detail. Discussion of the characters and the emotions takes up a considerable part of Aristotle's *Rhetoric*, and it is an important foreshadowing of the interest in psychology of British neoclassical rhetoricians. One importance of the idea is that it puts the audience on a full equality with the speaker and the speech in the rhetorical act. The major problem it raises is, as often in evaluating Plato's theories, the practical one. How can an orator know the souls of his audience in any full sense? And if he does, how can he fit his speech to the variety of souls likely to be found there? How can he keep from enflaming one at the same time he calms another? Plato shows a preference for rhetoric in a one-to-one situation: Socrates can indeed know the soul of Phaedrus, but he regularly speaks of souls in terms of genera and species, which suggests that they can be viewed as types rather than individuals. Aristotle's solution is to deal with souls in terms of the stages of life and the dominant passions and thus to carry through the study in terms of group psychology.

The discussion in the *Phaedrus* of what would constitute a true art of rhetoric is preceded by remarks about the orator's need for knowledge. It is followed, and thus framed, by a return to that same subject. In the lawcourts, we are told, it is commonly believed that the orator must prove what is plausible and probable, not what is true (272d7–32), and Socrates goes on to describe argument from probability as expounded by Tisias. But just as small differences in similarity cannot be detected except by a person with full knowledge, so the probable is a semblance of the true and can only be known by knowing truth (273d–e).

Finally, the entire discussion of knowledge and art is framed by a return to the first question discussed in the second half of the *Phaedrus*, that of the relative value of speaking and writing.[7] Here the view of writing is more negative than in the earlier passage. An Egyptian tale about Theuth and Thamus is told, with the conclusion that writing encourages forgetfulness. We know from Socrates' second speech in the first half of the *Phaedrus* what a bad thing forgetfulness is, since it separates us from the good and beautiful. Socrates makes the additional point here that a written work is like a painting and cannot speak. It can fall into the hands of those who do not understand it, and if so has no way of explaining itself, or if it is ill-treated it has no way to answer back. Writing is in fact an illegitimate brother of true, or oral discourse (275d–276a). If a man who knows truth and beauty uses writing it will be as a kind of plaything for his own amusement (276d).

As far as rhetoric goes, the major thrust of the passage is to assert the superiority of dialectic again, this time not in the sense of definition and division, but of the question-and-answer process of exploring an hypothesis. Rhetoric, in contrast, is like writing in being frozen into one form, that of the continuous speech with a thesis to be stated and proved. In a literary sense the passage helps to unify the dialogue, for it takes us back not only to the beginning of the second part, but to the beginning of the whole dialogue, where Phaedrus had appeared with a written text of Lysias' speech, a text which proved singularly unable to defend itself. Finally, the passage helps to restore the ironically playful tone with which the dialogue opened. Socrates, after all, did not commit his discourse to writing; Plato does, and suggests that he views it only as a kind of game for his own amusement. We see again the paradoxical side of Plato: the rhetorician who distrusts rhetoric, the poet who abolishes poetry from his state, and the admirer of oral dialectic who publishes dialogues worked out with extraordinary care.

There are two other passages in the concluding pages of the *Phaedrus* which deserve mention. One is the ostensibly complimentary reference to Isocrates as a promising young orator at the time the dialogue is imagined to take place (278e8). It is difficult not to take this as somewhat ironic in the context, for no Greek orator more developed the written forms of oratory and was less at home in dialectic. The other passage is Socrates' final picture of philosophical rhetoric as it emerges from all that has been said before. The passage contains nothing new, but it is a convenient summary of Plato's fully developed view. Although most translators chop it up into a series of short sentences, what Plato wrote was a long periodic sentence in which a true art of rhetoric is made dependent on the fulfillment of a series of previous steps:

Until someone knows the truth of each thing about which he speaks or writes and is able to define everything in its own genus, and having defined it knows how to break the genus down into species and subspecies to the point of indivisibility, discerning the nature of the soul in accordance with the same method, while discovering the logical category which fits with each nature, and until in a similar way he composes and adorns speech, furnishing variegated and complex speech to a variegated soul and simple speech to a simple soul—not until then will it be possible for speech to exist in an artistic form in so far as the nature of speech is capable of such treatment, neither for instruction nor for persuasion, as has been shown by our entire past discussion. (277b5–c6)

Among the implications of this passage is that there are various "styles" of discourse, appropriate in various settings and with various audiences. This idea, briefly touched on by Aristotle, was taken up by Theophrastus and developed by later writers into the "characters" of style, largely under the influence of the versatile successes of orators like Demosthenes and Cicero.

Plato's works were continuously read throughout antiquity, but his views on rhetoric exercised relatively little direct influence on classical rhetoricians. He was most often viewed as an enemy of all rhetoric, which is hardly entirely fair. What influence he had on rhetorical theory until the Renaissance came at second hand, through his student

Aristotle, Aristotle's student Theophrastus, Cicero, Longinus, and the Neoplatonists of later antiquity. Even in the Renaissance when Plato became immensely popular, his views of rhetoric were rarely given the serious attention they deserve. The primary reason is the strength of the tradition of technical rhetoric as taught in schools. Probably the best treatment of Platonic rhetoric in later times can be found in the *Dialogues on Eloquence* of Fénelon, written in the late seventeenth century, which will be discussed in chapter 11. In the eighteenth and early nineteenth centuries, especially in America, Plato's reputation suffered badly, but the twentieth century has again given serious attention to the issues about rhetoric raised in the *Gorgias* and *Phaedrus*.

Aristotle

Aristotle was born in northern Greece in 384 B.C., and though a Greek, he had close associations with the Macedonian court. He came to Athens to study with Plato in 367 and remained as a member of the Academy for twenty years. In many areas of study Aristotle apparently began with questions as Plato viewed them, but he lacked Plato's mystical side and was far more pragmatic than his master. He found it impossible to accept the Platonic theory of ideas as separate reality, and he was not attracted by the interest in mathematics which characterized Plato's later years. Doubtless realizing that he could not expect to succeed Plato as head of the school, and perhaps nervous at the growing hostility between Athens and Macedon, Aristotle left Athens shortly before Plato's death in 347 and moved to Assos, near Troy in Asia Minor, and then in 345 to Mitylene. In 343 he was invited to become the tutor of the thirteen-year-old Alexander, heir of Macedon. He continued in this capacity in Mieza or elsewhere until 340, when he returned to his native town of Stagira. The Macedonians defeated the Greek city states at the battle of Chaeronea in 338, and in 336 Alexander became king. In 335 Aristotle returned to Athens and opened a school in a covered walk or *peripatos* (hence the term "Peripatetic School") of the public gymnasium known as the Lyceum. Here he taught until 323, when he retired to Chalcis on Euboea to avoid the hostility to Macedonians which followed the death of Alexander, and he died there in 322. Theophrastus had succeeded him as head of the school in Athens.[8]

Aristotle's earliest writing on rhetoric was apparently the *Gryllus*.[9] Very little is known about the contents of this lost work, but it seems to have presented arguments against viewing rhetoric as an art (Quintilian 2.17.14). Gryllus was Xenophon's son, killed in 362 B.C. and the subject of several encomia (Diogenes Laertius 2.54–55). Aristotle may have criticized these encomia in a prologue and then constructed a dialogue, set in the recent past, in which Gryllus and his friends discussed the extent to which rhetoric and oratory constituted an art. If so, the discussions in Plato's *Gorgias* and *Phaedrus* would have been major influences.

The *Gryllus* may be dated around 360 B.C. Sometime thereafter, still as a member of Plato's Academy, Aristotle began to give a course on rhetoric, perhaps partially in reaction to Isocrates' teaching, and he continued to do so when he opened his own schools abroad and eventually in Athens.[10] These lectures are the basis of the *Rhetoric*. Like other surviving treatises by Aristotle, the *Rhetoric* is one of his "esoteric" works; that is, it is a draft of his theories without literary adornment, intended for his own use and for his students and not for publication. From time to time he revised the text, making additions or changes as his views on the subject developed. Footnotes and appendices were unknown in Aristotle's time, and material inserted in the text of his works sometimes elaborates a particular point at the expense of the orderly flow of the thought. Other points are sometimes left obscure, but perhaps were elaborated when Aristotle used a treatise as lecture notes. These characteristics are seen in his treatises on ethics, politics, metaphysics, and other subjects, as well as rhetoric. The treatises of Aristotle are thus living documents, and all the more interesting for that reason: the reader can see the philosopher's mind working out various stages of the argument, not always to full conclusion. Aristotle would not have objected to the further refinement of his ideas by his successors, ancient and modern.

There are references both in Aristotle and in later writers to a variety of other works on rhetoric or collections of material made by or for Aristotle. The *Synagoge Technon*, the summary of the handbooks of early rhetoricians mentioned in chapter 2, was probably compiled as background for Aristotle's lectures on rhetoric at some stage of his teaching, much as Plato in the *Phaedrus* finds occasion to consider, though more briefly, the contents of the handbooks he knew. The text of the *Rhetoric* which we have probably represents Aristotle's thinking on the subject during the major period of his teaching in Athens, 335–323 B.C. The latest datable reference to contemporary events is apparently the mention of a common peace (2.23.399b13) which can be taken as referring to the Peace of Corinth of 336 between Macedon and the Greek states.

Rhetoric was hardly a major interest with Aristotle. He seems to have taught it as a kind of extracurricular subject in the afternoon (see Quintilian 3.1.14), and probably not continuously. He was, however, interested in the nature and interrelationship of the sciences and the arts, and rhetoric thus has a place in his total system, as it was to have in the trivium and quadrivium of the Middle Ages or in the more philosophical system of Francis Bacon. Before turning to examine the *Rhetoric* it is desirable to have some understanding of Aristotle's total system.[11]

In the *Metaphysics* (6.1.1025b25) Aristotle says that all intellectual activity is divided into three categories: theoretical, practical, and productive. Theoretical intellectual activity is directed toward subjects like mathematics, where the objective is to know; practical intellectual activity toward subjects like ethics and politics, where the objective is doing something or doing it in a certain way; productive intellectual activity toward making something like creating a poem or a statue. The sciences differ from the arts in that the former deal with things which cannot be other than they are: in studying mathematics, for example, we discover what is necessarily true, not what is probably true. Art, on the other hand, is a capacity to realize a potentiality on the basis of reasoning. It is not concerned with things which exist by nature or by necessity, but rather with "the coming into being of something which is capable of being different from what it is" (*Nicomachean Ethics* 6.4.1140a10–15). At the very beginning of the *Rhetoric* (1.1.1354a9–10) Aristotle indicates that rhetoric is an art since we can ask "why some speakers succeed through practice and others spontaneously." Coming into being results from the operation of causes, of which there are four kinds, usually all present. A simple statement of the concept of the four causes, or ways things are said to be caused, can be found in the *Physics* (2.3.194b16–195a26). First is the material cause, such as metal as a cause of metal objects. Second is the formal cause, the pattern or genus which causes the form a product takes. The third is the efficient cause, the maker as cause of the product. The fourth is the final cause, that for the sake of which something is done or made, as the cause of exercise is health.

Aristotle does not systematically discuss how the four causes are to be applied to rhetoric, but it is probably consistent with his system and certainly with his treatment to say that the material cause of a speech is, in the final analysis, the words of which it is composed, but more immediately the arguments and topics which those words constitute; words, arguments, and topics are discussed at length in the *Rhetoric*. The formal cause is the genre to which the speech belongs, and Aristotle comes to the conclusion that there are three genres of oratory: judicial, deliberative, and epideictic. The efficient cause is the speaker. The final cause is persuasion.

It might be thought that the arts would be found exclusively among practical and productive activities, but this is not the case. An art will be theoretical as long as its objective is understanding something, rather than doing or making something. Now theorizing exists at two levels. What Aristotle calls *apodeixis*, or demonstration, is reasoning on the basis of logical necessities and should be thought of as a science. This is the subject of the *Prior Analytics*. But it is also possible to reason about probabilities, in other words the coming into being of something which is capable of being different from what it is, and this is dialectic, the subject of the *Topics*. (The *Posterior Analytics* contains discussion of both forms of reasoning.) Dialectic is thus a theoretical art.

What kind of an art is rhetoric? Insofar as it involves creativity, rhetoric, like poetics, might be a productive art, but Aristotle fails to make the identification. Rhetoric in his view does not produce oratory in the same sense that poetics produces poetry, for it stands at a different stage in the productive process. What rhetoric does, in Aristotle's view, is "to discover [*theoresai*] the available means of persuasion" (1.1. 1355b25-6). It is thus a theoretical activity and discovers knowledge. This knowledge, which includes words, arguments, and topics, is then used by the orator as the material cause of a speech. There is thus a theoretical art of rhetoric standing behind or above the productive art of speech-making. Conversely, one could imagine a theoretical art of poetics which would stand parallel with rhetoric as a form of knowledge one stage removed from poetry. Since in the *Poetics* the final cause of tragic poetry is catharsis, the end of such an art of poetics would be discovery of the available means of catharsis. The *Poetics* is sometimes criticized because, at least in the part preserved, it does not define catharsis. Neither does the *Rhetoric* define persuasion.[12] These and other ideas are implicit within Aristotle's thinking, and given world enough and time he would doubtless have worked them out in a logical fashion.

Aristotle's *Rhetoric* as we have it consists of three books. The first three chapters of the first book present in outline his view of a philosophical rhetoric. They constitute an answer to the objections of the *Gorgias* that rhetoric is not an art and develop the suggestions of the *Phaedrus* as to what constitutes a valid rhetoric. The rest of Book 1 and all of Book 2 work out the system in considerable detail. In Book 3 Aristotle adds a discussion of delivery, style, and arrangement. Recognizing that the *Rhetoric*, like Aristotle's other treatises, is a developing work, we should avoid imposing an artificial consistency on it. Aristotle simply has not revised the whole, so that words, even technical terms, are not always used with the same meaning, and he has not always reconciled material developed in detail in one part of the treatise with references in other parts. In addition to the problem of classification just mentioned, three major inconsistencies which appear are, in order of importance, (1) the inconsistency of Aristotle's complaints in the first chapter of Book 1 about earlier writers on rhetoric with the material he himself eventually adds in Book 2 on emotional appeal and in Book 3 on style and delivery; (2) his use of the term *topos* to mean different things in different passages, and especially his failure to make clear the relation of the "topics" described in Book 2, chapter 23, to other "topics"; and (3) varying degrees of emphasis on the *enthymeme*, or the *enthymeme* and the example, as the basis of proof. There are also some internal problems of consistency in the treatment of the virtues of style and the parts of the oration in Book 3.

Despite inconsistencies in its structure, the organization of the material in the *Rhetoric* strikes a major blow for philosophical rhetoric, consistent with the direction in which Plato had been looking. Aristotle begins with the relation of rhetoric to dialectic, the extent to which it can claim to be an art, the centrality of logical proof, the various kinds of knowledge and subject matter required, and then moves on to the way the orator applies his material to the kinds of soul he encounters in his audience. Some critics have been puzzled by the fact that whereas in discussing metaphysics and some other subjects Aristotle has much to say about the ways in which he differs from or is indebted to his predecessors, in the *Rhetoric* he says nothing about the relation of his ideas to those of the *Gorgias* and the *Phaedrus*. The reason surely is that his views are in fact an orderly development of the direction in which Socratic and Platonic thought had been moving for nearly a hundred years in contrast to the mainstream of classical rhetoric, represented by the handbook writers, the sophists, and Isocrates. Plato in the *Phaedrus* had already found some things he could utilize in specimen speeches and handbooks, and by the time the *Rhetoric* reached its present form Aristotle had found it convenient to include considerably more such material in a revised form, but his basic point of view about the nature of rhetoric remains that of his philosophical, not his sophistic predecessors.

To Plato, the only valid method of inquiry into truth is dialectic, which consists in a search for definition and a process of distinguishing genera and dividing up species. Philosophical or valid rhetoric should use this same method, though in continuous discourse rather than in question and answer, and in a movement which begins with the truth to be demonstrated rather than with a question to be explored. Dialectic is logically prior to rhetoric, which is the public demonstration of truths already privately determined.

In Aristotle's system dialectic is a somewhat more limited form of intellectual activity than it was to Plato. Superior to it is *apodeixis*, or demonstration, which is reasoning from scientifically true premises. Dialectic, in contrast, is the form of reasoning built on premises which are generally accepted, whether by everybody, by most people, or by those with some authority on a matter (see *Topics* 1.100a25–b23). Aristotle viewed dialectic as useful in three ways: as an intellectual training in argumentation; in unstructured discussions with individuals for the sake of determining the truth of some issue; and in connexion with the study of the various intellectual disciplines (*Topics* 1.2.101a25–b4). The first use is similar to that practiced by sophists; the second is essentially what goes on in most Socratic dialogues. The third involves the ability of the dialectician to raise difficulties on both sides of an issue, thus clarifying a problem, and it also facilitates the development of premises on which disciplines can be constructed. Aristotle's *Politics*, for example, begins with the premises that every state is a community, that a community is established for the sake of some good, and that men act in order to obtain what they regard as good. These premises are based on general agreement; they are not developed within the science of politics, and they can be demonstrated only by dialectic, not by scientific demonstration. It is characteristic of Aristotle's system that dialectic, like rhetoric, is more an art of communication than of the discovery of new truth; in the *Topics*, for instance, the student, like an orator, is usually assumed to have an hypothesis he wishes to prove, rather than to be engaged in an open-ended discussion. This feature of Aristotelian dialectic contributed to its rejection from the scientific method in the seventeenth century.[13]

If we turn now to the text of the *Rhetoric*, we find that Aristotle begins with the relationship of rhetoric to dialectic. "Rhetoric," he says in the first sentence, "is an *antistrophe* of dialectic." *Antistrophe* means "counterpart." We have seen that Plato and Isocrates used the related word *antistrophos* to indicate that rhetoric was a counterpart or correlative to some other art. The functions of rhetoric and dialectic, Aristotle means, are parallel movements, virtually identical in content; both deal with matters which are common subjects of knowledge among men; neither falls within any distinct science. Whether through rhetoric or through dialectic, all people have occasion to question or support an argument, to defend themselves or accuse others. The central concept of philosophical rhetoric, shared by Socrates, Plato, and Aristotle, is that rhetoric is essentially and logically a part or a form of dialectic.

The subsequent references to dialectic in the *Rhetoric* may represent earlier formulations of its relationship to rhetoric, but they are not significantly inconsistent with Book 1, chapter 1. We are told, for example (1.2.1356a25) that rhetoric is a *paraphues*, an "off-shoot," of dialectic and that it "dresses up" as political science. A few lines later (1356a30) rhetoric is called a *morion*, or small part, of dialectic and a *homoioma*, or likeness of it: neither dialectic nor rhetoric is knowledge of a distinct subject, but they are *dynameis*, or faculties of furnishing arguments. In chapter 4 (1359b9–14) we are told less technically that rhetoric is made up (*synkeitai*) of analytical knowledge and of the part of politics which is concerned with ethics and that it is like dialectic and sophistic argument; to treat dialectic and rhetoric as forms of scientific knowledge, rather than as faculties, is to destroy their true nature. The concept of a faculty is a convenient way for Aristotle to stress the fact that dialectic and rhetoric are forms of reasoning, unique in their functions, and without specific subject matters of their own; but faculties are included among the arts and Aristotle repeatedly speaks of rhetoric as an art or as artistic. The technical definition of rhetoric comes at the beginning of chapter 2: "Let rhetoric then be a faculty of learning in each case the available means of persuasion."

Aristotle is at pains to explain how rhetoric is similar to dialectic and says virtually nothing about how it differs from dialectic, which a modern reader would like to know. The reason for this is that rhetoric was much better known and more studied than dialectic, but its relationship to dialectic had not been stressed except by Plato. Aristotle takes up rhetoric as commonly understood by the sophists and Isocrates and largely reduces it to dialectic, but certain differences remain. One is formal: rhetoric is found in the forms of continuous discourse, whereas dialectic takes the form of debate. Rhetoric usually addresses a large audience, and the orator must sense his hearers' reaction; dialectic usually involves one-to-one argument and explicit agreement or refutation. There is, moreover, some difference in subject and in the treatment of subject. Dialectic usually deals with philosophical or at least general questions, rhetoric with concrete or practical ones. Dialectic is rigorous and constructs chains of argument; rhetoric is popular and expansive. It avoids complex argumentation and often employs things like maxims or fables which will appeal to an audience. As treated in the *Rhetoric*, rhetoric is limited to civic life and to three kinds of speeches: judicial, deliberative, and epideictic. Because Gorgias and Isocrates had treated rhetoric as an art of political discourse, Aristotle is at pains to show that it is a faculty and not a substantive art of politics, but he does view it as a faculty whose application or materials are political. Thus in the *Ethics* (1.1.1094b3–4) rhetoric is said to "come under" politics, which is the *architechne*, or master art, of the good for man. In the *Poetics* (chapter 19) rhetoric is seen in the speeches of tragedy and epic as well as in oratory, but these are analogous to political discourse. Both in oratory and in poetry rhetoric arouses emotion, rightly or wrongly, which dialectic does not do (to judge from the *Topics*), and the good character of the speaker has an important role in rhetoric, whereas in dialectic only the argument matters.

If rhetoric is a form of dialectic, the writers of the handbooks are sadly lacking: proofs alone are "artistic," everything else is supplementary, Aristotle claims. What the handbooks should discuss is the *enythmeme*; what they do discuss is arousing the emotions (*Rhetoric* 1. 1.1354a12–18). Aristotle's moral demands on the orator are consistently high. It is not right to pervert the jury by leading it to anger, envy, or pity (1354a24 25). We must not persuade what is wrong (1355a31). At no point in the *Rhetoric* do we find glorification of the orator, his power, his political or artistic success; such views are characteristic of sophistic but not of philosophical rhetoric.

The chapter divisions in Aristotle's treatises are creations of later editors, but what we call the first chapter of the *Rhetoric* is indeed an introduction to the subject as the philosopher sees it. Existing handbooks are inadequate, not only because of what they include, but because of their preoccupation with judicial oratory (which remained true of classical rhetoric) to the exclusion of the nobler form of political oratory, and because of what they do not include, the essence of rhetoric: *pisteis*, or modes of persuasion. *Pistis* is a kind of demonstration. (Aristotle here inconsistently uses the word *apodeixis* to include probable truth.) Rhetorical demonstration is the *enthymeme*, that is, a kind of syllogism; the study of syllogisms is the subject of dialectic (1355a3–a18). Rhetoric is useful, for the audience cannot be expected to come to the right conclusion if the truth is not presented so that people can understand it, and there are those whom it is difficult to instruct. Ability to persuade makes it easier to understand both sides of an issue and thus to see the facts. A man ought to be able to defend himself with speech, which is something characteristic of man. Speech can do great harm, but so can most good things (1355a19–b7). The point about the ability to argue on both sides of the issue is an important addition by Aristotle to the concept of philosophical rhetoric. We have seen that he included it in dialectic as well. The addition should be regarded not as a concession to sophistry, but as a logical conclusion from the function of dialectic and rhetoric as forms of reasoning and thus as techniques of clarifying ethical and political issues. In Plato philosophical rhetoric seemed authoritarian and antidemocratic, but in Aristotle the value of open debate is recognized.

Aristotle's systematic account of rhetoric begins in chapter 2 with the definition of rhetoric as a faculty for discovering the available means of persuasion and proceeds through the various forms of *pisteis*, or modes of persuasion. They are of two sorts: *atechnoi* and *entechnoi* (1355b35).[14] *Atechnoi*, or nonartistic or external modes, are outside the art of the orator to create, though he can use them. They include the evidence given by free witnesses, the evidence extracted from slaves under torture, written contracts, and other direct evidence discussed in chapter 15 of Book 1. Under the influence of the technical handbooks, with their judicial focus, Aristotle fails to consider external proofs available to deliberative or epideictic speakers, such as the important matter of the occasion on which they speak. *Entechnoi*, or artistic or internal modes of proof, are of three sorts, which we may call *ethos*, *pathos*, and *logos*. They derive from the three constituents of the speech-act: speaker, audience, and speech respectively. *Ethos* is the personal character of the speaker as seen in the speech; the orator should seem to be a good man and one who can be trusted. In Aristotle's view ethos should be accomplished through the speech and not be a matter of authority or the previous reputation of the orator (1356a9–10). The reason for this is that only ethos projected in this way is artistic. The authority of the speaker would be analogous to his role as witness and would thus be *atechnos*, something not created but used by the orator. This doubtless seemed all the more logical to Aristotle because of the common situation in Greek lawcourts, where the litigants were often persons of no particular reputation who had purchased speeches from logographers or professional speechwriters. A logographer's duties came to include the artistic creation of a credible ethos for the client.

Pathos occurs as a mode of artistic proof when the souls of the audience are moved to emotion: they will come to a different conclusion, for example, when they are angry than when they are pleased. Aristotle acknowledges that this is the same subject which he criticized writers of handbooks for treating to the exclusion of anything else and promises to discuss it in detail later in the work (1356a14–19); he was thus aware of the inconsistency. The orator must thus be able to understand character and the emotions (1356a22–24). This is a very brief statement of exactly what Plato concluded in the *Phaedrus*. Aristotle goes on to the statement discussed above, that rhetoric is a *paraphues* of dialectic, and that it sometimes tries to assume the form of politics.

He then takes up, for the rest of chapter 2, what we have called *logos*, or that mode of proof found in the argument and most characteristic of rhetoric (1356a35–1958a35). In chapter 1 this was said to be a matter of enthymemes, but here a twofold classification is made, parallel to that in dialectic. We are referred to the *Topics* for additional information. Argumentation, Aristotle says, can be inductive, based on

Forms of Proof in Aristotle's *Rhetoric*

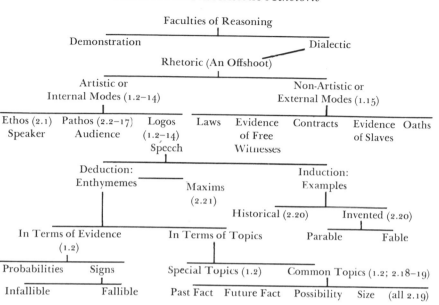

Faculties of Reasoning

Demonstration   Dialectic

Rhetoric (An Offshoot)

Artistic or Internal Modes (1.2–14)   Non-Artistic or External Modes (1.15)

Ethos (2.1) Speaker   Pathos (2.2–17) Audience   Logos (1.2–14) Speech   Laws   Evidence of Free Witnesses   Contracts   Evidence of Slaves   Oaths

Deduction: Enthymemes   Maxims (2.21)   Induction: Examples

Historical (2.20)   Invented (2.20)

Parable   Fable

In Terms of Evidence (1.2)   In Terms of Topics

Probabilities   Signs   Special Topics (1.2)   Common Topics (1.2; 2.18–19)

Infallible   Fallible   Past Fact   Future Fact   Possibility   Size   (all 2.19)

Kinds of Oratory in Aristotle's *Rhetoric*

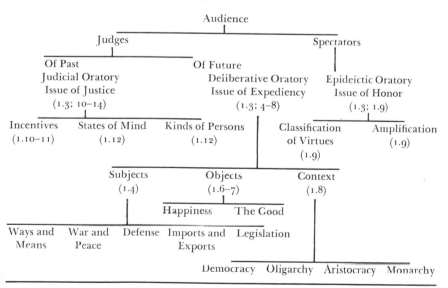

Audience

Judges   Spectators

Of Past Judicial Oratory Issue of Justice (1.3; 10–14)   Of Future Deliberative Oratory Issue of Expediency (1.3; 4–8)   Epideictic Oratory Issue of Honor (1.3; 1.9)

Incentives (1.10–11)   States of Mind (1.12)   Kinds of Persons (1.12)   Classification of Virtues (1.9)   Amplification (1.9)

Subjects (1.4)   Objects (1.6–7)   Context (1.8)

Happiness   The Good

Ways and Means   War and Peace   Defense   Imports and Exports   Legislation

Democracy   Oligarchy   Aristocracy   Monarchy

a series of examples which are then generalized into a conclusion; or deductive, in the form of an enthymeme. An instance of argument from example in oratory would be instances in Greek history when a popular leader had demanded a bodyguard in order to establish himself as tyrant, from which the orator concludes, "thus anyone who seeks a bodyguard seeks tyranny." The choice of proof by examples rather than by enthymeme is partly a matter of style (1356b18–27), but we are told later that proof by example is more suitable to deliberative than to judicial oratory, since we must predict the future on the basis of our knowledge of the past (1368a29–31).

In chapter 20 of Book 2 (1393a25) the subject of the use of examples is taken up again and they are classified into "historical" and "invented" examples. The instance just given would serve for the historical type. Invented examples are of two sorts: the parable, or comparison, as when Socrates ridicules the choosing of public officials by lot by comparing the process to choosing athletes or pilots by lot; and the fable, which is an imaginary historical example. Aristotle says that he favors using enthymemes where possible, and then adding an example as a kind of witness to the point. If the speaker puts examples first, he needs a number of them to establish their general implication (1394a9–16). But the orator might say, "Dionysius should not be given a bodyguard, for one who seeks a bodyguard seeks tyranny. If you don't believe me, look at the example of Pisistratus." Here a general observation, which could have been established by induction, is stated as an enthymeme, its premises being regarded as generally accepted, and then a specific example is added to clinch the point. In a passage in the *Prior Analytics* (2.23.68b30–69a19) Aristotle recognizes that proof from example can take syllogistic form, and elsewhere in the *Rhetoric* (2.25. 1402b14) he makes example one of the kinds of premises on which enthymemes are built. It may be that his view on this subject differed at different times or that he uses the term example in two different senses.[15]

Enthymeme is used by Isocrates (*Evagoras* 10) to mean a thought or idea uttered by an orator. In the *Prior Analytics* (2.27.70a10) Aristotle gives the word the technical meaning of a syllogism based on probabilities or signs. One thus might expect it to be commonly used in dialectic, which deals with probabilities, but in the *Topics*, Aristotle's discussion of dialectic, *enthymeme* is only used to refer to an argument in rhetoric (8.14.164a6), and dialectical arguments are called syllogisms. Aristotle seems to have thought that though argumentation in rhetoric, as in dialectic, rested in large part on the use of syllogisms, it was desirable to call rhetorical arguments by the different name to suggest the less rigorous logical context of oratory.[16] Enthymemes are certainly reducible to syllogistic argument, but their form of presentation is not always that of argument. In particular, the orator often suppresses one of the premises (1357a17–21). For example, "Doreus has been victor in a contest where the prize is a crown, for he has won the Olympic games" is an enthymeme which in its full form would consist of the major premise, "The prize in the Olympic games is a crown"; the minor premise, "Doreus has won the Olympic games"; and the conclusion, "Doreus has been victor in a contest where the prize is a crown." In Book 2 (22.1395b25) Aristotle seems to say that premises should not be fully expressed in rhetoric, but to judge from the context what he means is that a tight logical argument is not effective in rhetoric, which is addressed to a popular audience. Any syllogistic argument in a rhetorical context is an enthymeme, whether fully expressed or not. Is the argument only an enthymeme if the premises are probable? No. Despite the definition given in the *Analytics,* in a rhetorical context the argument is an enthymeme *even if the premises are certain* (see *Rhetoric* 1.2.1357a30–31).

Aristotle categorizes enthymemes in two different ways: one way is in terms of the material of the premises, whether probabilities or signs; the other way is in terms of the "topic" of the enthymeme as a whole, which is the more important logical distinction. Many of the enthymemes in a speech are in fact matters of political theory, economics, military strategy, or the like. These are particular topics of the arts or sciences under which they fall. Rhetoric of course makes use of them, but more characteristically dialectical or rhetorical are "common topics" (*koinoi topoi*) which have no special subject matter and do not make the listener knowledgeable about any one class of things (1.2.1358a21–22). Only one is identified here, the topic of the more and the less (1358a14), but in chapter 3 (1359a11–26), and chapters 18 and 19 of Book 2, four common topics are identified: the possible and the impossible, past fact, future fact, and size (the more and the less, the great and the small). One of the more characteristic common topics is what later came to be called *a fortiori* argument: if the harder of two things is possible, so is the easier; similarly, if the less likely of two things occurred in the past, the more likely probably occurred as well.

The Latin for *koinos topos* is *locus communis,* of which the English translation is "commonplace," but it is desirable not to use "commonplace" as a translation for Aristotle's common topic, since that will create confusion with the kind of commonplace found in sophistry or in secondary rhetoric throughout classical literature. Good examples of the latter from Aristotle's time are the trite observations for or against the validity of various kinds of direct evidence which professional orators inserted at need into any speech, or commonplaces about the gods or the laws of Solon or Xerxes' invasion of Greece. The third chapter begins with an identification of the elements in the speech-act as speaker, speech, and audience. Modern rhetoricians would add other factors, including the occasion, which might have proved useful to Aristotle in his subsequent discussion, but which he would apparently regard, like the speaker's authority, as an external influence. Here he next defines three kinds of rhetoric on the basis of three kinds of audience which a speaker can address in a speech: judges of past action, judges of future action, and spectators. This is the most influential of all his divisions. After consideration of the categories and their differences Aristotle takes up each in detail and his discussion extends through the rest of Book 1. Although the distinction is based on the kinds of audience, Aristotle clearly thinks of this part of the work as essentially an exploration of the subject matter of speeches (*logos*) and primarily as a definition of the material available to the orator for the construction of enthymemes (see, e.g., 1.7. 1365b19–20). He does not, however, narrowly restrict himself to that classification of the material, and he brings in the use of the example (1.9.1368a29). Some of the material he discusses would also be useful for an orator's understanding of ethos (e.g., 1.9.1366a25–27), and the addition at the end of Book 1 of a chapter on direct evidence in judicial oratory shows that he is trying to give an overall coverage of the contents of the three different kinds of oratory. This tendency to begin with a rather limited view and to expand it to include material of practical use to the orator, exemplified from Greek oratory as known to Aristotle's contemporaries, means that we gradually lose the clear focus on philosophical rhetoric as rational proof with which the treatise begins. The change is parallel to the movement within the *Rhetoric* as a whole, which begins with a limited philosophical view of the subject but in the course of three books expands to include style and arrangement and at times uses the prescriptive language of a rhetorical handbook. Aristotle was not able to resist bringing into the discussion most of the material of which he was aware, even at the expense of his original definition.

Up until Aristotle's time it had been recognized that there were various species of oratory, including prosecutions, defenses, funeral orations, and others, but these had not been classified into genres, and as far as we know Aristotle originated the concept of the three kinds of oratory, which became a permanent part of rhetorical theory. That he intended the classification to be a universal one can be seen in the universal terms in which it is originally laid out. A hearer of a speech must be a judge or not a judge. In the latter case he is described as a *theoros*, a spectator (1.3.1358b2–3). If he is a judge, he is being asked either to judge past fact (Did X perform this act?) or to make a judgment about what should be done in the future (Should the proposed policy be followed?). These two possibilities are the situations of judicial and deliberative oratory respectively, and each has, as Aristotle notes (1358b20–29), its final cause: litigants seek to establish what is just or unjust; the deliberative speaker is fundamentally concerned to establish that a course of action will be expedient for the audience, or at least not harmful to it. He may have something to say about justice, but that is secondary to his purpose. All of this is incisively, even brilliantly sketched. In chapters 4 through 8 of Book 1 the various subjects, objectives, and contents of deliberative rhetoric are examined in some detail, and in chapters 10 through 15 the materials of judicial oratory are considered: incentives for wrongdoing (10–11), the states of mind of wrongdoers (12), the kinds of persons wronged (12), the classification of just and unjust actions (13), and the comparative evaluation of unjust actions (14). In these chapters Aristotle summarizes a great deal of material, chiefly from politics and ethics, of which he believes the orator must have knowledge. Indeed, one is reminded of the sophist's claim in Plato's *Gorgias* that if a student did not know enough about a subject, Gorgias would teach him.

The treatment of the situation when the hearer is not a judge is less satisfactory. Aristotle calls such a speech "epideictic," or demonstrative, and says it refers to the present time in contrast with the focus on the past seen in judicial oratory, and on the future in deliberative (1358b18). He thinks of epideictic as the praise or blame of a man and that the final cause of such a speech is demonstration of the honorable or the shameful. The category is thus suitable for funeral oratory or for that kind of sophistic speech exemplified by the *Helen* or the *Evagoras* of Isocrates. In the detailed consideration of epideictic in chapter 9 the subject is somewhat enlarged to include the praise of gods, animals, and inanimate objects (1.9.1366a30). Slippage of the moral tone of philosophical rhetoric is first clearly evident in this chapter. For example, Aristotle says that "it is necessary to say that a quality honored by the audience is present [in the person being praised]" (1.9.1367b9–10). "Necessary" in what sense? To secure persuasion. It is also in this chapter that the prescriptive tone associated with rhetorical handbooks becomes evident, including the use of the verb in the second person. For example, "If you do not have enough to say about your subject himself, compare him to others, as Isocrates used to do . . ." (1368a19–20).

Aristotle admits (1367b37–38) that epideictic and deliberative overlap and suggests that the difference is often one of style. This is further confirmed by his discussion of epideictic style in Book 3, chapter 12. A great deal of what is commonly called epideictic is deliberative, written in an epideictic style—in most of the speeches of Isocrates, for example, where the object of the speech is to get an audience (in Isocrates' case readers) to make judgments about future policies for Athens or Greece. Much of Christian oratory is deliberative as well: the missionary sermon seeks to convert the heathen to a new faith to the end that the audience's actions will be consistent with Christian teaching. A speech of greeting to a visiting dignitary, a speech of thanks, such as Cicero's to the senate on his return from exile, or speeches of congratulation at birthdays or weddings, which were common in later antiquity, would fall within Aristotle's epideictic in so far as the objective is to get the audience to view the person or action in question as honorable or shameful. Many speeches of this sort, however, including encomia of public officials, are often intended, or partly intended, to urge the addressee to some future action or at least to a point of view about possible action. To that extent they logically fall into Aristotle's concept of deliberative oratory, but Aristotle's classification recognizes the fact that such speeches are distinctly different in structure and in style from the oratory of political debate.

The classification of epideictic has proved an important one historically, since at many times in history praise or blame has been the chief form of speech open to an orator to accomplish some other purpose; moreover, rhetorical conventions of praise and blame have been consistently borrowed by poets and other writers. It might be noted also that epideictic passages have often been inserted by orators into judicial or deliberative speeches to discredit an opponent or to win the good will of an audience—for example, Demosthenes' personal attacks on Aeschines in the lawcourts and Cicero's praise of Pompey in the Roman assembly to secure passage of the Manilian law. Perelman and Olbrechts-Tyteca in *The New Rhetoric* suggest that epideictic oratory is noncontroversial and aims at increased adherence to an accepted value, but this view, like Aristotle's, fails to provide adequately for the mixture of intentions found in actual oratory.[17] Sometimes the primary intent of an orator is to influence the audience's judgment of himself as a good or bad encomiast. Aristotle himself admits elsewhere (2.18.1391b15–17) that the *theoros*, or spectator, of epideictic is in a sense a judge; but he ordinarily prefers to restrict judgment to the narrower context of lawcourts and assemblies. It is possible to regard epideictic as a stylistic and topical phenomenon, evident in varying degrees in the two primary forms of oratory, judicial and deliberative, and capable of dominating other considerations in some contexts.

Another possibility is to add "occasion" to the factors in the speech-act and say that epideictic is "performance rhetoric," characterized by its association with formal occasions, such as funerals, whereas the other rhetorical forms are more independent of the occasion and characterized by the need to make a judgment.[18] In such a classification the orations of Isocrates again turn out to be deliberative, not epideictic, since their associations with occasions are literary fictions.

The second book of the *Rhetoric* opens by confirming the fact that the material in Book 1 has set forth the topics of enthymemes. It remains for Aristotle to discuss the other two modes of proof, the projection of ethos in the first chapter, and the emotions of the audience, which are the subject of discussion from chapters 2 through 17. These emotions are grouped into anger and calmness, friendship and enmity, fear and confidence, shame and shamelessness, kindness and unkindness, pity and indignation, envy and emulation (chapters 2–11 respectively). In the following chapters the various stages of life are considered in terms of their emotions and qualities. We have already noted that this represents Aristotle's attempt to construct an art of rhetoric along the lines plotted in the *Phaedrus* and that he solves the problem of how to address the soul by viewing it as belonging to a group of stereotypes.

The structure of the rest of Book 2 is confusing. After seventeen chapters devoted to ethos and pathos, we are suddenly taken back to the philosophical rhetoric of chapter 2 of Book 1, told that all that really matters is knowledge and decision, and advised that this is true even if only one person is addressed. Aristotle thus keeps alive Socrates' view that rhetoric is not limited to public occasions, though his account of the three kinds of oratory has hardly taken it very seriously. The rest of chapter 18 is a summary of the material from Book 1, chapter 3, through Book 2, chapter 17, followed by a resumption of the discussion of common topics where that subject was left in Book 1, chapter 2. It seems likely that the material stretching from Book 1, chapter 3, through Book 2, chapter 17, represents an insertion into an earlier stage of the text at a time when Aristotle became convinced that an art of rhetoric limited to the matter of rational proof did not adequately describe oratory as he knew it, and for that matter, did not even adequately fulfill the requirements of philosophical rhetoric as laid down by Plato in that it reflected no knowledge of the soul. He thus worked out that material, borrowing much of it from his studies of politics and ethics, and included it in a rather condensed and non-speculative form. Chapter 18 is then inserted as a link to take the student back to the train of thought of Book 1, chapter 2, with which this material or an earlier version of it was once contiguous. Chapter

19 elaborates the kinds of common topics found in the inserted material of Book 1, chapter 3 (1359a11–26). This earlier stage of composition is then continued in chapter 20, on the example, which we have already considered; in chapter 21 on *gnomai*, not otherwise anticipated; and in chapter 22 on the effective use of enthymemes.

Toward the end of chapter 22 Aristotle says that he wants to consider "the whole subject in general in another way" (1397a1) and introduces what is now chapter 23, on topics. The chapter discusses twenty-eight lines of reasoning, for example, inference from opposites ("temperance is good, for intemperance is harmful") or from correlatives ("if one person gave a benefit, the other received it"). These are also common topics in the sense that they are applicable to many different situations, and there is some overlap with the topics discussed earlier (for example, the fourth topic of chapter 22 resembles topics of chapter 19), but most are forms of argument rather than materials of argument. The passage is reminiscent of some parts of the *Topics* and is probably the remains of an earlier study in which Aristotle was seeking to discover how to describe rhetorical argumentation in terms of art. If so, it antedates his exposition of the enthymeme. He retained it, as he retained other material from various studies, because it seemed potentially useful to one studying rhetoric and oratory, even though it no longer fitted smoothly into his organization of the subject around the enthymeme. The topics of Book 2, chapter 23, are in fact enthymemes, and Aristotle's intention in chapter 22 is to join them into the text by recognizing that fact. If the appendix had been a literary phenomenon known to Aristotle, chapter 23 would have made an excellent one. The remaining material in Book 2 is a chapter on refutation and a short chapter on amplification and depreciation; both are based on the theory of the enthymeme and round out aspects of the subject for which no previous opportunity could be found.

With the end of Book 2 Aristotle's philosophical art of rhetoric is complete. The last sentence, however, states that we must now consider style and arrangement, and in Book 3 Aristotle proceeds to do so with no further reference to his abandonment of his original concept of philosophical rhetoric. Several explanations can be offered for this development. First, proof is certainly given pride of place in the *Rhetoric* and is the subject of the first two-thirds of the work, whereas the parts of the oration which constituted the framework and much of the substance of the handbooks is demoted into the third place as a kind of appendix. It is a characteristic feature of many Greek writings that the beginning of a work is the most important and that the emotional tone dissipates or the thought is diluted toward the end. Second, style and arrangement, whatever Aristotle says at the beginning of the

Rhetoric, are logical, if subsidiary, parts of rhetoric and inherent in Plato's view that different styles are appropriate for different audiences and that the logical structure and unity of a speech is an important consideration. Third, Aristotle was himself consistently interested in the organic unity of a whole and its realization of its potential; style and arrangement are part of artistic rhetoric and can be handled well or badly, and they thus need consideration. Fourth, the treatment of style and arrangement in the *Rhetoric* is considerably more philosophical than it was in the handbooks. Aristotle does not give a random list of techniques or figures but instead outlines the beginning of a concept of the virtues of style and considers what is essential to rhetorical structure.

Assuming that one were to develop the idea of philosophical rhetoric beyond what is said in the first two books, Aristotle's account in Book 3 is not an illogical step. Historically its major disadvantage is that it seemed a step in the direction of compromise with sophistic rhetoric and therefore diverted attention from the principles of philosophical rhetoric. A combination of the ideal and the real is, however, highly characteristic of Aristotle. It is seen in the *Politics* and in the *Ethics* and is one of the motivations in his systematic collection of data, including his summary of the handbooks of rhetoric. We should not jump to the conclusion that Aristotle added the third book to the *Rhetoric* late in his career at a time when the influence of Plato's ideas on rhetoric had faded. Aristotle's reference to the actor Theodorus (1404b22) implies that he is still alive, which means that Aristotle wrote at least a version of the sentence when he was teaching rhetoric in the Academy before Plato's death.[19] It is not unlikely that Aristotle studied matters of style in prose and in poetry in the earliest stage of his career, even though he may not have combined that material with Books 1 and 2 of the *Rhetoric* until a much later date.

Book 3 of the *Rhetoric* contains a number of important and influential features. First is the suggestion (1403b18–22) that the "natural" order of rhetoric is to consider first the materials from which a persuasive speech can be constructed, second the style in which the material can be set forth, and third the delivery of the speech. This is the basis of what later come to be called the five parts of rhetoric, which trace the act of composing a speech from "invention" of the subject, to its "arrangement," the casting of thoughts in an appropriate "style," the entrusting of the speech to "memory," and finally the "delivery" of the completed work. Aristotle's addition of an art of style to one of invention, together with his suggestion that an art of delivery is possible, may be said to have inspired this system, though it is not actually found until two hundred years or more later; and it must be remembered that Aristotle put arrangement after style rather than after invention.

Second is the proposal that delivery might become a part of rhetoric. Aristotle outlines what would be contained in a discussion of delivery, which no one had yet composed: the use of the voice to express various emotions, which is a matter of *megethos*, or volume, *harmonia*, or pitch, and *rhythmos*, or rhythm (3.1.1403b31). He did not regard delivery as a very dignified subject, since it was associated with acting, but his student Theophrastus took it up and composed the treatise which is here said to be needed. Aristotle reveals some defensiveness about this further step away from philosophical rhetoric. We cannot do without delivery, he says:

The just thing is to seek nothing in speech either to annoy or to delight the audience. It is just for cases to be tried on the basis of the facts themselves in such a way that everything other than their demonstration is irrelevant. But these other factors have great influence, as has been said, because of the depravity of the audience. Saying something in such and such a way makes some difference in making it clear, though not so much as is thought. All these things are forms of fantasy and directed to the hearer: nobody teaches geometry like this. (3.1.1404a5–12)

Third is the distinction between the language of poetry and that of prose (1404a28–29) and the rejection of "magical" qualities of language of the sort taught by Gorgias. Poetry was developed first and thus prose took on a strongly poetic quality, but Aristotle says that even poetic forms in his time were moving away from poetic language; he inserts a cross-reference to the *Poetics* for those interested in more detail. Even in the *Poetics* Aristotle stresses clarity (22.1458a18), not lyricism. The irrational powers of language have no attraction for him.

Fourth are the qualities or virtues (*aretai*) of good style. Style must above all be clear, or it cannot accomplish its purpose, and it must be appropriate. We are told in chapter 2 how these qualities can be attained through use of different kinds of words considered singly. Aristotle clearly wishes, however, that good style also have a quality of distinction, and a key ingredient in that is the proper use of the metaphor. Metaphor is especially important in prose, in his opinion, because the other forms of adornment are not available to the prose writer, and metaphor thus becomes the basis for clearness, charm, and distinction (1405a8). In chapter 3 various faults in the use of words are listed and in chapter 4 the simile is discussed, which Aristotle views not as a comparison, but as a subordinate type of metaphor.[20] In chapter 5 *hellenismos*, or correctness of Greek grammar, is discussed, a virtue which corresponds to clarity and appears particularly in the use of words in composition. Chapter 6 lists specific ways to achieve *ongkos*, or impressiveness in composition. Chapter 7 discusses the virtue of propriety, *to prepon*. These qualities were somewhat rearranged by Theophrastus in his treatise *On Style* and eventually became a standard list of four virtues of style: correctness, clarity, ornamentation, and propriety.[21] They are discussed in some form by many writers on classical rhetoric and reorganized by Dionysius of Halicarnassus and later by Hermogenes into a complex system of stylistic qualities.[22]

Fifth, in connexion with the virtues of style, Aristotle discusses prose rhythm and the periodic sentence in chapters 8 and 9. Interest in rhythm had developed in the late fifth century and was a major consideration to masters of fourth-century prose like Demosthenes. Aristotle attempts to conceptualize this interest around the principle that good prose should achieve a mean between the rhythmical regularity of verse and a complete absence of rhythm. Such a mean he finds in the two rhythmical feet called paeons.[23] His conception of a prose period is basically that of an antithesis, or two parallel motions.[24] He distinguishes a running style from a periodic style and recognizes a periodic quality even in a simple sentence, but he does not undertake analysis of the great prose periods of contemporary writers like Isocrates. Chapters 10 and 11 continue the discussion of qualities of style.

Sixth is the recognition in chapter 12 of various kinds of style. Aristotle is unaware of the categories of grand, middle, and plain style, which Theophrastus probably developed later.[25] He does, however, recognize that written discourse, which includes epideictic oratory, should be more finished than oral discourse and that the style of judicial oratory is worked out with greater detail than that of deliberative, which he compares to scene painting, intended to be seen from a distance (1414a8–11). An analogy between rhetoric and the arts is pointed out by many philosophical and technical writers on rhetoric.

Seventh is the discussion of arrangement, or the parts of the oration, which takes up chapters 13 to 19. The most striking feature of the discussion is the claim that basically an oration has only two parts, statement and proof. In chapter 13 we are thus briefly back in the world of philosophical rhetoric, but in what follows, proemium, narration, and proof, together with refutation, interrogation, and epilogue, are considered in terms of the actual needs of the Greek orator. The second-person verb of the prescriptive handbooks appears repeatedly. An important feature of the account is that Aristotle considers the arrangement not only of judicial but also of epideictic and deliberative oratory.

Aristotle's student Theophrastus and others in the Peripatetic School reexamined and altered several aspects of his work. Theophrastus' contributions included further development of Aristotle's suggestions about delivery, a reorganization of his ideas on the virtues of style, and definition of the epicheireme as a fully stated rhetorical argument in contrast to the enthymeme, or truncated argument.[26] The *Rhetoric* seems to have been known to the teachers of the Hellenistic period mostly through Theophrastus or other secondary sources. According to the first-century geographer Strabo (13.609), the treatises of Aristotle, which still remained unpublished at his death, were removed to Asia and lost until the early first century B.C., when they were found, brought to Rome, and edited. This tradition is perhaps exaggerated, for the Peripatetic School in Athens probably had copies of most of Aristotle's works, but it is generally confirmed by the fact that Cicero's *De Oratore* of 54 B.C. shows a knowledge of the *Rhetoric* considerably more profound than what is evident in his early treatise *De Inventione*. Subsequently the *Rhetoric* was occasionally read, more in the Greek East than the Roman West, but to many teachers it probably seemed outdated by Hermagoras' development of stasis theory in the second century, which adopted topics for use in lawcourts, and by the long lists of figures of speech compiled in late Hellenistic times.

Of all Aristotle's theories, unless one includes the five parts of rhetoric, for which he is indirectly responsible, the most generally accepted were the division of oratory into three kinds and the theory of the topics. We will return to the topics shortly. In the case of the three kinds of oratory the true basis of Aristotle's division was not well understood. For example, Quintilian (3.416–417) groups deliberative with epideictic as a form of oratory which does not call for judgment, perhaps reflecting the relative rarity of public deliberation under the caesars. And though the three categories of judicial, epideictic, and deliberative are noted by many medieval and renaissance writers on rhetoric, they did not particularly suit actual oratorical forms of the time. In the seventeenth, eighteenth, and nineteenth centuries rhetoricians in the classical tradition usually made a less philosophical, but more pragmatic division into the oratory of the pulpit, the senate, and the bar. Other concepts important in the *Rhetoric*, such as the modes of proof, the enthymeme, and the virtues of style, were watered down or restated in terms more congenial to the teachers of the sophistic tradition or the writers of handbooks. Particularly revealing is the history of the concept of logos, ethos, and pathos. In the Hellenistic period these three categories seem largely unknown. In Cicero's dialogue *De Oratore* (2.115), probably under the influence of the rediscovered text of the *Rhetoric*, they reemerge and eight years later in his *Orator* (69) are given the title *officia oratoris,* or duties of the orator: to teach, to charm, and to move. The focus on speaker, speech, and audience is thus reduced and attention turned to the orator of the sophistic tradition. The duties are then identified with use of the three kinds of style: plain, middle, and grand. Cicero also (*De Oratore* 2.183–185) blurs the distinction between ethos and pathos, a development carried on by Quintilian (6.2).

In a famous article, Friedrich Solmsen has made a detailed study of the history of Aristotle's influence on later writers concerned with rhetoric.[27] What he finds to recount is not a vital, independent tradition, but occasional influences on rhetorical writers like Demetrius, Cicero, Caecilius, the Anonymous Seguerianus, Minucian the Younger, and Martianus Capella. Among philosophical schools the Stoics gave greatest emphasis to the truth of the message and to logic, but their influence on rhetoric was undermined by their crabbed prose and dialectical pedantry. Christianity sought the truth, but no Christian writer specifically took up Plato or Aristotle's views on rhetoric. Aristotle's *Rhetoric* was read in Byzantium, but chiefly as a work on logic, ethics, or politics. In the Renaissance it was more widely studied but failed to replace the works of Cicero or Quintilian as major authorities. It was not until the twentieth century that rhetoricians began to cite Aristotle's work on a regular basis as a fundamental statement of rhetoric, even when they disagreed with the correctness of his views.

The major tragedy in the general neglect of Aristotle's *Rhetoric* is probably the fact that until the twentieth century it failed to play the role of which it is capable in mediating between philosophy and technical or sophistic rhetoric. The quarrel between rhetoric and philosophy was taken up in Hellenistic times in much the form seen in Plato's *Gorgias,* and despite the efforts of Cicero in *De Oratore,* has repeatedly exasperated partisans on both sides. In the West in late antiquity and the Middle Ages the philosophical prologue to *De Inventione,* which we will consider in the next chapter, was a better-known statement of the need to combine wisdom and eloquence.[28]

Discussion of the place of rhetoric among the arts and sciences is a part of the strand of philosophical rhetoric. We have seen that Aristotle made a basic division of knowledge into theoretical, practical, and productive and that he treated the logical science of investigation and the logical arts of dialectic and rhetoric as theoretical faculties applicable to many subjects. During the Hellenistic and Roman periods the commonest view was probably that of the Stoics, who divided philosophy into physics, which included metaphysics, ethics, which included politics, and logic, which consisted of three parts: canonics, or study of the criteria for truth, dialectic, and rhetoric (see Diogenes

Laertius 7.39–40). This division was taken up by Augustine (*De Civitate Dei* 11.25) and was commonly accepted until the twelfth century, though the Aristotelian scheme was known in the West through Boethius. In *De Doctrina Christiana* (2.19.29–39.58) Augustine outlines a different system based on a knowledge of things men have instituted (acting, painting, etc.) and things divinely instituted. The latter is subdivided into those pertaining to the senses (astronomy, medicine, etc.) and those pertaining to reason, which are dialectic, rhetoric, and mathematics. Medieval scholastic theologians made attempts to construct new systems, which usually include a place for rhetoric. In the *Didascalicon* Hugh of Saint Victor (1096–1141) developed a scheme of four arts: theoretical, practical, mechanical, and logical. The logical arts are divided into grammar and argument, and argument is subdivided into demonstration, probable argument, and sophistic, with probable argument again subdivided into dialectic and rhetoric. In *De Reductione Artium ad Theologiam* Bonaventure (1221–1274) made a division into superior, interior, inferior, and exterior *lumines*, or forms of knowledge. The interior *lumines* are divided into moral, natural, and rational processes, and the latter subdivided into grammar, logic, and rhetoric. Of many later attempts to describe the structure of knowledge, the most important for the tradition of classical rhetoric is probably that of Francis Bacon in *The Advancement of Learning*, which we will consider in chapter 10.

Dialectical and Rhetorical Topics

The theory of the topics has had a history of its own, and it is through this history that philosophical rhetoric exerted most of its influence on teaching and practice.[29] As we have seen, Aristotle presents rhetoric as a form of dialectic. He discusses dialectic at length in the work known as the *Topics*. On eight occasions the reader of the *Rhetoric* is referred to the *Topics* for further information on such matters as the difference between example and enthymeme (1356b12), and for several of the formal topics of Book 2, chapter 23. A reference at Book 2, chapter 22 (1394b4) sums up the relationship between the two works: the student of rhetoric needs a selection of arguments, such as those in the *Topics*, about questions which may arise in speeches.

Topos in Greek means "place" and a logical or rhetorical "topic" is thus a finding-place or pigeonhole for an argument; in Latin *locus*, plural *loci*, is similarly used. "Places" and "commonplaces" appear in older English writers, but as we have said, such usage invites confusion with "commonplace" in the literary or general sense and should be avoided. Aristotle probably borrowed the concept of the topic from the system of mnemonic devices being taught in his time (see *Topics* 8.14.163b28).

Aristotle's *Topics* is a treatise in eight books, to which his work *On Sophistical Refutations* is an appendage.[30] In Book 1 he distinguishes scientific demonstration from probable reasoning, or dialectic, and explains that a knowledge of topics is useful in mental training, in debate, and in establishing the premises of the sciences. Propositions are of three sorts, ethical, physical, and logical, and become the basis of inductive or deductive reasoning. Deductive reasoning is the more important and takes the form of the syllogism. Every logical proposition or problem involves four predicables: definition, property, genus, and accident (1.4.101b25). These are found in ten categories: essence, quantity, quality, relation, place, time, position, state, activity, and passivity (1.9.103b20–24). Aristotle also wrote a treatise called *Categories* which has a similar but not identical list. Syllogisms can be supplied by four means: the provision of propositions, an ability to distinguish different meanings of words, the discovery of differences, and the investigation of similarities (1.13.105a20–34). Books 2 through 7 then give a collection of topics, dealing with accidents, genus, property, and definition in that order. For example, one topic is to see if your opponent has treated a genus as an accident. White, for example, is not an accident of color, but a member of the genus color. The categories come into such matters in that, for example, white color is an essence (in Greek "some thing") and also indicates a quality. The eighth book of the *Topics* gives advice about reasoning—how to formulate or refute questions in debate. Thus the *Topics* deals both with the finding or invention of arguments and with their evaluation, which comes to be called judgment.

Dialectic, and the arguing of theses, was an important study in Greek philosophical schools of the Hellenistic period. Predicables and categories proved useful in many ways, for example, in the study of grammar, which was an important interest of the Stoics. In the middle of the second century before Christ the rhetorician Hermagoras reorganized the theory of topics in a form more adapted to lawcourts and more easily memorized by students in rhetorical schools. As such it is known as stasis theory and appears in Cicero's *De Inventione*, in the *Rhetorica ad Herennium*, and in many later handbooks of technical rhetoric. We will return to this subject in chapter 5. Interest in Aristotle's *Topics*, like interest in his *Rhetoric*, reappeared in the mid–first century B.C., and in 44 B.C. Cicero composed a short treatise called *Topica*, ostensibly a Latin version of Aristotelean topics, though in fact most of the topics he discusses are not from the *Topics*, but from the list in *Rhetoric* 2.23 or from Stoic sources.[31] Following the general lead of Aristotle, Cicero divides argumentation into two parts which he calls the art of invention, or topics, and the science of judgment, or dialectic. Invention was of course the first of the five parts of rhetoric, and the thrust of Cicero's discussion is to subsume invention and judgment within rhetoric. He had already discussed the topics of *Rhetoric* 2.23 in his dialogue *De Oratore* (2.162–173). Quintilian and Roman rhetoricians generally follow this same tradition. Dialectic was not a subject which appealed to the ancient Romans, but they saw the practical utility of rhetoric and made it a part of basic education.

Dialectic, however, continued to be an independent study in Greek philosophical schools and became even more important with the great revival of interest in Plato in the second and third centuries after Christ. The Neoplatonists achieved a kind of synthesis of the dialectic of Aristotle and the metaphysics of Plato. An important work in this new movement is the *Introduction* [*Eisagoge*] *to the Categories of Aristotle* by Porphyry, written about A.D. 280. Although not so intended, it became the basic introduction to Aristotelian logic for the next twelve hundred years. In the fourth century the Greek sophist Themistius wrote a commentary on the *Topics*, now lost, and in the years before 523 the Roman philosopher Boethius provided the basis for most early medieval study of dialectic in the West by translating into Latin Porphyry's *Introduction* and several of Aristotle's logical works and by composing a commentary on Cicero's *Topica* and a *Topica* of his own, *De Topicis Differentiis*, which includes (Book 3) a comparison of Cicero's and Themistius' treatment of the subject. In Book 4 Boethius then discusses the relationship of rhetoric to dialectic; the general thrust of his reexamination, in contrast to Cicero's, was to subordinate rhetoric again to dialectic.[32] Boethius also popularized the concept of the enthymeme as a truncated syllogism. The term *epicheireme*, in use by rhetoricians since Theophrastus, has usually been applied to the full rhetorical syllogism. Some of Boethius' works, including his translation of Aristotle's *Topics*, did not survive, but *De Topicis Differentiis* had a great influence in the Middle Ages, and in the thirteenth century Book 4 was made the basic text for the teaching of rhetoric at the University of Paris by the scholastic philosophers who then dominated education. As a result of their efforts the *Rhetoric* and the *Topics* were also made available in Latin in the West, but the *Rhetoric* was studied as a work on ethics.

Sometime in late Greek antiquity Aristotle's works on logic, including the *Topics*, came to be thought of as constituent parts, in an established order, of a unity called the *Organon*. The *Rhetoric* and *Poetics* were treated as the last two parts of this collection, and it was in this form that they were known to Boethius and studied in Byzantium, but neither work exercised much influence on rhetorical teaching.

Renewed study of Cicero and Quintilian in the fourteenth and fifteenth centuries encouraged the view that invention was a part of rhetoric, but Rudolph Agricola in the late fifteenth century and Peter Ramus in the sixteenth made invention, including topics, and judgment, including the syllogism, the two parts of dialectic as taught in many schools, and restricted rhetoric to style and delivery. The *Port-Royal Logic* of seventeenth-century France, influenced by the new science of Descartes and Pascal, subsequently rejected the topics as useless in logic and even pernicious, and that view spread to most neoclassical writers on rhetoric. Hugh Blair, for example, in the thirty-third lecture of his otherwise very classicizing work, outlines what the topics are and refers students to Cicero for more information, but advises them "to lay aside these commonplaces and think closely of their subjects." We will return to these developments in chapters 10 and 11.

Chapter 5
Technical Rhetoric in
the Roman Period

The classical phase of Greek history is usually said to come to an end with the defeat of the Greek states by Macedon at the Battle of Chaeronea in 338 B.C., followed by the short reign of Alexander the Great. He died in 323. Aristotle and Demosthenes, the greatest orator of the Athenian democracy, both died in 322. The next three centuries are known as the Hellenistic Age, the time when Greek culture, spread by Alexander's armies, adapted itself to native life all around the eastern Mediterranean. It was this process that brought Greek schools and Greek rhetoric in contact with Judaism and ultimately with early Christianity. During this period Greek prose style changed significantly. On the one hand, a simplified form of Attic Greek, known as *koine*, or the common language, gained ground everywhere as an international medium of communication. At the same time, however, professional rhetoricians showed an inclination for an artificial and undisciplined style more reminiscent of Gorgias than of the Attic orators of Athens. This movement is known as Asianism and the orators as Asianists, since many came from Asia Minor. According to Cicero (*Brutus* 325) there were two forms of Asianism, one sententious, smooth, and euphonious, the other voluble, excited, and given to ornamental words.[1] While these events were going on in the East, Rome developed from a small state in central Italy into the ruler of the peninsula and adjacent islands and by the first century before Christ had achieved dominance of the entire Mediterranean.

Theophrastus and Demetrius

The most important writer on rhetoric of the early Hellenistic period was Theophrastus, Aristotle's successor as head of the Peripatetic School. Theophrastus wrote *On Enthymemes* and *On Epicheiremes*, *On Amplification*, *On Humor*, *On Style*, *On Delivery*, and other works, none of which survives.[2] His studies, however, influenced later technical discussions, since they seem to have been read at a time when Aristotle's *Rhetoric* was little known, and sometimes can be reconstructed from these references. In general, what Theophrastus seems to have done is to take suggestions of a technical nature in Aristotle and work them out in greater detail, sometimes with significant changes. For example, he developed Aristotle's remarks about qualities needed in good prose style into an account of four "virtues"—correctness, clarity, ornamentation, and propriety—as applied to the two parts of style, choice of word and composition. This supplied the structure for most later discussions of the subject. Similarly, delivery was divided into matters of voice and matters of gesture or action, and rules given for each.

Not very much is known about the study of rhetoric in the third century B.C. Possibly the treatise of Demetrius, *On Style*, was written at this time, though it may be later. It shows how remarks of Aristotle were developed into a theory of several distinct kinds or "characters" of style. Theophrastus may have contributed to the theory of three kinds—grand, middle, and plain—each with its appropriate diction and composition. Demetrius, however, discussed four kinds: the plain, the grand, the elegant, and the forceful. He also further developed Aristotle's observations on the periodic sentence into three types: the rhetorical, the historical, and the philosophical. His work shows that interest in naming and defining figures of speech was gaining rapidly. Demetrius was clearly a follower of Aristotle, perhaps working in the Peripatetic School itself, but he is also clearly a part of the trend toward *letteraturizzazione*, which is one reason for thinking his work may have been written somewhat later. Some interest in rhetoric could be found in the other Hellenistic schools, such as that of the Stoics, who developed the theory of grammatical analogy and anomaly about this time and added the study of memory to the parts of rhetoric, and that of the Academics, who turned from Platonism to skepticism and the debating of both sides of an issue.[3]

Hermagoras

In the second century B.C. Hermagoras of Temnos wrote a very influential handbook of technical rhetoric in Greek. Little is known about him and his work has not survived, but it can be partially reconstructed on the basis of Cicero's *De Inventione*, the *Rhetorica ad Herennium*, and later references. Hermagoras defined the task of the orator as "to treat the proposed political question as persuasively as possible" (see Sextus Empiricus 2.62). He treated invention in the greatest detail; arrangement and style were grouped together under the rubric "economy"; there was probably also a brief account of memory and delivery.[4] Hermagoras is thus the earliest source we know for the full treatment of the five parts of technical rhetoric and a major authority for its identification with civic functions. He divided political questions, however, into two types: *theses*, which are general (for example, "Is it right to kill a tyrant?"), and *hypotheses*, or specific cases (for example, "Did Harmodius and Aristogeiton justifiably kill the tyrant Hipparchus?"). In his analysis of *hypotheses* Hermagoras laid down the basic lines of the important theory of stasis, or the basic issue of a case. For example, a defendant accused of murder may deny that he killed the victim at all. This is conjectural stasis, or stasis of fact. Or he may admit the action but claim that it was legal or that it was just, in which case the stasis becomes that of law or of quality. It is here that Hermagoras restated Aristotle's theory of topics in a system of categories adapted to the lawcourts, which a student of rhetoric could memorize and apply to any situation.

Hermagoras' system proved a major contribution to technical rhetoric; we will consider some of the details in reviewing Cicero's treatise *De Inventione*, which is the earliest surviving work in which the system appears. Hermagoras reemphasized the focus of technical rhetoric on judicial oratory, though stasis can be applied to other forms of civic speech, and he provided teachers of rhetoric with a much more organized body of material to present to their students. Later rhetoricians, of whom Hermogenes in the second century of the Christian era is the most important, invented new kinds of stasis or new ways of ordering the material, but stasis theory remained the heart of rhetorical invention until the end of the Renaissance and continues to have some influence today. An accidental result of the new approach was probably to make Aristotle's *Rhetoric*, since it lacks a discussion of stasis, seem less useful even among those who knew it, and thus further to undermine interest in philosophical rhetoric.

The Quarrel between Rhetoric and Philosophy

A second important development of the second century B.C. is renewed
hostility between teachers of rhetoric, like Hermagoras, and teachers
of philosophy.[5] As rhetoric became a more extensive discipline and
established itself more firmly in secondary education, and as it began
to compete for the serious attention of Romans interested in gaining
some culture or some speaking ability, the philosophers ceased to teach
it and scorned its claims as a humane study able to bring man to his
greatest fulfillment in society. Arguments used by Plato in the *Gorgias*
were taken up again and new arguments developed—for example, that
since rhetoric is found in Homer it could not have been "invented" by
Corax and Tisias. This dispute is the background against which
Cicero's dialogue *De Oratore* should be read. In that work, written in
54 B.C., Cicero seeks to reconcile the ideal orator with the eloquent
philosopher in a form which has both intellectual depth and civic use-
fulness. Such an ideal is a projection of the role Cicero himself sought
to play in Rome. It represents, on the one hand, a continuation of the
sophistic strand in classical rhetoric, and on the other, the Roman
concept of an orator as a statesman and "patron" who defends his
"clients."[6] The patron-client system in Rome, originating in social,
economic, and political needs, was thus extended to legal representation in a way not found in Greece. Cicero's ideal orator will appear
again in Quintilian, in the concept of the Christian orator of later
antiquity, in the Italian Renaissance, and in the neoclassical period in
France, England, and America, but the relationship of rhetoric and
philosophy continued to be regarded as a problem by many thinkers.

Theophrastus' work on style and delivery, the study of figures and
periods by writers like Demetrius, and Hermagoras' contributions, including stasis theory, largely complete technical rhetoric. Throughout
the rest of antiquity the same basic body of theory, accompanied by
exercises in composition and declamation, was taught to Greek and
Roman boys. There are variations in emphasis, terminology, and a very
few new theories favored by some authorities. Most rhetorical handbooks seem to have set forth the complete system, but there were
separate works on aspects of style, important for the history of literary
rhetoric. This standard theory of classical rhetoric, as taught from
around 150 B.C. to the end of antiquity, is set forth systematically in a
number of modern handbooks of the subject, usually with little historical attention.[7] Some modern critics call it Ciceronian rhetoric, since
it was known in Western Europe largely through writings of Cicero,

but it was also known in the East, and not from Cicero. Inasmuch as he made only small personal contributions to the theory it is better to call it technical, or prescriptive, or standard classical rhetoric.

Our knowledge of this standard classical rhetoric is dependent on some twenty-five works in Greek and Latin written between 100 B.C. and A.D. 500. They include major treatments by Cicero, Quintilian, and Hermogenes, as well as minor works to be found in the nineteenth-century collections *Rhetores Graeci*, by Christian Walz, and *Rhetores Latini Minores*, by Karl Halm.[8] The nature of the tradition will emerge if we consider *De Inventione* and *Rhetorica ad Herennium* and then note major later additions.

Cicero

Cicero (106–43 B.C.) was the greatest Roman orator and the most important Latin writer on rhetoric.[9] Fifty-eight of his speeches survive, and over nine hundred letters giving intimate details of his career, as well as a series of works designed to introduce contemporary Greek philosophy to the rather unphilosophical Romans, and seven works on rhetoric. *De Inventione*, or *On Invention*, was written when he was very young, and though it makes some claims to originality it is basically the system of technical rhetoric he had studied in his teens. *De Oratore*, or *On the Orator*, is a much more thoughtful work, published in 54 B.C. at the height of his career. Although it brings together, as we have said, some strands of philosophical and sophistic rhetoric, it also contains much of the tradition of technical rhetoric in a nontechnical form. *Partitiones Oratoriae*, of about 52 B.C., is a short rhetorical catechism, written for his son. *Brutus* is a history of Roman oratory, written early in 44 B.C. *Orator* is devoted primarily to style, especially composition, and was also written in 44. Another work of 44, *Topica*, has already been discussed. The final work, *De Optimo Genere Oratorum*, or *On the Best Kind of Orators*, was intended as an introduction to a Latin translation of two great speeches by Demosthenes and Aeschines.

De Inventione

Of all Cicero's writings on rhetoric, the most read for the next fifteen hundred years was *De Inventione*. Numerous commentaries were written on it from late antiquity to the Renaissance, of which the most important was that of Victorinus, and it was the major authority for all later knowledge of rhetorical invention.[10] The young **Cicero** had planned to complete similar surveys of other parts of rhetoric, but failed to do so at the time (the early 80s B.C.) and came to regard his early effort as unsatisfactory in comparison with the experience he later gained in speaking or the grander view of the orator which he later espoused.

The first book of *De Inventione* begins with a "philosophical" introduction (1.1–5) which for centuries became the classic statement of the nature of rhetoric.[11] Cicero inquires whether the accumulated knowledge of rhetoric, which is the basis of ability to speak, and *eloquentiae studium,* or a devotion to eloquence, have done more good or harm over the centuries, and he gives as his conclusion what becomes the premise of most thoughtful rhetoricians: "Wisdom without eloquence has been of little help to states, but eloquence without wisdom has often been a great obstacle and never an advantage." He then gives a picture of the development of human society, drawn from Stoic sources. There must once have been a great leader with persuasive power who brought mankind out of primitive conditions, but such great men are not interested in the day-to-day details of administration, and a lesser class of those skilled at speech took over petty disputes. In the course of time they became accustomed to stand on the side of falsehood. In the resulting strife the nobler souls withdrew into philosophical speculation. No specific names are mentioned, but presumably Cicero thought this process described the history of Greek oratory from the time of wise men like Solon to the sophists, followed by the rejection of rhetoric by Socrates and by Hellenistic philosophers. Roman statesmen like Cato, Laelius, and Scipio Africanus, in Cicero's view, have better combined wisdom and eloquence. The introduction ends with a eulogy of eloquence which thus incorporates one of the themes of sophistic rhetoric into the technical tradition:

From it the greatest advantages come to the state, if wisdom is present as moderator of all things; from it, to those who have attained it, flow glory, honor, and prestige; from it also is secured the most certain and safe defense of one's friends. To me it seems that although men are lower and weaker than the animals in many ways, they most excel them in that they are able to speak. Thus the man seems to me to have gained something wonderful who excels other men in that very way in which mankind excels animals. Since it is acquired not only by nature and by practice, but by some art, it is not irrelevant for us to see what they have to say who have left us precepts on the subject. (1.5)

The work then begins in earnest with the statement that rhetoric is *civilis ratio,* a part of politics. Its function is to speak in a manner suited to persuading an audience. We have said that *De Inventione* and rhetoric of this period in general show little influence from Aristotle, and one can see in these definitions that many of Aristotle's subtle distinctions have been lost. Aristotle is, however, cited (1.7) as the authority for the view that the material of rhetoric is not everything, as Gorgias had claimed, but falls into three classes, epideictic, deliberative, and judicial. Its parts, "most authorities" agree (1.9), are invention, arrangement, style, memory, and delivery. Invention is the reasoning out of truth, or that which is like the truth, to make a case probable. Arrangement is the orderly distribution of what has been found. Style is the fitting of suitable words to what has been found. Memory is a firm grasp in the mind of subjects and words. Delivery, or *pronuntiatio*, is the control of voice and body suitable to the subject and the words.

The rest of the work is devoted to invention. Cicero begins with stasis theory as developed by Hermagoras, but calls stasis *constitutio.* (Later writers sometimes adopted the Latin cognate *status.*) The *constitutio* is the first conflict of the two sides of a case, resulting from rejection of an accusation—for example, "You did it," and the response, "I did not do it." There are four kinds of *constitutio* in Cicero's view: *conjecturalis*, when the fact is at issue, *definitiva* when the definition of the action is debated, *generalis* when it is a matter of the nature, quality, or classification of an action, and *translatio*, when the jurisdiction of the tribunal is questioned. These *constitutiones* will be taken up in Book 1 and again in Book 2 in this order. Cases are simple, involving only one question, or complex, involving several questions or the comparison of questions (1.17). Here invention is extended into deliberative oratory: shall we destroy Carthage, give it back to the Carthaginians, or make it a Roman colony? Controversies involve either reasoning (*in ratione*) or written documents (*in scripto*) (1.17).

The system as outlined is intended to help the student find what to say. After he considers the nature of the case he must turn to the central question it involves, his explanation of that question, what the judge is to decide, and what argument can be advanced for that decision. To do the latter he must investigate topics, a subject to which the second book is devoted (see 1.50). Cicero leaves the details aside for the moment and goes on to the next step, which is to arrange the parts of a speech in order. There are six parts: exordium, narration, partition, confirmation, refutation, and conclusion (1.19). The rest of Book 1 takes up these parts in order, describing the qualities which each should have and some of the topics which can be included.

The exordium (1.20–26) prepares the audience to receive the speech and should make each listener *benevolus, attentus, docilis*, that is, well-disposed to the speaker, attentive, and receptive. Cases fall into five kinds, the honorable, the remarkable, the humble, the doubtful, or the obscure; and the exordium must be adapted to each type. In some kinds of cases where there is no problem the exordium can be a simple introduction, but otherwise there will be need of *insinuatio*, which by dissimulation or in a roundabout way will steal into the mind of each listener. In considering Cicero's suggestions about how to make a judge well-disposed, attentive, or receptive we begin to see how the theory of topics is applied to oratorical composition. There are four *loci*, places for the student to look, for goodwill: in his own character, such as a modest description of his good actions and services, or of his misfortunes or the like; in the character of the opponents, if they are hated, wicked, or unpopular; in the character of the judges, by paying tribute to their courage, wisdom, or mercy; or from the case itself if it can be praised or the opponents' case belittled. Similarly Cicero lists topics that will encourage attentiveness and receptivity, along with topics for use in insinuation.

The narration (1.27–30) may set forth the whole case or consist of a digression *extra causam*, beyond the narrow limits, to attack someone on the other side or make a comparison or amuse the audience. A narration in a speech should have three qualities (what are called in other writers the "virtues" of the narration): it should be brief, clear, and probable (1.28). For example, it will be clear if events are described in the order in which they occur and if clear words are used.

The partition (1.31–33) is of two sorts: the speaker can state the matters on which he agrees with his opponent and what remains in dispute, or he can list the points he will prove. In the latter event it is important to be brief, complete, and concise. Cicero notes that there are additional rules for partition in philosophy which are not relevant here.

The confirmation (1.34–77) is the part of the speech where, by argument, we make "our case" secure credence, authority, and strength Material for argument here is either of a general sort or is useful only in a particular kind of oratory and is derived from topics concerned with persons or concerned with actions. The attributes of a person are name, nature, manner of life, fortune, disposition, feeling, interests, purposes, deeds, accidents, and speeches. The topics of each are defined and discussed in turn. The last three, for example, involve a person's behavior, experiences, or words in the past, in the present, or in the future. Attributes of actions are of four sorts: connected directly with the action, connected with the performance of the action, adjunct to the action, or consequent upon the action. Each has its topics. For example, to find arguments relating to the performance of the action the student should consider place, time, occasion, manner, and facility. All arguments drawn from these topics, Cicero says (1.44), either will be probable or will be necessary, that is, irrefutable. Necessary argument usually takes the form of the dilemma, enumeration, or simple inference. Probabilities as used in argumentation are either signs, credibilities, official judgments, or comparisons. The form of argument is either induction or *ratiocinatio*, deduction (1.51). Examples of each are given, and Cicero considers at length how many parts a *ratiocinatio* has. He means, of course, an enthymeme, but neither that term nor epicheireme nor even syllogism is used; it is Cicero's habit in general to find a suitable Latin word wherever possible. His own view (1.67) is that *ratiocinatio* in full form has five parts: proposition, reason, assumption, reason for the assumption, and conclusion; at minimum, in Cicero's theory (not in his practice), it must have at least three parts: major premise, minor premise, and conclusion. At the end of the discussion of proof Cicero notes (1.77) that other intricacies studied by philosophers are not suitable for an orator.

The refutation (1.78–79) is of four kinds: either the premises are not admitted, or the conclusion is shown not to follow, or the form of the argument is invalid, or a stronger argument is set against what an opponent has stated. Examples of how to do each of these things are given. Arguments are defective if they are entirely false, general, commonplace, trifling, remote, badly defined, controversial, self-evident, controvertible, shameful, offensive, contradictory, inconsistent, or adverse to the speaker's purpose. Each fault is explained.

Digression, according to Cicero (1.97), was put by Hermagoras at this place in the speech, between the refutation and the conclusion. It might involve praise or blame of individuals or comparison with other cases or something that emphasized or amplified the subject at hand. Thus it is not literally a digression. Cicero criticizes the requirement as a formal rule and says such treatment should be interwoven into the argument. Ironically, ethical digressions of the sort here described are very characteristic of his greatest judicial speeches, like *Pro Caelio* and *Pro Milone*, and regularly and effectively occur at this very spot in the structure of the work.

The conclusion (1.98–109), sometimes called peroration by other rhetoricians, has three parts: summing up, or enumeration; the inciting of indignation against the opponent; and the *conquestio*, or arousing of pity for the speaker. Topics are given for each. Here and elsewhere Cicero treats the speaker himself as principal in the case and not as an advocate for a client. This is because he is relying on Greek theory, which reflects practice in Greek courts. The general use of advocates is an extension of the Roman patron-client system and not fully provided for in rhetorical treatises until Quintilian.

In the introduction to the second book of *De Inventione* (2.4) Cicero claims that he has utilized a variety of sources in the work. His claim may well reflect words of his teacher, whose identity we do not know. He then gives a brief survey of the history of rhetoric, including the development of the Aristotelian and Isocratean traditions, which he says (2.8) have now been fused into a single body of knowledge by later teachers. The purpose of the second book is to describe *certos confirmandi et reprehendi in singula causarum genera locos*, "specific topics of confirmation and refutation for use in each kind of speech." In the discussion he distinguishes general and particular topics for judicial, deliberative, and epideictic oratory, though the emphasis is still on judicial. Every inference, he says (2.16), is derived from the cause, from the person involved, or from the act itself. The four kinds of *constitutio* and their topics are discussed separately under the heading of judicial oratory, except that stasis of quality, which is the most important and most complicated, is put last (62–115). It is divided into two parts: legal topics (62–68); and juridical topics or topics of equity, which have a complicated set of subdivisions (69–115). A juridical question involves either absolutes of right and wrong or assumptive arguments which involve partially extraneous circumstances. The latter are used when the action is attacked or defended, not on its own ground, but on the basis of the circumstances under which it was committed. There are four subdivisions: an act may be defended by comparison to other possible actions, or by putting the blame for the action on the accuser, or by shifting blame to someone else, or by confession. Shifting responsibility may involve either the cause of the action or the action itself. Confession may take the form of purgation, in which the speaker claims ignorance, or an accident, or the necessity under which he acted and in any event denies the intent of harm, or it may take the form of deprecation, or plea for pardon. Each of these categories has appropriate topics to use both in accusation and in defense.

The next subject discussed is that of controversies involving written documents (2.116–154). The distinction between reasoning and written evidence had been made in 1.17 and is Cicero's version of Aristotle's concept of nonartistic or external evidence. Cicero discusses topics under the headings of ambiguity, conflict of letter and intent of the law, conflict of two or more laws, reasoning by analogy when no law specifically applies, and definition.

The relatively short discussion of deliberative oratory (2.156–176) hinges on topics of the honorable and the expedient, which should at best be combined. Aristotle had of course seen the expedient as the true issue in such speeches. What is honorable is found in the four cardinal virtues, wisdom, justice, courage, and temperance, each of which becomes a topic. The honorable when coupled with advantage consists of such things as glory, rank, influence, and friendship (2.166). How these might be worked out in an actual speech is well seen in Cicero's oration *On the Manilian Law*, of 69 B.C. *De Inventione* ends with a very brief discussion of praise and blame in epideictic oratory (2.177–178).

Cicero's survey of the technical rhetoric of invention ends here. As we have already noted, his emphasis is on the actual devices of a speech, generally in the order the student would use them in composition. Although the role of the orator and the reactions of the audience come in at certain points, they are minor considerations. The speech is what matters. This is a speech for a lawcourt, although we find a few additional remarks on other forms of civic oratory. The forms of argument and topics of dialectic are everywhere present, but rearranged into a system for teaching legal oratory to students. That system is based on the conditions of Greek, not Roman justice, though a great deal of the illustrative material has a Roman cast. Could one learn to compose a speech in this way? The answer seems to be that ancient teachers thought so and that boys in antiquity tried to follow the rules. Almost everything in *De Inventione* can be illustrated from Cicero's practice in his own speeches, but those speeches go far beyond anything here suggested in the subtlety of their art as Cicero acquired experience, self-confidence, and authority. Finally we should emphasize that *De Inventione* is totally concerned with primary rhetoric. Though the material could of course be applied to literary composition, that application is not the point.

The *Rhetorica ad Herennium*

Since Cicero did not write up his studies of arrangement, style, memory, and delivery, we may turn, as did students of rhetoric for a thousand years, to another handbook that does address those subjects. This is the *Rhetorica ad Herennium*, a treatise perhaps written by an otherwise unknown Cornificius and dedicated to an unidentified Herennius.[12] Its discussion of invention has many similarities to Cicero's *De Inventione*, and it thus probably represents the teachings of the same teacher and suggests some of what Cicero might have had to say on other parts of rhetoric. It was composed a few years later than *De*

Inventione, perhaps around 84 B.C. Through the Middle Ages and until the late fifteenth century the treatise was commonly regarded as a work by Cicero and often known as the *Rhetorica Secunda*.

The *Rhetorica ad Herennium* is in four books. The first two cover judicial invention but integrate the material in Cicero's second book into a single account of proof. Book 3 takes up deliberative and judicial oratory and then turns to the other parts of rhetoric.

The discussion of *dispositio*, or arrangement, is very short (2.16–18). The author says that there are two kinds, one arising from the rules of rhetoric, the other accommodated to the circumstances. The rules of rhetoric of course have provided for the exordium, narration, and the like, and the primary reason the discussion is so short is that these parts of the oration have already been discussed in detail. We noted in chapter 2 that these divisions are historically the earliest framework of technical rhetoric into which other material was inserted, such as stasis theory. Aristotle had attempted to change this, and the *Rhetoric to Alexander* shows his influence, but most teachers of rhetoric and the technical tradition as a whole clung to the old pattern. We are now told, however, that it is possible to vary this order if, in the speaker's judgment, something else is more effective. One might, for example, want to start with consideration of a very strong argument made by the opponent, or with the narration. Both Greek and Roman orators indeed do this. In the course of the first century B.C. this became an important issue between the schools of Apollodorus of Pergamum, who thought the canonical order should always be followed, and Theodorus of Gadara, who thought it should not.[13] Finally, we are given a paragraph on the order of arguments within the proof and refutation. The strongest ones should go first and last, with weak arguments in the middle.

Instead of turning next to style the author reserves that subject for treatment in a separate book and fills out Book 3 with his account of delivery and memory. This arrangement, which is imitated by George of Trebizond in the most important "rhetoric" of the fifteenth century, results primarily from the author's desire to treat style at greater length and in particular to include numerous examples of his own composition. He was perhaps also influenced by the fact that style was the subject of monographic treatment by others; some readers might only be interested in that subject.

The discussion of delivery (3.19–27) is the earliest we have, though it is not so vivid reading as Quintilian's account (11.3). Logically memory should go first, since the student must memorize his speech before he can deliver it, and indeed the order style, memory, delivery is the common one in the later tradition. But here the author puts delivery first, apparently because he thinks it is the more important of the two. He seems to be alluding to the famous story that Demosthenes, when asked what were the three most important things in oratory, replied "Delivery, delivery, and delivery" (see Quintilian 11.3–6). Delivery is divided into *vocis figura* and *corporis motus*, a distinction which probably originated in Theophrastus' study of the subject. Voice quality consists of *magnitudo*, or volume, *firmitudo*, or stability, and *mollitudo*, or flexibility. Volume is largely dependent on natural endowment, but can be improved. Stability is preserved by cultivation. Flexibility is primarily achieved by exercise and involves three tones or styles: *sermo*, or conversation, *contentio*, or debate, and *amplificatio*, or amplification. Each of these is further subdivided, and rules are given for achieving it. An analogy to styles of oratory is visible here and is further developed in Quintilian's account. Physical movement or gesture is coordinated with the three tones, and advice is given on use of the face, arms, hands, body, and feet. In moments of pathetic amplification it is even appropriate to slap the thigh and beat the head.

The discussion of memory in the *Rhetorica ad Herennium* (3.28–40) is the best account of the subject in any ancient treatise. Mnemonics has a history which apparently began in the fifth century b.c. Throughout the centuries the subject has been pursued in a series of separate treatises, as well as being given some treatment in the fuller rhetorical handbooks.[14] Most of the account here is given over to the artificial system of backgrounds and images which a student can use to memorize any kind of discourse. A background is a physical setting, familiar to the student, which he uses like a mental tablet. Against this background he imagines pictures which symbolize, in the order in which he wishes to speak, the ideas or words of his speech. The system works, but is cumbersome, especially for a long oration, and is probably most useful in exercising the memory to the point where it can unaided gain an ability to remember a composition. Ancient orators in practice sometimes used notes, but the reading of an entire speech was not customary. There are many ancient testimonies to the great potential of the human mind to remember material verbatim in a society which was far more oral than ours and put high value on such an ability.

Book 4 of the *Rhetorica ad Herennium* consists of an introduction defending the author's decision to write his own illustrative examples of style, followed by an account of kinds of style, virtues of style, and ornaments of style. Since there was probably more written on these topics than on anything else relating to rhetoric in the following centuries, his account here is less authoritative than his remarks on other

parts of rhetoric, but it is a good picture of the subject of style as understood in the first century B.C. and has been probably the most read
part of his work since late antiquity.

Three kinds of style are recognized (4.11–16): the grand, the middle,
and the plain. A passage illustrating each is given. Furthermore, the
three kinds of style have their defective counterparts, which may be
called the swollen, the slack, and the meagre, and each of these is illustrated. As is true throughout this book, the approach is less systematic
than in the earlier books. The student is not told when to use each
style or how to combine them.

The author then discusses qualities which good style should exhibit
(4.17–18). These correspond to what Aristotle and Theophrastus had
called "virtues." That term is not used, and Theophrastus is not mentioned, but the author does speak of *vitia*, or vices, of style. The qualities he approves are a rearrangement of Theophrastus' system, which
is clearer in *De Oratore, Orator*, and Quintilian's *Institutio*. Style, he
says, should have *elegantia, compositio*, and *dignitas*. *Elegantia* may
be translated "taste," but one must not think of the neoclassical concept of taste, which has no ancient authority. Here it consists of two
things, correct Latinity and clarity of expression. These are like the
first two virtues of Theophrastus' system. *Compositio* does not directly
correspond to anything in Theophrastus. It is a polished arrangement
of words and is defined as avoiding a series of faults, such as excessive
hiatus or alliteration. *Dignitas*, or distinction, is ornamentation of
style and consists in the use of figures. Neither the Greek word *schema*
nor the Latin word *figura* is used. The devices are called *exornationes*
and are divided into those of words and those of thoughts. Forty-five
figures of words are named, defined, and illustrated, some being broken
down into subdivisions. Sometimes comments are made about the effect
of a figure: *repetitio*, the first mentioned, is said (4.19) to have charm,
gravity, and vigor, but no effort is made to go beyond this to the psychology of effect. The last ten figures of words consist of those where
language departs from the usual meaning of a word (4.42). These are
what the Greeks and later the Romans call tropes, of which metaphor
is the most important. Then nineteen figures of thought are similarly
described. The author uses Latin names for the figures throughout his
discussion, whereas later Roman rhetoricians often adopt the Greek
names.

This is the technical system of classical rhetoric in its five traditional
parts, with its characteristic emphasis on judicial oratory and a textbook approach. We may now briefly consider the most significant addition or variations made in it by later writers.

The Duties of an Orator

Cicero made many contributions to rhetoric. His greatest legacy is his own oratory, which is closely associated with his vision of the orator as set forth in *De Oratore*.[15] Here he drew on both the philosophical and sophistic traditions of rhetoric. It is this that leads him to state his one major contribution to technical rhetoric, the concept of the *officia oratoris*, or duties of an orator. In Book 2 (115) Antonius is made to say: "The whole theory of speaking is dependent on three sources of persuasion: that we prove (*probemus*) our case to be true; that we win over (*conciliemus*) those who are listening; that we call their hearts (*animos . . . vocemus*) to what emotion the case demands." These clearly correspond to Aristotle's three modes of proof, and *De Oratore*, unlike *De Inventione* or *Rhetorica ad Herennium*, contains discussion of logical argument, ethos, and pathos. Later in the same book (2.183–185) Cicero treats ethos and pathos as degrees of appeal to the emotions, the former being the calmer and more pervasive attributes of character, the latter more violent stirrings of passion. In *Orator* (69) the same concept is taken up and given the name *officia oratoris*, or duties of the orator: *probare, delectare, flectere*, that is, to prove, to delight, and to stir.[16] They are then identified with the three styles: plain for proof, middle for pleasure, and grand for emotion. *Officia oratoris* are mentioned in this form by Quintilian (12.10.58–59) and become important concepts in Saint Augustine's discussion of Christian eloquence in the fourth book of *De Doctrina Christiana*.

Quintilian

Marcus Fabius Quintilianus (ca. A.D. 40–95) is the author of the largest Latin rhetorical treatise which survives from antiquity, *Institutio Oratoria*, or *Education of the Orator*, in twelve books.[17] Quintilian practiced as an orator in the Roman lawcourts but was more famous as a teacher of rhetoric. From about A.D. 71 to 91 he held an official chair of rhetoric paid for by government funds, giving lectures to large groups of students and criticizing their rhetorical exercises in declamation. On retirement from this chair he spent about two years on research and the revision of his lectures, and he published his only surviving work—a few others have been lost—around A.D. 94.

Quintilian's *Institutio* is primarily a treatise on technical rhetoric, setting forth the theory of invention, arrangement, style, memory, and delivery in that order and in great detail. He often begins with a historical survey of a subject or the differences of opinion which he finds in earlier authorities, and then tries to reach a reasoned judgment about what is best. His discussion of the various views of *stasis* (3.6) is a good example. Quintilian is above all a patient, moderate, reasonable man, dedicated to good teaching, clear thinking, and natural expression. He often appeals to nature as the best guide. Rhetoric he defines as *bene dicendi scientia*, "a knowledge of speaking well." Use of the term *scientia* does not imply that it is an exact science; use of *bene*, on the other hand, does imply both artistic excellence and moral goodness, for the orator in Quintilian's view must, above all, be a good man.

Quintilian is interested in primary rhetoric. He regards declamation only as a means to that end and wishes to train speakers in the lawcourts and public life. At several points in his work he adjusts Greek theory as seen in *De Inventione* to the actual circumstances of Roman oratory—for example, when he distinguishes several different roles for ethos in a trial, in contrast to the Greek concern only with the ethos of the actual speaker (4.1.6–15).

The system of technical rhetoric which Quintilian expounds from Book 3 through Book 11 contains many details which we would not otherwise know, but in most instances they do not represent innovations of his own. In comparison with *Rhetorica ad Herennium*, changes over the intervening century and a half seem most evident in the account of style, but this is partly because Quintilian is closer to the system of the Theophrastan virtues, which Cicero had expounded in nontechnical form in *De Oratore*. He does add a chapter on *sententiae* (8.5), the pointed or epigrammatic statements which had become very popular in the schools of rhetoric in the early empire; a long chapter on composition (9.4), drawn partly from Cicero's *Orator*; and a chapter on *copia*, or abundance of ideas and words (10.1). *Copia* is secured chiefly by reading and imitation of classical models. Quintilian's discussion here of what the student should read verges on literary criticism, but the paramount question throughout is what literature can most help the orator.

Quintilian not only adds to traditional rhetoric material being developed elsewhere, but he incorporates the whole subject into a total educational system. This is the greatest significance of his work. Rhetoric is to him the centerpiece in the training of the citizen. In Book 1 he begins with a newborn child and inquires into the earliest lessons in speech. Duly the child progresses through the school of the grammarian and in Book 2 comes to the rhetorician. His training there is then considered at length, in terms of both theory and practical exercises in declamation. In the earlier books Quintilian is chiefly addressing parents or teachers; in the later books he increasingly addresses the student as he becomes an orator. The twelfth and final book considers the adult orator. What knowledge does he need of law and history? What cases should be take? How should he round out his career? When should he retire?

Thus rhetoric is a part of education, and the goal of education is the great orator. This orator must be a good man, but he belongs to what we have called the sophistic tradition, not the philosophical. What Quintilian stresses is the orator's ability to lead, to influence, to dominate a situation (12.1 is the major passage). The orator is expected to know some philosophy and to be good at reasoning in the proof of speeches, but Quintilian has little sympathy with philosophy as it was understood in his time. He identifies it with trivial disputation or worse with social and political opposition to the state as seen in Cynic philosophers.

It is interesting to note that this eloquent statement of the ideal orator has been hardly affected at all by the fact that the Roman principate, or imperial government, had replaced the republic two generations before Quintilian's birth. He still sees great opportunities for oratory and hopes for an orator greater than Cicero (12.11). That would be very great indeed, since Cicero is very close to Quintilian's ideal. Quintilian sweeps away reactions against Cicero's ideas and style in the early empire—for example, in Seneca—and reasserts his works as the basis of great rhetoric. "Cicero," he says in a striking *sententia*, "is the name not of a man, but of eloquence" (10.1.112).

Quintilian's endorsement of the Ciceronian style was to prove a powerful witness in the Renaissance, when the humanists sought to recover classical standards of style. Similarly, his endorsement of the oratorical ideal helped ensure the survival of primary rhetoric as the major consideration of the schools throughout late antiquity and into the Middle Ages, when practical opportunities for speech were eroding. To be sure, Quintilian's influence varies somewhat over the centuries and is a less constant factor than the influence of *De Inventione* and *Rhetorica ad Herennium*. His work was really too vast to be used as a handbook by students, but it was always read by leading teachers interested in its thoroughness. In late antiquity it was quarried by rhetoricians writing abstracts, of whom C. Julius Victor is probably the best example. After the Carolingian period the text of Quintilian was known only in a mutilated form, but even so, it exerted a powerful influence on John of Salisbury, primarily as a work on education. In the fifteenth century, as we shall see, the full text was recovered, and thereafter its influence was great, at times exceeding that of Cicero. To Hugh Blair, in the second half of the eighteenth century, the authoritative statement of classical rhetoric was still that in Quintilian.

Declamation

In both Greek and Latin the major rhetorical phenomenon of the Roman Empire is declamation. Originally intended as training for the lawcourts or senates, the practice became not only an educational exercise but an intellectual game for adults. The writings of Seneca the Elder are the best source of information on Latin declamation, which stressed judicial speeches (*controversiae*).[18] In Greek its greatest practitioners were the orators of the Second Sophistic, who gave displays of their ability at prepared or extempore declamation and taught the art to others. They favored deliberative and historical themes. *The Lives of the Sophists* by Philostratus gives a vivid picture of the sophistic schools. Most sophists also delivered public and private "occasional" orations, and their popularity encouraged application of the systematic analysis of technical rhetoric to forms of epideictic oratory. A handbook on epideictic in eight chapters is preserved among the works of Dionysius of Halicarnassus but was probably written by someone else in the late second or early third century. Encomia for festivals, for marriages, for birthdays, and for the arrival of a bride are included, as well as addresses to rulers, funeral orations, and speeches of exhortation at athletic games. A more extensive treatment of epideictic forms is found in two works attributed to Menander of Laodicea, a rhetorician of the third century.[19] Sophistic forms of oratory continued to have widespread use through the Byzantine period and often conform to Menander's rules.

Hermogenes

The single most important Greek rhetorician of Roman imperial times is probably Hermogenes of Tarsus, who began life as a sophistic prodigy in the mid–second century and to whom four works of technical rhetoric are attributed.[20] They achieved an authoritative status among medieval Greeks comparable to that of *De Inventione* in Western Europe. One work is a textbook of *progymnasmata*, or elementary exercises, which was translated into Latin by the grammarian Priscian, and unlike Hermogenes' other works, was thus known in the West in the Middle Ages. The other handbooks are devoted to invention, stasis theory, and style. Although Hermogenes' works have practical applications for judicial and other forms of rhetoric, he wrote primarily for sophists and students in the school of declamation.

The two areas of rhetoric where Hermogenes made the greatest changes were stasis theory and the kinds and virtues of style. His stasis theory has similarities to Hermagoras' system as we saw it in *De Inventione*, but instead of having four coordinated *constitutiones* (fact, definition, quality, and transference), it subordinates each kind to the one previously discussed. A matter is either uncertain or certain. If uncertain, the stasis is one of fact. If certain, the matter is either undefined, which requires stasis of definition, or defined. If defined, it is either qualified in some way by the circumstances, requiring stasis of quality, or it is not. If it is not, the speaker may hope to deny the court's jurisdiction (transference). The student of declamation is to proceed down the sequence, conceivably ending up with the conclusion that the case cannot be undertaken. We know that sophists engaged in acrimonious discussion about the proper stasis to use in fictitious cases.

The other part of rhetoric on which Hermogenes had the most to say was style. There were essentially two schools of thought about theories of style in antiquity, though the lines of influence sometimes crossed.[21] One tradition is that of the three kinds of style—the grand, the middle, and the plain. These were often called the "characters" of style and their definition was perhaps influenced by Peripatetic ideas about types of character. This tradition was followed by the author of the *Rhetorica ad Herennium*, by Cicero, and by Quintilian and remains the authoritative view in the West, as seen, for example, in Saint Augustine's *De Doctrina Christiana*. The other view, which is almost exclusively Greek, is that there is an ideal form of style, made up of various qualities or virtues combined in different ways. This theory was developed by Dionysius of Halicarnassus, as seen in his work *On Composition*. An unknown writer of the second century after Christ, whose works are preserved among the speeches of the sophist Aristides, sought to define twelve different qualities of style. Hermogenes' *On Ideas of Style* is a complex continuation of this tradition. The "ideas" or qualities of style which he describes are clarity, grandeur, beauty, vigor, ethos, verity, and gravity, but some of these are broken down into subdivisions for a grand total of twenty "ideas." Examples are sought in classical Greek writers, but especially in Demosthenes, who occupies in Hermogenes' thinking the place of the ideal orator. Hermogenes' theories have great specificity and appealed to the categorizing instinct of Neoplatonists during the third, fourth, and fifth centuries;[22] the concept of an "idea" of style comes perhaps from Isocrates' use of that word but is easily coordinated to Platonic ideas.

Hermogenes' theories also appealed, as did his stasis system, to teachers of rhetoric, and both works became textbooks of the Byzantine period, inspiring many commentaries, as we shall see in chapter 8.

George Trebizond introduced the ideas of style into western Europe in 1426, where the concept became widely known in literary circles. Hermogenes' works again became school texts, and the ideas themselves exercised considerable influence in renaissance literature.

Rhetores Latini Minores

From later Roman times there are several Latin works which give summaries of all or part of the system of classical rhetoric, partially as textbooks for students of declamation. Their authors are known collectively as the Minor Latin Rhetoricians. Julius Victor, mentioned in our discussion of Quintilian, is one.[23] Another is Aquila Romanus, who wrote a treatise on forty-eight figures of speech, probably in the late third century. At some later time Julius Rufinianus added thirty-eight more figures. In the fourth century Sulpicius Victor produced his *Institutiones Oratoriae*, a dry compendium of definitions and categories with a title borrowed from Quintilian. Sometime later Consultus Fortunatianus composed an *Ars Rhetorica* in the form of questions and answers. Its most unusual feature is its theory of *ductus*, or treatment of the orator's intent (1.5 7), which George Trebizond took up in the fifteenth century.[24] Commentaries on *De Inventione* were written by Victorinus, who shows the influence of Neoplatonist philosophy, and Grillius and had considerable use in the Middle Ages.[25] The *Rhetores Latini Minores* are of some importance for their later influence—they were briefer and easier to read than Quintilian—and they also suggest something of the functions of rhetoric in later antiquity. Although the Ciceronian tradition survived, there are also signs of a separate and more Greek tradition going back to Hermagoras. Interest in stasis theory clearly remained strong, but interest in style, except for figures, and in memory and delivery declined. This probably reflects in part changed conditions in the lawcourts: stasis theory continued to be useful in planning a defense or accusation, but procedures in court now debarred the kind of full scale opening address or summation of a case in which Cicero had won his fame. Judicial rhetoric thus outlived judicial oratory.

Donatus

The most influential technical writer of the fourth century, however, was not any of these rhetoricians, but the grammarian Aelius Donatus, whose works were the basic grammatical texts for the Middle Ages. He also wrote important commentaries on the Latin poets Terence and Virgil. The *Ars Minor* of Donatus is limited to discussion of the eight parts of speech (noun, pronoun, verb, and the like), but his fuller *Ars Grammatica* goes on to discuss, in Book 3, grammatical faults like barbarism and solecism, and the ornaments of style.[26] He distinguishes *schemata lexeos*, or *figurae verborum*, from *schemata dianoias*, or *figurae sensuum*. The latter, the figures of thought, he says belong to the orators; that is, they are part of the study of rhetoric. Figures of speech, however, he includes in grammar. He gives no general definition of a figure, but he names, defines, and illustrates with a single example each of seventeen figures of speech: prolepsis, zeugma, hypozeuxis, syllepsis, anadiplosis, anaphora, epanalepsis, epizeuxis, paronomasia, schesis onomaton, parhomoeon, homoeptoton, homoeoteleuton, polyptoton, hirmos, polysyndeton, and dialyton. It is clear that the Greek names had become standard in Latin rather than the attempts at translation seen in the *Rhetorica ad Herennium* and in Cicero. After treating these figures, Donatus turns to tropes, which he says are expressions transferred from their "proper" meaning to another for the sake of ornament or necessity. A trope is necessary if there is no "proper" word in good usage. Thirteen tropes are named and defined, each illustrated with one Latin example: metaphora, catachresis, metalepsis, metonymia, antonomasia, epitheton, synecdoche, onomatopoeia, periphrasis, hyperbaton, hyperbole, allegoria, and homoeosis. Donatus' treatment of figures and tropes had great authority and is substantially repeated by later writers like the Venerable Bede. Since grammar was always more widely studied than rhetoric, and often out of Donatus' textbook, his discussion insured that these ornaments of style were known in later centuries even to students who did not study rhetoric as a separate discipline.

Technical rhetoric is technical. It often seems dry, and in antiquity it had to be learned by rote by students in their teens, though their studies were enlivened by practice in declamation, with its bizarre themes of pirates and ravished maidens. It is the nature of technical writing to impose rules, to regularize, and to codify—thus not to provide for subtlety or finesse. Of particular interest in this respect is the way classical rhetoric traditionally viewed style as a set of qualities "laid on" to the thoughts which invention had provided and disposition set out, rather than as something integral to the whole speech. This was, of course, not the view of Gorgias, and it may well be that it is a heritage of Aristotle's efforts to reduce the importance of style in rhetoric.

One strength of technical rhetoric in contrast to most other ancient critical writing should be noted. It has a concept of unity of the material: it deals with the whole argument, the whole speech, and in the case of Quintilian the whole of education. As such it tends to balance the obsessive concern of those other important disciplines, grammar, dialectic, and poetics, with words, single lines, short passages, or separate arguments. Plato's demand for a living discourse had filtered through to the rhetoricians as long as they held to the concept of primary rhetoric.

Chapter 6
Literary Rhetoric

During the last century, much of the study of the history of rhetoric has been the work of scholars of the history of literature. In order to understand the composition of written works, both in prose and in verse, in periods such as the Middle Ages and the Renaissance, they turned to the system of rhetoric taught in the schools of the time, and they naturally saw rhetoric in terms of their original interests, as a phenomenon of literature. It is an objective of this book, however, to view the history of rhetoric, and the classical tradition in particular, in wider terms, and when that is done, the primacy of speech is clear. To cite a few of the most important signs, the study of rhetoric in Greece originally emerged as a way to learn how to speak in courts and assemblies. The goal of the influential schools of declamation of the Roman Empire was the training of public speakers. The rhetoric taught in the Middle Ages, as we shall see in chapters 8 and 9, was basically the civic and oral rhetoric of antiquity, even though its principal contemporary manifestation was in written forms such as the epistle. Rhetoric blossomed in the early Renaissance when opportunities for speech in the Italian municipalities increased. Serious interest in and important contributions to rhetorical theory came in the neoclassical period when opportunities for speech in the pulpits of France and before the bar and the parliament of Britain expanded. This interest waned in the nineteenth century under the influence of romanticism, belles lettres, and the elocutionary movement, but the study of speech emerged again in the twentieth century when a new and more general orality came to characterize society. There has thus been, through history, a repeated reinspiration of the discipline of rhetoric from oral speech.

To approach rhetoric solely in literary terms distorts its history by obscuring the thread of orality. It also distorts literary history. Literary criticism, ancient and modern, has used the system of rhetoric without giving adequate attention to important differences between speech and literature. Although speech may create a text, which can then be analyzed like a written work, it is in itself an act and not a text. Delivery is an important part of rhetoric. The time, the place, and the immediate reaction of the audience are also important factors, as they are not in the case of literature. A number of successful speeches fail to persuade readers in their written form; a number of great published works in oratorical form were rhetorical failures when delivered.[1] In particular, a speech is linear and is usually given but once. A speaker has greater need to repeat his main points than does a writer. The audience has little opportunity at any moment to look back at what the orator said ten or twenty minutes before; it has little opportunity to consider the structure of the whole; many effective literary features such as complex structure or imagery are easily lost on an audience which is carried away by the emotions of the moment; devices of ethos and pathos cleverly obscure lack of evidence or logical inconsistencies once an audience has the will to believe. Careful study of the orations of Cicero reveals all of these oral characteristics. Literary critics of antiquity, even the great "Longinus," borrowing the system of rhetoric for literary analysis, usually treat a literary text as similarly linear and say nothing about the structural and imagistic devices peculiar to a written work. One reason for this is presumably the fact that works of literature in antiquity, including poetry, were usually read aloud and thus regarded as a speech-act even though, unlike a true speech, they were intended for repeated readings. Rhetoric had been conceptualized and was readily at hand as a system of analysis for literary critics; the peculiar features of literary composition were not conceptualized and presumably existed as a kind of secret among a guild of poets who learned them by imitation, experimentation, and something which they regarded as inspiration. Careful comparison of the subtle literary techniques of Horace in his *Odes* with the warmed-over rhetoric of his verse treatise, *The Art of Poetry*, well illustrates the gulf between practice and theory.

In chapter 1 we used the term *letteraturizzazione* to describe the repeated slippage of rhetoric into literary composition. In this chapter we shall try to examine some of the reasons for that slippage, a few of its manifestations, the ancient view of the relationship of rhetoric to poetry and literature in general, and the particular case of the theory of imitation, developed in classical times and taken up by critics of the Renaissance and later centuries.

Factors Encouraging *Letteraturizzazione*

Letteraturizzazione was made easier by the fact that all Greek literature was originally oral. That does not mean that it should be identified with speech. A speech was delivered on a particular occasion; it was heavily influenced by that occasion, and lacked a preexisting text. Early Greek orators did not memorize speeches, they spoke extempore, using formulae and commonplaces. Oral literature had a text, even if it was a somewhat more fluid text than that of a written work. Its length, but not its content or style varied with the occasion. An oral poet like Homer repeatedly published the text of the *Iliad* in more or less similar form by delivering it at festivals.

Letteraturizzazione was also made easier by the fact that a great deal of Greek literature is in some sense public, and like oratory, had religious or political functions within the society. This is clearest in the case of epic and drama. Lyric poetry, such as that by Sappho or Archilochus, is a partial exception and has a personal element, but even here public function is often a factor. Most Greek lyric falls into genres such as wedding hymns, odes for the victors in athletic games, exhortations to military virtue, and the like, all of which, in a different society, could have been the occasion for oratory. There was in antiquity nothing quite like the romantic, personal poetry of the nineteenth and twentieth centuries, in which a poet seems alone in the universe.

Letteraturizzazione was further facilitated by the fact that early Greek literature, imitating the society of which it was a part, made much use of the forms of oratory. We have only to think of the "speeches" in Homer or in lyric poetry or later in drama. Formal debates are also a part of Greek historical writing from the beginning in Herodotus and Thucydides. Rhetoric was thus brought into Greek literature even before rhetoric was "invented" or conceptualized. As seen in Homer these speeches are intended to imitate attempts at persuasion, but it was relatively easy for later writers to imitate the technique for more decorative purposes. In the third book of Herodotus (80–83),. for example, written in the third quarter of the fifth century, occurs a famous debate about constitutions for the Persian Empire; the situation is historically improbable and Herodotus has used the form of speech, under sophistic influences, to summarize in a vivid way the characteristics of monarchy, oligarchy, and democracy as he understood them.

The use of oratorical forms in literature continued throughout antiquity and was imitated in later centuries, especially in the Renaissance and early modern period. It was not until the nineteenth century that historians abandoned the convention of writing speeches for characters in their narratives. Furthermore, the fiction of orality was preserved in a great deal of literature. Poets throughout antiquity "sing" and their successors sometimes still use the term. Pamphleteers and controversialists "speak out." And the formal line between the literary oration and the epistle is often a narrow one. Finally, as we have said, even when classical literature was written it was often orally published. Herodotus read his history, or parts of it, in Athens; Virgil read books of the *Aeneid* to Augustus; Asinius Pollio established the custom of public recitations of literature in Rome. When a Greek or Roman wanted to "read" a book, he is very likely to have asked his slave to read it aloud to him, and even if he read it alone, he read it aloud.

The introduction of writing into Greece tended to freeze speech into texts. Plato saw this and in the *Phaedrus* objects to it on dialectical grounds. As his contemporary Alcidamas realized, it was inimical also to the vitality of primary rhetoric.[2] With Isocrates oratory itself became established as a literary genre. His speeches show great amplification and a lack of concern for immediate effect on an audience. They were intended as texts to be read and studied with care, not to be heard only once in linear progression. Aristotle recognizes the trend in chapter 12 of the third book of the *Rhetoric*. The change from the use of the scroll to the codex, or leaved book, during the early centuries of the Christian era made it easier to turn back and forth to different portions of a work. The revolutionary effect of the introduction of writing then is reproduced on a much larger scale in the Renaissance with the introduction of printing. The relative importance of the spoken as contrasted with the written word steadily decreased until the twentieth century, when the process began to be reversed by radio and television.

Rhetorical theory, intended as a training for the ability to speak in the Greek city-state, was useful, was neatly conceptualized, and could be learned with relative ease. Beginning in the fourth century before Christ it became a central discipline in the education of the young, replacing the more informal imitation of orators or sophists as the way to learn to speak. Not only in Greece and Rome, but in medieval and renaissance Europe, rhetoric was studied at such an early age that like language itself, it tended to become an instinctive part of students' mental framework and to influence their formal expression in writing. In contrast, literary criticism was slow to develop in antiquity and was never fully conceptualized.

At the end of the fourth century in Greece and again at the end of the first century B.C. in Rome, opportunities for significant oral discourse declined. This decline was occasionally the result of systematic efforts by tyrants to prevent freedom of speech, but in larger part it resulted from transference of decision-making from the local level to the centralized bureaucracy of large states like Macedon, Syria, Egypt, and Rome and from the development of Roman law, which provided equitable solutions to many problems on the basis of formulae and precedent rather than through argument from probability, ethos, and pathos. From the period of the early Roman Empire we have a series of discussions of this trend and of how it related to literature.[3] The last chapter of "Longinus' " *On the Sublime* is devoted to the question, as is the splendid little *Dialogue on the Orators* of Tacitus, written around A.D. 100.[4] The leading character in the dialogue has given up oratory for rhetorical poetry, and Tacitus himself, the greatest orator of the time, turned from public life to the writing of history.

The result of these factors, and perhaps certain other forces inherent in the makeup of the human brain or the culture of man, was that rhetoric, thoroughly a part of the framework of thought, found application in forms of creative expression other than spoken oratory and that these other forms became relatively more common and more important. Teachers were perhaps dimly aware of the trend even from an early time and stressed those aspects of rhetoric, such as arrangement and style, which were easily applicable to writing. The use of topics, the structure of exordium, narration, demonstration, and conclusion, and the tropes and figures of speech are the clearest marks of rhetorical literature.

Manifestations of Literary Rhetoric

Among manifestations of literary rhetoric which contributed reinforcement to the theoretical side of its development are the monographs on aspects of style written in the late Hellenistic and early imperial period. These works, rediscovered in the Renaissance, had a major influence on the development of later literary rhetoric. The treatise *On Style* by Demetrius, the works by Dionysius of Halicarnassus, and *On the Sublime*, attributed to "Longinus," are a part of this trend, as is Hermogenes' later work, *On Ideas of Style*. Cicero's *Orator* shows a Latin tendency in the same direction, though Cicero continues to make the role of the public speaker central to his concern. It is this interest in writing among ancient writers that produced handbooks on composition. The earliest example is Dionysius of Halicarnassus' *On Composition*, written toward the end of the first century before Christ.[5] Dionysius considers how words are put together into sentences, the various styles of composition and poetical elements in prose, and also prose

elements in poetry. He approaches the material as linear, to be analyzed in small units of text.

The famous treatise *On the Sublime* was probably written during
the first century of the Christian era by a Greek rhetorician familiar
with the trend toward *letteraturizzazione* seen in the works of Dionysius and others of the time.[6] The author's name may have been Longinus, but he was subsequently confused with a rhetorician named Cas-
sius Longinus who enjoyed some fame in the third century. He defines
"sublimity," Greek *hypsos*, or "elevation," as the quality of excellence
found in great poets and prose writers; it is thus a literary feature. Five
sources are identified (8.1): the power to conceive great thoughts;
strong emotion; the use of elevated figures of thought and speech;
noble diction; and dignified word arrangement. Emotion is left for
separate treatment in a continuation, now lost, but the other sources
are discussed and illustrated in turn, with considerable insight into literature. The basis of "Longinus'" critical system, however, is rhetoric,
from which he borrows his categories and terminology. Great thought
and strong emotion are aspects of rhetorical invention; the remaining
sources of sublimity are parts of the rhetorical theory of style. The
work is intended to be a practical aid to composition, and "Longinus"
thinks that a student can, to some extent, achieve sublimity by study and
imitation of the literary excellences of Homer, Thucydides, Plato, and
Demosthenes. The work also contains, unique among classical writings,
a discussion of genius (32.8–36.4), which had much to do with the popularity of "the Sublime" in the eighteenth century, as did the author's
citation (9.9) of the opening of Genesis as an example of the quality
which he seeks to define. At the end of the work as we have it he adds
a chapter on the decline of eloquence. The central role of political oratory is here recognized, but the author concludes that the real problem
is a pervasive moral decline, resulting from materialism, which infects
all the arts.

Although Hellenistic Greek poetry shows some signs of literary rhetoric, the literature of the Silver Age in Rome, starting with Ovid at the
beginning of the Christian era and including such writers as Seneca,
Lucan, Martial, and Juvenal, is the first truly rhetorical literature.
Much of it is influenced not only by rhetorical theories of arrangement
and style but also by the schools of declamation, where highly unreal
themes were given rhetorical development in an ostensibly oratorical
situation. The *Heroides* of Ovid show the influence, as do the tragedies
of Seneca. The latter, very popular in the Renaissance, consist of series
of speeches by characters seeking to develop the rhetorical possibilities
of their situations, with little real communication between characters
and little overall development. Roman poets like Juvenal, although

seeming to write out of personal experience, are often developing the rhetorical possibilities of a theme or situation with little relationship to their own lives. This artificial literary trend should be distinguished, if possible, from the tendency of writers like Tacitus to abandon speech for safer literary forms as a vehicle for political criticism, but it is often difficult to draw the line. Is Lucan's epic *On the Civil War* a serious political attack on Nero, and thus like a work of primary rhetoric in literary form, or an extravagant display of secondary rhetoric as learned in declamation? Both elements seem present.

In chapter 7 we will consider the relationship between rhetoric and Christianity. It seems clear that some Christians were attracted by secondary rhetoric and regretted the generally nonliterary character of the Scriptures. With the acceptance of Christianity as a legal religion in the fourth century it became possible to give Christianity more literary expression, and Christian rhetoric thus experienced a kind of *letteraturizzazione* of its own, moving from the simple, oral homily to the elaborate, epideictic sermon.

In the Middle Ages, when limited teaching of rhetoric at an elementary level survived with reduced opportunities for civic expression, the literary use of classical tropes and figures is the mark of the classical tradition. It finds its theoretical exposition in the *dictamen*, in the development of *artes poetriae*, rather superficial statements of the conventions of rhetorical expression in verse, and in handbooks on preaching based on scholastic models. The Renaissance saw the brief appearance of a true primary rhetoric, with a renewed influence on rhetorical expression in oratory, as well as the development of rhetorical dialogues and historiography and the continuation of rhetorical poetry along the lines known in the Middle Ages. In France the term "First Rhetoric" is applied to prose composition, "Second Rhetoric" to poetry, as practiced by the *grands rhétoriqueurs*, and in Holland the *Kamers van Retorica* are part of a comparable movement.[7] The failure of primary rhetoric in the Renaissance to establish a new theoretical tradition at a high intellectual level resulted in the survival of rhetoric primarily as an elementary, if almost universal, study in the schools, with significant implications for the form of renaissance literature, not only in Latin, but in all European vulgate languages.

The Arts of Rhetoric and Poetry

The question of the relationship of rhetoric to the art of poetry has often been raised in modern times and has been made the subject of many theories and complex speculations. Within the pure classical tradition that relationship is rather clear, even if not always understood. In the classical world there were many different arts. Some of them were more basic than others. As we have seen, Aristotle thought of rhetoric as an art of communication, parallel to dialectic, whereas he saw poetics as a productive art, like painting. As seen in the so-called liberal arts of later times, basic arts were regarded as limited to grammar, rhetoric, and dialectic, which are the three arts of communication, and geometry, arithmetic, astronomy, and music, but certain other arts are probably nearly as primary, including physics and medicine. Some arts, however, are clearly secondary developments, built upon one or more of the basic arts. Secondary arts include some of the noblest forms, such as architecture, which involves both physics and geometry.[8] In the purest classical tradition, poetics, or the art of poetry, is also a secondary art which uses the three arts of communication—grammar, rhetoric, dialectic—and also uses music in the creation of a text. Poetics is properly the study of the specific compositional needs of the poet working within the poetic genres. These needs include plot (or at least unity of narrative), characterization, the choice of appropriate poetic diction, and not least an understanding of the conventions of the genres within which the poet works. The classical art of poetry is not an art of free composition. These topics are what Aristotle in the *Poetics* and Horace in *The Art of Poetry* discuss. They are also the topics of the classicizing poetics of sixteenth-century Italy and seventeenth and eighteenth-century France and England.

The view of poetry as something less than the complex interplay of other arts existed in antiquity. Plato flatly calls poetry a form of rhetorical public address (*Gorgias* 502d2). In the Hellenistic period poetry was taught by the grammarians and poetic criticism was regarded as a part of grammar. In late antiquity we find an attempt by rhetoricians to take over poetry as a subdivision of epideictic. During the period of the Roman Empire and extending into the Byzantine age, there is no first-rate Greek poetry at all, though there are occasional attempts to write encomia in verse. The best late Greek poetry is seen in the epigram, equivalent to a versified *sententia*. The absorption of poetry into rhetoric can be well seen in the prose hymns in oratorical form created by sophists like Himerius, who lived in the fourth century. Latin poetry of late antiquity is more extensive and of somewhat higher literary quality, but as already noted, it is dominated by rhetorical forms. True poetry reemerges in Christian hymns, both in Greek and Latin, which go outside the classical tradition to the Hebrew psalms for their inspiration.

The opposite view, that poetry is something much more than the interplay of classical arts, also existed in antiquity, where it is best seen in the lyric poets. Horace, for example, in his *Odes* speaks as a priest of the Muses, but he makes little effort to conceptualize this art, least of all in his own *Art of Poetry*. Ancient literary criticism never succeeded in describing the characteristics of carefully edited, written texts, including the complex use of imagery seen in writers like Virgil. Literature continued to be analyzed as though, like oral speech, it were entirely linear, each word spoken in order, with no opportunity for the audience to reread or to compare portions of the text. Modern celebrations of poetry as superior to rhetoric largely represent the efforts of romanticism to free poetry from convention and rule and to make it either the unlimited expression of the poet's personal genius, speaking primarily to himself, or a philosophical glimpse of a higher reality unapprehended by the other arts. Critics of the seventeenth and eighteenth centuries seized upon the concept of the sublime as a classical authority for such a view, but they significantly distorted "Longinus' " account of a quality which the Greek writer had analyzed in terms of the parts of classical rhetoric. Although Boileau was a leader in this movement, his own work *L'Art poétique* reveals him as a classical critic. The work of his successors, among them Dennis, Burke, and Kant, on the sublime represents a step even beyond *letteraturizzazione* to include painting, music, and the rhetoric of natural beauty.

Imitation

The concept of *mimesis*, or imitation,[9] has historically been fundamental to theories of poetics and important in theories of literary rhetoric; it is thus appropriate here to define it briefly and assess its place in classical rhetoric. The celebrated work of Eric Auerbach, *Mimesis: The Representation of Reality in Western Literature*, is often regarded as central to the study of imitation but is of little help in understanding the history of rhetoric. Indeed, the word *mimesis* was used by the Greeks in several different but related ways.

First is what may be called dramatic imitation. Aristotle, in the *Poetics*, defines tragedy as the imitation of an action. Aeschylus' *Persians*, for example, is the imitation of a possible scene at the Persian court when the news of Xerxes' defeat was received there. Similarly an actor imitates or mimics a character who is an individual or a type. An actor in Aristophanes' *Clouds* thus imitates Socrates. But art as a whole imitates life or nature, with varying degrees of fidelity. "O Menander, o life!" exclaimed an ancient critic, "Which one of you imitated the other?"[10] Here photographic detail is not so important as an imitation of the spirit, passions, and essential nature of life in such a way that the product seems real in itself. Often the crucial factor is the ethical and emotional quality of the action or person imitated. The concept of imitation was extended by Plato and the Neoplatonists to describe the relationship between our physical and visible world of change and the unchanging world of metaphysical reality or ultimate being. Life as we know it imitates the forms and the idea of the Good.

These concepts or levels of imitation, important in poetics, aesthetics, and philosophy, constitute a background for the specific and more limited use of imitation in the theory of classical rhetoric. It should be remembered that a kind of imitation occurred in the composition of oral literature in Greece. At least to judge from modern oral poets, the young poet learned by listening to and imitating the older, and the young orator did likewise. Further, we have seen that the teaching methods of the sophists were based on imitation. The sophist spoke and only occasionally perhaps reduced his technique to rules; the student listened, admired, and imitated, sometimes verbatim, as Phaedrus seeks to do, sometimes not verbatim, but in the spirit of the master. This kind of imitation would involve subject, arrangement, style, and delivery, but it is likely that style was often the most conspicuous element. To speak like Gorgias means to speak in Gorgias' style. Students in Isocrates' school learned his methods and his philosophical, moral, and political ideas, but above all learned to imitate his style.

In the Hellenistic period grammarians began to establish a canon of models of each genre of writing; Quintilian (10.1.54) mentions Aristarchus and Aristophanes of Byzantium as doing so. That would be around 200 B.C. This reflects the beginnings of classicism and a sense that the great creative efforts in literature were largely past. Homer is the model in epic, and his works are imitated by later writers of epic, such as Apollonius of Rhodes. Who are the models for imitation in oratory? They are, above all others, the so-called Ten Attic Orators. We do not know whether this list originated with Aristarchus and Aristophanes or whether it is later. Caecilius of Calacte in the late first century before Christ wrote a book, now lost, called *On the Character of the Ten Orators*, and among the *Moralia* of Plutarch is a little treatise, which he did not write, called *On the Lives of the Ten Orators*.[11] In any event, by the time of the Roman Empire there existed a canon (which in Greek means "rule" or "measure") of ten orators of the fifth and fourth centuries whose works were preserved in writing: Antiphon, Andocides, Lysias, Isaeus, Isocrates, Demosthenes, Aeschines, Hyperides, Lycurgus, and Dinarchus. Great orators like Pericles were not included because their speeches were not written down. Gorgias was probably omitted as not an appropriate model for imitation in the view of later teachers.

The earliest work to discuss literary imitation of orators is the small, partially fragmentary, treatise *On Imitation* by Dionysius of Halicarnassus, written at the end of the first century before Christ. The concept of imitation, however, is fundamental to all of Dionysius' writings on rhetoric. His study *On the Ancient Orators* is intended to define the stylistic virtues and characteristics of several of the classic models, both as a basis of judging which of their works are genuine and to enable students to understand and imitate these qualities.[12] We have already noted that imitation is also discussed in the treatise of "Longinus." The later work of Hermogenes, *On Ideas of Style,* is a more complicated effort to identify characteristics which a student can imitate. Most critics agreed that among the features to be studied in the model were choice of word and composition, including use of figures and the way the model puts together sentences or varies expression.

Imitation has a special place in Roman literary history, for all of Latin literature is in origin an imitation of Greek. There was no Latin literature until the third century before Christ, when Romans became familiar with Greek epic and Greek plays and set out to translate and then to imitate them in Latin. Roman oratory was similarly an imitation of Greek orators, especially of ambassadors who came to negotiate with the Roman senate in the second century B.C.[13] Imitation in Latin of Greek models of course primarily meant imitation of contents, topics, and arrangement, but tropes, figures, and other devices of ornament could be imitated in Latin as well. With growing sophistication in Latin in the mid–first century B.C. a movement grew up in Rome which sought to imitate the stylistic qualities of the purest and simplest Greek models like Lysias. This movement was called Atticism, a term which refers to the classical Greek dialect of Athens and which as far as we know had not been used by Greek critics of style. Cicero's *Brutus* and *Orator* are in large part intended to counteract this Atticist movement and to establish Demosthenes as a more trusty "Attic" model of style. Cicero was in turn accused of "Asianism," that is, of imitating the undisciplined excesses of orators of Asia in the Hellenistic period, but he always insisted that he was more truly Attic than his opponents. Atticism as a term to describe fondness for the simple style persists in Rome for a century or so, and use of the term to describe English style is primarily derived from Roman sources.

To judge from Dionysius of Halicarnassus' introduction to his work *On the Ancient Orators,* Greek critics of the late first century B.C. were influenced by Roman practice in their development of a concept of Atticism in Greek, but as we have seen there are signs of classicism in Greek earlier in Alexandria. In any event, the major period of Greek Atticism begins about the time of Dionysius, reaches a height in the mid–second century with the Second Sophistic, and extends throughout the Byzantine period. In its extreme form this Atticism is the rule that the Attic orators and such other Attic writers as Thucydides and Plato are the only sound models for choice and use of words. This doctrine "froze" literary Greek into a classical pattern which was regarded as the only vehicle for formal discourse for well over a thousand years, even though spoken Greek changed considerably during the same period. A similar phenomenon on lesser scale occurred in the Renaissance, when some teachers made the usage of Cicero the standard of all good Latin. Erasmus ridicules the view in his dialogue *Ciceronianus*.

The tenth book of Quintilian brings together many of the topics which have been discussed here. Quintilian's purpose, however, is that of primary rhetoric: "What can the prospective public speaker learn from study of literature?" He devotes the long first chapter of the *Institutio Oratoria* to explaining how to secure a *copia*, or supply of ideas and words, from a study of Greek and Latin literature. In this connexion he reviews the qualities of the major literary genres and takes up each of the classical models in turn, first Greek, then Latin literature. This chapter was a major inspiration for the study of stylistic abundance that flourished in the Renaissance and it was a source for Erasmus' influential treatise *On Copia*. The second chapter of Quintilian's tenth book deals with imitation. Quintilian recognizes its dangers and limitations but thinks the orator has much to learn from careful study and imitation of the style of a variety of great models.[14]

Literary rhetoric is an important study. An understanding of the world's great writings depends upon it. Its future lies in a careful balance of awareness of the history of primary rhetoric with analysis of the internal rhetoric, the dynamism and unique artistic features, of great artists in all periods.

Chapter 7
Judeo-Christian Rhetoric

Judaism, Christianity, and to a lesser extent Islam, are highly verbal religions. They are based on sacred writings, and they have developed preaching into a high art. It is thus not surprising that these religious movements play a role in the history of rhetoric. Christianity had, in particular, a commandment to preach the gospel. It sought to convert the world, basically through the grace of God, but with testimony, sermons, saints' lives, letters, and other appeals or demonstrations, by example or a way of life, including martyrdom in the final necessity, and later in its history by the use of rhetorical arts like sculpture, painting, music, and liturgical pageantry. This chapter will examine some rhetorical features of the Old Testament, the concept of rhetoric inherent in the beginnings of Christianity, and the relationship between Christianity and classical rhetoric during the first four centuries of the Christian era, culminating in Saint Augustine's influential treatise *De Doctrina Christiana*.[1]

Old Testament Rhetoric

The rhetoric of the Old Testament is preconceptual. Although, as in the Homeric poems, there are many speeches and examples of oral and written literary forms, there is no passage which analyzes the nature, purpose, and forms of speech. Indeed, rhetorical consciousness is entirely foreign to the nature of biblical Judaism. As a result, there is no established critical tradition of approaching the Old Testament as primary rhetoric, but it seems fairly obvious that both as a whole and in its various books there are signs of oral, persuasive intent. The identification of various purposes and the analysis of their techniques is rendered difficult by multiplicity of authorship and by the fact that different books were written at different times, not in the sequence in which they now appear, and are often the product of redaction, or composition by editors out of earlier material which was sometimes very different both in form and in purpose. What is known as "form criticism" has brought about the recognition of types of narrative, prophecy, poetry, and wisdom literature and of their *Sitz im Leben*, or setting in society, which includes the purpose for which they were written and the often different purposes for which they were used.[2] Future research can probably build on form criticism and on the comparison of rhetoric in the Old Testament to other rhetorical traditions in order to produce an historical picture of the primary, preconceptual rhetoric of the Jews, as well as the literary rhetoric evident in the Bible as we know it. It may be necessary to take into account recent hypotheses about the origin of consciousness and particularly about the speech of "gods" and prophets.[3]

Taking the Bible as we have it, the evidence begins with the first chapter of Genesis, where the creation is described not in terms of God's actions, but of speech: "And God *said*, 'Let there be light'; and there was light." In contrast to this creation by enunciation, the second chapter records a different tradition in which God *acts*, forming man, for example, out of the dust of the ground. Whoever put the first chapter first had a strong sense of the power of speech and in particular of the authoritative speech of God.

The essential rhetorical quality of the Old Testament is this assertion of authority. God has given his law to his people. They are convinced because of who he is, what he has done for them, and how this is revealed to them. In the New Testament the authoritative message of God is extended from a national group to all individuals in the world. Authority is analogous to ethos in classical rhetoric, but at a different metaphysical level. It is bolstered by something like pathos in the remembrance of the past suffering of people and by their fears of future punishment or hopes of future reward. In its purest form Judeo-Christian rhetoric shows similarity to philosophical rhetoric: it is the simple enunciation of God's truth, uncontaminated by adornment, flattery, or sophistic argumentation; it differs from philosophical rhetoric in that this truth is known from revelation or established by signs sent from God, not discovered by dialectic through man's efforts. We have seen a hint of such a possibility in the divine voice which came to Socrates. However, like Greek philosophical rhetoric, Judeo-

Christian rhetoric gradually came to use features of classical rhetoric to attain its ends. Judaism in the Hellenistic period already shows some influence of classical rhetoric, and Christianity makes an increasing use of classical rhetorical forms.

A passage in the Old Testament in which the nature of Judeo-Christian rhetoric emerges clearly is the fourth chapter of Exodus. God has commissioned Moses to bring the children of Israel out of Egypt, but Moses distrusts his ability to persuade them. "But behold," he says, "they will not believe me or listen to my voice, for they will say, 'The Lord did not appear to you'" (Exod. 4:1). He feels the lack of personal authority. The Lord's reply is typical of the subsequent tradition; it is a series of signs or miracles proving the authority of the commission: the rod is cast down and becomes a serpent, but Moses picks it up and it becomes again a rod; the hand becomes leprous and is restored; the Nile water will become blood. Authority is confirmed by miracle, and this, rather than logical argument, will be the primary mode of persuasion.

Moses, however, is not content with authority. "Oh, my Lord," he says (Exod. 4:10), "I am not eloquent, either heretofore or since thou hast spoken to thy servant; but I am slow of speech and of tongue." The Lord replies (Exod. 4:11–12), "Who has made man's mouth? Who makes him dumb, or deaf, or seeing, or blind? Is it not I, the Lord? Now therefore go, and I will be with your mouth and teach you what you shall speak." The preacher is thus to be a vehicle through which an authoritative message will be expressed. If not Moses, Aaron will do equally well, and in fact it is Aaron who becomes the "orator" of the Jews. Some practical recognition is given to natural ability, but the Judeo-Christian orator, at least in theory, has little need of practice or knowledge of an art as required by the orator in the classical tradition. He needs only the inspiration of the Spirit. The role of the speaker in Judeo-Christian rhetoric is generally incidental, except in those cases where the speaker is God or Jesus or in later instances where a bishop or pope speaks with authority.

Moses is to go back to Egypt and try to persuade Pharaoh to let Israel leave. In this effort he will encounter another crucial feature of Judeo-Christian rhetoric. His success will depend entirely on the extent to which God allows Pharaoh to listen. "When you go back to Egypt," the Lord tells him (Exod. 4:21), "see that you do before Pharaoh all the miracles which I have put in your power; but I will harden his heart, so that he will not let the people go." And so it is. Moses does not persuade Pharaoh until the Egyptians are utterly despoiled and eager that the Jews depart. Persuasion takes place when God is ready, and not through the verbal abilities or even the authority of Moses. Similarly in Christian rhetoric God must act, through his grace, to move the hearts of an audience before individuals can receive the Word, and if he does pour out this grace, the truth of the message will be recognized because of its authority, and not through its logical argumentation. In its purest and most fundamental form, therefore, the basic modes of proof of Judeo-Christian rhetoric are grace, authority, and logos, the divine message which can be understood by man. These correspond in a very incomplete way to the pathos, ethos, and rational logos of Aristotelian rhetoric.

It is, however, frequently the case that the Judeo-Christian orator is addressing an audience on whom the Spirit has worked in the past and for whom the prerequisite grace has been provided earlier, but whose experience of conversion is no longer vivid. There is a possibility of reminding such an audience of the religious experience it has already known, recalling individuals to the truth through rational or emotional means. We have here something analogous to recollection as described by Plato in the myth of the *Phaedrus* or in other dialogues. Under these circumstances Judeo-Christian rhetoric still retains characteristic features of its own, including a strong element of authority, but the character of the speaker, the evidence he can present in his speech, and the extent to which he can arouse feelings of emotion, including hope of future reward or fear of punishment, become crucial to the success of his speech.

In the Old Testament the most characteristic form of speech to an audience already disposed to believe is the "covenant speech," an address built on the assumption of a covenant between God and the people of Israel. The general pattern of a covenant speech is, first, to strengthen the authority of the Lord by reminding the audience of what he has done; second, to add new commandments; and third, to conclude with a warning of what will happen if the commandments are disregarded. In a general way the Old Testament as a whole constitutes a vast covenant speech, consisting of the narrative of God's actions toward the people of Israel, his commandments to them, and the warnings of the prophets when the people fall away from their duty. Within the Old Testament there are, however, many specific examples of covenant speeches. Deuteronomy is made up in large part of three (chapters 1–4, 5–28, and 29–30), each containing a narrative of what has happened in the past, commandments, and warnings about the consequences of disobedience or promises of the blessings of obedience.

The pattern can also be seen in speeches closer to the circumstances of classical public address. An example is the speech in the twenty-fourth chapter of Joshua. This consists of a narration of what God has done in Jewish history, put in the mouth of God himself and therefore given heightened authority (24:2–13). Joshua then adds his own injunction: "Now therefore fear the Lord and serve him in sincerity and faithfulness. . . . Choose this day whom you will serve . . . but as for me and my house, we will serve the Lord" (24:14–15). The people accept Joshua's examples as authoritative and agree that they will serve a lord who has done what the Lord has done. Joshua then reminds the people that the Lord is a jealous God and gets them to commit themselves completely to the covenant, of which he sets up a stone as witness. The covenant speech of 1 Samuel 12 follows the same general pattern but prefaces it with a personal introduction. A characteristic of the covenant speech is that whatever the specific occasion, the basic message of Judaism—the covenant with God—is incorporated in the speech. This survives as a feature of some Christian preaching, where whatever the text or starting point of the orator, the message tends to come down to a single theme of overriding importance, the kernel of the gospel, that "God sent into the world his only begotten son that through him we may have eternal life."

A second form of rhetoric in the Old Testament is that of prophecy. If the covenant speech deals with the past, and thus has resemblance to classical judicial oratory, prophecy looks to the future and adapts the message of the covenant to future circumstances, thus resembling deliberative oratory. The twenty-fourth chapter of Ezekiel shows how a covenant speech can be adapted to the circumstances of prophecy. Old Testament prophecy is very influential in Christian rhetoric. Prophecy of the coming Messiah in Isaiah, for example, was converted into a basis of authority for Christianity as early as the preaching of the apostles and the composition of the gospels.

Students of form criticism distinguish several different kinds of prophecy in the Old Testament.[4] One is the "prophecy of disaster," which usually consists of an introductory word, an indication of the situation, a prediction of disaster, and a concluding characterization. There is some (perhaps superficial) similarity here to the proemium, narration, proof, and epilogue of classical oratory based on the natural logic of development of ideas. Another kind of prophecy is "prophecy of salvation," and there are also some secondary forms, including one based on a trial situation,[5] seen, for example, in Isaiah 41:21–29 or 43:8–15.

A considerable part of the Old Testament, including much of the oldest material, is poetry and wisdom literature.[6] In the first chapter of Proverbs, for example, can be found a poetic speech by Wisdom. In classical terminology this is a prosopopoeia, analogous to the speech of the Fatherland in Cicero's first oration against Catiline. There is in Wisdom's address no logical argument nor any definition of what is meant by wisdom or knowledge, only assertions delivered with authority. Wisdom rebukes fools who have no knowledge. Then she threatens to ignore them when they appeal to her in time of trouble. Finally she prophesies their repentance. Passages like this exercised considerable influence on later preaching. Even more influential is the allegory common in Hebrew poetry—for example in Psalm 80, verses 8–11:

> Thou didst bring a vine out of Egypt;
> thou didst drive out the nations and plant it.
> Thou didst clear the ground for it;
> it took deep root and filled the land.
> The mountains were covered with its shade,
> the mighty cedars with its branches;
> it sent out its branches to the sea,
> and its shoots to the River.

In classical rhetoric allegory is a figure of speech, and though allegorical poems occur in classical Greek or Latin (for example, Alcaeus' poem on the ship of state and Horace's imitation of it), allegory is not a pervasive factor in most classical poetry. It becomes an important element in the Christian style in Greek, Latin, and modern languages. Christian orators draw on all parts of the Bible, but especially the Psalms and the more emotional parts of the prophets, to create a non-classical prose with its own rhythms and exotic imagery, much of it allegorical. Allegory also becomes important for the exegesis of the Bible.[7]

New Testament Rhetoric

Jewish Sabbath services in the Hellenistic period (that is, the last three centuries before Christ) and in later times included the reading of lessons from the Scriptures, followed by interpretation of the passages read and exhortations to the congregation to follow the law or to strive for moral excellence. This form of preaching, rather informal, rather spontaneous, shared among different members of the congregation, is the ancestor of the homily, the informal sermon of the early

Christian church. It seems to have been influenced to some extent by Greek rhetorical forms, in particular the diatribe of the Stoic and Cynic philosophers, and eventually by Greek philosophical ideas.[8]

In the fourth chapter of Luke, Jesus is described as coming into Galilee and teaching in the synagogues in the way just described. In Nazareth he reads the lesson for the day, which is Isaiah's prophecy of the Messiah. Then he interprets what he has read: "Today this Scripture has been fulfilled in your hearing" (Luke 4:21). There is murmuring against him, but he refuses to perform miracles here to demonstrate his authority in his own country and with some difficulty escapes from the town. Later at Capernaum he again teaches on the Sabbath, and "they were astonished at his teaching, for his word was with authority" (Luke 4:32). This time he confirms his announcement by expelling an unclean demon from a man, and the reaction in the congregation is "What is this word? For with authority and power he commands the unclean spirits, and they come out" (Luke 4:36). Similar accounts can be found in Matthew, chapter 4, and Mark, chapter 1.

As a result of Jesus' preaching in the synagogues he attracted crowds from all parts of the country and according to Matthew (5:1) preached to them the Sermon on the Mount. It may be a composite document put together later by one of Jesus' followers on the basis of a variety of sermons; in Luke verbally similar material appears in different contexts. The Sermon on the Mount is, however, the most extensive example of Jesus' preaching as envisioned by the early Church. It consists of five parts, the first being a poetic introduction, the Beatitudes with their marked anaphora, or repetition of the same initial word in each clause. Second comes an expression of assurance not unlike a classical proemium (5:13-17). Then a statement of the relation of Jesus' teaching to Jewish law (5:17-48), followed by a series of injunctions about almsgiving, praying, fasting, and the like (6:1-7:20). Finally there is an epilogue with a strong warning, and a parable comparing those who build on the rock of authoritative knowledge and those who build on the sand of foolishness (7:21-27). Although some elements are reminiscent of classical rhetoric, the techniques employed, including the parable, are largely drawn from Jewish traditions of speech. The persuasive quality of the sermon comes primarily from the authority projected by the speaker, seen especially in his relation to the law, but in the second half supporting statements are frequently given, thus creating enthymemes. "Do not lay up for yourselves treasures on earth. . . . For where your treasure is, there will your heart be also" (6:19-21) would be regarded by Aristotle as an enthymeme. Jesus as seen in the gospels is quite adept at argumentation. His encounters with the

Pharisees show an ability even at dialectic (for example, Matthew 15:1–9 and 22:15–22).

It seems clear, however, that the basis of persuasion in Jesus' view did not lie in rational proof and that his rhetoric is much like that we have found in the Old Testament. He says to the disciples, for example:

> But take heed to yourselves; for they will deliver you up to councils; and you will be beaten in synagogues; and you will stand before governors and kings for my sake, to bear testimony before them. And the gospel must first be preached to all nations. And when they bring you to trial and deliver you up, do not be anxious beforehand what you are to say; but say whatever is given you in that hour, for it is not you who speak, but the Holy Spirit. And brother will deliver up brother to death, and the father his child, and children will rise against parents and have them put to death; and you will be hated by all for my name's sake. But he who endures to the end will be saved. (Mark 13:9–13)

Among the points to be noted in this passage are the importance of testimony up to and including the example of martyrdom; the fact that no special eloquence is required, for as in Exodus God will provide the words; and an apparent assumption that the disciples cannot expect to persuade their judges of the righteousness of their cause: that is God's work, and as with Pharoah, he seems to intend to harden their hearts. All of this is completely contrary to the situation of the classical orator, who uses his eloquence to overcome enormous opposition in defense of himself and his clients.

The word for "preach" in Mark 13:10 and commonly in the New Testament is *kerusso*, which literally means "proclaim." It is what a herald (*keryx*) does with a message, a law, or a commandment. The message is a *kerygma*, or proclamation, and constitutes the gospel ("good news," *euangelion*). Christian preaching is thus not persuasion, but proclamation, and is based on authority and grace, not on proof. Augustine says (*De Doctrina Christiana* 4.21) that a good listener warms to it not so much by diligently analyzing it as by pronouncing it energetically. Its truth must be apprehended by the listener, not proved by the speaker. The reaction of a person in the audience to the *kerygma* is like his reaction to a miracle, the direct evidence of authority: he believes or he does not.

A repeated message of the gospels is that not all will comprehend: some lack the strength for the gospel. In the parable of the sower (Mark 4) some seed falls along the path, some on rocky ground, some among thorns, and some in good soil. The parable ends with "He who has ears to hear, let him hear"; but even the disciples do not understand and have to have the parable explained to them. There is irony in the failure of those who hear or see Jesus to believe in him, and this irony is developed in other ways as well, particularly in Matthew's gospel. The first will be last, the last first; the humble great, the great humble; the one who loves his life shall lose it, the one who gives his life shall save it; and so on (cf. 16:25, 18:3, 20:26–28, 23:11). These paradoxes become a permanent part of the Christian style of preaching, as do the vivid metaphors contained in the first-person proclamations so characteristic of John's gospel: "I am the living bread" (6:51); "I am the door to the sheep" (10:7); "I am the true vine" (15:1); and so on.

The gospels are unique works which do not exactly fit any classical literary genre and which have a subtle internal rhetoric of their own. In *The Language of the Gospel: Early Christian Rhetoric*, Amos N. Wilder summarized the characteristics of this rhetoric as a creative novelty in style (including imagery), a dramatic immediacy with dialogue features, a use of common idiom and media, an addiction to narrative, and a subordination of the personal role or talent of the writer to the spirit in the community.[9] He says that Jesus and his followers created a new speech, in that they quickened and revised the existing images by which men lived, and that the form in which Jesus and his followers spoke and wrote could not be separated from what they communicated;[10] that is, the gospel form is an expression of Jesus' teaching, much as the dialogue is an expression of Socrates' teaching. In a series of short chapters Wilder considers dialogue, story, parable, poem, and image, symbol, and myth. His book succeeds in conveying the rhetorical intensity of Jesus, though it probably exaggerates the novelty and uniqueness of that rhetoric, and it significantly fails to relate the developing internal rhetoric of Christianity to the traditions of Judaism of which it is a part.

It seems inappropriate to leave the gospels without brief mention of the famous words with which John's gospel opens: "In the beginning was the Word, and the Word was with God, and the Word was God." As the editors of the *Oxford Annotated Bible* say in their note on the passage, "the *Word* (Greek logos) of God is more than speech: it is God in action, creating . . . , revealing . . . redeeming. Jesus is this *Word*." The concept is probably influenced by Greek philosophy, but is consistent with Jewish thought. It fulfills the pattern of creation which we noted in the first chapter of Genesis and is celebrated in the Psalms (33:6): "By the word of the Lord the heavens were made, and all their hosts by the breath of his mouth." The concept of the Word carries within it the three factors of Christian rhetoric we have identified—grace, authority, and the message "proclaimed" to mankind—and has provided an image elaborated by Christian preachers through the centuries.

The Apostles

A picture of preaching in the early Church is given in the book of Acts. Unfortunately, the picture may not be entirely historical. Many New Testament scholars believe that Acts is influenced by the conventions of Greek historical writing and that the speeches in Acts, like those in Greek historians, are not evidence for what was actually said.[11] That may be the case, but the speeches in Acts are not classical Greek orations; they are generally consistent with Jewish rhetorical traditions and those developing in early Christianity as seen elsewhere. The speech of Stephen (7:2–53), which enrages the high priest and precipitates the first martyrdom, is similar in structure to Old Testament rhetoric as we saw it in the speech of Joshua and may be derived from a Jewish homily.[12] It furnishes a model for the resolute rhetoric of later martyrs and is a Christian analog to Socrates' apology. Better known are the seven speeches in Acts attributed to Peter and the six attributed to Paul. Paul's speech of farewell at Miletus (20:18–35), his speeches while on trial at the end of the book, and Peter's first speech proposing a replacement for Judas (1:16–33) have special features, but the rest fall into the category of what is known as the "missionary sermon," the Christian counterpart of the Jewish covenant speech. A few examples may be considered briefly.

In the third chapter of Acts, after healing a cripple, Peter stands on Solomon's porch and addresses the people. He begins with the miracle just performed: "The faith which is through Jesus has given the man this perfect health in the presence of you all" (3:16). In explaining how this can be, Peter recapitulates the prophecy of the Messiah and the life and death of Jesus. He warns the people to repent and supports his warning with the authority of Moses, and at the end he returns to the miracle God has performed. The rhetorical elements are thus the familiar ones of authority or the law, prophecy and fulfillment, and warnings of the future.

Simpler in structure is the sermon delivered by Paul on a sabbath day in the synagogue at Antioch in Pisidia (Acts 13:16–41). The law has been read, an invitation to speak is extended, and Paul rises. He rehearses Jewish history and the prophecy of the coming of the savior. He proclaims Jesus to be that savior and supports his claim with the prophecy of two psalms. And he ends with a warning to those who do not believe. The only miracle cited is God's raising Jesus from the dead.

The most famous of all missionary sermons is that of Paul on "Mars' Hill," the Athenian Areopagus (Acts 17:22–31).[13] Here the message is adapted to Greek ears: it is not the prophecy of the Old Testament which is fulfilled, but the Greeks' own search for the unknown god, who is the God of all mankind. Of course Paul does not attempt the dialectical reasoning of a Greek orator or philosopher; he proclaims the gospel, but the proclamation is supported by a Greek quotation: "As even some of your poets have said" (17:28). Then comes the usual call to repentence and warning of judgment. Up to this point God has repeatedly been mentioned, but not Jesus, who is only referred to at the very end as the man through whom the judgment will come. God has given assurance of this by raising his son from the dead, so that we have the miracle as a sign, but its truth is dependent, as is the proclamation as a whole, on the willingness of those present to accept Paul's authority.

Rhetorical schools were common in the Hellenized cities of the East when Paul was a boy, and he could have attended one; certainly he was familiar with the rhetorical conventions of speeches in Roman lawcourts, the oral teachings of Greek philosophers, and the conventions of Greek letter-writing. Some biblical scholars see in his epistles a strong influence of the arrangement of contents, argumentation, and figures of speech of classical rhetoric which also appear in the diatribes of Stoic and Cynic philosophers.[14] The Epistle to the Galatians, for example, can be analyzed in terms of an "apology" of the classical sort, with exordium, narration, proposition, proof, and conclusion, and rhetorical structure and devices have been seen in some of his other letters as well.[15] What Paul has to say about rhetoric in his epistles, however, is a refinement of what we found in the gospels and in Acts. Probably the most important passage is the opening of the 1 Corinthians. There were factions in the church at Corinth, and Paul's preaching had apparently been criticized as philosophically simplistic (3:1–4). In reply he says:

For Jews demand signs and Greeks seek wisdom, but we preach [*kerussomen*, "proclaim"] Christ crucified, a stumbling block to the Jews and folly to Gentiles, but to those who are called, both Jews and Greeks, Christ the power of God and the wisdom of God. For the foolishness of God is wiser than men, and the weakness of God is stronger than men. (1:22–25)

The message is proclaimed, not proved; it is persuasive to those who are called or chosen by God. Paul employs an oxymoron, "wise foolishness," which ironically reverses the expectations of those who seek rational wisdom.

He continues:

For consider your call, brethren; not many of you were wise according to worldly standards, not many were powerful, not many were of noble birth; but God chose what is foolish in the world to shame the wise, God chose what is weak in the world to shame the strong, God chose what is low and despised in the world, even things that are not, to bring to nothing things that are, so that no human being might boast in the presence of God. He is the source of your life in Christ Jesus, whom God made our wisdom, our righteousness and sanctification and redemption; therefore, as it is written, "Let him who boasts, boast of the Lord." (1:26–31)

The emotional intensity of the passage is built up by its constant repetition and by the way it plays on the paradox of the wise and the foolish, the weak and the strong. This is all part of God's plan and it is all summed up in one figure, Christ. Nothing else matters. Paul continues:

When I came to you, brethren, I did not come proclaiming to you the testimony of God in lofty words of wisdom. For I decided to know nothing among you except Jesus Christ and him crucified. And I was with you in weakness and in much fear and trembling; and my speech and my message were not in plausible words of wisdom, but in demonstration of the Spirit and power, that your faith might not rest in the wisdom of men, but in the power of God. (2:1–5)

The orator himself is nothing; his words are not plausible; all lies with God. He continues:

Yet among the mature we do impart wisdom, although it is not a wisdom of this age or of the rulers of this age, who are doomed to pass away. But we impart a secret and hidden wisdom of God, which God decreed before the ages for our glorification. None of the rulers of this age understood this; for if they had, they would not have crucified the Lord of glory. But as it is written, "What no eye has seen, nor ear heard, nor the heart of man conceived, what God has prepared for those who love him," God has revealed to us through the Spirit. For the Spirit searches everything, even the depths of God. For what person knows a man's thoughts except the spirit of the man which is in him? So also no one comprehends the thoughts of God except the Spirit of God. Now we have received not the spirit of the world, but the Spirit which is from God, that we might understand the gifts bestowed on us by God. And we impart this in words not taught by human wisdom but taught by the Spirit, interpreting spiritual truths to those who possess the Spirit. (2:6–13)

This passage may be said to reject the whole of classical philosophy and rhetoric. For rhetoric the Christian can rely on God, both to supply words and to accomplish persuasion if it is God's will. In place of worldly philosophy there exists a higher philosophy, only dimly apprehended by man. Much of the work of Christian exegesis in the following centuries is built on the assumption that there is a wisdom in the Scriptures, deliberately obscure, which man can, in part, come to understand with God's help. Augustine's view, influential on many Christians, was that God had deliberately concealed his wisdom to keep it from those who were indifferent to it, but would allow those who sought the truth to find a road to understanding (see *On the Psalms* 103.3.2).

Rhetoric in the Early Church

The history of rhetoric in the Church in the 350 years from Paul to Augustine involves consideration of several subjects: the survival of a distinctive Christian rhetoric, the utilization of classical rhetoric, the development of forms of preaching, and the interrelationship between Christian exegesis and doctrine on the one hand and Greek dialectic and philosophy on the other. A great mass of material is available in the writings of the Fathers, though only occasionally do they comment on the nature and functions of rhetoric. Examples of Christian oratory and preaching are relatively rare until the fourth century, when Gregory of Nazianzus, Basil the Great, and John Chrysostom in Greek and Ambrose and Augustine in Latin achieved reputations for eloquence which can be studied in the surviving collections of their sermons. Perhaps the relation of the Church to rhetoric can best be approached if we consider first the contexts in which early Christians found need for rhetoric.

The audience addressed by a Christian writer or orator is either not yet converted to a belief in Christ or is assumed to be converted. If the audience is already Christian it may either be inclined to heresy or be orthodox. The degree of education, and thus rhetorical sophistication, varied from place to place and gradually increased as Christianity expanded from a small group of humble believers living in Jewish communities of the East to all levels of society in the Roman Empire. The Church remained illegal and was periodically persecuted until the Edict of Milan, on toleration of the Christians, issued by Constantine in A.D. 313. Subsequently the Church became more worldly and the phenomenon of the nominal Christian with a good education (the poet Ausonius is an excellent example) made its appearance. During the course of the fourth century the legal standing of the Church changed from one of persecution, to toleration, to official status, and finally to a position of exclusive religious authority when Theodosius prohibited pagan worship in A.D. 392. Worship of the old gods survived privately or among country folk (*pagani*) for two or three centuries, but with little influence.

The Apologists

The best examples of address to the nonconverted are, first, missionary sermons of the first century, chiefly addressed to Jewish communities in urban centers where Christianity was beginning to take hold, and second, the apologetic literature of the second century, pamphlets written by Christians who sought to refute charges made against the new religion. This apologetic literature is addressed to influential and educated Greeks and Romans and makes use of Greek philosophy and rhetoric in hopes of persuading those in positions of power to take a more sympathetic view of the Christians and especially to cease legal persecution of them. The apologists probably did not expect their arguments to convert the addressees to Christianity—that could happen only through the grace of God—but they could hope to improve the public image of Christianity. The charges made against Christians were often outrageous slanders, such as the allegation that they met at dawn to kill small children, drink their blood, and eat their flesh. Tertullian replies to these in his *Apologeticus* (8.3–5). About A.D. 125 a Greek named Quadratus composed a defense of Christianity and presented it to the emperor Hadrian on one of his visits to Athens, which was, of course, a center of schools of sophistry and philosophy. The single fragment of the defense which is preserved (in Eusebius, *Church History* 4.3.2) emphasizes that the miracles of Jesus were genuine and well attested by many people. More philosophical in tone are the extant works of Justin Martyr, who addressed his *Apology* to the emperor Antoninus Pius and also wrote a philosophical dialogue with the Jew Trypho, arguing for the fulfillment of prophecies of Christ. Athenagoras composed his *Apology* or *Appeal for the Christians* about A.D. 180 in Alexandria, using references to Greek philosophers and poets to support his claims that Christian worship and teaching were innocent, reasonable, and moral.

The Greek apologist who makes the greatest use of the techniques of classical rhetoric is perhaps Tatian. He composed the *Oration to the Greeks* around A.D. 167. This is largely an invective against Greek claims of intellectual and moral achievement. Tatian's oration is an odd mixture of sophistic cleverness and Christian piety. He seeks to show that Moses was older and greater than Homer and that the Greeks have learned most of what they know from barbarians, but he says it with figures of speech, a care for composition, and quotations from the Greek poets. Even the Greek language does not escape his criticism, and there are a few nasty words about Greek rhetoric: "You have contrived rhetoric for injustice and slander, for a price selling the free power of your speech, and often representing something as now just, and again as not good, and [you have contrived] the art of poetry to describe battles and the loves of the gods and the soul's corruption" (1.2c). The use of rhetoric to denounce rhetoric is not rare among Christians, but of course it could also be found in the works of Greek philosophers ever since Plato. Tatian's rhetorical apology is not unique. Another example from about the same time is the *Letter to Diognetus* by an unknown author, who attacks paganism and Jewish sacrifices in an artificial, antithetical style.[16]

Pagan criticism of Christianity before the fourth century ordinarily took the form of encouraging rumors and complaints to authorities rather than reasoned criticism, but around A.D. 178 a Greek Platonist named Celsus became alarmed at what he viewed as the threat of Christianity to Roman society and security, and he sought to check the growth of the new religion and persuade Christians to become more responsible in a work called *The True Teaching*. It does not survive, but it inspired Origen's reply, *Against Celsus*, which was published much later, in 248, and is usually regarded as the greatest of Christian apologetic treatises.

Most great oratory and rhetorical writing has been against something even when it has been for something: Pericles against the Spartans; Demosthenes against Philip; Cicero against Verres, Catiline, and Antony. There is, especially in Latin, a vigor in early Christian preaching and writing lacking to its pagan counterparts, and this derived in no small part from the intensity of Christian feeling against paganism. The first great Latin representative of Christian invective is Tertullian (ca. A.D. 160–ca. 225), a native of Carthage who practiced as an advocate and taught rhetoric in Rome, but was converted to Christianity and returned to Africa to devote himself to the Christian cause. His apologetic works include the fiery appeal *To the Heathen*, which pleads against repression of Christianity, and the *Apologeticus*, written in A.D. 197, which is addressed to the governors of Roman provinces and seeks to refute the arguments against Christians in judicial terms. Tertullian also wrote on moral and doctrinal subjects and attacked various heretical groups. When Tertullian became a Christian he did not cease to be a rhetorician. Not only does he fully exercise the stylistic techniques of rhetoric, such as figures of speech, but he follows the rules for judicial oratory as a basis of the structure of his works, he makes use of stasis theory in defining issues, and he draws on traditional topics or finds their counterparts in the Scriptures.[17]

Polemicists

Polemic against heretics is the second category of Christian rhetoric. It develops in the second century in response to the ideas of agnostics, Monatists, Quartodecimanists, Marcionists, and other sects which fractured Christian unity or seemed to depart from the apostolic faith. The first major polemicist is Irenaeus, a Greek from Smyrna who became bishop of Lyons in Gaul in the second half of the second century. His treatise *Against Heresies* not only attacks splinter groups but includes a systematic presentation of Christian doctrine.[18] A later and larger work of the same sort is the *Refutation of All Heresies*, written about A.D. 200 by Hippolytus, bishop of Rome, but almost all major Christian writers, including Augustine, engaged in attacks on heresy.

Preaching

None of the works by early Christians discussed so far were publicly delivered as a speech, with the possible exception of Tatian's *Oration to the Greeks*. When we come again to Christian addresses to other Christians, however, we are dealing at last with rhetoric in its most familiar form. There are four major forms of preaching in the early Church. One of these is the missionary sermon, discussed earlier, which has similarities to the Jewish covenant speech. A second is prophecy, a continuation of the Jewish form which is referred to occasionally (e.g., Acts 11:27). It is characterized by inspiration and might be practiced by anyone and in any kind of setting. No very good example of it survives unless we use the term to describe the so-called *Second Epistle of Clement to the Corinthians*.[19] This is not an epistle and not the work of any known author; the imagery in its seventh chapter suggests that it may be a sermon delivered at Corinth in the second quarter of the second century on a day when the city was thronged with visitors to the Corinthian games. Passages of Scripture from the Old and New Testaments are taken up and an exegesis offered. There is some allegorical interpretation. The language, even when the Bible is not being quoted, is often biblical. There is no clear outline or structure, but the various quotations and themes are strung together to accomplish an exhortation to the Christian life, more moral than theological in emphasis. The greatness of salvation imposes duties on men, in the author's view, which they dare not refuse for fear of punishment. Unity is given chiefly by the repeated call to repentance, which becomes more insistent as the end of the work approaches. It is this tone which justifies calling the work an example of the prophecy sermon.

The third and most important form of early Christian preaching is the homily. *Homilia* is a Greek word for "conversation," or informal address, which came to be used to describe an oral interpretation of a text of Scripture for a Jewish or Christian congregation. The word is eventually also used in Latin (*homilia*), though the Latin word *sermo* also meant "conversation," and not a formal sermon. The structure of a homily is basically determined by the order of material in the text, to which may be added material from other texts. By nature homily is lacking in artifice and subtlety and does not aspire to systematic exposition of theology. The speaker simply tells his congregation what he feels they should know to understand the sacred text and make it a part of their lives. In an early Christian context the speaker would ordinarily be a bishop, whose chair, like that of a teacher or sophist, gave him the right to speak, and the congregation would be made up of catechumens (people preparing for admission to the church) or of fully baptized members.

As the Church gradually began to employ more artificial rhetoric addressed to cultured audiences, homilies were not always simple words addressed to simple hearts, either in style, structure, or content. Around A.D. 165 Melito, bishop of Sardis, composed a sermon on Easter which is a homily since it is based on a text, but it is characterized by the most flamboyant literary style imaginable, reminiscent of the sophist Gorgias or the excesses of Hellenistic Asianism. This is how Melito begins:

> This account of the Hebrew exodus has been read,
> and the words of the mystery have been made clear,
> how the Lamb has been sacrificed
> and how the people have been saved.
> Learn then, beloved,
> how the paschal mystery is new and old,
> eternal and transitory,
> corruptible and incorruptible,
> mortal and eternal:
> but new according to the Word,

ancient according to the Law,
transitory in prefiguration,
　　eternal in grace,
corruptible through slaughter of the Lamb,
　　incorruptible through the life of the Lord,
mortal through his burial in the tomb,
　　immortal through his resurrection from the dead.

Melito intended this as prose, but setting the words as poetry illustrates the affinity of his style to Hebrew poetry. More particularly has he been influenced by Greek Jewish writing of the Hellenistic period, especially the Septuagint. There is also a clear influence of the sophists of second century Asia Minor who surrounded Melito in Sardis and were popular with the masses in those sophisticated cities.[20]

Less flamboyant in style, and even more sophistic in spirit, is the homily *What Rich Man is Saved?* by Clement of Alexandria, dated from around A.D. 200. Clement was a learned Greek, a student of Platonism, but a teacher in the Christian catechetical school in Alexandria. In his numerous and often elegant writings Clement began to make serious use of Greek philosophy and to take steps toward the Christian Platonism of a century later. Clement's sermon is a homily on Mark 10:17–31 and was addressed to a prosperous congregation which found biblical injunctions against wealth rather inconvenient. After a proemium comparing rich men to athletes, a prayer, and a reading of the text, Clement enters on its exegesis. Ostensibly simple passages, he says, often require more careful attention than obscure ones. In telling the rich man to sell all that he has and give to the poor, Jesus is not literally talking about wealth, but enjoining man to strip his soul of its passions. The style of this homily is antithetical and the thought is often complex. Most quotations are from the Bible, but there are references to pagan philosophy (for example, in chapter 11).

Domination of early Christian preaching by the homily reflects an important difference between classical and Christian oratory. The classical orator had a free field in choice of a proposition and the topics for proving it. He used or invented arguments from many sources, and the only check upon his arguments was their inherent probability, defined as what was acceptable to an average audience. The primary function of the Christian orator, in contrast, was to interpret and bring into practice the holy word. Homiletic preaching was basically "a projection of the eloquence of Scripture"[21] and not an achievement of the eloquence of the preacher. This pure homiletic conception was, of course, compromised by some preachers before some congregations, but it has never been entirely abandoned by the Christian clergy.

Origen

The history of the homily is closely related to the history of exegesis. Exegesis, or hermeneutics, explores and seeks knowledge of a text; homiletics seeks to discover the available means of presenting that exegesis persuasively. Thus what dialectic is to rhetoric in the Aristotelian system, hermeneutics is to homiletics in Christian rhetoric. The most important figure in the development of Christian exegesis and the greatest Christian thinker between Paul and Augustine is Origen (ca. 184–254), who passed his life in times of trouble and persecution in Egypt and Palestine. It is largely because of Origen's labors that the homily abandoned casual structure, even when keeping a simple style of expression, and took on the complexity of analysis of a text at several layers of meaning.[22]

In the fourth book of his treatise *De Principiis*, or *On First Principles*, Origen discusses the interpretation of the Scriptures. The discussion is important for the history of allegorical interpretation and was widely known both in Greek in the East and in the West in the Latin translation of Rufinus. Origen regarded the Bible as in every respect inspired. Just as man consists of body, soul, and spirit, so does the Scripture have three similar levels, arranged intentionally by God for man's salvation (4.1.11). The corporeal level is that of the letter, the literal meaning, and is addressed to those who are still children in soul and do not yet recognize God as their father. This level of meaning imparts edification. The interpretation is one of soul when the passage is interpreted to have a specific but nonliteral application to the audience addressed. This might often be regarded as the moral level. Origen has the least to say about it, but cites 1 Corinthians 9:9, where Paul interprets a verse from Deuteronomy about muzzling the mouth of the ox: "Is it for oxen that God is concerned? Does he not speak entirely for our sake?" Finally, the interpretation is spiritual when we recognize in it essential truths of Christianity. This might be called the theological level.

Since all of the Bible is inspired, all of it contains the spiritual level. In contrast, however, Origen thought that there were many things in the Scriptures which could not possibly be literally interpreted. Such otherwise incomprehensible passages include metaphors or figures to be interpreted allegorically. Origen calls these figures *typoi*, or types (4.1.9), and explains their function: "God has arranged that certain stumbling-blocks, as it were, and offences, and impossibilities should be introduced into the midst of the law and the history in order that we may not, through being drawn away in all directions by the merely attractive nature of the language, either altogether fall away from the true doctrine, as learning nothing worthy of God, or by departing from the letter come of the knowledge of nothing more divine" (4.1. 15).[23] Origen is not troubled by the possibility that many different meanings can be found in a single text interpreted allegorically, for we may be sure that the inspiration of Scripture contains far more meaning than we can ever succeed in fathoming (4.1.26). Nor is he disturbed at the possibility of misinterpretation, since by definition the spiritual meaning is a portion of the universal message of Christianity, and therefore valid. He concludes the discussion (4.1.27) by saying that we must not be concerned about words and language, for every nation has its own, but look beyond to the meaning of the words, remembering at the same time that there are things which cannot be conveyed by the words of human language and are made known directly through apprehension. The truth of the Christian message is apprehended by the soul. This perception is then strengthened and explored by study of the words of Scripture, where meaning exists at an immediate logical level, but where there are one or more parallel and higher levels of meaning which the Christian can hope to perceive. Such a view opens the floodgates of mysticism and allegory but is neither inconsistent with Christian rhetoric as it has earlier been defined nor with the use of myth in the works of Plato, which Origen knew well.

Origen's exegesis was set forth in scholia, homilies, and large scale commentaries on books of the Bible. We have 21 homilies in Greek and another 186 in Latin translations made by Jerome and by Rufinus of Aquileia (A.D. 345–411). They became an important part of the homiletic tradition, and like the homilies of other famous Fathers of the Church, were read in churches in later times in place of original sermons. Some seem addressed to a general congregation, some to catechumens, some to a small group of disciples. According to Eusebius (6.36) Origen allowed shorthand writers to take down his *dialexeis*, or disquisitions, which he delivered in public late in life at Caesarea. It is occasionally possible to compare Origen's treatment of a text in a homily with his treatment in a commentary. The content is generally similar, but the style is different. In the homily the speaker is mindful to persuade his audience not only to understand and believe the text but to live in accordance with it, whereas the commentaries are generally limited to exposition of the meaning. The three levels of meaning discussed in *De Principiis* can all be illustrated in the homilies, but the emphasis is on the moral and spiritual levels. The homilies are in a simple, generally Attic, style, filled with direct address, imperatives, and rhetorical questions to maintain audience contact. The structure is essentially that of the text, but considerable intensity of emotion is sometimes achieved. This is chiefly because of the spiritual nature of the material and the fact that since all the text is inspired, the great features of the Christian message are inherent in every verse.

Gregory Thaumaturgus

From A.D. 230 until his death in 254 Origen was head of a school of Christian studies at Caesarea in Palestine. One of his students was Gregory of Pontus, usually distinguished from the many other Gregorys by the name Gregory Thaumaturgus, "The Wonderworker." Gregory was born around A.D. 215, studied rhetoric and Latin in Pontus, and at the age of about fourteen was sent to the famous school of Roman law which had developed at Beirut. Because of family connexions he ended up in Caesarea instead, and under circumstances which are not clear entered Origen's school. He remained there eight years before returning to play an important role in the Christianization of his native province. On departing from Origen's school about A.D. 238 Gregory delivered a speech, of which a text survives. It is the first true example of Christian epideictic oratory, one of the very few surviving speeches of the third century, and the only extant example of a Greek farewell speech.

The manuscripts describe Gregory's oration as a *logos prosphonetikos*, or speech of address, but that term is more correctly used of an address to some important person on his arrival, not in taking leave of him. In the text (31 and 40) Gregory refers to the speech as a *logos charisterios*, or speech of thanks, which is not otherwise known as a form of epideictic. The sophistic form which it most approximates is the *logos syntaktikos* as described by the rhetorician Menander, although Gregory omits the required praise of the city he is leaving.[24] Despite a general movement away from rhetorical conventions as the speech unfolds, there can be no question that Gregory set out to create an epideictic speech in the manner of the sophists. The style, for which he apologizes on the grounds that for some years he has been studying Latin and law and not Greek oratory, is the affected Greek of a rather inept sophist, filled with elaborate sentences and amplification. The proemium, which is by far the most sophistic part, utilizes commonplaces from the schools, including the inexperience of the orator and the analogy of oratory and painting. There are echoes of Homer, Euripides, Demosthenes, and Plato and a quotation (141) from the Delphic oracle. Although the point of view is certainly Christian, Christianity is treated as a philosophy and there is no mention of Christ. It is very much the kind of speech that a student leaving the school of a sophist might give as a tribute to his teacher if the latter were a Christian and if the audience were made up of individuals educated in the conventions of sophistic rhetoric.

It is clear that some tension existed between rhetoric and religion in Gregory's society. He attempts to meet this problem by careful definition. He says (4–5) that it is not the case that Christian philosophers do not desire beauty and accuracy of expression for their thoughts, but rather that they give a second order of priority to words, and faced with the choice between cultivating holy and divine power of thought or practicing speech, they choose the former. Origen, says Gregory (74), had used every resource of speech to persuade him to join the school, although he regarded the teaching of rhetoricians as a small and unnecessary thing (107). In fact, Gregory found Origen's love and moral influence the most persuasive thing about him (84). He treats Origen as almost deified (10, 13) and describes the relationship between them in terms of David and Jonathan (85). This is a remarkable return to the circumstances of Socrates and Phaedrus and to the philosophical love of Plato, though there is no specific reference. Gregory criticizes pagan philosophers at length (160–169). They are irrational, choose doctrines by chance, and stick to them unreasonably without considering the evidence, as opposed to the more objective and truth-loving Christian philosophers. Origen in particular has encouraged his students to study widely in all but the atheistic writers and to draw conclusions on the basis of the evidence. This is a clever rebuttal to the claims of pagan philosophy.

It would, of course, be interesting to know what Origen thought of this performance. His reaction seems to have been negative. We have the text of a letter from Origen to Gregory advising him on his future course, probably written after the oration. It is time, Origen says, for Gregory to move beyond philosophy to Christianity and to become a partaker of Christ and of God.[25]

Eusebius

Gregory's speech is not a sermon and thus not an example of Christian preaching, but it serves as an excellent introduction to the fourth form of preaching, which is Christian epideictic, sometimes also called the panegyrical sermon. This is chiefly a development of the fourth century, when Christianity and public life came together. Unlike other

forms of preaching it has no Jewish antecedents. An early figure in it
is Eusebius (A.D. 260–340), who had been trained in the same Christian
school in Caesarea which Origen had once headed and is a leading
authority for our knowledge of Origen. After escaping the persecutions of the opening years of the fourth century, Eusebius became
bishop of Caesarea and later a friend and adviser of Constantine, the
first Christian emperor. His most famous work is his *Church History* in
ten books, which includes the panegyrical sermon he delivered at Tyre,
probably in 316 or 317.[26] It ostensibly honors Paulinus, bishop of Tyre,
for his reconstruction of the church there, which had been destroyed
in the persecutions. Eusebius says that all of the rulers of the church
delivered panegyrics to the assembly in the rededicated church. "One
of moderate talent," that is himself, then came forward, having prepared an arrangement of a speech. This probably means that he had
premeditated his topics and their order, but perhaps not his expression,
for which he relied on extempore inspiration and experience. Possibly
a shorthand transcription of the speech was made at the time; in any
event it was written up and polished and published in the *Church
History* (10.4).

Although Eusebius calls his speech a panegyric, it has few of the
elements of sophistic encomia. We are told nothing at all about
Paulinus except that he directed the rebuilding of the church. The
church itself, however, is described in some detail (10.4.37–46), in which
we may see an example of rhetorical *ecphrasis*. The visible and material church is made a counterpart of a greater and invisible spiritual
Church; God has chosen the emperor to cleanse and reconstruct the
spiritual world. The speech has a powerful religious movement, and
the issues involved were life-and-death matters to the speaker, who had
witnessed the persecutions and the victory of his faith. On the particular occasion at hand he symbolically recapitulates the whole history of Christianity and sees it justified. Another source of vigor is the
invective included in the speech. We have already noted the rhetorical
advantages to the Christians of being not only for, but against something. In Eusebius' speech the devil's frustrations at Christ's power are
said to have led him to attack the building of the church. This leads
Eusebius to a comparison (*synkrisis* in classical rhetoric) of Christ and
Satan (10.4.14); but Christ is the cornerstone, and the devil is foiled
again.

A second panegyrical sermon by Eusebius is the speech he delivered
in A.D. 336 in honor of Constantine's thirtieth jubilee.[27] The first ten
chapters seem to be addressed to the court and celebrate the emperor's
rule and his theological, political, and moral virtues. There is very
little use of Scripture here, but neither does the speech observe the

specific topics of classical encomium. The second half (chapters 11–17) is addressed to Constantine and is a sermon on the glory of God, intended to lead the uninitiated to the truth and to show the religious basis of Constantine's deeds. This part of the speech draws more heavily on scriptural sources and makes a spirited attack on pagan cults.

The great masters of the panegyrical sermon are the three Cappadocian fathers, Gregory of Nazianzus (ca. A.D. 329–389), his friend Basil the Great (ca. 330–379), and Basil's younger brother, Gregory of Nyssa (ca. 331–395). Gregory of Nazianzus and Basil studied together in the schools of sophistry and philosophy at Athens in the 350s. One of their teachers was the pagan Himerius, whose highly artificial declamations and orations survive; another was Prohaeresius, who was a Christian, although his school seems to have differed very little from those of his pagan counterparts.[28] All three of the Cappadocians were intimately familiar with classical Greek writers, especially with Plato. All three are masters of Greek prose, Gregory of Nazianzus being perhaps the most ornate and Basil perhaps the most restrained. Virtually every figure of speech and rhetorical device of composition can be illustrated from their sermons, treatises, and numerous letters; they were also influenced by rhetorical theories of argumentation and structure, and probably by theories of memory and delivery as well, though direct evidence there is lacking. Yet all three are repeatedly critical of classical rhetoric as something of little importance for the Christian, and none of them made, or even seriously attempted, a synthesis of classical and Christian rhetorical theory. They were considerably more successful in uniting Greek philosophy with Christian theology.

Gregory of Nazianzus

Forty-four orations by Gregory of Nazianzus are extant.[29] A number of these deal with specific occasions in his life or events involving members of his family. Others are doctrinal, such as the sermon on baptism (40) or the five "theological" sermons preached in Constantinople in 380. Two (4 and 5) are invectives against the emperor Julian, who attempted to reestablish paganism, and are interesting for Gregory's outrage at Julian's prohibition against Christians teaching classical literature and rhetoric. Eight speeches are encomia showing strong influence of the structure and topics of such works as delivered by sophists of the period or as described in the handbook on epideictic by the rhetorician Menander. Funeral orations for Gregory's father, his sister Gorgonia, and his brother Caesarius, as well as his encomium for Basil, are especially close to sophistic models. The latter is probably the masterpiece of sophistic Christian oratory, an extraordinary tour de force, replete with subtle variations on familiar topics, figures of speech, rhetorical comparisons, reminiscences of Plato, Greek history, and mythology, and an emotional peroration. A passage may be quoted to show some of the equivocation, or at least complexity, of Gregory's feelings about the place of eloquence and pagan learning in Basil's life:

When he was sufficiently instructed at home, as he was to neglect no form of excellence, nor to be surpassed in diligence by the bee which collects what is most useful from every flower, he hastened to the city of Caesarea to attend its schools. I mean this illustrious city of ours, since she was also the guide and mistress of my studies, and not less the metropolis of letters than of the cities which she rules and which have submitted to her power. To rob her of her supremacy in letters would be to despoil her of her fairest and most singular distinction. Other cities take pride in other embellishments, either old or new, depending, I think, on their annals or their monuments. This city's characteristic mark, like the identification marks on arms or on plays, is letters.

What followed, let those tell the story who instructed him and profited by his instruction. Let them tell of his standing in the eyes of his masters and his companions, as he equaled the former and surpassed the latter in every form of learning. Let them tell what glory he gained in a short time in the sight of all, both of the common people and the leaders of the city, exhibiting a learning beyond his years and constancy of character beyond his learning. He was an orator among orators even before the sophist's chair, a philosopher among philosophers even on questions of philosophical theory. And, what constitutes the highest tribute in the eyes of Christians, he was a priest even before the priesthood. In such wise did all defer to him in everything. With him, eloquence was only an accessory, and he culled from it only what would be helpful for our philosophy, since its power is necessary for the exposition of thought. For a mind incapable of expression is like the movement of a paralytic. But philosophy was his pursuit, as he strove to break from the world, to unite with God, to gain the things above by means of the things below, and to acquire, through goods which are unstable and pass away, those that are stable and abide.[30] (section 13)

Gregory goes on to describe their years together in Athens, "the home of eloquence, Athens, a city to me, if to anyone, truly golden, patroness of all that is excellent."

Basil himself is not so outspoken about the glories of eloquence.[31] He delivered several panegyrical sermons, but even in one of these (*On Gordius the Martyr* 142d–143a) he belittles the rules of encomium which he sometimes employs. As a preacher he is best known for his homilies, especially the *Hexahemeron*, which is a series of homilies on the six days of creation. A work of considerable interest is a short address, *To the Young On How They Should Benefit from Greek Litera-ture*.[32] This is in the general tradition of Plato's exclusion of the poets from his ideal state, but it takes a moderate point of view: pagan literature can be usefully read by young Christians, but careful choice should be exercised to avoid mythological stories contrary to truth and morality. Portions of Homer, Hesiod, Theognis, and Prodicus' *Choice of Heracles* are approved. Nothing is said about the study of oratory or prose style.

John Chrysostom

The finest Christian orator in Greek is John Chrysostom ("John the Golden-Tongued," A.D. 347–407), a student of the sophist Libanius and later patriarch of Constantinople. A number of his panegyrics survive, of which seven on Saint Paul are the most famous, but he was most at home in the homily. Even so, the style and mannerism of rhetoric are a part of his nature, and he cannot resist flamboyant comparisons, jingles, and parallelisms.[33] His most striking homilies are probably the twenty-one entitled *On the Statues*, delivered in 377, which illustrate his compassion as well as his responsibility and sincerity as a preacher at a time of political crisis. He admits that style can be helpful in relieving the tedium of an audience (e.g., *On the Psalms* 41.1–55 Migne) and in securing variety: "When we have the care of the sick, we must not set before them a meal prepared at haphazard, but a variety of dishes, so that the patient may choose what suits his taste. Thus we should proceed in the spiritual repasts. Since we are weak, the sermon must be varied and embellished; it must contain comparison, proofs, paraphrases, and the like, so that we may select what will profit our soul" (*On the Obscurity of the Prophecies* 56.165 Migne).[34]

The rhetorical practice of Gregory of Nazianzus and John Chrysostom, and to a lesser extent of Basil and Gregory of Nyssa, go considerably beyond anything they would seem to tolerate in theory. The reason for this is partly their education; they were so thoroughly imbued with figures of speech and devices of composition that these had become second nature to them. Partly their audiences are responsible. Chrysostom tried in vain to prevent congregations from applauding in church (see *Homilies* 30.4 = 60.225 Migne). We need not charge such thoughtful Christians as Gregory or Chrysostom with pandering to the mob, but they were concerned with moving the hearts of their audience and inspiring their lives, and the devices of sophistic rhetoric had become the cues to which their audiences responded and by which their purposes could be best accomplished. This trend is in many ways a victory for classical rhetoric. Ambitious young Christians now did not hesitate to study in the schools of rhetoric, and as the fourth century advanced, the Christian communities were less and less a simple company of simple folk content with the message of the gospel.

A case in point, and the most thoroughly classical of fourth-century Christians, is Synesius of Cyrene (ca. 370–ca. 413), who became a Christian bishop on the stipulation that he be allowed to have a wife and to retain his Neoplatonic philosophical beliefs. Among his works is a striking epideictic speech, *On Royalty*, delivered to the emperor Arcadius in 400, urging him to be a ruler in the image of God; such royal discourses were a tradition among Greek sophists. There is also preserved his encomium of baldness. His treatise called *Dion* is named for the sophist Dio Chrysostom and starts with him, but becomes an apology for Synesius' Greek way of life and his interest in philosophy and rhetoric. In a search for truth Synesius is superior to the sophists, but he retains a sense of culture and independence.[35]

The Latin Fathers

By the end of the fourth century the Greek church had thus reached an accord with classical culture which made it possible for Christian thinkers to draw on the rich tradition of Greek philosophical thought and to utilize classical rhetoric, but no theoretical restatement of a Christian Greek rhetoric was made. Consideration of this subject will be resumed in the next chapter. In the Latin-speaking West the situation was somewhat different. There was, long before Christianity, some Roman hostility to Greek culture, and in the case of philosophy that suspicion never entirely faded away. For example, Gn. Julius Agricola, governor of Britain in the late first century of the Christian era and father-in-law of Tacitus, always remained grateful to his mother "for preventing him from going more deeply into the study of philosophy than was suitable for a Roman senator" (Tacitus *Agricola* 4.4). The teaching of rhetoric had met with initial hostility at Rome in the second and early first centuries B.C., but by the Augustan period rhetoric was entirely acclimatized throughout the Roman Empire. Unlike philosophy it seemed to be useful, concrete, and manly. This distrust of philosophy and acceptance of rhetoric is generally reflected in the Christian Latin writers. In addition, it is a remarkable fact that of the eight greatest Latin Fathers of the Church, five (Tertullian, Cyprian, Arnobius, Lactantius, and Augustine) were professional rhetoricians before they became Christians, while the other three (Ambrose, Hilary, and Jerome) were thoroughly trained in the rhetorical schools.

Tertullian (ca. A.D. 160–ca. 225) had a deep distrust of Greek philosophy; it was he who phrased the famous question "What has Athens to do with Jerusalem? What concord is there between the Academy and the Church?" (*De Praescriptione Haereticorum* 7), but the next sentence, and the context as a whole, shows that what really concerned him was the way philosophy had become the basis of heresy, particularly of agnosticism. Tertullian speaks with respect of Demosthenes and Cicero (*Apologeticus* 11, 15–16), and he never directly attacks rhetoric as such. Christians should not teach it; they can and must study it (*De Idolotria* 10).[36] We have already seen how deeply colored by rhetoric is Tertullian's own writing.

Cyprian (*Ad Donatum* 2), writing in the mid–third century, and Arnobius (*Adversus Nationes* 1.58–59), writing late in the third century, both distinguish secular from Christian rhetoric, claiming that in the latter the subject and not the style matters, although Arnobius regards syllogisms, enthymemes, and the like as useful to the Christian controversialist. Ambrose (ca. A.D. 337–397) anticipates Augustine in finding eloquence in the Scriptures, especially in what he calls the "historical" style of Luke (*On Luke*, prologue 1). He was himself an orator of great power, both in the homily form, where he follows the exegetical method of Origen and shows the influence of Basil, and in the panegyrical sermon, such as his funeral orations for Valentinian II and Theodosius. These are the earliest Christian panegyrics in Latin.

Of all the Fathers, Jerome (ca. A.D. 348–420) is the one most torn between a feeling for style or love of eloquence and a belief that the art of rhetoric is a worldly product, at best of no true importance for a Christian and possibly inimical to the Christian life. His greatest achievement, of course, was his Latin translation of the Bible, and he says that translations of Scripture should avoid deliberate literary qualities in order to speak more directly to the human race than to schools of rhetoric or philosophers (*Epistulae* 48). Characteristic of Jerome is the story he tells in the long epistle to Eustochium (*Epistulae* 22).[37] "What has Horace to do with the Psalms, Virgil with the Gospels, Cicero with the Apostle?" he asks (22.29); we ought not to drink both the cup of Christ and that of the devils. Jerome had tried to cut himself off from pagan learning, but he could not forego his library. He would fast, but he would then read Cicero. When he read the prophets, their style revolted him. He became distraught and ill; preparations were made for his funeral. Suddenly, in a dying condition, he had a vision (22.30) in which he seemed to be caught up to heaven and the judgment seat. He threw himself on the ground and averted his eyes before the judge, who asked him to state his "condition." Jerome replied that he was a Christian. "You lie," came the answer. "You are a

Ciceronian, not a Christian. 'For where your treasure is there will your heart be also' [Matthew 6:21]." The bystanders prayed for forgiveness and Jerome himself promised to mend his ways: "Lord, if I ever have secular books, if I ever read them, I have denied thee." Like Saint Peter, it is doubtful that he kept his promise.

Lactantius

Two Christian Latin writers attempted statements of rhetoric in terms that might resolve the tensions felt by Christians like Jerome. The earlier of these is Lactantius (ca. A.D. 250–320), whose major work was written forty years before Jerome's birth. Although Lactantius' literary abilities were appreciated in antiquity, the synthesis he attempted was not widely understood until the Renaissance, when he emerged as a founder of Christian humanism, "the Christian Cicero."

Lactantius was a North African teacher of rhetoric who acquired fame and was appointed by the emperor Diocletian to teach Latin rhetoric in the Greek-speaking city of Nicomedia in Bithynia, which functioned as the eastern capital before the foundation of Constantinople. There he was converted to Christianity and lost his chair under the oppressive Galerius, but later in life Constantine named him the tutor of his son Crispus. Lactantius is the master of a beautiful Ciceronian prose style and was very familiar with Latin literature and classical philosophy. As a Christian he saw in the latter numerous superstitions and errors which needed refutation, but he also saw a reflection of the same divine truth which was more authoritatively revealed in the Bible. It troubled Lactantius that educated pagans would not give serious attention to Christianity because of the illiterate style in which the Scriptures were written and because Christian apologists defended their faith with prophecies and revelations which seemed absurd to many intellectuals. He thus took upon himself the mission of setting forth the teachings of Christianity in a style which would win the respect of the most discriminating reader and with arguments based on evidence in Greek and Latin writers, not on that in the Bible. The most important result of this effort was the treatise in seven books entitled *Divinae Institutiones*, completed around A.D. 313. The time was a crucial one. Constantine had not yet been baptized, but had decreed the toleration of Christianity, and there were many people beginning to give serious attention to the new faith for the first time.

The introductory chapters to the separate books of the *Divinae Institutiones* contain discussion of Lactantius' objectives and methods, and from these and a few other passages (e.g., 3.13) a philosophical

Christian rhetoric emerges. Although Lactantius had probably read Plato, his sources are the writings of Cicero, the Neoplatonists of his own time, and other secondary Latin sources. Lactantius' basic position is not unlike Aristotle's: if the truth is defeated, we have only ourselves to blame; if the attention of the audience is once secured, the truth can be demonstrated, and good will prevail. But to Lactantius of course the truth is divine truth, the Word. He does not reject inspiration, revelation, and miraculous conversion, and he claims (e.g., 6.1.1) the tutelage of the Holy Spirit, but he associates divine intervention in the rhetorical act with the mind's recognition of truth when effectively presented. The Christian orator thus has much he can do. The passage where this view is best summed up is the introductory chapter to the third book.[38]

Though a learned, reasonable, and eloquent man, Lactantius was not a powerful thinker. His work probably had the greatest appeal to an audience already favorably disposed to a religion being adopted by the court, but unwilling to put aside everything that education and tradition had taught it to admire. As we have seen already, Lactantius' synthesis did not satisfy a Christian like Jerome, who was still troubled by the conflicting claims of Christian and classical learning. A more successful and more widely accepted answer was to be that of Augustine.

Augustine

Augustine was born 13 November A.D. 354 at Thagaste, about two hundred miles southwest of Carthage on the edge of Numidia.[39] In the *Confessions*, completed about 400, he has left a remarkable portrait of his psychological, religious, and intellectual development from birth to middle age. Although Monica, his mother, was a devout Christian and a strong influence upon him, Augustine was thirty years old before he fully embraced Christianity. He has much to say about her and other influences upon him and about his education. After elementary studies at Thagaste he was sent to the larger town of Madaura to begin rhetoric. His father, however, wanted more for him and decided to keep him home for a year while money was accumulated to pay for studies in Carthage. These he began in 370 and continued for three years, planning a career as a pleader in the lawcourts (*Confessions* 3.4. 6), but at this point there occurred the first step in what proved eventually to be his conversion to Christianity: "In the usual order of study I came to a book of a certain Cicero, whose tongue almost all admire, but not his heart to the same extent. But there is a book of his containing an exhortation to philosophy and called *Hortensius*. That book changed my perception and changed my prayers, O Lord, to you . . . (*Confessions* 3.4.7).

As he goes on to explain, what pleased him in Cicero was the advice to love and search for wisdom, though what gave him pause was the absence of the name of Christ (3.4.8). Under the influence of his mother, it was Christianity to which he tended to look for "philosophy"; thus he turned, apparently for the first time, to the serious reading of the Scriptures. And he was totally put off. The whole object of his education up to this point had been the cultivation of literary taste. What he found in the Bible seemed quite "unworthy to be compared to the dignity of Cicero" (3.5.9). Dissatisfied with Christianity, he turned to Manichaeism, which combined some phenomena of Christianity with a dualism of good and evil, derived from Zoroastrianism. He says (4.1.1) that from his nineteenth to his twenty-eighth year he was led astray and led others astray. What he means is that he continued his association with the Manichaeans and that he supported himself as a teacher of rhetoric, first in Thagaste (4.4.1–7), after 376 in Carthage (4.7.12). He tells only a little about his school (4.2.2–3), but claims he was motivated by a desire to make money and that though he taught how to save the guilty, he did not teach how to condemn the innocent. Cicero had followed similar principles (*De Officiis* 2.51).

In 383 Augustine decided to go to Rome and teach rhetoric there. Friends urged him to do so, and he claims he was persuaded not because of the greater fees and glory of Rome but because student discipline was so much better there than in Carthage (5.8.14). About this time he became increasingly dissatisfied with Manichaeism and interested in Academic philosophy, by which he means the sceptical tradition known to us best from Cicero's philosophical writings. He spent less than a year in Rome (5.12.22–13.23). Although his school seems to have been successful, and discipline was indeed better than at Carthage, he was not really very satisfied with the situation. When the great pagan orator Symmachus was asked to nominate candidates for the chair of rhetoric at Milan, Augustine applied. Symmachus listened to him declaim and gave him the nomination. Thus Augustine arrived in the city which was the administrative capital of the western empire and far more thoroughly Christianized than either Carthage or Rome at the time. In Milan he taught rhetoric for two academic years (384–386), but he also heard the sermons and enjoyed the friendship of Ambrose, bishop of Milan, and from him learned the manner of explaining the Old Testament figuratively which made it possible for him to embrace the Scriptures with full faith (5.14.24).

Augustine's intellectual and spiritual quest culminated in the summer of 386 in the scene in the garden which he describes in the eighth book of the *Confessions* and which involved the act of will that made him in his own eyes a Christian. One consequence of that conversion was the resignation of his chair of rhetoric, but he resigned quietly, waiting until the fall vacation and alleging poor health as a reason (9. 2.2–4 and 9.5.13). With a group of relatives and friends he withdrew into the country to engage in meditation, study, and conversation, which resulted in a series of philosophical dialogues including *Contra Academicos, De Beata Vita,* and *De Ordine.* In the spring of 387 he returned to Milan and was baptized by Ambrose on Easter Sunday. In the following years he went to Ostia, to Rome, to Carthage, and home to Thagaste. In 391 he was ordained a priest at Hippo and in 395 was consecrated as bishop there, a position which he retained until his death in 430.

Augustine's output of sermons, commentaries, treatises, and letters was enormous and is in large part preserved. Those that are most directly related to rhetoric are reviewed in the following paragraphs.

In Milan, in the spring of 384, Augustine undertook a series of books on the liberal arts. He apparently completed the one on grammar, though it does not survive. In the case of other arts including rhetoric he wrote some notes, but only those on dialectic survive. There is a small Latin treatise on rhetoric printed in Halm's *Rhetores Latini Minores* that is attributed by one manuscript to Augustine, but it has no relation to his thought and is not his work.[40]

The early dialogue *De Ordine* is a discussion of divine providence in terms which remind Augustine of his earlier composition of a panegyric (1.9.27). It culminates in a description of the introduction appropriate for those who wish to understand the order of the universe and to live in accordance with God's law. Knowledge comes by authority or by reason, he says (2.9.26), and reason embraces a somewhat purified exposition of the liberal arts, including grammar, dialectic, rhetoric, arithmetic, music, geometry, and astrology. Dialectic deals with how to teach and how to learn, in which reason reveals its nature, desires, and powers. But ordinary men follow their feelings and habits, and for them to be taught the truth it is necessary not only to make use of logical reasoning, but to arouse their emotions. Here is the realm of rhetoric, which is described as a seated allegorical figure with a lap full of charms to scatter to the crowd in order to influence it for its own good (2.13.38). This view may be taken to reflect Augustine's preliminary reaction against his rhetorical career in the winter between his conversion and his baptism. It was to be followed by more profound considerations of the role of rhetoric in Christian knowledge.

The dialogue *De Magistro,* or *On the Teacher,* was finished around

389. From the outset the tone is more religious and Christian than in *De Ordine*, but references to Cicero and Virgil still came naturally to Augustine. The basic argument is to deny the possibility of human communication through rational signs (words) without a knowledge of reality (God). Persuasion cannot be accomplished by rhetorical means unless the truth is first known or simultaneously revealed by divine grace.

The *Confessions*, written in 397–398, is Augustine's spiritual autobiography. As such it traces his change of commitment from a student and then a teacher of rhetoric to a Christian and a preacher. The work itself has a remarkable internal rhetoric or style by which Augustine seeks to dramatize the history of his life.

Augustine wrote many controversial or polemical works intended to refute heresies. His antagonists were at first Manichaeans, later Donatists, and toward the end of his life Pelagians. About A.D. 400 he composed a treatise attacking a Donatist bishop named Petilian. In reply the grammarian Cresconius took up Petilian's cause and attacked Augustine. The latter then composed the four books *Against Cresconius* around 406. Cresconius had not only attacked Augustine's arguments but had criticized his eloquence and his dialectic as unchristian, and it is to this point that Augustine devotes three-fourths of the first book. His position is that neither eloquence ‛nor skill at disputation is unchristian, which he seeks to prove by numerous scriptural examples, especially those of Jesus and Paul. Eloquence, he says (1.2), is the faculty of speaking, or explaining appropriately what we feel. It is to be used when we have perceived the truth. The utility of eloquence is a function of the utility of what is being said, and the speaker is comparable to the soldier. We cannot fail to take up arms for the state, because arms are sometimes used against the state—an Aristotelian view. The true disputator seeks first to be sure he is not himself being deceived (1.19). Then he tries to use his audience's knowledge of some of the truth. Although Augustine does not explain here how knowledge of the truth is to be discovered, it is clear from his method that consistency with Scripture is an important test. Not only may a Christian use dialectic and rhetoric, but a Christian bishop must do so. He cannot allow error to continue, and his responsibility is not limited to his own church, but extends to the world around him. As often, Augustine advances his views vigorously and pushes Cresconius hard, but without personal abuse; he is chiefly concerned to show the inconsistency of his opponent's view and to confront him with dilemmas. For example, if Cresconius is not himself an able dialectician, why does he engage in dialectic? If he is, why does he object to dialectic (1.16)? Some of the contents foreshadow the fourth book of *De Doctrina Chris-*

tiana, and in one passage (1.20) there is even allusion to the existence of different kinds of style.

De Doctrina Christiana is Augustine's major contribution to the history and theory of rhetoric. From the references to it in the *Retractationes* (2.4.1) and elsewhere it seems likely that the first two-thirds of the work (through 3.25.35) was written in the early months of 397, shortly after Augustine became bishop of Hippo. The rest of it was completed in 426 and 427. It is thus a fully mature work, and the discussion of rhetoric in it represents Augustine's views at the end of a lifetime of Christian study and preaching. What Augustine says about Christian rhetoric here is generally in accord with his own practice as seen, for example, in his sermons on the gospel of John.[41]

In a short prologue Augustine states that he is writing precepts for treating the Scriptures which will be useful to teachers and proceeds to a *praemunitio,* or anticipation of the objections which some may make. One category of objections is that everything which should be known about the obscurities of Scripture will be revealed by divine assistance to the preacher or teacher. Augustine's answer to this claim is that it is a form of pride and leads to the extreme position in which one would not go to church nor read the Scriptures at all (prologue 5): "The condition of man would be lowered if God had not wished to have men supply his word to men" (6).

Book 1 then begins with the statement that there are two things necessary in the treatment of the Scriptures: discovery of what is to be understood there, and teaching of what has been learned there. The first subject is discussed in Books 1 through 3, the second in Book 4. They correspond respectively to dialectic and rhetoric in Aristotle's system. In Augustine's view, all doctrine concerns either "things" or "signs" (1.2). A natural object like a stone is a "thing," but it may be also a "sign" of something else, as when in Genesis 28:11 Jacob places a stone on his head. This distinction becomes the basis of separate levels of meaning in the sacred text. Book 1 is devoted to things. Some are to be enjoyed, some to be used, some to be enjoyed and used (1.3). Things to be enjoyed are the Father, Son, and Holy Spirit (1.5), discussed in sections 5 through 21. Things to be used include four kinds of things to be loved: those above us, ourselves, those like us, and those below us. These are discussed in sections 22 through 38. The direction of Augustine's thought emerges clearly at the end of Book 1 (sections 39–40), where he says that the sum and end of the Scriptures is the love of God. The whole temporal dispensation was made that we might know and implement this love, and the basis of all interpretation of Scripture is love: "Whoever, therefore, thinks that he understands the divine Scriptures or any part of them so that it does not build the double love of God and of our neighbor does not understand it at all. Whoever finds a lesson there useful to the building of love, even though he has not said what the author may be shown to have intended in that place, has not been deceived, nor is he lying in any way" (1.40).[42]

Books 2 and 3 are devoted to signs. Signs are natural or conventional (2.2); known, unknown, or ambiguous (2.15); literal or figurative (2.15). God has provided unknown and ambiguous signs "to conquer pride by work and to combat disdain in our minds, to which those things which are easily discovered seem frequently to become worthless" (2.7). That which is sought with difficulty is discovered with more pleasure (2.8). Knowledge is the third of the seven steps to wisdom (2.9–11), and Augustine inquires as to what knowledge is necessary for the Christian teacher, much as Plato, Aristotle, Cicero, and Quintilian had considered what knowledge was necessary for their conceptions of the orator. Augustine's orator needs first a thorough knowledge of the Scriptures. He can thus use those things which are clear to explain those which are not. All teaching involving faith is said openly in the Scriptures, as is that which is necessary for the Christian life. If we know this we have a basis for explaining what is obscure (2.14). In subsequent chapters Augustine considers knowledge of languages, numbers, and music.

More delicate is the matter of knowledge of literature and philosophy. Should the Christian study pagan writings? Yes. "We should not think that we ought not to learn literature because Mercury is said to be its inventor" (2.28). Doctrines current among the pagans are said to involve either institutions (2.36–40) or things men perceive (2.41–58), the latter through the body or through reason. Augustine dislikes sophistry and criticizes eristic (2.48), but thinks that valid inference was instituted by God and then observed by men (2.50). Definition, division, and partition are part of the order of things (2.50). The Christian has every right to take true ideas from the Platonists and transform them as "Egyptian gold" (2.60). It is in this part of the work (2.59) that Augustine suggests that it would be useful to have an index of the various signs used in the Scriptures, a suggestion which was taken up by later students and led to the collections of *distinctiones* current in the Middle Ages.[43]

Book 3 deals with ambiguous signs. When literal interpretation causes ambiguity, the rule of faith should be consulted as found "in the more open places of the Scriptures and in the authority of the Church" (3.2). There is considerable danger in too literal interpretations (3.9): "The letter killeth, but the spirit quickeneth," as Paul said (2 Corinthians 3.6). If an admonition in Scripture is to something useful or good, it is not figurative; if to something criminal or vicious it must be figurative (3.24). Figurative signs do not have the same meaning in all passages (3.35); the context must be judged. Augustine is not concerned that something may be read into a passage which the author did not intend (3.38). What is important is the intent of God, who foresaw whatever is found in the passage and more. The rule of faith and the context are the best guides to the interpretation of Scripture. In the last resort, reason can also be used, but it is dangerous (3.39). Book 3 ends (42–56) with a critique of the *Rules* of Tyconius. These are categories of figurative language which resemble topics, some more than others. For example, the third rule, "of promises and the law," deals with matters of the spirit and the letter, and the fourth rule with matters of species and genus.

Having completed his discussion of the discovery of the meaning of Scripture, Augustine turns in Book 4 to Christian preaching and the teaching of what has been discovered. This fourth book falls into six parts: a brief introduction (sections 1–5), a description of Christian eloquence (6–26), an examination of the duties of the orator as stated by Cicero and as applied to Scripture and Christian preaching (27–33), a similar examination of the three kinds of style (33–58), a discussion of ethos (59–63), and a conclusion (64).

Augustine does not set forth all the rules of rhetoric. They are useful, he says (4.2), but should be learned elsewhere. Yet he summarizes many of them in one characteristic sentence:

Who would dare to say that truth should stand in the person of its defenders unarmed against lying, so that they who wish to urge falsehoods may know how to make their listeners benevolent or attentive or docile in their presentation [i.e., in the exordium], while the defenders of truth are ignorant of that art? Should they speak briefly, clearly, and plausibly [in the narration] while the defenders of truth speak so that they tire their listeners, make themselves difficult to understand and what they have to say dubious? Should they oppose the truth with fallacious arguments and assert falsehoods [in the proof] while the defenders of truth have no ability either to defend the truth or to oppose the false? Should they, urging the minds of their listeners into error, ardently exhort them, moving them by speech so that they terrify, sadden, and exhilarate them [in the peroration], while the defenders of truth are sluggish, cold, and somnolent? Who is so foolish as to think this to be wisdom? While the faculty of eloquence, which is of great value in urging either evil or justice, is in itself indifferent, why should it not be obtained for the uses of the good in the service of truth if the evil usurp it for the winning of perverse and vain causes in defense of iniquity and error? (4.3)

Rhetoric may be studied by the young and by those not engaged in something more important, but the Christian speaker must beware of forgetting what should be said while considering the artistry of the discourse (4.4). In fact, study of rules is not necessary at all, for eloquence can be learned from imitation of eloquent models (4.5). Imitation had of course been a part of classical rhetoric, side by side with theory, since the times of the early sophists and had led to the canonization of stylistic models such as the Attic orators. Augustine would replace that canon with a new canon of the Scriptures.

The description of Christian eloquence (4.6–26) begins with the statement that the expositor and teacher of the Scriptures should teach the good and extirpate the evil. Christian rhetoric, like the three kinds of classical oratory, thus has a positive and a negative form. Augustine anticipates in this passage his later discussion of the duties of the orator, saying that the Christian teacher should "conciliate those who are opposed, arouse those who are remiss, and teach those ignorant of his subject." In the subsequent discussion he finds many examples of classical rhetorical techniques in the writings of Paul and Amos, including climax, the various parts of the periodic sentence, and several tropes. But, he concludes of Amos: "A good listener warms to it not so much by diligently *analyzing* it as by pronouncing it energetically. For these words were not devised by human industry, but were poured forth from the divine mind both wisely and eloquently, not in such a way that wisdom was directed toward eloquence, but in such a way that eloquence did not abandon wisdom" (4.21). As to the virtues of style as seen in the Scriptures or practiced by a Christian, clarity is the only real consideration (4.23). Augustine has, however, earlier remarked on the appropriateness of the style in the Scriptures (4.9). Ornamentation and correctness are not of great importance (4.24).

From sections 27 to 33 Augustine considers the three duties of the orator—to teach, to delight, and to move—which Cicero developed out of the Aristotelian modes of proof. The first of these relates to the subject matter, the second and third to the manner. Augustine thinks that it is necessary to delight a listener in order to retain him as a listener; it is necessary to move him in order to impel him to do what is right. Moving is equated with persuasion (4.27). Moreover, "When that which is taught must be put into practice and is taught for that reason, the truth of what is said is acknowledged in vain and the eloquence of the discourse pleases in vain unless that which is learned is implemented in action" (4.29). Persuasion thus lies with the orator and is not left entirely to God. Ultimately, though, the orator needs both expertise and divine guidance: "He who would both know and teach should learn everything which should be taught and acquire a skill in speaking appropriate to an ecclesiastic, but at the time of the speech itself he should think that which the Lord says more suitable to good thought" (4.32). And then Augustine quotes the familiar passage from

Matthew (10:19–20): "For it is not you that speak, but the spirit of your father that speaketh in you."

In sections 33 through 58 Augustine ties the three duties of the orator to the three kinds of style, teaching to the plain style, delighting to the middle style, and moving to the grand style, as Cicero had done in the *Orator*. Examples of each are given, both from the Scriptures and from the Fathers (Cyprian and Ambrose). The three styles should be mingled, "but the whole speech is said to be in that style which is used most in it so that it predominates" (4.51). He concludes, "It is the universal office of eloquence in any of these styles, to speak in a manner leading to persuasion; and the end of eloquence is to persuade of that which you are speaking. In any of these three styles an eloquent man speaks in a manner suitable to persuasion, but if he does not persuade he has not attained the end of eloquence" (4.55).

Addressing the fifth topic in Book 4 (sections 59–63), Augustine points out that the life of the speaker has greater weight than any grandness of eloquence. He thus revives ethos as a major rhetorical factor, though not ethos as projected in a speech, which is what Aristotle had in mind. That quality has been transmuted into the second of the duties of the orator, to delight. To Augustine ethos is Christian works, the life of the teacher, and the extent to which it accords with his teaching. Under certain circumstances, however, a bad man may become a good orator. Quintilian would have been surprised. Augustine recognizes that there may be someone who can speak well but cannot think of anything to say. Such a preacher can take eloquent sermons composed by another speaker and deliver them to his congregation. "Whence it may happen that an evil and wicked man may compose a sermon in which truth is preached which is spoken by another not wicked but good. And when this is done, the wicked man hands down to another what is not his own, and the good man accepts what is his from another" (4.62). As it happens, Augustine's own sermons were often read to Christian congregations during later centuries.

Several observations may be made about *De Doctrina Christiana* as a whole. First, it is not concerned with the rhetoric of conversion. Augustine, like earlier Christians, regarded conversion as an act of the Spirit in which eloquence has no true role. The work is addressed to Christian teachers, chiefly the clergy, and explains how to discover Christian knowledge and how to expound it to a converted, but ignorant or lethargic, audience. The function of Christian eloquence in Augustine's system is to convert belief into works, to impel the faithful to the Christian life. This had become an important consideration and remained one permanently now that Christianity was the established religion of the state and that the Church numbered many nominal members who lacked the intensity and dedication characteristic of earlier Christians.

Second, Christian rhetoric as viewed by Augustine is popular rhetoric. Christianity is addressed to all sorts and conditions of men, and the Christian preacher should be able to move the illiterate and unlearned or the sophisticated and erudite. The importance of preaching and the challenge of the Christian audience was especially evident to Augustine because of his rhetorical background and helped maintain his interest in rhetoric throughout his life.[44]

Third, Augustine deals with two related matters: in Books 1, 2, and 3 with discovery of the meaning of the Scriptures, in Book 4 with exposition of that meaning. It has already been suggested that these correspond to dialectic and rhetoric in Aristotle. In religious studies they are regularly given the names of hermeneutics and homiletics, respectively, and are the arts of exegesis and of preaching.

Fourth, the subject matter of Christian rhetoric is limited to the exposition of the Scriptures and their meaning for the Christian life, especially for the development of the love of God and of fellow men. Classical rhetoric had already become highly respectful of models of imitation such as Demosthenes in Greek or Cicero in Latin, but Christian rhetoric gives exclusive honor to the Old and New Testaments as the totality of wisdom and eloquence. Proof in Christian rhetoric is primarily a matter of discovery of the authoritative utterance in the text and its clear explication.

Fifth, as a consequence, logical reasoning and argumentation play a very subordinate role in Christian rhetoric, despite its search for truth, and style plays a correspondingly greater part. The fourth book of *De Doctrina Christiana* canonized the view that rhetoric is largely a matter of style. Christians of course engaged in argumentation among themselves, but Augustine's view of rhetoric left open to dialectic the whole area of religious disputation, which was much cultivated in later centuries.

Sixth, even Christian exegesis is more strongly influenced by the factor of style than by reasoning, since much of exegesis involves the interpretation of figurative signs. Peter Brown points out how characteristic this is of a writer of late antiquity: "No one else would have made such a cult of veiling his meaning. Such a man lived among fellow-connoisseurs, who had been steeped too long in too few books. He no longer needed to be explicit: only hidden meanings, rare and difficult words and elaborate circumlocutions, could save his readers from boredom, from fastidium, from that loss of interest in the obvious that afflicts the overcultured man. He would believe . . . that the sheer difficulty of a work of literature made it more valuable."[45]

Seventh, Augustine does not distinguish Christian rhetoric from classical or other rhetorics. It is characteristic of him to secularize human institutions: even the Roman Empire itself, in *The City of God*, is stripped of its pagan associations, and Augustine's work in grammar, dialectics, music, rhetoric, and other subjects equally shows his effort to make them religiously neutral, capable of utilization by a Christian for Christian purposes.[46]

Eighth, *De Doctrina Christiana* has often been viewed as a repudiation of the sophistic tradition.[47] This is only partially true. In common with other Christians and with philosophically minded pagans, Augustine rejected empty bombast and the trivial forms of declamation practiced in rhetorical schools in the later empire. On the other hand, certain features of sophistic are retained, including emphasis on the function of the orator as well as on imitation and style. Christian rhetoric has a new subject, the divine truth and the Christian life, a subject with much greater vitality than the message of Hellenism set forth by the sophists at their best.

Ninth, Augustine's rhetoric belongs largely in what we have called the technical tradition, with some threads of the sophistic strand. Insofar as philosophical rhetoric is involved, it is represented by Christianity, not by the influence of Plato and Aristotle. Indeed, Augustine knew little Greek. His primary source was Cicero, and the divergence of classical rhetoric into separate Greek and Latin traditions is already evident in his work. This was to continue until the fifteenth century.

Finally, *De Doctrina Christiana* exemplifies clearly two sound critical principles which had been more appreciated by the rhetoricians than by grammarians and dialecticians: interpretation must be based on an understanding of the context in which a word or passage occurs and also on the overall meaning or structure of the work in which it occurs. Christianity, with its consciousness of its message, would have everything consistent with one theme.

De Doctrina Christiana is an authoritative statement of Christian rhetoric and had significant influence in Carolingian and later medieval times. Among other writers, Hrabanus Maurus, Thomas Aquinas, Alan of Lille, Humbert of Romans, Robert of Basevorn, Hugh of Saint Victor, and Peter Lombard made significant use of it, and Augustine's defense of scriptural obscurity became a part of poetic theory from Petrarch to the sixteenth century. The great virtue of *De Doctrina Christiana* is that it made it possible for Christians to appreciate and teach eloquence without associating it with paganism. The weakness of Augustine's treatise is that it encouraged the identification of rhetoric with style and gave still greater authority to the categorization of styles and figures which was already an obsession of classical rhetoric. Just as

technical and sophistic rhetoric had absorbed and diluted philosophical rhetoric in the centuries after Aristotle, Augustine made it possible
for classical rhetoric to absorb Latin Christian writing and preaching
into its discipline and prescriptions. *De Doctrina Christiana* is thus to
rhetorical theory in the West what the panegyrical orations of the
Cappadocian Fathers are to rhetorical practice in the East, a synthesis
of rhetoric and Christianity.

Chapter 8
Greek Rhetoric in
the Middle Ages

Classical rhetoric survived through the Middle Ages both in the East in the Greek-speaking Byzantine Empire[1] and in western Europe, where Latin remained the international language of politics, religion, and scholarship. The two traditions are somewhat different: in the East it is the sophistic strand which is the strongest; in the West the technical strand. In both cultures rhetoric maintained a place in education—in the West precariously at times, but with increased strength after the Carolingian age. In both cultures rhetorical education affected speaking and writing, in the East primarily through imitation of classical models, through exercises in composition like those in the rhetorical schools of late antiquity, and through collections of exemplars by famous men. In the West new handbooks were developed applying rhetoric to letter-writing, to poetry, and to preaching, a phenomenon less evident in the East.

Some basic reasons for the difference between East and West are clear. First of all, sophistry was much more strongly established in the Greek portion of the Roman Empire than in the West. The Second Sophistic had only feeble western imitations; Greek rhetorical schools concentrated less on judicial exercises than did their Roman counterparts; the major technical writings in Greek focus on declamation, as seen in the case of Hermogenes, or epideictic, as in the case of Menander. The serious application of epideictic to Christianity began in the East in the works of the Cappadocian Fathers, especially Gregory of Nazianzus, and in John Chrysostom, though there is imitation of this in the West, for example, in orations by Ambrose. Western interest in rhetoric was closely connected with Roman interest in the procedures and institutions of civil administration, a tradition that never entirely faded away.

However, the continuity of civilization in the East was much greater than in the West. The functions performed by Greek sophists of later antiquity continued to be performed throughout Byzantine history once they had been adapted to Christianity. Although there were serious threats to the survival of the eastern empire (for example, in the eighth and thirteenth centuries), survive it did. The western empire did not survive as such, despite the creation of the Holy Roman Empire. In the East, Greek was continuously spoken, although the popular dialect significantly deviated from the official language. In the West, the new rulers brought new languages with them, even though Latin continued to be important throughout the region.

Perhaps because of this continuity in the East and because of relatively less introduction of new traditions, Byzantine civilization was extremely conservative and extremely in awe of classical models. To a medieval Greek scholar, Homer, Plato, and Demosthenes held a position in his own culture which exceeded anything possible for even Virgil or Cicero in the West. As great authorities as the latter were, they were foreigners in language and in experience. In the case of rhetoric, Byzantine conservatism is seen in adherence to classical textbooks like Hermogenes and Menander and in its preservation of sophistic forms.

Byzantium had been made the eastern capital of the Roman Empire by Constantine in A.D. 324 and was refounded as Constantinople in 330.[2] After the death of Theodosius in 395 the empire was permanently split into an eastern and a western half, and as the western parts slipped into the control of Germanic rulers in the course of the next century, the eastern empire emerged as the sole remnant of Roman power. Subsequent Byzantine history is usually divided into three periods. The first has no sharp break with antiquity. It includes the vigorous age of Justinian (527–565) and ends with the siege of Constantinople by the Arabs in 717. The second period gradually emerges into a renaissance of learning in the ninth century, associated especially with the name of Photius, patriarch of Constantinople. This development continues in the tenth century during the reign of the scholar-emperor Constantine VII Porphyrogenitus and reaches a climax in the eleventh century, the time of the greatest Byzantine writer, Michael Psellus. Photius and Psellus were both students of classical rhetoric who sought to reestablish standards of language and eloquence. The second period shows some decline in the twelfth century, which nevertheless produced the classicizing historian Anna Comnena and Eustathius, author of an enormous commentary on Homer. It may be said to end with the fall of Constantinople to the Latin crusaders in 1204. The final period of Byzantine history begins in 1204 and includes the Byzantine recovery of Constantinople in 1261 and the succeeding cultural renaissance under the dynasty of the Palaeologi, which facilitated the transmission of Greek learning to the western Renaissance. Constantinople fell to the Turks in 1453, in whose hands it still remains under the corrupted name Istanbul.

Grammar Schools

As heir to the educational system, the language, the literature, and above all, the Christianity of Greece, Byzantium sought to maintain and transmit them to future generations as unchanged as possible. The truth had been revealed; methods of study had been canonized; but standards were difficult to maintain. Grammar schools taught the rudiments of the Greek language, reading of the Greek classics, and graded exercises in Greek composition. Secondary education, where it existed, continued to be based on the schools of rhetoric.[3] A few students might then continue to study dialectic, thus completing a program analogous to the Trivium in the West. A counterpart of the Quadrivium is also discernible at times.[4] The only significant addition to the subject matter of late classical education was study of the Bible and of the Fathers of the Church.

Students in ancient grammar schools studied the language, read the poets, and composed a series of exercises in composition. The basic grammatical textbook was that by Dionysius Thrax, written about 100 B.C. It remained authoritative for the next fifteen hundred years and received many commentaries. Homer and other poets continued to be staples of Byzantine education and also received commentaries, such as those of Eustathius. Exercises in composition, called *progymnasmata*, are known from treatises by Theon (first century), Hermogenes (second century), and Nicolaus (fourth century), as well as from examples by writers like Libanius (fourth century); but the most influential textbook of composition, partly because it provided an example of each exercise, proved to be that of Aphthonius of Antioch, probably written about the beginning of the fifth century.[5] It too received many commentaries.[6] Among them are one by John of Sardis dating from the ninth century and one by John Geometres dating from the tenth. The first of these contains no reference to Christianity, but the second draws on examples from Gregory of Nazianzus. The "homilies" of John Doxapatres, composed in the eleventh century, are also discussions of Aphthonius' exercises. Aphthonius had described fourteen different exercises, and the Byzantine commentators characteristically divided these up among deliberative, judicial, and epideictic rhetoric. Myth, *chria* (ethical thought), and maxim belong in the first group; confirmation, refutation, introduction of a law, and commonplace in the second; encomium, invective, comparison, and *ethopoeia* (dramatic characterization) in the third. In addition there are three other exercises which fall under more than one form: narration, thesis, and *ecphrasis*, or description.

Many examples of Byzantine progymnasmata survive.[7] Those by Nicephorus Basilices, for example, written in the mid–twelfth century, combine exercises about Zeus or Ajax with those about Samson and the Virgin and an ethopoeia on what the Greek god of the underworld, Hades, said when Lazarus was raised from the dead.[8] These forms of exercise directly influence composition in almost all literary genres, being incorporated into homilies or histories or saints' lives as a writer felt moved to do so. The phenomenon of *letteraturizzazione* thus persisted. A good example of *synkrisis*, or comparison, is the essay by Theodorus Metochites (ca. 1260–1332), *On Demosthenes and Aristides*.[9] The exercise called ethopoeia influenced the epistle, which had become a favorite literary form by late antiquity and continued to flourish in Byzantium.[10] Another favorite Byzantine form was the *ecphrasis*, which was given a Christian treatment as a description of a church or a work of Christian art. Probably the most famous example, and certainly one of the most ambitious, is the work *On Buildings* by Procopius of Caesarea (d. 565), with its celebrated description of the church of Sancta Sophia.[11] Procopius intended the work as an encomium of Justinian, whom he did not admire but thought it prudent to praise.

Hermogenes' handbook of progymnasmata was translated into Latin by the grammarian Priscian about A.D. 500 and became known in western Europe, where the exercises were called *praeexercitamina*. Not until the Renaissance, however, did they become as popular as in the East. In the fifteenth century Rudolph Agricola translated Aphthonius into Latin, and this work became a major school text for the next two hundred years.[12]

Rhetorical Schools

What Dionysius Thrax and Aphthonius were to the grammer schools, Hermogenes of Tarsus was to the schools of rhetoric throughout the

Byzantine period. Hermogenes' popularity in Byzantium resulted from several qualities in his work. First, his treatises constituted a comprehensive account of those aspects of rhetoric which were of interest and use to Byzantines: the statement of a question, its orderly presentation, and some aspects of style. Stasis theory had application to judicial procedure; the "ideas" of style were useful in the composition of occasional speeches, such as funeral orations, in homilies and other forms of sermons, in religious polemic, and in the secondary rhetoric of literary composition, especially in letters, in lives of the saints,[13] and in historiography. Second, Hermogenes is strongly classicizing. His great rhetorical model is Demosthenes, who more than any other writer seemed to combine all "ideas" of style. This classicism constituted an initial appeal to early Byzantine scholars, but the acceptance of Hermogenes as a standard text, especially in the middle Byzantine period, certainly helped to perpetuate classicism, including the admiration for Demosthenes at a time when political and social conditions were the antithesis of what Demosthenes had known. Third, Hermogenes is systematic, specific, and generally clear. He defines his terms, gives examples of what he means, and above all is given to categorization and subdivision of concepts in a highly academic manner. His work is prescriptive and seems authoritative. These numerous categories and this rather pedantic approach appealed to the Byzantine mind, which proceeded along similar channels in theology, philosophy, law, political structure, court ceremonies, and other aspects of life. Hermogenes thus combined complex details of considerable subtlety into a unified structure which paralleled Byzantine feelings for human life as a microcosm of eternal life. And in addition, his twenty forms of style could be mingled, combined, and varied to produce a kaleidoscope of aesthetic effects congenial to the Byzantine taste for color, symbol, and mystical expression, as seen, for example, in their mosaics. A good instance are the homilies of Photius, which seem to reflect a knowledge of the Hermogenic system even though Photius never mentions Hermogenes by name.[14]

Hermogenes' treatises were the subject of repeated commentaries throughout the Byzantine times.[15] For the work on stasis, for example, commentaries include one from the fifth century by Syrianus, a well-known Neoplatonist, and from about the same time commentaries by two lesser-known rhetoricians, Sopater and Marcellinus. From the thirteenth century comes the commentary of Maximus Planudes, a well-known scholar and poet who also commented on Hermogenes' works on invention, on ideas, and on method, drawing chiefly on earlier discussions and demonstrating little originality. For the work

CLASSICAL RHETORIC

on ideas of style there is a commentary by Syrianus again, and an anonymous commentary probably dating from the tenth century which draws on older material but adds references to Christian writers, chiefly Gregory of Nazianzus, as well as a more original and more Christianizing commentary by John Siceliotes from the eleventh century, and again the commentary by Planudes.[16]

Most commentators to Hermogenes begin with a *prolegomenon*, or introduction to the study of rhetoric, similar to the introductions to philosophy composed by Neoplatonists. These discuss the definition of rhetoric, its use among the gods and heroes and its beginning among men. They are important, if rather uncertain, sources for information about the beginnings of rhetoric in Greece.[17] There are also various Byzantine works on figures of speech which show Hermogenes' influence, and synopses of Hermogenes' rhetoric (for example, those by Michael Psellus and by Georgius Pletho).

Declamations do not seem to have been practiced in middle or later Byzantine times to the same extent that progymnasmata were, perhaps because of the lack of interest in memory and delivery which had characterized declamation in the sophistic schools. Some Byzantine declamations do survive, however, such as those by Georgius Pachymeris, a writer of the thirteenth century who also composed progymnasmata. In his fifth declamation, faithful to the tradition of the sophists, he imagines himself as Demosthenes advising the Athenians what to do about Philip's seizure of Elatea.

It is because of the work of Byzantine scribes that the texts of Plato, Aristotle, Demetrius, Dionysius, "Longinus," and other classical Greek writers on rhetoric were preserved. We cannot, therefore, say that the *Gorgias*, the *Phaedrus*, and the *Rhetoric* were unknown. Plato was indeed much read, especially in the first Byzantine period, when Christian and pagan Neoplatonists dominated the schools of philosophy. Neoplatonist critical and aesthetical theory is an important influence on Byzantine art and writing.[18] Hermias of Alexandria wrote a commentary on the *Phaedrus* in the mid–fifth century, and Olympiodorus one on the *Gorgias* in the late sixth century.[19] In later Byzantine periods Aristotle was more read than Plato, largely because of the place of his logical works in the curriculum, but there were enthusiastic Platonists, of whom Michael Psellus is a good example.[20] The *Rhetoric* was thought of as a part of the *Organon*, or collection of Aristotle's logical treatises, and read in that connexion. At least two Byzantine commentaries on it are preserved, probably dating from the middle Byzantine period. Nevertheless, there is little sign of direct influence of the ideas of Plato and Aristotle about rhetoric.

Advanced Education

In the fourth century of the Christian era teachers of rhetoric could be found in every city, and students traveled many miles for advanced instruction and to hear the great sophists of Athens, Antioch, and Constantinople. There was some study of rhetoric in Alexandria, but it was primarily known for its school of philosophy. Athens seems to have declined as a center of rhetorical studies during the fifth century. Her philosophical schools were closed by Justinian in 529, but the importance of that event has probably been exaggerated by modern historians who like to couple it with the establishment of the monastery at Monte Cassino in Italy in the same year to designate the end of the classical and the beginning of medieval institutions of learning. More significant at the time was Justinian's termination of the municipal payment of salaries of teachers throughout the empire (see Procopius, *Secret History* 26.5); most cities probably could not afford the cost. In the fifth and sixth centuries Gaza in Palestine was a leading center of advanced rhetorical studies under teachers like Zosimus of Gaza, Proclus of Gaza, and Choricius.[21] Panegyrics, ecphrases, prose monodies, and commentaries on the Attic orators were composed here. These rhetors of Gaza were Christians and contributed to the integration of Christian and pagan models of style and of examples drawn from Christian and pagan classics.

In Constantinople a school of advanced studies, called by modern scholars "the University," had been organized in 425 by an edict of Theodosius II (*Codex Theodosius* 14.9.2).[22] The faculty consisted of ten teachers of Greek grammar, five of Greek rhetoric, ten of Latin grammar, three of Latin rhetoric, two of law, and one of philosophy, but there was no chair of theology. Indeed, the curriculum as a whole was remarkably secular. How long this institution survived is not known, but it may well have collapsed in the sixth century. The view to be found in older books on Byzantium, that the university survived with a series of refoundings and reforms until 1453, is without substance. There was no continuous tradition of higher education in Constantinople and no policy of government support.[23] There were private teachers of rhetoric and philosophy and some other subjects, and occasionally one of these achieved national eminence, as did Caesar Bardas in the ninth century and Michael Psellus in the eleventh. Psellus and Xiphilinus, an eminent legal scholar, were the heads of competing schools, and Constantine IX Monomarchus intervened in the dispute between them and briefly provided some subsidy for a school of law and a school of rhetoric and philosophy under Psellus' direction, but the system soon collapsed.[24] Our best source of information is Psellus' *Funeral Eulogy* of Xiphilinus.

Michael Psellus (1018–ca. 1078) was an official at court, an orator, professor in a school of advanced studies, a Platonist whose philosophical views were condemned by the Church, and the author of many works, of which the best known is the *Chronographia*, a rather personal history of his own times. He also wrote on scientific and philosophical subjects and composed a versified summary of Hermogenes.[25] The importance of sophistic rhetoric in Psellus' thinking emerges clearly in a speech he composed on the rhetorical character of Gregory of Nazianzus.[26] This employs the theory of ideas of Hermogenes and in form is modeled on Dionysius of Halicarnassus' essays on the ancient orators. Gregory is found to be the exemplar of all "ideas"; each quality of style is taken up in turn. Psellus' own major speeches are three funeral orations on three distinguished contemporaries, each of whom served as patriach of Constantinople: Gerularius, Leichudes, and the legal scholar Xiphilinus. In the *Chronographia* (6.41) he speaks of learning as divided into two parts, rhetoric and philosophy. He describes as his personal goal to mold his tongue by rhetorical discourse to eloquence and by philosophy to purify his mind (6.107). Statements in Psellus' letters are consistent with this goal. Writing to a correspondent about Hermogenes, he says, "Perhaps you know philosophy and rhetoric, but you do not know how to put them together; there is a philosophizing rhetoric as well as a rhetoricizing philosophy"; and elsewhere, "Just as Plato in the *Timaeus* combines theology with physical science, so I write philosophy by means of rhetoric and fit myself to both through the use of both."[27] This represents the Greek tradition in rhetoric at its best, but it is a nobler vision than that of most in Byzantium.

Perhaps more continuous than "the University" was the patriarchal school of Constantinople, which is first heard of in the seventh century and best known from the twelfth, when its three teachers of Scripture were joined by a fourth, the master of the rhetors.[28] The faculty of the patriarchal school at that time had important public oratorical functions: the delivery of panegyrics, funeral orations, and other official speeches. Their sermons and speeches were preserved and published. Among the masters of the rhetors were Nicephorus Basilices and Eustathius, best known for his commentary on Homer, which makes considerable use of Hermogenic concepts of style.[29] Constantinople dominated Byzantine culture of the middle and late periods, but there were some other centers of education, including Antioch, Nicea, and Thessalonica, and there were important monasteries in Asia Minor and

Greece and on the islands which preserved classical texts throughout the later centuries. The monasteries of Mount Athos are best known.

Attic Greek

The official language of the Byzantine Empire was the literary Greek of late antiquity, artificially preserved by educated persons for over a thousand years.[30] Although generally referred to as "Attic," in contrast to the language of daily life or the speech of the uneducated, this dialect had its start as the common language of Hellenistic times and is the Greek of the New Testament. It was refined by the Atticist movement of the early centuries of the Christian era, continually reinforced by the attention paid to true Attic prose models like Demosthenes and Plato, as well as to Atticizing prose like that of Aristides and Libanius, and expanded somewhat by the inclusion of words and phrases from Homer and the tragic poets. Byzantine writers like Psellus repeatedly tried to reassert the standards of classical Greek; Anna Comnena "dislikes to record even the names of barbarians, for fear that they may defile the pages of her history."[31] Not only the diction and grammar of classical Greek, but classical literary genres, commonplaces, and allusions were expected in serious writing. One result is that it is often impossible to date a Byzantine literary work unless one has external sources of reference to it or its writer.

The anachronistic use of Atticizing Greek for all serious cultural communication, including the writing of personal letters, sharpened the division between the educated and the uneducated. It was made possible by the continuation of traditional grammatical and rhetorical education encouraged by the Church, which of course drew its authority from the Greek Scriptures and the writings of the Fathers and was anxious to preserve knowledge of their language. This extraordinary value put on classical language and style, exceeding the role played by Latin in the West, was also in part a search for cultural stability and permanence in the face of the destruction of the classical world and the dangers from the alien societies of Slavs to the north, Arabs to the south, Turks to the east, and a varied horde of semibarbaric "Latins" to the west.

Functions of Rhetoric in Byzantium

One reason why rhetorical studies did not significantly change throughout the Byzantine period is that there was little significant change in the need for rhetoric, its functions, or its forms, as perceived by the leaders of society. It must be recognized that in a subtle way rhetoric contributed to the power of the elite establishment. To a degree evident in few societies, knowledge of the right language and right forms was the prerequisite for a career in church and state, and the attitudes inculcated with that knowledge were extremely conservative. It is ironic that Greek rhetoric, which was "invented" in the fifth century B.C. as an instrument of social and political change, became under the Roman and Byzantine empires a powerful instrument for preservation of the status quo.[32]

In such a situation, and especially considering the Church's interest in the language but not the content of the classics, it is easy to see that style would become the most important aspect of rhetoric. Study of stasis theory in Byzantium kept alive the logical side of the subject to some extent, and the Byzantines studied Aristotelian logic, but without developing that subject into the scholastic discipline so congenial to western scholars. Byzantine rhetoricians made no important contributions to rhetorical theory. Their willingness to acknowledge deliberate obscurity as a virtue of style, in contrast to Aristotle's insistence on clarity, is one of their unusual themes, which is parallel to the use of rhetoric to retard rather than facilitate social and political change, but even this concept develops out of Hermogenes and the aesthetics of late antiquity rather than being entirely new and has some counterpart in Augustine and other western writers.[33]

The Byzantine Empire had a senate and a system of lawcourts, descended in both cases from institutions of the Roman Empire, but neither deliberative nor judicial oratory are major forms of discourse in the East. The function of primary rhetoric in Byzantium is to present decisions to the public and to strengthen loyalty to church and state through the use of the forms of epideictic. The church year presented a series of opportunities for panegyrical sermons, especially in Constantinople, and many of these are preserved, as are many funeral orations of famous men. Both types are consistently modeled on the great works of Gregory of Nazianzus and John Chrysostom, which were studied as classics. Literally thousands of homilies also survive, again often indebted to Chrysostom, some highly rhetorical, some in the simpler form of the ancient homily, and collections of homilies were also made such as the Patriarchal Homiliary of John Agapetos. The emperor Leo the Wise (886–912) seems to have been especially influential in the development of these collections.[34] Outside the specific functions of the Church, though not outside her influence, are numerous epideictic orations given on public occasions. The most important group are probably the encomia of emperors and members of the imperial family by officially approved orators.[35] Examples of these survive from all periods, including the encomium of Anastasius I by Procopius of Gaza, encomia by Psellus of the empress Theodora, of Constantine IX Monomachus, and of Michael VII Ducas, and encomia by Nicetas Choniates of Isaac II and Alexis III. There are also encomia of patriarchs, such as that by Eustathius on the patriarch Michael III (1170–1178). Other epideictic oratory is cast in the form of funeral orations for the great and monodies, or prose laments, such as Psellus' for Andronicus Ducas, son of Constantine X. The monody was a classical form for which models could be found among the works of Aristides (for Smyrna after an earthquake) and Libanius (on the death of Julian the Apostate). In addition there are *prosphonetics*, or speeches of official welcome, *propemptics*, or speeches of farewell, *genethliacs*, or birthday speeches, and many other sophistic forms, all described in the handbook of Menander, to which Byzantine orators generally conform.[36] In addition to real speeches there were also composed written addresses to influential persons in the tradition of Isocrates' *To Nicocles*, and rhetorical autobiographies, of which the first oration of Libanius was a model.[37]

The static quality of Byzantine rhetoric does not mean that the period is not important in the history of rhetoric. Just the opposite. The grammatical and rhetorical schools of Byzantium and the activities of Byzantine orators preserved classical rhetoric as a living tradition for a thousand years. It is because of them that Greek writings and ideas and great models of Greek literature survived and could be carried to Italy for study and imitation, which became the basis for cultural change when increased wealth and motivation made higher levels of culture in the Renaissance possible, and when Byzantine civilization itself was terminated by the Turkish conquest. Byzantium is a time capsule in which the teachers of rhetoric sealed the best of the past as they saw it, including works of philosophical rhetoric by Plato and Aristotle. The Church connived at this preservation, because of her own vested interest in the status quo, but she did not institute it, as she did in the West, and among the monks a strong distaste for wordly knowledge always lingered. The Greek Church cannot be said to have loved the classics. She loved the language of the New Testament and the writings of the Fathers, but study of rhetoric had became one of the roads to knowledge of the Scriptures and patristic literature.

The last important figure in Byzantine rhetoric is George Trebizond.[38] Born in Crete in 1395 and educated in Greek rhetoric, he arrived in Italy in 1416 and brought with him a knowledge of the

Hermogenic tradition, unknown to the West. This he set forth in the first complete rhetorical treatise of the Renaissance, *Rhetoricorum Libri V*, or *Rhetoric in Five Books*. It is in large part a conflation of Hermogenes and Cicero. Published in manuscript in Venice in 1434, it became widely known in printed form before the end of the century. From this point the histories of eastern and western rhetoric are again woven into the same fabric.

Chapter 9
Latin Rhetoric in
the Middle Ages

The context in which classical rhetoric developed, was taught, and was practiced was the civic life of Greek and Roman cities. Although the Roman Empire brought restrictions on the cities' freedom, it preserved political institutions and traditions at the local level and encouraged education in rhetoric to meet their needs. As long as the Roman Empire survived in the West, technical rhetoric remained the basis of secondary education and thus of much of cultural life. The strand of sophistic rhetoric survived in the concept of the orator as an ideal and in declamations and ceremonial speeches by panegyrists of the emperors and the imperial families. We have seen that in the fourth century sophistry was Christianized by Latin preachers like Ambrose. The strand of philosophical rhetoric became largely reduced to study of the topics as organized within stasis theory and to awareness of dialectic as a study relating to rhetorical invention. Secondary rhetoric remained strong: indeed, literary composition in later antiquity is virtually synonymous with the exploitation of figures of speech and other ornaments of style and with the application of rules of rhetorical structure and the theory of imitation.[1] Ausonius, Claudian, and Symmachus are good examples from the fourth century; Rutilius Namatianus and Sidonius Apollinaris from the fifth.

Although classical rhetoric triumphantly survived the victory of Christianity over paganism, it almost succumbed to the collapse of its native environment as the cities of the empire were destroyed or abandoned in the face of barbarian attack beginning in the early fifth century. With the end of orderly civic life there disappeared not only state support of education but most of the reasons for rhetorical education in its traditional form. The last person known to have held the chair of rhetoric at Rome was Melior Felix in 534.[2] Few senates remained in which an orator could speak; legal procedures were disrupted; and barbarian kings did not perceive the need of being extolled in Latin. Poverty, fear, and poor communications became endemic; libraries were destroyed; books disintegrated and were not recopied; knowledge of Greek faded throughout the West.[3]

But classical rhetoric did not die. A few private teachers of grammar and rhetoric could probably be found at most times in cities of Italy and Gaul. In the mid–sixth century Cassiodorus introduced the liberal arts into monastic schools. The literature of the seventh century shows some knowledge of classical rhetoric and occasions for persuasive speech. By the eighth century the first glimmerings of a new civic life emerged in Italy: Venice in the relative safety of her lagoon began to elect her doges and manage her own affairs. In the ninth and tenth centuries Pisa, Pavia, Bologna, and other cities became important commercial centers, and by the eleventh century the commune movement had created assemblies, councils, and courts of law with a jury system in many Italian municipalities. It was in this setting, not totally different from the city-states of antiquity, that rhetoric reemerged as a practical subject of study in Italian schools and communities in the period between the eleventh and fourteenth centuries.

North of the Alps, in the ninth and tenth centuries the Carolingian age brought to western Europe the first of several "renaissances," which found a place for rhetoric in the schools on the basis of the need to understand the eloquence of the Scriptures and which also generated a need for rhetoric in civil and ecclesiastical courts. Although progress was by no means steady, the restoration of education in the Carolingian age eventually led to the French and English cathedral schools of the eleventh and twelfth centuries, in which rhetoric was an established discipline within a framework of liberal arts. It found application in courts, in religious disputation, in letter-writing, in preaching, and in poetry. This is the period of many commentaries on *De Inventione* and the *Rhetorica ad Herennium* and a revived interest in Quintilian. With the development of universities in the twelfth century, especially at Oxford and at Paris, dialectic came to dominate higher education, and rhetoric was chiefly studied as an adjunct to it. Boethius' *De Topicis Differentiis* replaced Cicero as the favored rhetorical authority, and new preaching manuals were composed emphasizing thematic development of argument. The thirteenth century is something of a low point for classical rhetoric in many parts of Europe despite the recovery of Aristotle's *Rhetoric* in Latin translation at that time. The fourteenth century, however, saw renewed study of Cicero, not only in the Italian cities, but in France and England, shown again in new commentaries on *De Inventione* and the *Rhetorica ad Herennium*.

The history of rhetoric in the western Middle Ages thus has three main phases: the early medieval period of the fifth to the eighth centuries, in which the study of classical rhetoric survived precariously in monastic schools and the chief authorities were the encyclopedists Martianus Capella, Cassiodorus, and Isidore; a period from the ninth to the twelfth centuries, in which Ciceronian authority was strong, primary rhetoric found some scope, especially in Italy, and the liberal arts flourished, especially in France; and the late medieval period, when practical needs brought the study of rhetoric back from the subordinate role assigned to it by scholastic philosophers. We may now consider these developments in greater detail, noting where possible the continuity of primary rhetoric. Most histories of medieval rhetoric have been written from the point of view of literature and style, for *letteraturizzazione* is certainly a strong trend in centuries of chaos or autocracy; but recent studies are revealing a practical function for persuasive, oral arts throughout the Middle Ages.[4]

Martianus Capella

The seven liberal arts can be traced back to the *enkyklios paideia*, or comprehensive education of Greek thinkers like Plato or Isocrates, and were manifested in the broad cultural interests of a few Romans like Cicero. They were, however, more an ideal in the minds of philosophers or a program of reading and study for leisured (*liberi*) adults than a series of graded levels of study undertaken either in Greek or Roman schools. Grammar and rhetoric were the two stages of ancient education, both supported from public funds in towns of any size, but dialectic, the other "art" of the *trivium* (as these three introductory studies later came to be called), was a part of philosophy, which was an advanced discipline undertaken by only a few and confined to a few centers. Cicero's contemporary Varro wrote an "encyclopedia" of nine liberal arts, including not only the three which became the trivium and the four which became the *quadrivium* (geometry, arithmetic, astronomy, and music), but also medicine and architecture. Varro's work did not survive the fall of Rome, and its section on rhetoric seems never to have been influential. More than anything else it was the encyclopedia of Martianus Capella which made rhetoric one of the liberal arts of the Middle Ages. Martianus was certainly familiar with the form of Varro's work, and he also utilizes a combination of prose and verse (called Menippean satire) which Varro had favored, but the actual content of his books is drawn from other standard sources. His primary source on rhetoric is Cicero's treatise *De Inventione*, to which is added an account of figures of speech based on that in the work of Aquila Romanus and some other material.

Modern scholars have usually reacted with distaste to Martianus Capella's work. But the very features which make it least attractive today insured its medieval popularity. It was composed in Carthage between 410 and 439 and is thus almost exactly contemporary with Augustine's *De Doctrina Christiana*. The title is *De Nuptiis Philologiae et Mercurii*, or *The Marriage of Philology and Mercury*,[5] and the first and second books are a fantastic, cumbersome allegory in which Satire tells Martianus how Mercury desired a wife and at Apollo's suggestion decided to marry Philology. All sorts of divine and allegorical figures are introduced, of whom the most important are seven handmaids who are personifications of the seven liberal arts. In subsequent books each handmaid presents her discipline: rhetoric is allotted the fifth book. The technical parts are written in a simple, if pedantic style, but the allegorical portions are presented in the highly artificial and obscure Latin which passed for eloquence in late antiquity. Medieval readers appear to have loved the allegory, excused the paganism because of it, and delighted in trying to penetrate the obscurity. The technical portion of the seven arts also appealed to them because of its very superficiality: it was concise, authoritative, and could be learned by rote. In any event the popularity is undoubted: at least 243 complete or partial manuscripts exist in European libraries. A significant percentage of these come from the ninth and tenth centuries, the Carolingian age, when both the trivium and quadrivium were of special interest in the cathedral schools of France.

Martianus' influence helped make rhetoric a part of this system, but a limited part. The goal of classical education was primarily to train effective citizens. Martianus' objective in *The Marriage of Philology and Mercury* is apparently the personal one of demonstrating his own eloquence and learning, but if a product of the studies he describes can be envisioned at all, the product is an amateur philosopher. Dialectic, which is here a part of the trivium equally with grammar and rhetoric, tends to replace rhetoric in philosophical dispute, while the quadrivium moves entirely beyond the need or interests of civic life. Rhetoric thus seems and indeed was a less important part of education than it had been in earlier times. To judge from references to it, Martianus' book on rhetoric was one of the least popular parts of his work. Fortunately, he made clear where a reader should turn for a more authoritative discussion, namely to Cicero, whom he mentions with the highest praise. By Martianus as by Varro rhetoric was put in third position, after grammar and dialectic, but it was later moved by Cassiodorus back to second position, probably because of the custom of the ancient schools. One effect of the change, however, was further to reduce rhetoric to a link between grammar and dialectic and to rob it of its position as the capstone of an ordinary education.

Cassiodorus

Martianus was a pagan, and his authority would not have ensured the survival of technical rhetoric in the Middle Ages if his work had not been taken up by Cassiodorus a hundred years later. Even the great authority of Augustine would not have been enough to ensure a place for rhetoric in the training of the clergy if Cassiodorus had not created a system which made minimal intellectual demands and which was enforced by the discipline of monastic life.

Born in southern Italy around 480, Cassiodorus was well educated himself and held high office in Ravenna under the Ostrogothic kings, but after the victories of the Greek Belisarius he withdrew to a monastery of his own founding at Vivarium, near Squillace in the toe of Italy. This establishment was remarkable for the emphasis it placed on the preservation of texts, both Christian and secular, and on the education of its monks. In addition to collecting, editing, copying, and commenting on texts, Cassiodorus composed, around 551, a work called *Institutiones Divinarum et Humanarum Lectionum,* or *Introduction to Divine and Human Readings.*[6] It became a basic reference work and educational handbook for centuries and was to be found in almost every medieval library. Cassiodorus addresses his monks about the importance of secular studies as follows:

We can understand much in sacred literature as well as in the most learned interpreters through figures of speech, much through definitions, much through the art of grammar, much through the art of rhetoric, much through dialectic, much through the science of arithmetic, much through music, much through the science of geometry, much through astronomy; it is thus not unprofitable in the book which follows to touch briefly upon the elements of instruction laid down by secular teachers, that is, upon the arts and sciences, together with their divisions, in order that those who have acquired knowledge of this sort may have a brief review and those who perhaps have been unable to read widely may learn something from the compendious discussion. Beyond any doubt, knowledge of these matters, as it seemed to our Fathers, is useful and not to be avoided, since one finds this knowledge diffused everywhere in sacred literature, as it were in the origin of universal and perfect wisdom. When these matters have been restored to sacred literature and taught in connection with it, our capacity for understanding will be helped in every way. (*Institutiones* 2.27.1)

This becomes a common view of technical rhetoric in the early Middle Ages. Clearly many of Cassiodorus' monks had little or no education in such things as grammar or rhetoric, while he himself regarded some knowledge of those subjects as essential for the understanding of the Scriptures. The knowledge he expects, however, is of a very limited sort. In the second book, after a short chapter on grammar based on the fourth-century grammarian Donatus, whose work the monks are expected to study (2.1.1), he turns to rhetoric, which is treated in hardly greater detail (2.2.1–17). Sources cited are Cicero's *De Inventione* and *De Oratore*, Fortunatianus, Marius Victorinus, Quintilian, Augustine, and Martianus Capella. Although Cassiodorus had earlier mentioned figures of speech as a subject common to grammar and rhetoric (2.1.2), his discussion of rhetoric is chiefly devoted to summaries of stasis theory and rhetorical argumentation. Thus its logical side is emphasized.

Boethius

Boethius (480–524) came of a noble Roman family and held high office under Theodoric, Ostrogothic king of northern Italy, delivering panegyrics at the court and speaking in what passed for a senate, but in 522 he was accused of conspiring against Theodoric on behalf of the eastern emperor, Justin I, was imprisoned, and in 524 executed. Boethius' *De Consolatione Philosophiae*, or *Consolation of Philosophy*, recounts in prose, interspersed with poignant verse, the visit of Philosophy to him in prison and the consolation which she offered. It had been the boast of classical orators that they could bend the most stubborn heart, but Boethius does not address his eloquence to Theodoric or to his own friends at court, as Seneca, for example, had done five hundred years before. He prepares himself for death. The decline of civic rhetoric, which had begun with the advent of the empire, is thus evident. Boethius is not the only one to turn away from speech to pursue the eternal life. We have already seen that his friend Cassiodorus withdrew from a public to a monastic life, and Gregory the Great, fifty years later, also laid down office in Rome for the cloister.

Boethius was one of the last Romans to know Greek well, and as has been discussed in chapter 4, his works were the source of knowledge of Aristotelian logic, including the topics, throughout the Middle Ages.

His most important work on rhetoric is the fourth book of *De Topicis Differentiis*, which subordinates the whole study of rhetoric to dialectic. "We have," says Boethius, "received no tradition from the ancient authors on this subject [the whole discipline of rhetoric], for they taught the particulars but did not work at the whole at all. Let us undertake this missing part of their teaching as best we can. Accordingly, we will talk about the genus of the art, its species, matter, parts, instruments, parts of the instrument, work, function of the speaker, the end —and after that about questions to topics" (4.1206c26).[7] He goes on to say that the genus of rhetoric is discipline and its species are judicial, epideictic, and deliberative. The matter is every subject proposed for a speech, but usually a political question. The parts are the traditional five: invention, arrangement, style, memory, and delivery. The instrument is discourse. The parts of the instrument are the parts of the judicial oration. The work is to teach and to move. The function of the orator is to speak appropriately for persuasion. The end is to have spoken well or to have persuaded. The ensuing account chiefly deals with stasis theory. Boethius' discussion of rhetoric, brief as it is, is beautifully systematic, and it is not surprising that it was taken up by the scholastics in Paris as a major rhetorical authority in the thirteenth century.[8]

Early Medieval Preaching

Much of the preaching in the early Middle Ages was of a very simple sort, but in major ecclesiastical or political centers there was some need for a preacher to demonstrate knowledge of theology and perhaps some rhetorical sophistication. The Second Council of Vaison in 529 extended the right to preach from bishops to priests and provided that if no priest were available a homily by one of the Fathers was to be read by a deacon.[9] Augustine's treatise *De Doctrina Christiana* was of course a very important work in establishing a tradition of rhetorical preaching, but its influence was not great in the early Middle Ages. A more widely read work, but one which contributed to *reducing* the role and influence of rhetoric, was the *Cura Pastoralis*, or *Pastoral Care*, of Gregory the Great (pope 590–604). It became a basic handbook of church administration. Although Gregory stresses the importance of preaching and of adapting a sermon to the congregation, he restricts his remarks to the content of sermons and says nothing about their rhetorical qualities.[10] Gregory had held high office in Rome, served as ambassador to Constantinople, played a political role as pope, and encouraged missionary activity. He himself wrote a highly rhetorical

Latin, but his attitude toward classical literature was negative, as seen in a celebrated letter rebuking Bishop Desiderius for teaching grammar and poetry (*Epistulae* 11.54).[11]

Isidore

The final figure who contributed most to the survival of classical rhetoric in the early Middle Ages was Gregory's contemporary, Isidore of Seville (ca. 570–636). He was the author of a vast work entitled *Origines* or *Etymologiae*, which served as an encyclopedia throughout the following centuries.[12] It outlines the trivium and quadrivium in the first three books. The brief and "timid"[13] account of rhetoric (2.1–22) is based on that in Cassiodorus and is really a series of snippets on various subjects with little organization. The longer chapters are on stasis theory, the syllogism, and figures of speech and thought. A chapter on law (2.10) is inserted between the discussion of the syllogism and that of style and is important in suggesting that rhetorical invention was useful in the courts of the time.

The Role of Rhetoric in the
Early Middle Ages

Within the Church it is clear that rhetoric was part of basic education, that it was thought to contribute to an ability to interpret the Scriptures along the lines outlined by Augustine, and that it had some implications for preaching. It was chiefly taught in monastic schools, which were open to the public but were primarily intended to train those entering the life of the Church. Discussions of stasis theory and forms of argument, like the syllogism, bordered closely on dialectic and could serve as an introduction to theological disputation for those who went on to that level. The definitions of rhetoric given by Martianus, Cassiodorus, and Isidore indicate that the origins of conceptual rhetoric in civil life were not forgotten, and Isidore's insertion of a chapter on law into his sections on rhetoric points to the same conclusion. Legal procedures of course chiefly took the form of hearings before a civil or ecclesiastical official, and both the official and the petitioner needed some knowledge of law, of public speaking, and of argumentation. Another application of rhetoric was perhaps found in the addresses of ambassadors sent back and forth between warring kings and officials of the Church. The best picture of the practical uses of rhetoric in the sixth century, as well as the dangers and disruptions on all sides, can be found in the *History of the Franks* by Gregory of Tours, completed in 594.[14] To cite only one example, Gregory gives a full account of the trial of Praetextatus, bishop of Rouen, before an ecclesiastical court (5.18). Although no lengthy addresses were permitted, stasis theory and rhetorical forms of argument play a leading role.

Bede

Glimpses of the role of rhetoric in seventh-century Britain can be seen in writing of the Venerable Bede (673–735). His homilies show how he applied his knowledge of rhetoric to preaching, but the only one of his works to discuss rhetoric directly is a small book, entitled *Concerning Tropes and Figures*.[15] It is intended to help readers of the Bible identify these devices, and the illustrations are entirely biblical. Bede's source here, as was usually true with such material, was the grammarian Donatus rather than any rhetorical treatise. More interesting are references to speech to be found in Bede's great *Ecclesiastical History of the English People*.[16] Missionary preaching was clearly important at this time, as seen, for example, in Bede's description of the arrival in Britain of Augustine, who was to become the first archbishop of Canterbury. The pagan king Ethelbert gave Augustine a hearing in an open field on an island (1.25), and Bede vividly describes how Augustine and his company advanced to meet the king, singing the litanies and preceded by a cross of silver and a painted image of the Christ. All then sat down and Augustine preached to the king and his household "the word of life." Bede apparently had no sources about what Augustine said, though he does quote the reply in which the king refuses to abandon the traditions of his people but grants Augustine the necessities of life and freedom to preach. The later missionary activities of Wilfrid in Frisia are also described by Bede (5.19). Some additional information on missionary preaching in this period can be found in saints' lives and letters, such as those of Boniface. It seems clear that the rhetoric was basically that of the Christian rather than the classical tradition, with strong reliance on authority and external means of persuasion.

An occasion for more sophisticated speech was provided by the synods of the Church, of which the best described is that at Whitby, in 664, when Bishop Colman of the Scots contended against the same Wilfrid, advocate for Bishop Agilbert of the West Saxons, on the true date for Easter, with King Osway as judge. Bede gives a version of the speeches on both sides (3.25), and one can see that Wilfrid in particular had considerable skill in argumentation. The central issue is one of authority, an "external" topic in Cicero's *Topica*, but more characteristically a feature of Christian than of classical rhetoric. At the end the king reduces the question to the issue of whether Columba had any special authority to match that of Saint Peter, which Wilfrid had invoked. Bishop Colman has none to cite, and the king declares that Wilfrid has prevailed and orders the church to observe the orthodox date for Easter.

Bede himself never seems to put a very high value on eloquence. As a Christian he doubtless trusted in the power of the spirit to work belief in the truth. He did, however, value learning, in which he would include the liberal arts and secular literature. For example, he describes (4.2) how Theodorus, in 669 the first archbishop to be accepted by all the English church, encouraged the liberal arts, though rhetoric is not specifically mentioned among them, and how he himself as abbot at Jarrow played a major part in educational efforts in Northumberland which marked the first steps toward the improved intellectual conditions of the Carolingian period on the continent.

In England, however, interest in rhetoric seems to show a decline after Bede. Although the works of Martianus Capella and Isidore, and probably also of Cassiodorus, were available, Christian distrust of rhetoric increased in the time of Aelfric, perhaps encouraged by the austere discipline of Benedictine monks. The synthesis of Christianity and rhetoric made by Augustine seems to have been forgotten, and *De Doctrina Christiana* was apparently unknown.[17]

Alcuin

Out of the English tradition of Bede, however, Alcuin, called in Latin Albinus (ca. 732–804), emerged to bring some remnants of ancient learning back to the continent when he was invited by Charlemagne to take charge of the palace school at Aachen in 781. In this capacity he not only taught many individuals in the court but seems to have contributed to Charlemagne's mandate encouraging verbal education, *De Litteris Colendis*, issued about 795.[18] The objective of the mandate was to encourage churches and monasteries to provide instruction in grammar and rhetoric so that each individual in the realm could attain his own full capacity of verbal skills and thus be able to read the holy writ with full understanding. Charlemagne and Alcuin were clearly concerned at the general low level of literacy. Instruction in grammar was the primary aim, but the mandate mentions "figures, tropes, and other things like them commonly found in the sacred writings." The better a student understood those devices, the better he would understand the text. Although it made no specific provisions for enforcement, Charlemagne's mandate contributed to the improved educational opportunities offered by the Church. Eventually monastic schools such as Bec in Normandy or Bobbio in Italy and cathedral schools such as Chartres or Rheims in France became major educational forces. Grammar was restored to something like its role in antiquity. Rhetoric did not recover its old influence, but it had an established place as a link between grammar and dialectic, which the controversial needs of the Church gradually elevated into the most important of the liberal arts in the medieval period.

Toward the end of his life Alcuin wrote a *Disputatio de Rhetorica et de Virtutibus* in the form of a dialogue between himself and Charlemagne.[19] Though rather little read in succeeding centuries, it is important as the first attempt in the Middle Ages to consider the secular uses of rhetoric. In the opening paragraph Charlemagne points out that the strength of the art of rhetoric lies entirely in dealing with "civil questions." He himself is involved in such matters on a daily basis and he would therefore like Alcuin to open to him "the gates of the rhetorical art of dialectical subtlety." Much of what follows is a catechism in which Charlemagne asks a brief question and Alcuin replies. The practical utility of the subject is mentioned again at the end of section 3, and Alcuin has specifically adapted the judicial rhetoric of antiquity to contemporary conditions at some points.[20] The technical parts of the treatise are primarily excerpts from Cicero's *De Inventione* and from the rhetorical handbook of Julius Victor for subjects not discussed by Cicero. Although the distinction of three kinds of oratory is made (section 5), the actual discussion is devoted entirely to judicial oratory. There is one brief passage on sophistic discourse (section 35), inserted to show the absurdities to which dialectical controversy could be reduced. This had apparently become a fashion in the palace school, foreshadowing the development of scholasticism. After surveying the five parts of rhetoric, Alcuin concludes with a brief consideration of the four cardinal virtues, also based on Cicero and here recommended as a good subject for practice in speaking (44).

Alcuin's treatise clearly reveals how strong was the authority of Cicero and how rhetorical theory remained tied to judicial oratory. The strength of that tie may well have encouraged the development of dialectic as a more suitable study of discourse in the conditions of medieval intellectual life. The Carolingian period, however, did produce another institution which eventually was to have a major function in the history of rhetoric: the antecedent of the modern jury system. This began in the ninth century, when Carolingian kings convened small groups of neighbors to give evidence in support of royal right. The system was imitated in Italy and in England, though it long functioned for the crown's benefit. Juries did not begin to determine the truth of charges in criminal trials in England until the thirteenth century. Medieval and modern juries were, of course, much smaller than the classical juries which had done so much to encourage development of judicial rhetoric as an art form, but they did provide need for systematic statement of a case to a popular audience and an opportunity for ethical and pathetical appeal.

Hrabanus Maurus

A second important writer on rhetoric in the Carolingian period is Hrabanus (or Rabanus) Maurus (778–856), a student of Alcuin. The third book of his treatise *De Clericorum Institutione,* or *On the Education of Clerics,* is the major treatment of preaching in the early Middle Ages.[21] Hrabanus makes no claim to originality; indeed, any such claim would have been foreign to the age in which he lived, which expected to find truth only in the Scriptures and the writings of the Fathers, but he does show a greater appreciation of the potential role of classical rhetoric in preaching than had been evident during the preceding three centuries. Hrabanus' major source is Augustine's *De Doctrina Christiana,* which he excerpts (3.27–39) in the order of Augustine's text, including the discussions of the three kinds of style and the duties of the orator, with lesser borrowings from Cassiodorus and Gregory. There are also short chapters on each of the liberal arts. That on rhetoric (3.19) points out that it is useful not only for civil questions but for the ecclesiastical discipline, and stresses that it should be part of the trivium of introductory studies but not be allowed to take up the attention of an adult preacher.

Rhetoric in Medieval Italy

Latin survived as a spoken language in Italy well into the Middle Ages, and with it spiritual affinity to the verbal arts of the classical period. Adaptation of these to Italian was not difficult. Conversely, Italy did not develop that consuming interest in systematic theology and dialectic which tended to overwhelm other disciplines in France in the twelfth and thirteenth centuries. Among the writers who were educated or worked in Italy and show the influence of the rhetoric of their times is Ratherius (ca. 887–974), bishop of Liege and later of Verona, who used rhetoric to denounce the vices of the clergy and required them to be trained in it.[22] Of particular interest is his *Praeloquia*, which is fundamentally a work of moral instruction but which served as a consolation to him in prison and thus makes an interesting contrast with Boethius' consolation at the beginning of our period. Boethius' work is symptomatic of the death of Roman rhetoric, Ratherius' perhaps of the rebirth of new rhetorical possibilities. Others who show some of the same spirit are Gerbert of Aurillac, who reigned as Pope Sylvester II from 999 to 1003, Peter Damian (1007–1072), and perhaps best of all, Anselm of Besate (ca. 1000–ca. 1060). Anselm was trained in secular rhetoric by a certain Aldeprand. His most interesting work is *Rhetorimachia*, three books written between 1046 and 1048.[23] It takes the form of an invective against the imagined rhetorical ignorance and moral failings of his cousin Rutiland. Anselm speaks of the work as a *controversia* (like those of the Roman schools) and uses the invective as a way to expound and exemplify rhetorical theory, here derived from Hermagoras (indirectly), Cicero, Servius, Quintilian, Victorinus, Grillius, and Boethius, and a bizarre combination of other ideas.

But for all these signs of interest, traditional rhetoric had not yet recovered a place in education in tenth and eleventh-century Italy comparable to what it had had in classical times. The primary reason is that classical rhetoric was an oral art. It taught how an orator could compose and deliver an effective speech in the presence of a living audience. Although these conditions existed to a limited extent in medieval Italy, the uses of the art of persuasion in writing, and especially in written documents, were somewhat more important, and for these rhetoric in its traditional form was ill-suited. A revival of interest in and knowledge of Roman law began to overwhelm rhetoric as the core study of civic or ecclesiastical communication; Justinian's *Digest*, unknown in western Europe in the early Middle Ages, became an important influence on jurisprudence in the eleventh century. Twelfth-century Bologna produced Irnerius, who first taught rhetoric and the other arts but later became the greatest medieval authority on Roman law.

Dictamen

To meet the needs of the time in Italy, the major development within the discipline of rhetoric was the *dictamen*, the rhetorical art of letter-writing.[24] This seems to have emerged from the school of Monte Cassino, and its first great teacher there was apparently Alberic, who flourished around the middle of the eleventh century.[25] Alberic's *Flowers of Rhetoric* deals primarily with ornamentation of the style of letters, his *Breviarium* with the form and content. In the twelfth century, dictamen, like law, was taught in the University of Bologna. Dictamen (from Latin *dictare*, to dictate a letter) is a derivative of classical rhetoric, reflecting especially the figures of speech and the parts of the oration, which were adapted into a standard five-part epistolary structure: the *salutatio*, or greeting; the *captatio benevolentiae*, or exordium, which secured the goodwill of the recipient; the *narratio*; the *petitio*, or specific request, demand, or announcement; and a relatively simple *conclusio*. The dictamen was strongly influenced by the conventions of diplomatic and legal correspondence, both civil and ecclesiastical, in medieval courts. The papal court in particular sought high standards of accuracy and dignity of statement. There was considerable demand for persons trained in the proper forms of communication, and the art was thus both taught in schools and set forth in numerous handbooks. Before the development of these handbooks there had existed formulary letters which scribes could adapt to particular purpose, just as commonplaces were available for fifth-century Greek orators for use in various situations in court, and handbooks of dictamen, like Greek handbooks of progymnasmata, are often accompanied by model letters. This is true, for example, of the treatises of Adalbertus Samaritanus and of Hugh of Bologna, two of the most famous writers on dictamen in the early twelfth century. About the middle of the thirteenth century *ars dictaminis*, as a study at the University of Bologna, was replaced by *ars notaria*, which was less rhetorically and more legally oriented. Meanwhile, the study of dictamen had begun also in France.[26] The French schools encouraged a more artificial style and composed models on fantastic subjects.

Although the handbooks of dictamen are concerned with letter-writing, they often initially define that art broadly as the art of writing and distinguish several kinds, such as qualitative poetry, accentual poetry, and rhythmical prose, before concentrating on the latter. Beginning in late antiquity, feeling for the quantity of long and short syllables had waned in both Greek and Latin and was replaced by an increased perception of word accent. This became the basis of a new system of accentual prose rhythm, replacing the quantitative system discussed by Quintilian (9.4) and other classical writers. The new system is called the *cursus*; it involves a rhythmical flow of accents deliberately put at the end of a phrase or clause or sentence, and its three main forms can be illustrated by the English phrases "help and defend us," which is *cursus planus*; "governed and sanctified," which is *cursus tardus*; and "punished for our offenses," which is *cursus velox*. First developed in Latin, the cursus was imitated in the formal prose of English and other languages in the late Middle Ages and Renaissance.[27]

Although the dictamen is the most distinctive development of Italian medieval rhetoric, as already noted the circumstances of life in Italian cities made useful a variety of kinds of public address; these include funeral orations, speeches for academic occasions, and other kinds of epideictic, as well as speeches by ambassadors and some judicial oratory. Writings on rhetoric in the thirteenth century include models for such speeches and also discussions of rules for their composition. Guido Faba (ca. 1190–1244), who wrote an important handbook of dictamen, also wrote model letters and speeches,[28] and other model speeches can be found in the anonymous *Oculus Pastoralis*, written between 1179 and 1190, and in treatises for instruction of city officials.[29] One of the most interesting works is the *Rhetorica Novissima* (1235) by the eccentric and aggressive Boncompagno of Signa, modestly intended as a replacement for Cicero.[30] It consists of thirteen short "books" on the origin of law, the parts of rhetoric, exordia, narratives, arguments, and the like. Much of it is in the form of question and definition. Although the work applies to letter writing, there are sections on memory and public speaking at the end; the material as a whole would be useful to an advocate. Another sign of the thirteenth-century Italian interest in judicial rhetoric is the *Ars Arengandi*, or *Art of Haranguing*, by Jacques de Dinant, apparently a monk and teacher of rhetoric in Bologna at the end of the thirteenth century.[31] It is made up of a short introductory poem and extracts from the *Rhetorica ad Herennium* on the parts of rhetoric and the form of judicial oratory. Dinant also wrote on dictamen. Brunetto Latini (1220–1294), teacher of Dante, wrote a treatise on the liberal arts called *Tresor*,[32] which resembles those popular in France at the time, and also an Italian translation of *De Inventione*, which shows clearly the importance of political oratory in the late thirteenth century.[33] These mark the beginning of the study of rhetoric in the vernacular languages.

The teaching of technical rhetoric in Italy in the later Middle Ages is an important antecedent for the flowering of rhetoric in Italy in the time of the renaissance humanists. The humanists of the fourteenth and fifteenth centuries added their great enthusiasm for classical models and their acquaintance with many more texts to a living art of speaking and letter-writing which already utilized Ciceronian rhetoric.

Rhetoric in French Cathedral Schools

Early Italian proclivity toward rhetoric may have contributed to some increased interest in the discipline in French schools in the eleventh century. Lanfranc, for example, born in Pavia around 1005, was educated in rhetoric and law in Italy, but went to Bec in Normandy to teach, became a friend of William the Conqueror, and ended his life as archbishop of Canterbury (1070–1089). But the schools of northwestern France, and especially the cathedral school of Chartres, already gave serious attention to all parts of the trivium and quadrivium.³⁴ The leading figure in the rise of Chartres to eminence was Fulbert, bishop from 1006 to 1028. He was followed by other distinguished teachers over the next century and a half, among them Bernard, his brother Thierry, and their student, John of Salisbury.³⁵ The fullest expression of the liberal arts as understood in the Middle Ages is probably that found in the enormous (never printed) encyclopedia by Thierry, the *Heptateuchon*, written about the middle of the twelfth century. Its treatment of rhetoric is said to be based on Cicero's *De Inventione*, the *Rhetorica ad Herennium*, and Cicero's *Partitiones Oratoriae*, with some reference to Julianus Severus and Martianus Capella.³⁶ Thierry also composed a commentary to *De Inventione*. Throughout this period manuscripts of that work became very common, manuscripts of the *Rhetorica ad Herennium* became more common than at any other time, and commentaries were written on both. It would thus seem than Ciceronian rhetoric was being thoroughly taught at least in some parts of France. Study of these commentaries has only recently been undertaken but seems to show that rhetoric was conceived of as a practical civic tool.³⁷ The mutilated text of Quintilian was also unusually popular in Chartres in the twelfth century, especially its discussion of elementary education and grammar.³⁸ Quintilian influenced the teaching of Bernard and John and was frequently cited by John as an authority in his *Metalogicon*, *Policraticus*, and other works. In the later twelfth and in the thirteenth centuries compendia of the liberal arts continued to be written: Alan of Lille (ca. 1128–1202) in his versified treatise *Anticlaudianus* reduces rhetoric to specious adornment; ³⁹ Vincent of Beauvais (ca. 1190–1264) in his *Speculum* essentially repeats the discussion in Isidore. Rhetorical instruction in Spain apparently followed along the same lines as in France.⁴⁰

The "renaissance of the twelfth century," as some scholars have called it, brought a renewed interest in classical Latin writers and in a deeper education in the liberal arts for humanistic goals—greater literacy, greater understanding.⁴¹ Rhetoric played a part in this study, especially at Chartres, but for many students its contribution was an indirect one contributing to their verbal and mental skills, which received full development in the study of logic and theology. Classical rhetoric also had considerable influence on handbooks of poetic composition of the late twelfth and thirteenth centuries, such as the *Ars Versificatoria* of Matthew of Vendome, the versified *Poetria Nova* of

Geoffrey of Vinsauf, and the *Poetria* of John of Garland, which also includes discussion of dictamen.[42] These works and others like them are primarily presentations of methods of rhetorical ornamentation and are to be associated with Latin verse composition in schools. They are historically important because medieval poets had studied them, even though their art goes beyond anything in such works, and because they foreshadow the development of literary criticism in the Renaissance, which explores in greater depth and scope the implications of classical rhetoric for all of literature. An interesting feature of some *artes poetriae* is the theory of "material" style, which seeks to adapt the classical theory of the three kinds of style to medieval hierarchies; the grand style is applied to aristocratic subjects, the middle to bourgeois subjects, and the plain to humble or rural subjects.[43]

Rhetoric in Medieval Universities

Rhetoric did not play a major role in most medieval universities. Bologna is the chief exception, but even there a period of neglect ensued around 1300. Rhetoric was then revived in 1321 with the appointment of a professor to teach Cicero, Latin composition, and dictamen.[44] A statute of 1215 of the University of Paris mentions rhetoric, but in a way that indicates it was overshadowed by dialectic.[45] The text of Aristotle was the basis of the teaching of philosophy at Paris and elsewhere, and efforts were made to recover additional parts of the Aristotelian corpus which had been heard about from Arabic commentators or were thought to exist in Byzantium. About 1240 Hermannus Allemanus made a Latin translation of an Arabic commentary on the *Rhetoric* attributed to Al-Farabi. Soon thereafter the *Rhetoric* itself was translated into Latin, in what has been called the "old translation," attributed sometimes to Bartholomew of Messina, though the author is not known with certainty. Around 1270 William of Moerbeke produced a second translation which became much more widely known and which survives in many manuscripts. William was a member of the Dominican religious order, born in Flanders, who had spent several years in Greece and on his return to the West was urged by Thomas Aquinas to translate texts of Aristotle. In addition to the *Rhetoric* he made versions of the *Politics* and *Metaphysics* and of some Greek commentators on Aristotle, all rather literal. About ten years later Aegidius (or Giles of Rome as he is sometimes known) wrote a Latin commentary on William's version. The emphasis of this commentary, along with the groupings of the *Rhetoric* with other texts in bound manuscripts of Aristotle, seems to make it clear that the *Rhetoric* was read in the thir-

teenth and fourteenth centuries primarily as a moral and political treatise because of the discussions of those subjects in Books 1 and 2 and
that it was little used for the study of rhetoric.[46]

A rather different example of this trend is the art of memory as studied in the Middle Ages. Memory was of course the fifth part of classical
rhetoric and was known to medieval scholars from the discussion in the
Rhetorica ad Herennium and brief mention in Martianus Capella and
other writers. The subject was comparatively neglected until the thirteenth century, when it was taken up by Albertus Magnus as part of
his treatise *On the Good* and by Thomas Aquinas in the *Secunda Se-
cundae* of the *Summa Theologiae*. In both cases the philosophers draw
on the *Rhetorica ad Herennium*, but their interest in the subject is
ethical. They also wrote commentaries on Aristotle's philosophical
treatise *On Memory*.[47]

Late Medieval Preaching

The form of rhetoric which came closest to developing new theory in
the Middle Ages was preaching.[48] Augustine's treatise *De Doctrina
Christiana* was excerpted by Hrabanus Maurus and became widely
known in the later Middle Ages, but Augustine's lofty stylistic concepts
were beyond the reach of most medieval preachers. Gregory's *Cura
Pastoralis* had greater influence but did not contain a developed theory
of preaching. Its most important rhetorical feature is Gregory's insistence on the importance of adapting a sermon to the audience. Otherwise, in the early Middle Ages there seems to be a decline in preaching
as in other arts. Improvement is evident in the eleventh century. The
most effective medieval sermon ever preached was probably that by
Pope Urban II at the Council of Clermont (1095): it was the efficient
cause of the First Crusade.[49] Manuals of preaching begin to appear in
the twelfth century, and from the thirteenth to the fifteenth century
they were compiled in large numbers. During this period preaching
became a popular art throughout western Europe. Harry Caplan associates this phenomenon with the rise of new preaching orders in the
Church (such as the Franciscans and Dominicans), the spread of mysticism, the growth of scholasticism, and a generally improved level of
culture.[50]

The earlier stages of the development can be represented by works
by Guibert of Nogent (ca. 1084) and Alan of Lille (ca. 1199). Guibert's
Liber Quo Ordine Sermo Fieri Debeat, or *Book about the Way a Sermon Ought to be Given*, discusses the purpose of preaching and forms
of scriptural interpretation, of which four are distinguished: the histor-

ical or literal, the allegorical, the tropological or moral, and the anagogical or mystical.[51] These four levels are developments of the three levels distinguished by Origen and were probably canonized in late antiquity. They appear first in the writings of Eucherius and Cassian in the fourth century[52] and become standard features of manuals of preaching from the time of Guibert to the nineteenth century. Guibert's treatise was an introduction to his commentary on Genesis and is as applicable to exegesis as to an oral sermon.

Alan of Lille's *Anticlaudianus* has been mentioned earlier as an allegorical poem about the seven liberal arts. His treatise *De Arte Praedicatoria*, or *On the Preacher's Art*, is strongly influenced by Gregory the Great's *Cura Pastoralis*.[53] Much of it consists of models of how to rebuke sinners, in which Alan seems to follow a systematic method of distinguishing different meanings of a word and supporting each with the authority of Scripture. His divisions are reminiscent of the topics of rhetoric as found in Cicero or Boethius, but he has nothing to say about the organization of a sermon or about style.

In the early thirteenth century handbooks of thematic preaching began to appear, perhaps first in England with the manuals of Alexander of Ashby and Thomas Chabham of Salisbury.[54] These works adapt the parts of the oration as described in the *Rhetorica ad Herennium* to the needs of the preachers. They reflect an interest in the form and technique of sermons, rather than just the contents, and foreshadow the thematic preaching which became popular at the University of Paris and elsewhere in a few years.[55] By "thematic preaching," in its fully developed form, is meant a systematic, logical form of preaching, as opposed to the informality and lack of structure of the homily or of the simple preaching of Saint Francis. The theme takes the form of a quotation from Scripture. The preacher then divides the theme into a series of questions, which may be as numerous as the number of words in the quotation. He takes up each of these divisions in turn, interpreting them by other quotations from Scripture and applying them to his congregation. Richard of Thetford's *Ars Dilatandi Sermones*, or *Art of Amplifying Sermons* (ca. 1245), describes eight modes of "dilating" or amplifying divisions of the theme.

Thematic preaching is not missionary preaching. The congregation is assumed to believe in Christ; the preacher instructs them about the meaning of the Bible, with particular emphasis on moral action. The thematic sermon is thus, like the homily, closely related to Biblical exegesis. Just as the dictamen combined features of rhetoric and law to meet a perceived need, so the preaching manuals drew on a variety of disciplines to outline their new technique. Biblical exegesis was one. Scholastic logic was a second; the manuals became popular about the same time that scholasticism reached its height. A third influence was rhetoric as known from Cicero and Boethius. There is also some influence from grammar and other parts of the liberal arts in the amplification of divisions of the theme.

Manuals of preaching were very common in the late Middle Ages and Renaissance, but no one manual became the standard work and none is comparable in achievement to the major works of classical rhetoric. An easily available example of a late medieval treatise on preaching, one representative of the genre, is the *Forma Praedicandi*, or *The Form of Preaching*, by Robert of Basevorn, written around 1322.[56] The word "form" in the title is important, since Robert's interest is the method of constructing thematic sermons. In the prologue he compares the method of preaching on every subject to logic, which is the method of syllogizing on every subject. Preaching he defines as "the persuasion of the multitude, within a moderate length of time, to worthy conduct"; it is thus moral and instructional. There follows a brief consideration (chapters 2–5) about who can be a preacher and a description (6–13) of earlier methods of preaching: those of Christ, Paul, Augustine, Gregory the Great, and Bernard of Clairvaux (1090–1153). This section ends with a quotation from Pope Leo: "This is the virtue of eloquence, that there is nothing foreign to it that it cannot be extolled. Who will hesitate to say that wisdom and eloquence together move us more than either does by itself? Thus we must insist upon eloquence and yet not depart from wisdom, which is the better of the two." The view is reminiscent of the preface to *De Inventione*, Book 1, and of Augustine. Indeed, Robert cites Augustine's formulation of the duties of the preacher: to teach, to please, and to move.

The body of the treatise consists of twenty-two "ornaments employed in the most carefully contrived sermons." These are a strange mixture of devices with antecedents in classical rhetoric, relating to invention, arrangement, style, and delivery, but all deal with the statement of the theme, its division, and the amplification of the divisions. Examples are given and the treatment of most of the ornaments involves the process of division. The fourth ornament, for example, is introduction (31). It can be formed by authority, by argument, or by both together, and each of these is further divided. Fifteen of the ornaments, Robert says (50), apply to the form or execution of the sermon. The last seven contribute to its beauty. These are coloration, including the rhetorical colors, for which the reader is referred to the fourth book of the *Rhetorica ad Herennium*; voice modulation as described by Augustine; gesture as described by Hugh of Saint Victor; humor as described by Cicero; allusion to Scripture; a firm impression, which seems to be systematic repetition of allusion to a scriptural passage; and reflection, or the consideration of who is to speak to whom, what, and how much.

A greater work on preaching could easily be imagined, one which would put together the inventional thinking of classical handbooks, Cicero's *Topica*, Augustine's discussion of style, Gregory's concern with fitting a sermon to an audience, and the distinctive nature of Christian rhetoric as seen in the Bible and practiced by missionaries. Robert's treatise, however, seems to have been a practical aid to the composition of the kind of sermon approved in his time. He mentions Oxford and Paris as two centers of preaching, each characterized by a slightly different style.

Aristotle divided the subject of rhetoric into that which did not demand a judgment from the audience and that which did. The former was epideictic. The latter either involved judgments of the past, which was judicial rhetoric, or of the future, which was deliberative. The adjustments made in rhetoric by the later Middle Ages seem to call for a different basis of distinction. For that age, even though classical authorities remained dominant, it would be truer to say that the art of persuasion was regarded as either oral or written. If oral, its main practical forms were those of preaching and oral controversy, though we have seen in Italy the appearance of opportunities for political and legal oratory, and this probably existed elsewhere as well to some extent. If written, it was the art of dictamen and could be either in verse or in prose. If in verse, it inherited the traditions of ancient epideictic and poetic and manifested itself in topics, tropes, and figures. If in prose, it was best found in the epistle. Thus, the three most characteristic forms of rhetoric in the later Middle Ages were preaching, rhetorical poetry, and letters. In none of these areas did theory or criticism make a significant advance; in all three, systems were devised which were regarded as useful for the times.

Of the three elements in the rhetorical act—speaker, speech, and audience—that of the speaker, which had dominated sophistic rhetoric, lost ground in the western Middle Ages, though the tradition was preserved in the East. The speech itself, the central focus of classical treatises, remains central in western medieval thinking, an attitude probably reinforced by medieval study of grammar and dialectic. Some interest in the audience is demonstrated by writers on dictamen and on preaching.

This chapter has been devoted to the history of rhetorical theory in the classical tradition as it persisted in the western Middle Ages. The tension between this tradition and Christianity is occasionally evident, especially in the early Middle Ages, as seen, for example, in Gregory the Great, and early medieval missionaries turned back to Christian rhetoric, but in general the Augustinian solution to the problem was accepted: rhetoric was regarded as an important element in Scripture, and its study could be justified on that ground as well as for some potential utility in civic life. Throughout the period, secondary rhetoric was practiced with enthusiasm. Ernst R. Curtius's important book, *European Literature and the Latin Middle Ages*, can be read as a history of the devices of style and exposition and of the rhetorical topics in which medieval authors exulted.[57] For most English readers the poems of Chaucer are the finest application of rhetoric in this period.[58]

There are in the Middle Ages a variety of rhetorics: most conceptualized is the classical tradition; Christian rhetoric is often evident; a non-artistic rhetoric of brute force, intimidation, and authority is often visible in the demands of kings and nobles; native forms of expression are to be found in the vernacular languages, that in Irish being the most distinctive. The conflicts and interworkings of these rhetorics deserve more study than they have been given. Finally, two other medieval rhetorical traditions should not pass unnoticed even though they lie outside the subject of this book. One is the Hebrew rhetoric of the Middle Ages, for which Harry Caplan has suggested some materials;[59] the other is Arabic rhetoric, on which some information is also available.[60]

Chapter 10
Classical Rhetoric in
the Renaissance

We have seen that rhetoric was a useful tool in the Italian cities of the later medieval period. This partly took the form of the dictamen and the associated arts of the notary, but there are signs of the importance of judicial oratory, and perhaps some deliberative oratory, as well as preaching. The needs of these rhetorical forms were mostly met by simple handbooks; the ultimate authority, however, was Cicero. *De Inventione* and the *Rhetorica ad Herennium* were well known to teachers and serious students of rhetoric.

Italian civic life serves as the environment for a remarkable enthusiasm for classical rhetoric in the fourteenth, fifteenth, and sixteenth centuries.[1] First here and then in other parts of Europe rhetoric rises briefly from the valley between grammar and dialectic to become a major force in education and cultural life. A knowledge of Greek and of works of Greek literature, including rhetorical treatises and orations, was recovered in the West; important Latin rhetorical works, long thought to have been lost, were discovered in early manuscripts lying neglected in out-of-the-way monasteries; translations, commentaries, and new works were written in considerable numbers; finally, the invention of printing greatly facilitated the dissemination of learning. Cicero's *De Oratore*, *Brutus*, and *Orator* in 1465 and *De Inventione*, the *Rhetorica ad Herennium*, and the complete treatise of Quintilian in 1470 were among the earliest texts printed.

The Humanists

The individuals known as the Italian humanists were the efficient cause of this development. A humanist was not a humanistic philosopher, but a teacher or advanced student of the subjects collectively known as *studia humanitatis*, embracing grammar, rhetoric, history, poetry, and moral philosophy, all studied on the basis of classical models and theories.[2] These came to constitute the basic curriculum which began in schools and extended through the arts course in universities. With the exception of a very few remarkable writers like Petrarch (1304–1374), the humanists usually earned their living either by teaching rhetoric or some aspect of classical studies or by working as a chancellor, or public secretary to a prince, a pope, or a commune. In this capacity they put to practical use their knowledge of rhetoric, including dictamen, in the composition of Latin letters and speeches. To consider only the most famous Italian humanists, Coluccio Salutati (1331–1406), Leonardo Bruni (ca. 1370–1444), and Poggio Bracciolini (1380–1459) served variously as secretary of the papal chancery and of the Florentine republic. Lorenzo Valla (1407–1457) was papal secretary and also lectured on rhetoric in Rome. Politian (1454–1494) was tutor to the children of Lorenzo de Medici and gave public lectures on Greek and Latin literature to large classes in Florence.

In function the Italian humanists were thus a continuation of the teachers of grammar and rhetoric and the notaries of the later Middle Ages. What was new, however, was an extraordinary enthusiasm for classical literature which spread among these functionaries in the fourteenth and fifteenth centuries, analogous to an interest in classical architecture, sculpture, and other arts which is to be seen in the same period. This classicism had not characterized Italian culture earlier and seems to have been imported from France, where an admiration for classical models was already found at the school of Chartres, as we have seen, and later in Paris. In any event, the humanists were intoxicated with the language and literature of antiquity and sought to recover all possible knowledge of it and to make that knowledge the basis of the twin ideals of wisdom and eloquence in the culture of their times, which they regarded as awakening from a long sleep.[3] The two factors of rhetoric and classicism of course greatly reinforced each other, since the more the humanists learned about the classics, the more they discovered that rhetoric was the discipline which had created the forms, disposed the contents, and ornamented the pages which they admired and sought to imitate. Rhetoric proved to be not the arid study of the medieval trivium or the technical teachings of *De Inven-*

tione and the *Rhetorica ad Herennium,* but a noble and creative art, characteristic of man at his best. In many ways the humanists thus resemble the leading figures of the Second Sophistic, who were also teachers of rhetoric, admirers of the classics, orators, and letter writers.

In the Italian Renaissance, not only rhetoric but Latin oratory reemerged as a major form of human communication. As we have seen, there was political, academic, judicial, and occasional oratory in Italy in the later Middle Ages. With the Renaissance the quantity and the quality of this oratory greatly increased. Quality includes not only the Latinity, of which Ciceronian standards were again achieved, and the use of figures, but also the rhetorical effectiveness of the whole work. Eloquence was an ideal of the age: speeches or works in the form of speeches were published, read, and copied. For example, Leonardo Bruni's *Laudation of the City of Florence* (ca. 1403–1404), composed in the spirit of the Second Sophistic, was widely admired and imitated by Pier Candido Decembrio for Milan and Enea Silvio Piccolomini for Basel. The most famous renaissance work in oratorical form is doubtless Pico della Mirandola's *Oration on the Dignity of Man* of 1487. A great deal of renaissance oratory is basically concerned with praise and blame and fits comfortably into the limits of classical epideictic,[4] but in Florence and Venice and other free cities there developed around 1400 a new sense of civic responsibility and appreciation of liberty, and oratory, as well as the writing of epistles, histories, dialogues, and poetry, thus took on a practical political purpose, which became primary rhetoric, even in the hands of scholars. Within the Church medieval forms of preaching were abandoned and classical models were enthusiastically embraced, with attendant discussion of the theoretical problems involved, especially in the period after 1450.[5] Considering the uses of rhetoric by the humanists and their successors and by renaissance preachers and letter writers, it is not surprising that style, rather than invention, seemed to many the most important part of the discipline.

Petrarch, in many ways the founder of the humanist movement, envisioned a synthesis of wisdom and eloquence in oral expression and in both civic and academic contexts, and this view was taken up by some of his successors like Coluccio Salutati and Lorenzo Valla.[6] Their efforts ultimately failed; the devastation and disruption caused by French, German, and Spanish invasions in the sixteenth century frustrated the earlier political initiative, and there revived among educators the feeling inherited from the Middle Ages that rhetoric was essentially a discipline to be studied by the very young or to be absorbed into the aesthetics of literary criticism, but for some two centuries rhetoric made a claim to be queen of the arts.

The recovery of texts crucial to the revival of classical rhetoric in the Renaissance can be said to begin with the new Latin translations of Aristotle made in the thirteenth century, including the *Rhetoric*, even though these were not immediately put to rhetorical use.[7] Petrarch's discovery in 1345 at Verona of a manuscript of Cicero's previously unknown letters to Atticus, Quintus, and Brutus brought to life the fascinating career of the greatest Roman orator with an intimacy never before known and contributed to renaissance interest in the individual, his role in the state, and the complexity of the problems of the orator. The fourteenth century also saw the beginning of a general recovery of a knowledge of Greek in Italy. Petrarch's friend Giovanni Boccaccio (1313–1375), whose writings included the *Decameron* and a work on classical mythology, studied Greek with a Calabrian named Leonzio Pilato and secured his teacher's appointment as a public professor of that language in Florence in 1361. More influential was Manuel Chrysoloras, who came to Italy as an ambassador from Constantinople and held a Greek chair in Florence from 1396 to 1400. Leonardo Bruni combined his active life as chancellor in Florence with a study of the classics, translating Plato's *Gorgias*, *Phaedrus*, and other dialogues into Latin as well as speeches of Demosthenes and Aeschines. Even more influential were the Latin translations of all of Plato, by Marsilio Ficino, begun in 1463 and completed about 1470.

In terms of immediate effect on renaissance knowledge of rhetoric and enthusiasm for classical sources, the most important discoveries were those of Poggio. He had already recovered eight speeches of Cicero, including *Pro Roscio*, *Pro Murena*, and *Pro Cluentio*, when in 1416 at Saint Gall he found, dirty and neglected, an old manuscript of the complete text of Quintilian's *Institutio Oratoria*, as well as a manuscript of some of Asconius' commentaries on speeches of Cicero and other works.[8] Since the early Middle Ages available texts of Quintilian had contained significant gaps, specifically the beginning of Book 1, the end of Book 5, all of Books 6 and 7, portions of 8, 9, 10, and 11, and the end of Book 12. The complete Quintilian enjoyed an enormous popularity in the fifteenth and sixteenth centuries as an authority both on technical rhetoric and on education. His educational theories profoundly affected schools of the liberal arts, such as that of Vittorino da Feltre in Mantua (founded in 1423), and his rhetorical theory is reflected in such otherwise diverse writers as Lorenzo Valla, Rudolph Agricola, Erasmus, Juan Luis Vives, Peter Ramus, and Francisco Patrizi.[9] Poggio made many other discoveries of Latin texts, but the canon of major Latin rhetorical treatises was completed in 1421 when Gerardo Landriani, bishop of Lodi, found a complete manuscript of Cicero's *De Oratore*, *Orator*, and *Brutus*. The first two works had been known for centuries only in mutilated versions; the *Brutus* had been totally unknown. *De Oratore* was to inspire a series of dialogues on eloquence during the next two centuries.[10] It would probably be possible to write a history of renaissance rhetorical thought in terms of the successive impact of rediscovered works: Cicero, Quintilian, and the Greek treatises, especially Dionysius of Halicarnassus' *On Composition*, Hermogenes' *On Ideas*, Demetrius' *On Style*, and finally "Longinus' " *On the Sublime*. The first three of the Greek works were printed in a popular edition by Aldus Manutius in Venice in 1508.

Knowledge of Greek was acquired by the humanists primarily from Greeks who came to Italy in the fourteenth and early fifteenth centuries. This process was complemented by westerners' travels to Greece in search of manuscripts; Giovanni Aurispa (1376–1459) and Guarino of Verona (1374–1460) were among the most important travelers. The increasing Turkish threat to Constantinople, ending with the fall of the city in 1453, gave a sense of urgency to the effort to preserve and translate into Latin all that could be found of Greek writing.

George Trebizond

Of the Greek emigrants to Italy, the most important for the history of rhetoric is George Trebizond (1395–1472), who introduced Hermogenes and the Byzantine Greek rhetorical tradition to the West.[11] Surnamed Trebizond from a grandfather who came from the Greek city of that name on the Black Sea, George himself was born in Crete and came to Italy in 1416 to work in the library of the Venetian humanist Francesco Barbaro. The patronage of influential Venetians continued to be important to him throughout his career. A few details about his life may help to make clear the kinds of rhetorical activities practiced by fifteenth-century humanists.

Trebizond had been well educated in Greek grammar and rhetoric, but on arrival in Italy had to begin by learning Latin. He soon distinguished himself and became one of the best Latin stylists of his time. As early as 1421 he delivered Latin orations at Vicenza—his *In Praise of Eloquence*[12] and *In Praise of Cicero*. He probably taught private pupils at this time and completed a Latin synopsis of Hermogenes' work *On Ideas*. In 1426 he published a Latin treatise, *De Suavitate Dicendi*, or *On the Sweetness of Speaking*, based on Hermogenes' discussion of *glykytes*, and was appointed to the public chair of Latin in Vicenza. Discharged at the end of the following year for unknown reasons—he could be very difficult in personal relations and like many others of his time was quick to engage in acrimonious debate—he devoted himself to teaching privately and to the composition of his greatest work, *Rhetoricorum Libri V*, or *Five Books of Rhetoric*, which he published in 1433 or 1434. This is the first full-scale rhetoric of the Renaissance; it integrated the Greek tradition of Dionysius of Halicarnassus and Hermogenes into the standard Latin sources with examples from Cicero and Virgil. Trebizond himself apparently thought of it as a rival to Quintilian's treatise, which was then at the peak of its popularity. He also dared to criticize the Latin style of others, including the humanist Guarino of Verona, author of a major commentary on the *Rhetorica ad Herennium*. This involved him in extended disputes. In 1437 he issued his *Reply to the Invective of Guarino and Defense of His Own Rhetoric*. Meanwhile he had delivered the *Funeral Oration for Fantino Michiel* before the doge and senate of Venice and had completed his *Compendium*, a treatise on the parts of speech that was based on the grammar of Priscian. This became a very popular work for the teaching of Latin grammar throughout the rest of the century.

In 1437 Trebizond moved to Bologna, where he may have lectured on rhetoric at the university and where he delivered his *Oration in Praise of Pope Eugenius IV* before Eugenius himself and the papal court, then in residence there. He also published a letter in Greek to the Byzantine emperor, which is the opening document in what becomes an obsessive apocalyptic vision of the union of the eastern and western Churches under a Turkish sultan converted to Christianity. In 1440 he published *Isagoge Dialectica*, or *Introduction to Dialectic*, which is the first humanist textbook on logic. Trebizond regarded dialectic as a small subject, useful for one entering into the greater field of rhetoric; from it one could learn something about reasoning processes as a basis for study of invention. Ironically, in northern Europe in the sixteenth century the *Isagoge* became popular with those interested in removing invention from rhetoric. By 1440 Trebizond was in Florence, where he taught poetry at the university and lectured in private on Greek and Latin, logic, rhetoric, and philosophy. The papal court was now also in Florence and he began work there as a secretary. He also wrote a commentary on Cicero's speech *Pro Ligario* and completed a translation of Basil's *Against Eunomius*. The latter was done at the request of Cardinal Bessarion, another Greek immigrant, who was, however, to become one of Trebizond's most bitter opponents.

In 1443 Trebizond moved to Rome and the following year was sworn in as a secretary in the apostolic court. This association, with some interruptions, lasted much of the rest of his life. The routine duties were apparently slight, and his time went largely into the translation of Greek works not yet available in Latin, an activity in which the new pope, Nicholas V, was much interested. Trebizond worked on scientific writings of Aristotle, Plato's *Laws*, sermons by John Chrysostom and Gregory of Nazianzus, and other works. He thus made available to the West the classic models of Greek Christian epideictic, although panegyric of saints was already being practiced in Italy by Pier Paolo Vergerio and others at the end of the fourteenth century on the basis of Latin models. Trebizond also made a new translation of Aristotle's *Rhetoric* and a version of Demosthenes' speech *On the Crown*, one of at least six done in the fifteenth century. In 1452, after a nasty brawl with Poggio, he left for Naples but returned to serve under a new pope, Calixtus III, in 1455 and continued under Pius II.

The fall of Constantinople in 1453 reawakened all of Trebizond's private prophetic visions and led him to a new, ill-advised activity. It was indeed primarily in this connexion that he became involved in the dispute between Platonists and Aristotelians, on the side of Aristotle, and published in 1457 *A Comparison of the Philosophers Plato and Aristotle*, to which Cardinal Bessarion eventually replied in a work entitled *Against the Calumniator of Plato* (that is, Trebizond). The latter claimed that his dislike of Plato originated with Plato's treatment of Gorgias in the dialogue of that name, and his own views of rhetoric as seen in his oration *In Praise of Eloquence* and the preface to his own *Rhetoric* echo those of the Greek sophist. Though he translated Aristotle's *Rhetoric* and admired its author, he was not strongly influenced by Aristotle's views on rhetoric.[13]

In 1460 Trebizond left Rome to become professor of rhetoric and humanities at Venice, but returned to the papal court in 1464 when his former pupil Pietro Barbo was elected Pope Paul II. In 1465/66 he paid a secret visit to Constantinople, but failed to see the sultan, much less to persuade him of the religious destiny which Trebizond envisioned. On his return, however, he published a highly injudicious address to the sultan entitled *The Eternal Glory of the Autocrat*. The result was his imprisonment in Castel Sant'Angelo for four months. After his release he remained in Rome, continued his involvement in the Plato-Aristotle debate and other controversial matters, and died in 1472 or 1473. It would be a mistake to describe his career as typical, and his apocalyptic religious enthusiasm was almost unique, but the activities of this indefatigable rhetorician and sophist touched almost every aspect of the professional life of a renaissance humanist, with the exception of the discovery of new manuscripts of Latin classics. That effort had been largely completed by others. Trebizond, however, played a major role in bringing the Greek classics to the West.

When Trebizond arrived in Italy, teachers of rhetoric had already begun to make significant improvements in the depth and perception of rhetorical traditions in the form of either commentaries or monographs, but solely within the Ciceronian tradition as known in the Middle Ages. Antonio Loschi's commentary on eleven orations of Cicero and Gasparino Barzizza's Ciceronian treatise *On Composition* are examples.[14] Trebizond took the framework of the Ciceronian tradition, but in the full form including all five parts of rhetoric. The structure of his *Rhetoric* is that of the *Rhetorica ad Herennium*, but with one additional book. This framework is expanded with considerable material from other Roman writers on rhetoric like Quintilian, though Trebizond names Quintilian only to criticize him, and by Greek material; very little, however, comes from Aristotle, though he is repeatedly named.

Book 1 begins with a short preface on the utility of oratory in society, reminiscent of the sophistic tradition of antiquity or *De Inventione*.[15] It then proceeds to define rhetoric: "a science of civic life in which, with the agreement of the audience insofar as possible, we speak on civil questions." He defines what he means by questions and the kinds of oratory and then takes up the parts of the oration: exordium, narration, and "contention" or proof; he subdivides proof into division, confirmation, and refutation. This leads to the question of *status* and completes Book 1. Book 2 is largely a paraphrase of Hermogenes' *On Staseis*, though Trebizond fails to adopt Hermogenes' method of division. Book 3 is entitled "On Argumentation"; it is here that Trebizond incorporates into rhetoric a considerable amount of material on dialectic, including twenty-two dialectical topics derived from Themistius, Boethius, and Peter of Spain. The book ends with an account of the peroration. Book 4 discusses deliberative oratory, demonstrative oratory, the theory of *ductus*, arrangement, memory, and delivery. Book 5, like the last book of the *Rhetorica ad Herennium*, is devoted to style. It begins with a preface in which Trebizond explains that style, unlike invention, can be easily taught to the young. In what follows he treats both the three kinds of style of the Ciceronian tradition, which he regards as a broad view of the subject, and Hermogenes' ideas, or *formae*, treated as a more advanced and subtle analysis of the subject.

Trebizond's *Five Books of Rhetoric* is a classical rhetorical treatise in the technical tradition: it is written in good classical Latin; its examples are classical, drawn from Cicero in the earlier books but expanded to include Greek and Latin poetry and historical writing in the last book; its sources are Cicero and Quintilian, into which are melded Hermogenes, Dionysius, and a few other Greek sources. Trebizond's own contribution is his knowledge of these sources, his ability to organize the material into a consistent whole, and his polished Latin style, which won the confidence of humanistic readers. He himself has no new ideas on rhetoric, but as one who had frequent occasion to speak in public, he has a sound instinct for what is important.

Trebizond's *Five Books of Rhetoric* was widely studied, first in manuscripts and then in a series of printed editions, for about a hundred years after his death. In the treatise *On the Transmission of Knowledge*, published in 1531, Juan Luis Vives cites Trebizond twice (4.3) side by side with classical authorities, the only modern so honored. But soon after, Trebizond began to be neglected: the works of Hermogenes and other Greek rhetoricians had been printed in Greek and translated into Latin and Italian, and teachers and students were now able to go directly to the Greek as well as to Latin sources. Neither Trebizond's nor any other renaissance treatise ever established itself as a permanent competitor, not to say replacement, of Cicero, the *Rhetorica ad Herennium*, and Quintilian, though Erasmus' *De Copia* became a minor classic in its limited field.

Much of renaissance writing on rhetoric after Trebizond is restricted to matters of style, but full-scale Latin rhetorics in the Ciceronian tradition were occasionally written and had some influence. Among them are the *Rhetorica* of Gulielmus Fichet, rector of the University of Paris, dated to 1471, and the *Nova Rhetorica* of Lorenzo Guglielmo Traversagni, an Italian who visited England and completed his work there in 1478.[16] The *Institutiones Rhetoricae* (1521) of Philipp Melanchthon is an adaptation of the full tradition. In the sixteenth century full-scale rhetorics are found in the vernacular languages, including, in English, Leonard Cox's *The Art or Crafte of Rhetoryke* (ca. 1530), which is based on Melanchthon, and *The Arte of Rhetorique* by Thomas Wilson (1553), and in Italian, *La Retorica* in seven books by Bartolomeo Cavalcanti (1558). The tradition in Latin was continued by the work of Cypreano Soarez, a Spanish Jesuit, whose *De Arte Rhetorica Libri Tres ex Aristotele, Cicerone, et Quintiliano Deprompti*, first published around 1560, went through many subsequent editions.

As seen in the career of Trebizond and other humanists, rhetoric had become again a feature of education in the liberal arts analogous to what it had been in antiquity and rivaling grammar and dialetic, which had overshadowed it in the Middle Ages. Trebizond taught rhetoric at various times to young boys, to university students, and occasionally in public lectures to adults, and these three levels can be seen in the teaching of others in his time; but once humanistic excitement about rhetoric began to fade it was in the schools, in company still with grammar and dialectic, and in the introductory stages of university arts courses, that most instruction in rhetoric was given. It must be stressed that students of rhetoric in the Renaissance were largely young boys; even university students at the time were considerably younger than today. Thus a typical rhetorical treatise aimed at being simple, clear, and capable of rote memorization. Philipp Melanchthon's somewhat later *Elementorum Rhetorices Libri II* is a good example. Though written by one of the major intellectuals of the sixteenth century, it is addressed to two adolescents who have been studying dialectic for two years and now need a simple introduction to rhetoric. In the preface Melanchthon expresses the hope that they will go on to study Aristotle's *Rhetoric* at some time in the future or to read the rhetorical works of Cicero and Quintilian. Similarly Juan Luis Vives, the great Spanish humanist, in the preface to *De Ratione Dicendi* speaks about the knowledge the orator ideally should have and the irony of the study of rhetoric by those who are still mere boys. We have already seen that Trebizond thought style, as contrasted with invention, was a subject the young could understand. Some humanists preferred to defer rhetoric to a later stage of study, at least after dialectic, and practice varied in different schools, but in general rhetoric remained antecedent to dialectic.[17]

The elementary nature of most rhetorical studies in the Renaissance contributed to the failure of Aristotle's *Rhetoric* to become a major influence. New translations of the *Rhetoric* into Latin and vernacular languages were repeatedly made;[18] university professors sometimes lectured on the text and occasionally published commentaries, and parts of the *Rhetoric* influenced theories of poetics or politics or moral philosophy, but no true Aristotelian rhetoric was composed in the Renaissance.[19] There were of course some additional reasons for this. The great strength, and easy accessibility, of the Ciceronian tradition is clearly one. Cicero, the *Rhetorica ad Herennium*, and Quintilian remain the ultimate authorities behind simpler handbooks, and even when university professors lectured on rhetorical texts, it was usually one of these works they chose. Further, Plato enjoyed great popularity in renaissance Italy, and opposition to Aristotle was often involved in love of Plato, without, however, leading to the development of a new Platonic rhetoric. The Italian dialogues on rhetoric by Francisco Patrizi (published in 1562) are Platonic and vigorously anti-Aristotelian; they advance something like the views of the *Gorgias* without attempting any development of the concepts of the *Phaedrus*. Sperone Speroni's *Dialogo della retorica* of 1542, though more moderate, had preferred modern expression to ancient rhetoric and asked whether the training of the Latin orator is really a suitable discipline for expression in other languages.[20] The increasing importance of the vernacular languages seemed to many to add point to these inquiries.

Enthusiasm for rhetoric, in the broad sense of the five parts of the classical art, waned in Italy after 1500 except in the case of preaching. Political conditions were now quite unfavorable for deliberative oratory, and the tendency of rhetoric to take on a literary cast reasserted itself, based on its role in elementary education. This was reinforced by a keen interest in developing Italian literature to a level rivaling the classics, which produced an important body of literary criticism that became influential as well in France and England. Aristotle's *Poetics* had been known in the later Middle Ages in a Latin version, but like the *Rhetoric* exercised rather little influence until brought to public attention in a new translation by Gorgio Valla in 1498. Subsequently a series of works examined critical questions and laid down rules for composition in the classical genres, especially epic and drama, in Italian. Among the more important writers are Trissino, Minturno, Castelvetro, and Julius Caesar Scaliger.[21] Meanwhile an interest in rhetoric was developing in northern Europe.

Erasmus

Within the discipline of rhetoric a major figure who contributed his authority to viewing the subject primarily as a literary tradition is Desiderius Erasmus (1469–1536). Born in Rotterdam, he studied in Paris, lived several years in England, paid an extended visit to Italy, and spent the last quarter of his life largely in Basel in Switerland and Freiburg in Germany. He is thus the most international of the humanists, and rightly called himself a "citizen of the world." His life's work was the revival of Christian piety through study of the classics and his greatest achievement was his edition of the Greek New Testament, but he did much for the study of the Fathers of the Church, editing several whose names have appeared in this history—Origen, Chrysostom, Jerome, and Augustine—as well as a variety of classical authors, among them Demosthenes. He was moreover a major writer in his own right: *The Praise of Folly* and the *Colloquies* may rightly claim to be the last truly great imaginative works of Latin literature. Although Erasmus knew thoroughly the whole system of classical rhetoric, the only part of the discipline to which he made a major contribution was style. The basis of his interest was the achievement and teaching of a sound knowledge of Latin as a flexible and subtle tool of communication and education. Here his standards were based on good sense and utility, as can be seen in his influential *Ciceronianus* of 1528.[22] Among other important publications by Erasmus were his works on letter writing, *De Conscribendis Epistulis*, and on preaching, *Ecclesiastes sive de Ratione Concionandi*, which turned back from late medieval preaching theory to classical rhetoric and homiletics.

Most influential was Erasmus' treatise of 1511, *De Duplici Copia Rerum et Verborum*, or *De Utraque Verborum ac Rerum Copia*. It is usually called simply *On Copia*.[23] The word *copia* might be translated "abundance." The major classical source for the concept is the first chapter of the tenth book of Quintilian's *Institutio*, where two kinds are identified, abundance of matter or ideas and abundance of words. Erasmus discusses how to attain this facility in writing Latin prose. Other renaissance writers, including Melanchthon, were also interested in the subject. In Book 1 Erasmus discusses abundance of words, which is secured chiefly by an imaginative use of tropes and figures, for which he cites examples from classical Latin sources, including but not restricted to Cicero, and by the study of formulae, which shows how the same idea can be differently expressed. Some of this is a tour de force, as when Erasmus shows (1.33) one hundred and fifty ways to say (in Latin) "Your letter pleased me very much" and two hundred ways to say "I shall remember you as long as I live." Book 2 deals with abundance of thought, of which ten methods are cited. Erasmus expanded the work in three revisions, and partly as a result the structure of the discussion is confused; but schoolmasters immediately saw the utility of the treatise for teaching composition, and it continued to be reprinted until the early nineteenth century. It was also the subject of commentaries and was translated into vernacular languages.

Erasmus was familiar with the work on dialectic by Agricola, to which we will shortly turn, and thought highly of it. He seems to have approved of Agricola's efforts to transfer invention and arrangement from rhetoric to dialectic or logic, with the resulting limitation of the study of rhetoric to style and delivery, but unlike Agricola he does not treat style as something of secondary interest, left when dialectic is given a new place in education. He is actively interested in style for its own sake, and in this sense belongs here in our discussion and not with the philosophical critics of rhetoric, to whom we may now turn.

Many other texts on style were written in the sixteenth century; among those which had repeated printings and school use over a long period of time and in many countries are the *Tabulae de Schematibus et Tropis* of Petrus Mosellanus, first published about 1529, and the *Epitome Troporum ac Schematum* of the south German schoolmaster Joannes Susenbrotus, from around 1540.[24]

Rhetoric and Dialectic

The strand of philosophical rhetoric in the Renaissance is primarily represented by the efforts of teachers of dialectic to assert the supremacy of their discipline and to limit the field of rhetoric. This movement, which is found chiefly in Germany and France, parallels the reduction of rhetoric to style in Italy and thus leads to similar results, but for entirely different reasons. It is somewhat reminiscent of Plato's criticism of rhetoric, to which some renaissance dialecticians refer, but is primarily concerned with method and with logical validity, not with philosophical truth. Its formulators, however, were doctrinaire classicists who found their concepts and the authorities for rearrangement of the system of teaching dialectic and rhetoric in classical sources and who represented their teachings as a return to the classics after the scholasticism of the later Middle Ages.

In Italy in the second quarter of the fifteenth century there arose an apparent interest in restating the relationship of dialectic and rhetoric on the part of those whose primary interest was in rhetoric. As we have seen, rhetoric's place in education in the verbal arts was limited throughout the Middle Ages. In general, it fell between the two more important arts of grammar and dialectic, where Cassiodorus had put it. In contrast, interest in rhetoric greatly increased in Italy in the fourteenth and fifteenth centuries and seemed to demand a new place in the scheme of things. Trebizond's solution to this problem was both to produce a simple, introductory work on dialectics, which was to be preliminary to serious study of rhetoric, and also to include a book on argumentation (Book 3) in his large treatise on rhetoric. He did not, however, attempt to deny the existence of scientific logic as discussed by Aristotle in the *Analytics*. The humanist Giovanni Tortelli seems also to have sought to redefine the relationship of dialectic and rhetoric about this time,[25] but the most extreme view is that of the distinguished humanist Lorenzo Valla (1407 1457).

Valla was a rival of Trebizond, overshadowed him in popularity as a teacher of rhetoric in Rome, and like him served the pope as secretary.[26] He did major scholarly work on the text of Livy and the New Testament, translated Thucydides into Latin, and wrote a series of studies called the *Elegantiae Latini Sermonis*, perhaps the most influential work of its time rediscovering the standards of classical Latinity. Valla was the most enthusiastic admirer of Quintilian to be found in the Renaissance and was a critic of Aristotelianism and scholasticism. In addition to his philological works he wrote on philosophy and religion, and his treatise entitled *Dialecticae Disputationes contra Aris-*

totelicos was published about 1438, soon after Trebizond's *Isagoge*. (Publication of course still meant circulation in manuscript form, since printing was not to be introduced for another generation.) In this work Valla takes the view of demonstration found in Quintilian (5.10) and absorbs dialectic entirely into the discipline of rhetoric: "What else is dialectic than a species of confirmation and refutation? These are parts of invention; invention is one of the five parts of rhetoric. Logic is the use of the syllogism. Does not the orator use the same? Certainly he does, and not only that, but also the enthymeme and the epicheireme, in addition to the induction. . . ."[27]

Rudolph Agricola

The next stage in this movement to redefine the relationship of dialectic and rhetoric is the work of the Dutch scholar Roelof Huusman, usually known by the Latin version of his name, Rudolphus Agricola (1444–1485).[28] After studies in Erfurt, Louvain, Cologne, and Paris he went to Italy about 1468 to study law, but became converted to the way of life of an Italian humanist, with its emphasis on study of the classics. While still in Italy he began *De Inventione Dialectica*, in three books, which was completed on his return to Germany about 1479. Next to Erasmus, Agricola is the leading link between Italy and the intellectual life of northern Europe. In addition to his influential work on dialectic, Agricola translated the *Progymnasmata* of Aphthonius into Latin. We saw in chapter 8 that this was the major schoolbook of rhetorical composition for centuries in Byzantium. Agricola did for Aphthonius what Trebizond did for Hermogenes, and for the next two hundred years the schoolboys of western Europe found themselves studying Agricola's text.[29]

De Dialectica Inventione opens with a short prologue in which Agricola makes immediately clear that rhetoric, which he does not mention by name but which is represented by the Ciceronian "duties of the orator," is in his view a subordinate part of dialectic.[30] The first and proper objective of speech is to teach. Teaching involves exposition and argumentation, which involves probable reasoning from something that is well known to something that is less well known. In so doing it is most useful to understand the seats of arguments, which men call *loci*, or places. Chapter 2 then proceeds to define a *locus* and show how one is used in argument. "This part of the subject, which involves thinking out the middle term or argument, is what dialecticians call invention; there is another part which is called judging [*iudicandi*]," or judgment (*iudicium*), whose function is to evaluate all forms of syllogism used in invention and to reject those which are not in accord with reality. In the following chapters of Book 1 Agricola considers the loci discussed by Aristotle, Cicero, and Themistius (as known from Boethius) and describes his own list of twenty-four: definition, genus, species, property, whole, part, etc. There is considerable similarity in lists of loci in classical and classicizing writers, but no agreed-upon canon. Although Agricola's three books are concerned only with invention, not with judgment, he returns to the matter of judgment in the proemium to the second book and indicates that the content is drawn from Aristotle, Cicero (especially *Topica* 6), and Quintilian (3.3.5).

Book 2 is devoted to dialectic in a broader sense and the place of rhetorical invention in it. The end of dialectic is to speak with probability about the subject proposed. To move and to delight are subordinated to this. The material of dialectic is the question, and its divisions are discussed. Among them is stasis theory. The instrument of dialectic is speech, and Agricola considers the parts of an oration, for which he prefers a four-part division: exordium, narration, confirmation, and peroration. All of this material can be found in some form in classical sources, and Agricola presents it with liberal illustration from Cicero and other classical models.

The third and shortest book is given over to *affectus*, that by which the mind is impelled to seek or avoid something. It deals with the emotions and with what in a more traditional ordering would have been found in rhetorical discussions of arrangement and some parts of style, including amplification or copia, and practice. Agricola does not discuss the ornaments of style, which are thus left to be the subject of a much more limited art of rhetoric.

Agricola's work was very influential. Erasmus thought highly of him and approved his views, though as discussed earlier it seems likely that Erasmus' own contributions to rhetoric are more a part of the literary tradition to be found in Italy. Another who followed Agricola's treatment of dialectic and rhetoric was Philipp Melanchthon (1497–1560), the Protestant leader and friend of Luther. His popular *Elementorum Rhetorices Libri II* (1546), already mentioned, uses Agricola's division of dialectic and rhetoric; his earlier *Institutiones Rhetoricae* treats judgment and arrangement as part of rhetoric and shows a less strong influence of Agricola. Melanchthon was very influential in the German schools and beyond, and his writings on rhetoric deserve to be made more easily available to modern students.[31]

Another writer on rhetoric influenced by Agricola is Juan Luis Vives (1492–1540). Born in Spain, he studied in Paris, taught at Louvain, served as a tutor to the future Queen Mary of England, and died in Bruges. His treatise *De Corruptis Artibus*, or *On the Corruption of the Arts* (1531), which attacks scholasticism and the teaching in the universities of the time, includes a book on rhetoric (Book 4), which rejects invention. He also wrote a work on rhetoric in three books, *De Ratione Dicendi* (1532): Book 1 is devoted to words, taken alone or in composition; Book 2 to style and ornament; and Book 3 to rhetorical exercises. The chapter on rhetoric (4.3) in his important treatise *De Tradendis Disciplinis*, or *On the Transmission of Knowledge* (1531), has similarities with the larger work. This latter treatise has been translated into English and together with Erasmus' *On Copia* and *Ciceronianus* furnishes perhaps the best introduction to Renaissance rhetoric now available to the nonspecialist modern student.[32] In short compass Vives brings out well the importance assigned to rhetoric, the enormous authority of classical writers on the subject, (chiefly the Romans, but also the Greeks as introduced by Trebizond), and the moral and philosophical issues involving rhetoric as seen at the time; he also gives a picture of rhetorical exercises in declamation as taken over by renaissance schools from the Romans. The tendency to view rhetoric as style is very clear, and this is emphasized in his next chapter, which is devoted to imitation. Quintilian and Rudolph Agricola are cited as models for imitation in questions of language or style.

Peter Ramus

Most influential of the followers of Agricola is Peter Ramus (1515–1572). Like Agricola and most other renaissance rhetoricians, Ramus lectured and wrote in Latin and thus is usually known by the Latin version of his name, Petrus Ramus.[33] In his native French, and in many American library catalogues, he is Pierre de La Ramée. He spent most of his life in Paris, where he became head of the Collège de Presles and professor of eloquence and philosophy on royal appointment at the Collège de France. As such it seems possible that he was the only person ever to hold a chair of rhetoric in Paris, which would be ironic in that much of his professional effort went into a method of study and classification of the arts which increased the importance of dialectic, taking up where Agricola had left it, and greatly decreased the importance of rhetoric. His dialectic, like Agricola's, is divided into invention and judgment. The former of these is based on the theory of loci. The latter includes *dispositio*, or arrangement, traditionally the second part of rhetoric, and apparently absorbs memory also, though that part of rhetoric is largely abandoned.

In his *Institutiones Dialecticae* of 1543 Ramus says that a complementary work on rhetoric will be provided by Omer Talon.[34] Talon, or in Latin Talaeus (ca. 1510–1562), was a teacher in colleges of Paris and closely associated with Ramus for most of his life. In 1545 he published his *Institutiones Oratoriae* under his own name, but was clearly dependent on Ramist principles. The title is derived from Quintilian, who probably exercised more influence on Ramist rhetoric than any other authority, but it is rather ironic in that Quintilian's meaning is the education of an "orator," and neither Ramus nor Talon can be said to have been seriously interested in training an orator. They wanted to train young boys to write Latin with tropes and figures in the most efficient method they could find. Yet Ramus himself was apparently famous as a colorful and eloquent lecturer.

In addition to the version of 1545 there is a *Rhetorica* in one book of 1548, a *Rhetorica* in two books of 1562, and further editions of 1567 and 1569, after Talon's death.[35] Talon's name is dropped and Ramus' part in the work increases in each edition, parallel to the development of his work on dialectic. He seems first to have tried to divide up the subject in accordance with classical categories which can be found in Quintilian, such as nature, art, and practice, but in the edition of 1548 and later editions rhetoric is divided, like other arts in Ramus' method, into two parts—*elocutio*, or style, and *pronuntiatio*, or delivery—and each of these in turn is divided into two parts: *elocutio* into tropes and figures (the latter itself divided into figures of diction and figures of thought), and *pronuntiatio* into voice and gesture. These topics are of course to be found in Quintilian, though much else there is omitted, including the virtues of style, *sententiae*, amplification, and copia. Ramus' definition of rhetoric, *doctrina bene dicendi*, is an adaptation of Quintilian's *scientia bene dicendi*, but speaking (or writing) well in Ramus means far less than in Quintilian.

Ramus, Talon, and other teachers taught rhetoric to boys at about the age of junior high school students today; clarity, simplicity, and a content which could be easily memorized were desirable features in such teaching. It would have been a logical application of Ramus' theory for students to study dialectic first and then learn rhetoric, putting as it were a cap of eloquence upon their logical dress, but he and most of his successors taught rhetoric before dialectic. It thus remained, what it often had been in the Middle Ages, an adjunct to grammar.

The specific concepts, definitions, and materials of rhetoric as taught by Ramus, and to a considerable extent those of dialectic as well, are to be found in classical authorities. Ramist rhetorical works are written in good classical Latin, the examples they cite are drawn from classical models, and the objective is to teach how to write eloquent Latin. In this sense Ramist rhetoric is firmly in the classical tradition. That was not to be fundamentally challenged until the next century. Perceptive critics of Ramus and his followers, however, have noted several features of Ramism which negate or even vitiate the principles on which classical rhetoric is based. Classical rhetoric is essentially civic and essentially oral; Ramism is neither. The attempt of the Italian humanists to recreate a civic rhetoric of public address which would, among other things, be useful in courts and assemblies, was of no interest to Ramus. For all his classicizing, what he describes is an elementary course in rhetoric which is a continuation of the limited subject taught in the trivium of the Middle Ages. *Pronuntiatio* in theory remains a part of his system, but he has little to say about it and his successors usually omitted it. More fundamentally, his whole way of looking at dialectic and rhetoric is not in terms of speech and debate, but in terms of visual images.

The appeal of Ramism was great and his rhetoric is a powerful force throughout the seventeenth century in France, England, and Puritan America. Ramus became a Protestant near the end of his life and was killed in the Saint Bartholomew's Day Massacre, thus becoming elevated to the stature of a Protestant saint, but perhaps more important, his emphasis on dialectic was consistent with Puritan sentiments about preaching and plain thinking. Many editions of Ramus' works were published, and other rhetorics were written in Latin or vernacular languages adapting his views. In England these include Gabriel Harvey's *Rhetor* and *Ciceronianus* of 1584,[36] Abraham Fraunce's *Arcadian Rhetorike* of 1588, and Charles Butler's *Rhetoricae Libri Duo* of 1598, which was reprinted throughout the seventeenth century.[37] The appeal of Ramism was largely its "neatness"; the objection to it was its superficiality and the continued strength of the Ciceronian tradition which Ramus had only somewhat rearranged. Thus it is not surprising that a reassertion of the fuller tradition of classical rhetoric soon emerged.

Cicero's work continued to be taught and studied in the universities, thus reinforcing the tradition; for example, the great Dutch classical scholar Gerhard John Vossius produced his *Commentaria Rhetorica*, six books on Ciceronian rhetoric, in 1605 and also wrote three popular works on rhetoric. Furthermore, especially in England, the practical opportunities for persuasive oratory began to increase in public life and in the Church. In 1629 the same Charles Butler just mentioned, without totally abandoning the Ramist principles of thirty years before, published *Oratoriae Libri Duo*, which includes discussion of all five traditional parts of rhetoric, the "duties of the orator," and the classical oration in six parts, and resurgent Ciceronianism can be seen on the continent about the same time in the *Orator Extemporaneus* of the Jesuit Michael Radau. Jesuit schools did much to keep alive the discipline of classical rhetoric for centuries. In England and America a major Ciceronian rhetoric of the seventeenth century is the *Index Rhetoricus* of Thomas Farnaby, published in 1625 and in many later editions. Preaching too was brought into this movement, in works such as the *Sacred Eloquence* of John Prideaux (1659). Throughout the period the teaching of rhetoric built on formulae and the practice of declamation remained vigorous in the schools. Examples include Ortensio Landi's *Paradossi* of 1543, adapted into English by Anthony Mundy in *The Defense of Contraries* (1593), and the work of Le Sylvain of 1581, adapted in Lazarus Piot's *The Orator* of 1596.[38]

The technical tradition of the schools, and especially that part of it devoted to style, was increasingly applied to the national languages of Europe. The history of this expression in the vernacular literatures, especially in English, has been well told by a number of modern scholars.[39] It is an important subject for the understanding of the art of almost all great writers from the sixteenth to the eighteenth centuries, not the least that of Shakespeare, whose works are in a very concrete way perhaps the greatest achievements of classical rhetoric. From his early education Shakespeare was not only fully conscious of the rules and conventions of rhetoric, to which he sometimes directly alludes or which he sometimes satirizes, but he fully exploits them in his composition for the highest artistic purposes.[40] Until the Romantic movement, poetry was not a matter of free expression but an application and development of the thought of the poet within the arts of grammar, rhetoric, and dialectic, learned at a tender age and natural to all subsequent expression.

Ciceronian and Baroque Prose

Classical rhetoric also bequeathed an important legacy to the modern world in the development of prose style. This movement runs parallel to, and thus may be viewed as a microcosm of, the wider impact of classical rhetoric from the fourteenth to the seventeenth century.

Late medieval Latin prose, according to the late Morris Croll, shows two contrasting styles.[41] One of these, the product of the teaching of rhetoric in the trivium, is characterized by its use of classical figures of speech, but is not strongly classical otherwise in composition and even less so in diction. This style strongly influenced preaching and can also be found in saints' lives, devotional treatises, and speeches in chronicles. It was strongest in France and England and represents the tradition and survival of medieval rhetoric, but it can be seen in elementary instruction in rhetoric throughout the Renaissance. This tradition most influenced poetry in the vernacular languages, and also some forms of prose, such as the so-called euphuism of John Lyly in English or the similar style of Antonio de Guevara in Spanish in the late sixteenth century.

The other late medieval Latin style is the style of the chanceries and law schools, associated with dictamen. In this tradition the tropes and figures are neglected, being thought too poetic and artificial, but as we have seen, other aspects of rhetoric, such as the structure of the oration, continue to have a strong influence.

The humanists, taken as a whole, reacted against both these late medieval Latin styles as inelegant and sought to bring spoken and written Latin back to a classical standard of eloquence as an international medium of communication.[42] They varied among themselves, however, in the extent to which they insisted on Cicero as the touchstone. Humanists of the early fifteenth century, including Leonardo Bruni, Poggio Bracciolini, George Trebizond, Guarino of Verona, and Lorenzo Valla, show the classicizing movement without establishing Cicero as the single model of correctness. The late fifteenth and early sixteenth centuries are the period of the most doctrinaire Ciceronianists, of whom Pietro Bembo and his student Christopher Longolius are probably the best examples. They sought to use no Latin word which could not be found in Cicero, as well as to imitate his composition. Mario Nizzoli (or Nizolius) published his *Lexicon Ciceronianum* in 1585, which set a new and definite standard of Ciceronian Latinity.

There were numerous reactions against this extreme Ciceronianism in style. Erasmus' *Ciceronianus* of 1523 is the most famous statement of classic, but flexible Latin style. Erasmus drew his vocabulary from a wide variety of ancient authors and he sought to keep Latin a vigorous, living, useful tongue. J. C. Scaliger and others attacked Erasmus, but his views had great influence, and in the matter of Latin style he might be said to occupy a position parallel to that of Agricola in the question of the relationship of rhetoric and dialectic: classical but not Ciceronian.

A more general reaction against the Ciceronian prose style, parallel to Ramus' stronger reaction against the full form of classical rhetoric, then appears in the mid–sixteenth century. The crucial figure in this development is apparently Justus Lipsius (1547–1606). He was strongly attracted to the Latin prose writers of the early empire, who were in their own age anti-Ciceronians. The clipped, epigrammatic, but simple Latin of Seneca is one such model; the more complex, sometimes pregnantly obscure style of Tacitus is another. These and other Latin writers, including Sallust, became the inspiration first of anti-Ciceronian Latin prose of the late sixteenth and seventeenth centuries, which then extended, just as Ramism did, from Latin over into the Baroque prose of the vernacular languages, of which the works of Montaigne in French and Francis Bacon in English are important examples.[43] The Ciceronian style, however, like Ciceronian dialectic and rhetoric, continued to have admirers and eventually blossomed forth again in the neoclassicism of the later seventeenth and the eighteenth centuries.

The application of theories of rhetoric outside of the field of oral expression was not limited to literature. Ancient rhetoricians had noted an analogy between rhetoric and painting, and renaissance art theorists exploited the view. Among them are Paolo Pini, author of *Dialogo di pittura* (1548), Lodovico Dolce in his *Dialogo della pittura* (1557), and Franciscus Junius in *Painting of the Ancients* (1638). Junius was the brother-in-law of the classicist and rhetorician Vossius, noted above, and Vossius also wrote a discussion on painting in terms of rhetoric which constitutes part of a larger treatise, *De Artium et Scientiarum Natura ac Constitutione*, not published until 1697.

The analogy between rhetoric and music was not much discussed in antiquity, though Quintilian devoted a chapter to music (1.10) in terms of ethos and pathos. The Renaissance took up the matter and elaborated it. Nicola Vicentino in 1555 compared the musician to the orator who speaks loudly or softly, slowly or quickly, to move the souls of his audience. In Germany Joachim Burmeister produced an introduction to musical composition; the second edition of 1601, under the title *Musica Autoschediastike*, eulogizes music as a higher form of oratory. In 1606 he expanded this in his *Musica Poetica*, which makes use of rhetorical divisions and identifies a series of musical figures based on the figures of speech studied in schools. Other writers of the sixteenth century continued this approach to music as secondary rhetoric.[44]

Francis Bacon

Far more important than any of these writers, however, both in terms of reaction against Ramism and in the profundity of his thought, is Francis Bacon (1565–1621), lord chancellor of England and the herald of the new age of science.[45] Bacon was a distinguished orator in the House of Commons and the lawcourts, a fact which gave him an understanding of primary rhetoric unknown to most of the writers we have discussed. Ben Jonson said of him that "He commanded where he spoke, and had his judges angry and pleased at his devotion. No man had their affections more in his power. The fear of every man that heard him was lest he should make an end."[46] He served in the House of Commons at a time when real political debates on important issues produced major orations for the first time in English, and thus in modern, history. The subjects included the religious policy of the court, the privileges of the House of Commons, and the control of finance. Primary rhetoric in general and deliberative oratory in particular are always closely linked to each other, and in Bacon's speeches they reappear together after sixteen hundred years of quiescence.

Bacon discusses aspects of rhetoric in several of his works, but our brief account can be limited to *The Advancement of Learning* of 1605 and its expanded Latin translation of 1623, *De Dignitate et Augmentis Scientiarum.*[47] *The Advancement of Learning* is an ambitious and imaginative attempt to restructure human knowledge on rational principles useful for the modern world with its emerging new sense of science. There are many similarities to Aristotle's theory of knowledge in this structure, but a restatement was badly needed for several reasons. One is that Aristotle's own accounts, as we saw in his remarks about the relationship of rhetoric to dialectic, were not entirely clear; they reflect different stages in his thinking and are not worked out in detail. A second reason is that Aristotle's authority had been somewhat weakened by being associated with scholasticism in the popular mind of the Renaissance, for it shared with scholasticism a reputation of being pedantic and unrealistic. A third is that the issues had been somewhat confused by Ramism and its facile solution of the problem of rhetoric and dialectic. Although the one reference to Ramus by name in *The Advancement of Learning* (2.17.12) is complimentary, Bacon clearly criticizes Ramism in his discussion of method (2.17.1) as "weakly inquired," and in fact, he provided a much more satisfactory answer to Ramus than did those who simply reverted to the Ciceronian tradition in the seventeenth century.

Bacon divided human learning into three parts: history, which is based on memory; poetry, based on imagination; and philosophy, based on reason. He takes these up in turn. Philosophy is given the most attention and is divided into divine, natural, and human. Human philosophy is either segregate, dealing with men as individuals, or congregate, dealing with men in social groups. The study of men as individuals involves either the body (medicine, cosmetics, athletics, or sensual arts) or the mind. Bacon's approach to the mind is functional, and here he distinguishes intellectual functions and moral functions. The intellectual functions include four arts: invention, judgment, custody (either by writing or memory), and tradition or transmission. The art of tradition (from Latin *tradere*, "to hand over") is broken down into three parts: study of the organ of transmission, which is speech and grammar; study of the method of transmission, which is logic; and study of the illustration of transmission, which is rhetoric, discussed in the eighteenth chapter of Book 2. Rhetoric is "a science excellent and excellently well laboured." Though in the abstract inferior to wisdom, as God said to Moses in Exodus 4:16 (cited above in chapter 7), it is "more mighty," for which the authority of Solomon in Proverbs 16:21 is cited. Bacon continues:

> Elequence prevaileth in an active life. And as to the labouring of it, the emulation of Aristotle with the rhetoricians of his time, and the experience of Cicero had made them in their works of rhetorics exceed themselves. Again, the excellency of examples of eloquence in the orations of Demosthenes and Cicero, added to the perfection of the precepts of eloquence, hath doubled the progression in this art; and therefore the deficiencies which I shall note will rather be in some collections, which may as hand-maids attend the art, than in the rules or use of the art itself. (2.18.1)

We may pause at this point to stress major features of what Bacon has said. Rhetoric is given a secure place of its own in the structure of knowledge, equal in importance to logic, because of its great practical utility. Nothing is said here about style, which is not central to rhetoric in Bacon's scheme. The fundamental work on the discipline is attributed to classical authorities, especially to Aristotle; Cicero contributes "experience," and the art is best illustrated by the achievements of Demosthenes and Cicero, that is, by political oratory, whether deliberative or judicial. Throughout the work, not just in the discussion of rhetoric, Bacon goes directly to classical sources and most of his illustrations are classical, though there are occasional contemporary references. He gives special weight to the Greek sources as more primary, and in Book 1 (2.9) had referred to Cicero as "the best, or second orator," correcting himself at the thought of Demosthenes. Bacon believes his contribution to rhetoric will be to fill in "deficiencies," that is, "lacks," not errors, in the fundamental system of Greek rhetoric, which remains valid.

Bacon then proceeds to define "the duty and office of rhetoric" as "to apply reason to imagination for the better moving of the will" (2.18.2).[48] This definition is significant in several ways. It focuses, as had Plato and Aristotle, on the *function* of rhetoric, and thus on the primary art, not on its secondary ornamentation. It makes clear, as we stated in chapter 1, that the element of *purpose* is essential to rhetoric. It introduces the concept of imagination as rhetorically important. Antecedents can be found in Plato and are clearly illustrated by Socrates' second speech in the *Phaedrus*, but they were not taken up by Aristotle. Something similar can be found in Quintilian's insistence (6.2.29–36) on the orator's use of *visiones* in visualizing the scenes he describes and involving himself personally in his subject, and in "Longinus'" account of the sublime, which was to become an important document in neoclassical rhetoric and criticism. Imagination thus reenters rhetoric. It brings with it emphasis on the role of the orator, and in Bacon's definition great emphasis also on the role of the audience. The orator's imagination moves the will of his audience. Not since Plato's requirement that the orator know the souls of his hearers and how to move them, an idea taken up in Aristotle's concept of ethos and pathos but diluted by Cicero and his successors, has the audience been an important factor in rhetoric. It was to remain so in neoclassical rhetoric.

Bacon goes on to explain that the very factors which disturb the judgment of reason—sophism, impression, and affection—are the very factors which are equally used "to establish and advance it": "The end of rhetoric is to fill the imagination to second reason, and not to oppress it" (2.18.2). This is reminiscent of Aristotle's remarks in Book 1, chapter 1, of the *Rhetoric* about why the possibility of the abuse of rhetoric is not an argument against its legitimate use. Bacon then continues with a brief criticism of Plato's objections to rhetoric in the *Gorgias* and quotes with approval an observation from the *Phaedrus*, showing that these works are in his mind as he writes. Rhetoric can no more be charged with making the worse seem the better cause than can dialectic. Aristotle was right in placing rhetoric between logic on the one hand and ethics and politics on the other, "for the proofs and demonstrations of logic are towards all men indifferent and the same; but the proofs and persuasions of rhetoric ought to differ according to the audience" (2.18.5). As Plato had demanded, "if a man should speak of the same thing to several persons, he should speak to them all respectively and several ways," a matter Bacon recommends "to better inquiry."

Bacon makes no reference to the five parts of Ciceronian rhetoric or to other categories as taught in the schools. They are of course secondary to the essence of philosophical rhetoric. In the last part of chapter 18, greatly expanded in *De Augmentis Scientiarum* (6.3), he considers the specific "deficiencies" of Aristotle. These are slightly disappointing at first sight, but their utility to a practicing orator like Bacon was considerable, and they are elaborations of categories described by Aristotle or Cicero.[49] The first are the "colours of good and evil, both simple and comparative, which are as the sophisms of rhetoric." An example of a comparative sophism is "What men praise and celebrate is good; what they criticize and reprehend is bad." This truism can be refuted because, Bacon says, men may praise the bad out of ignorance, bad faith, zeal for a cause, or weakness of character. Second are "antitheta," or arguments for or against something, such as the classic conflict between the letter and the intent of a law. The Latin edition details forty-seven such arguments. Third are commonplaces to be used within a speech in preface, conclusion, digression, transition, or excuse. Bacon says they are of special ornament and effect, but in fact they are useful to the extempore orator in maintaining the flow and structure of his speech. These devices take the student of classical rhetoric back to the early days of the sophists, to the model arguments of Antiphon, and to the collection of proemia made by Demosthenes.

Bacon's work exercised some specific influence on rhetorical theory during the next two hundred years,[60] but his general influence on later thinkers is considerably more important than any of his specified doctrines. For the history of classical rhetoric he represents the completion of the recovery of the strand of philosophical rhetoric, the slenderest thread since antiquity, and a sign of a new rhetorical maturity in an age of effective oratory.

Chapter II
Neoclassical Rhetoric

In the seventeenth and eighteenth centuries rhetoric experienced a remarkable development which was both classical and nonclassical, both a return to a more profound understanding of the original strands of classical rhetoric as they existed in Greece, and a more radical departure from the philosophical assumptions of classical rhetoric than anything previously encountered. This development is more often viewed, and quite properly, in terms of the impact of the new science, especially the new logic of Descartes and Pascal in France and of Locke and the British Empiricists in England, upon the understanding and exposition of rhetoric. Through the work of the Port-Royalists, the schools of France, Britain, and America were directly affected in the teaching of logic, but new conceptions of rhetoric only slowly influenced teaching at more elementary levels, which clung to the technical Ciceronian tradition or to the lists of tropes and figures of literary rhetoric.

It is also possible, however, to approach some new developments in terms of the neoclassical movement which flourished in France in the reign of Louis XIV (1643–1715) and reached England after the restoration of Charles II in 1660. This approach is appropriate in a study of the tradition of classical rhetoric, for the history of rhetoric in those years is analogous to a renewed classicism in literature evident in the seventeenth and early eighteenth centuries and to the neoclassical movement in architecture, sculpture, and painting of the eighteenth century.

Neoclassicism in all these forms represents a turn from late renaissance mannerism and the baroque style to a more profound, and more historically accurate, standard of classical taste, seen primarily in Greek rather than in Roman models. Knowledge of Greek, recovered by the humanists of the fourteenth and fifteenth centuries, first produced Latin translations of Greek works, but in the sixteenth and seventeenth centuries Italian, French, and English translations of literary merit became popular, and awareness of the aesthetic superiority and greater originality of Greek forms was widely diffused. This new knowledge of the Greek classics made possible the classicizing literature of the next two centuries, seen in France, for example, in the tragedies of Corneille and Racine, which are close to Greek models in contrast to Shakespeare's earlier reliance on the Roman tradition. Similarly, the first-hand knowledge of Greek architecture by travelers to Greece and the Levant in the early eighteenth century made possible a much purer use of classical forms by the architects of the following century.

The classicism of the Renaissance had been largely manifested in Latin, and one of its aims was the restoration of a purer Latinity. The classicism of the seventeenth century was pursued in the interests of raising the levels of the vernacular languages to equal Greek or Latin, just as neoclassicism in architecture was applied to domestic buildings and uses materials of western Europe foreign to classical construction. In the case of rhetoric, neoclassicism can be seen in the preference among intellectual leaders for Plato and Demosthenes over Cicero and Quintilian, already emerging in Bacon, in a new role for primary rhetoric in French and English oratory, and in the writing of rhetorical treatises in French and English concerned with the eloquence of those tongues. Bacon's treatise *De Dignitate et Augmentis Scientiarum* is the last major work to discuss rhetoric in Latin, though Latin continued to have some use in school texts, or in dedicatory epistles, academic lectures, or reference works to the end of the eighteenth century. Ernesti's dictionaries of technical terms, published in Leipzig in 1795 and 1797 and still in some use today, are at the end of this stream.[1]

Seventeenth-century classicism received official sponsorship from the French Academy, established in 1635. The goals of the Academy from the start included the publication of authoritative works on French language, rhetoric, and poetics.[2] The most essential part of the program, the *Dictionary*, finally appeared in 1694. Oliver Patru, who became a member of the Academy in 1640, was apparently expected to produce the *Rhetoric* and was occasionally referred to as "the French Quintilian," but he never got beyond an informal prospectus. Two treatises did eventually appear under the title *La Rhétorique française*, one by René Bary in 1659 and one by sieur Le Gras in 1671, and although both seek to take a broad view of the subject and to adapt it to the French language and the circumstances of seventeenth-century life —by the division of oratory, for example, into the two contemporary forms of preaching and judicial oratory—neither is an imaginative and creative expression of the new classicism. More influential were two treatises of René Rapin of 1684, which, however, represent again the tendency of *letteraturizzazione* in their development of the concept of *belles lettres* and which cling to the Latin tradition.[3]

During these same fifty years, however, important developments were taking place in logic which do not replicate, but are analogous to, the criticism of rhetoric voiced by Socrates and Plato in Greece. The starting point of these criticisms is the *Discourse on Method* of René Descartes (published 1637) and their most specific manifestation is the *Port-Royal Logic* of 1662, largely the work of Antoine Arnauld.[4] A third important contributor to the same development was Pascal, in the work called *De l'esprit géométrique* but known also as *L'Art de persuader* (1664).[5] The effect of these works was to challenge traditional rhetoric, whether Ciceronian or French. Put in an extreme form, the new logic claimed that the only sound method of inquiry is that of geometry, proceeding from self-evident axioms to universally accepted conclusions. The topics of dialectic and rhetoric are useless in discovering the truth or in demonstrating it, and the five traditional parts of rhetoric are a form of deception. The role of an orator seeking to dominate communication is inappropriate, and to stir the emotions of an audience is unacceptable. The positive side of the new logic was to establish a new method of communication needed for the emergence of modern science; its negative side was its denial, or its ignorance, of psychological realities in politics, law, and religion. One result, however, was to restore the question of truth, central to the strand of philosophical rhetoric, to serious discussions of rhetoric, including the rhetoric of preaching.

Fénelon

It is against this background, and taking into account neoclassical sympathy with things Greek, that one should read the greatest work on classical rhetoric written in French and the finest statement of the philosophical strand of the tradition since antiquity. This work is a literary dialogue in three books, written in the late 1670s (but published posthumously in 1718) by François de Salignac de la Mothe Fénelon (1651–1715): *Dialogues sur l'éloquence en général et celle de la chaire en particulier*.[6] As the title suggests, Fénelon treats rhetoric in general but gives particular attention to the eloquence of the pulpit (*la chaire*). Since he was Archbishop of Cambrai, he had a special interest in the subject, but preaching was the single most important oratorical form in seventeenth-century France; judicial oratory was a poor second in importance and deliberative oratory hardly existed. Ecclesiastical orators like Saurin, Bourdaloue, Massilon, and Bossuet achieved enormous popularity.[7]

In this fashion for elegant preaching Fénelon saw dangers analogous to those Plato had seen in the speeches of the sophists, and his *Dialogues* are a neoclassical version of the *Phaedrus*, both in the dramatic situation and in much of the contents. The interlocutors are labelled A, B, and C.[8] A corresponds to Socrates and states the views of Fénelon himself; he is knowledgeable and authoritative, but not much individualized. B is a young man passionately interested in preaching and like Phaedrus easily taken in by meretricious adornment, but fundamentally sensible. C plays only a small role in the first two books, which are chiefly devoted to rhetoric at large, but pushes A hard in the third dialogue to achieve an understanding of early Christian rhetoric and its significance for the modern preacher. Here he emerges as a worthy interlocutor of A. The work has elegance and unity, and well brings out the major questions about rhetoric in general and Christian rhetoric in particular, though it lacks the charm of an original Platonic dialogue. While written in French and expressly devoted to the question of French rhetoric, it is thoroughly classical: the sources to which A and C turn are primarily Plato, Aristotle, and Augustine. The models of noble eloquence cited are Demosthenes, Cicero, and other Greeks and Romans, the writers of the Bible, and the Fathers of the Church. Vitiated contemporary sophist-preachers are not named, but Isocrates is repeatedly taken as the classic model of their faults. References to recent or contemporary discussions are disguised or indirect, as when A seems to use Cicero and Augustine against Ramist rhetoric (Book 2; Howell, p. 92), but there is one conspicuous exception: Boileau's recent translation of "Longinus" is spoken of favorably, and the admiration for "Longinus" throughout the work is clearly derived from Boileau. Moreover, Boileau's *Art of Poetry* is also highly praised. Boileau "is a man who well knows not only the basis of poetry, but also the solid goal toward which philosophy, the superior of the arts, should guide the poet" (Book 1; p. 71). To this we will return.

Rhetoric as understood by Fénelon is primary rhetoric: it is spoken and persuasive; focus is on function, on the effect on the audience. "Why should you speak," says A, "if not to persuade, to instruct, and to proceed in such fashion that the listener remembers what you say?" (p. 58). B thinks that simple persuasion is all right for the common people, but that "gentlemen have more refined ears" (p. 61). A admits that there are two goals of speaking, to persuade and to please, reminiscent of Horace's statement of the goal of poetry, to teach and to charm. "But," says A, when they seek to please, they have another, a more distant, aim, which is nevertheless the principal one. The good man seeks to please only that he may urge justice and the other virtues by making them attractive. He who seeks his own interest, his reputation, his fortune, dreams of pleasing only that he may gain the bow and esteem of men able to satisfy his greed or his ambition. Thus, even his case can be reduced like that of the good man to persuasion as the single aim which a speaker has; for the self-interested man wishes to please in order to flatter, and he flatters in order to inculcate that which suits his interest. (pp. 61–62)

Fénelon's concept of the poet and the orator is very close to that of Plato. He is to lead a simple life, to be free of passion and self-interest. The people give him honor and accept him as an authority:

In the dialogue where he makes Socrates speak with Phaedrus, Plato shows that the great defect of the rhetoricians is that they strive for the art of persuasion before they understand, by the principles of philosophy, what are the things which they ought to seek to convince men of. . . . The speaker will be obliged to know what man is, what is his destiny, what are his true interests; of what he is made, that is to say, body and soul; what is the true way to make him happy; what are his passions, what excesses they may have, how they may be regulated, how they may be usefully aroused in order to make him live in peace and to keep society together. . . . Thus does Plato show that the role of true orator belongs only to the philosopher. It is with this in mind that we must interpret everything he says in the *Gorgias* against the rhetoricians; that is to say, against the kind of person who devises his own art of speech and persuasion, without putting himself to any trouble to know in terms of principles what one ought to seek to convince men of. . . . Cicero has virtually said the same things. (pp. 82–83)

The definition is reminiscent of Bacon's. It is on this note that the dialogue of the first day ends. A has laid the foundation for an identification of Plato's philosophical orator with the Christian preacher of Augustine.

In Book 2 this identification is carried forward. A claims (p. 92) that "all eloquence can be reduced to proving, to portraying, and to striking. Every brilliant thought which does not drive towards one of these three things is only a conceit." Fénelon rejects the dry argumentation of the scholastics and equally rejects "the literary scholars, who sought only purity of language and works elegantly written" (p. 90). The heart of rhetoric is neither in dialectic nor in style, but in persuasive function. Delivery is thus given a prominence not usually found in rhetorical treatises since antiquity: "The entire art of the good orator consists only in observing what nature does when she is not hampered. Do not do what bad speakers do in striving always to declaim and never to talk to their listeners. On the contrary, each one of your listeners must suppose that you are speaking particularly to him" (p. 104). Memory is similarly approached. Men are "not given to following nature; they have only sought to learn to write, and to write with affectation, at that; never have they aspired to learn to speak in a lofty, strong, and natural way" (p. 110). What about order? The common system of thematic preaching is scorned: "The ancients did not divide a discourse. But they carefully distinguished therein all the things which needed to be distinguished; they assigned each thing to its place; and they carefully considered in what place each thing must be put to make it most likely to have an effect" (p. 112).

By the end of Book 2 Fénelon has thus touched upon matters of invention, arrangement, style, memory, and delivery, but in each case taken truth and nature and the persuasion of the audience as the criteria of excellence, without any of that fondness for rigid rules commonly attributed to neoclassical criticis. In Book 3 he returns in greater detail to preaching. The argument is built on what Augustine says in his *De Doctrina Christiana*. The history of early Christian rhetoric is perceptively reviewed, the influence of vitiated style on Tertullian and some other writers recognized, and the homiletic preaching of the Fathers of the Church strongly recommended as a model in content, arrangement, and style.

Fénelon's *Dialogues* are a fine statement of the tradition of primary classical rhetoric. They complement and further develop the thought of Plato and Augustine on eloquence as those ideas might be practical guidelines for Christian oratory in seventeenth-century France. Equally important, they make constructive use of the insistence of the Port-Royalists on the logical integrity of the thought of a speech, but without sacrificing an important role for speaker and audience in the speech situation. Fénelon has no interest in the old system of topics as the basis of oratorical invention. Not only does he not mention them, he insists instead that the speaker must have a deep knowledge of his subject. In the case of preaching this knowledge can be a matter of certainty, though in the case of other forms of oratory it must be one of probability. In contrast to the Ramists he thinks rhetoric is first of all a matter of invention. Style and delivery are important in performing its function, and Fénelon's concept of rhetoric extends to all literature, including poetry, but rhetoric itself is something other than literary technique.

Fénelon's *Dialogues* appeared in numerous French editions and was translated into German, Spanish, Dutch, and English. Its influence in Britain was considerable. William Stevenson published a free English translation in 1722, which was reprinted in 1750 and 1760 and occasionally later, and the ideas of Fénelon entered into the work of British writers who made the major contributions to rhetoric in the eighteenth century.[9] Before turning to them, however, we should consider briefly a second classical influence which received an important statement in late seventeenth-century France, one of which Fénelon thought highly.

Neoclassical critics sought to establish a sound basis for good taste.[10] They found this in the principles of classical critics, fully developed and extended in all their implications, and illustrated by the models of classical works of art and literature. The object of all art was the imitation of nature; these words "nature" and "imitation" embody the tensions that give life to neoclassicism, and eventually destroy it. "Nature" is the final cause of neoclassicism and the basis of its claim to meaning; "imitation" is its formal cause and the basis of its creative act. The two principles in classical rhetoric are very well illustrated in Quintilian, who constantly appeals to "nature" and who states the rules of traditional rhetoric in their fullest (though not in their most rigid) form, but even in Quintilian the tendency of rules to dominate is clear, and the besetting flaw of neoclassicism is the persistent tendency of rules to overshadow invention. Good examples are the limitations put on the literary genres, and doctrines such as the three dramatic unities.

Boileau

From the point of view of the history of rhetoric the most important of the French neoclassical critics is Nicolas Boileau-Despréaux (1636–1711). His verse treatise *L'Art poétique* (1674) is probably the best statement of the neoclassical theory of poetry, including the concept of the genres and of imitation of the classics. It balances nature and art in good taste, good judgment, and good humor. The same year Boileau published a French translation of "Longinus'" *On the Sublime*, together with an introduction and notes, followed in 1694 by a series of essays, *Réflexions critiques sur quelques passages du Rhéteur Longin*.[11] "Longinus" had been rather little noticed during the preceding century, but *On the Sublime* added to neoclassical rhetorical criticism an element it badly needed, a theory of genius and inspiration to rise above pedantic rules of composition without contradicting them. This was particularly valuable to those critics like Boileau who sought to defend the greatness of the classics in the debate between the Ancients and Moderns which waxed hot over the next century.[12]

Interest in the sublime grew in France, England, and Germany and finally burst its neoclassical limits completely into the aesthetic of romanticism. The major treatment of the sublime in English was the work of the parliamentary orator Edmund Burke, entitled *A Philosophical Enquiry into the Origin of Our Ideas of the Sublime and Beautiful* (1757). Burke equated the sublime with the strongest emotions which the mind can feel and saw its sources in "the ideas of pain, and danger, that is to say, whatever is in any sort terrible, or is conversant about terrible objects, or operates in a manner analogous to terror," and further associated it with vastness, obscurity, infinity, and magnificence, both in nature and in art. In contrast, the beautiful is that which causes love or a passion similar to love, like smallness in size, proportion, smoothness, and grace.[13] Some of these concepts are reminiscent of the "ideas" of Hermogenes.

John Locke

The British counterpart of the French Academy was the Royal Society of London, which began as an informal group shortly before the middle of the seventeenth century and received a charter from Charles II in 1662.[14] In contrast to the linguistic and literary interests of the French Academy, the Royal Society was much more concerned with science; but fundamental to that interest was the development of a new logic, as was also the case in France in the same period, and discussion of logic in the seventeenth century necessarily involved the question of the province of rhetoric. Several early members of the Royal Society had something to say about rhetoric, including its greatest member, John Locke, who had even been lecturer on rhetoric at Oxford in 1663. What he said at that time is not known, but in *An Essay Concerning Human Understanding* (1690) he described traditional rhetoric as "an art of deceit and errour" and wanted to exclude figures of speech and other rhetorical devices from serious discourse.[15] But he conceived of something like Plato's philosophical rhetoric which would have three legitimate functions: "First, to make known one man's thoughts or ideas to another. Second, to do it with as much ease and quickness as is possible; and Thirdly, thereby to convey the knowledge of things."[16]

During the course of the eighteenth century in Britain, four different approaches to rhetoric became evident. One of these was the survival of the technical, largely Ciceronian tradition. A second was the peculiar Elocutionary Movement, which shares some of the features of sophistry. A third was the neoclassical philosophical rhetoric somewhat as expounded by Fénelon, with its roots in Plato. A fourth, in contrast to the third, was the development of a new philosophical rhetoric based on the new logic, with the addition to it of a new psychology as developed by the British Empiricists, paying some lip service to classical rhetoric, but differing from it in fundamental ways. During the course of the century all these movements showed some signs of *letteraturizzazione*, and all of them treated the three forms of oratory as pulpit, senate, and bar. It should be remembered that a major function of British universities, and American colleges, was the training of the clergy. Attention to preaching was thus very appropriate in courses on rhetoric.

John Ward

The first approach is probably best seen in the teaching of rhetoric at the elementary level, which continued in schools much as it had throughout the Renaissance.[17] The strongest part of this tradition continued to be its teaching of tropes and figures.[18] At the more advanced level, however, it is exemplified by the lectures of John Ward at Greshman College, London, which were published in 1759 under the title *A System of Oratory*.[19] Ward's fifty-four lectures set forth Ciceronian rhetoric in a thorough, rather pedantic way. Although he had read Fénelon, he was untouched by his spirit, and although he knew of attacks on the system of topics, he set it forth in the old way. Ward's rhetoric was praised at the time of publication but soon overshadowed by newer approaches, and it was not reprinted until the twentieth century.

The Elocutionary Movement

A second approach to rhetoric in the eighteenth century was the Elocutionary Movement.[20] Oratorical delivery had been given rather little attention by rhetoricians since the collapse of the ancient schools of declamation, but interest in it began to revive with the effort in the seventeenth century to achieve classical standards of excellence in the modern languages, especially in the Church and in the theatre. The French Jesuit Louis de Cressoles wrote a Latin treatise on the subject early in the seventeenth century, and his influential *Traité de l'action de l'orateur, ou de la prononciation et du geste* was published soon after his death in 1657. Fénelon of course also discussed delivery as an important part of rhetoric in the classical tradition, but the movement flourished more in the British Isles, where its leading proponent was the Irishman Thomas Sheridan, father of Richard Brinsley Sheridan. Sheridan tried to establish a school of correct English speech, which he hoped would attract students from England, Ireland, Wales, Scotland, and the British colonies and would contribute to the cultivation of a standard English. He lectured widely and published several works, of which his *Course of Lectures on Elocution* (1762) is the best known.[21] To Sheridan, the only part of ancient rhetoric that really mattered was delivery, and his overall understanding of classical rhetoric was very shallow. At most he refers vaguely to "the ancients" or "the Greeks." He attracted much attention, however, and the Elocutionary Movement has a history in Britain and America which even stretches into the twentieth century, though it lost the theory and method which characterized it in the eighteenth and nineteenth centuries. Demonstrations of elocution on religious or patriotic themes are a part of the sophistic strand of classical rhetoric. Plato's *Menexenus* is supposed to have been recited annually in Athens in the Hellenistic and Roman period, and Greek orators of the Second Sophistic repeated their best speeches with appropriate gestures all over the Roman Empire.

John Lawson

The third approach, along the lines of the philosophical rhetoric of Fénelon, does not have a "classic" exposition in Britain, but awareness of it can be seen in a number of writers. John Lawson taught rhetoric at Dublin and in 1758 published his *Lectures Concerning Oratory, Delivered in Trinity College.*[22] Lawson regarded rhetoric as "the Handmaid of Truth" and sought to answer the objections of Locke by taking up Bacon's view that rhetoric, though inferior to wisdom in excellence, was superior in common use: to impart truth it is necessary to "soften the severity of her aspect" and thus to "borrow the embellishments of rhetoric." In approaching the parts of rhetoric he sought to reconcile Bacon and Aristotle, and in treating the topics he noted the objections to them but felt they were useful for beginners. He viewed the study of rhetoric in his own time as aiming primarily at the improvement of eloquence in English, and especially in preaching. Style was an important part, but Lawson rather scorned the artifices of tropes and figures. Most interesting, perhaps, is his eighteenth lecture. Here he turns from Aristotle and Cicero's *De Oratore* as his main sources to Plato's *Phaedrus*, of which he gives a summary. He says that the *Phaedrus* contains "the fundamental precepts of rhetoric, enlarged afterwards and reduced into a regular system by Aristotle, to which succeeding writers have added little new; even the eloquence and experience [Bacon's word] of Tully [the common neoclassical name for M. Tullius Cicero] did not much more than adorn these." Lawson ended his lecture with enthusiastic praise of Plato's "poetic" style and a poem of his own composition, modeled on the popular myth of the choice of Heracles, in which the young Plato is faced with a choice between the two allegorical figures of Philosophy and Poetry. He chooses Philosophy, but is rewarded by the gift of Poetry as well.

David Hume

A rather different expression of admiration for classical rhetoric well shows how intense was the feeling that English had far to go in equaling its achievements. This is the essay *Of Eloquence* by the great Scottish philosopher, David Hume (1743).[23] In comparison with the Greeks and Romans, Hume says, "if we be superior in philosophy, we are still, notwithstanding all our refinements, much inferior in eloquence." This is strange, he thought, since "of all the polite and learned nations, England alone possesses a popular government, or admits into the legislature such numerous assemblies as can be supposed to lie under the dominion of eloquence. But what has England to boast of in this particular?" What Hume means is that ancient eloquence "was infinitely more sublime than that which modern orators aspire to." On the lips of "our temperate and calm speakers" Demosthenes' oath by those who fell at Marathon or the pathetical passages of Cicero's speeches against Verres would sound absurd. Equally absurd would seem the vehement delivery of the ancient orators. Hume continues:

> One is somewhat at a loss to what causes we may ascribe so sensible a decline of eloquence in later ages. The genius of mankind, at all times, is, perhaps, equal: the moderns have applied themselves, with great industry and success, to all the other arts and sciences: and a learned nation possesses a popular government; a circumstance which seems requisite for the full display of these noble talents; but notwithstanding all these advantages, our progress in eloquence is very inconsiderable, in comparison of the advances, which we have made in all other parts of learning.

Hume then takes up three reasons to explain this failure and finds each unsatisfactory. It is true, he admits, that modern legal procedure and rules of evidence put constraints on judicial oratory, but it was deliberative oratory which in antiquity most elevated the genius and gave full scope to eloquence. It is also true that modern customs, "or our superior good sense, if you will, make our orators more cautious and reserved than the ancient, in attempting to inflame the passions, or elevate the imagination of their audience." But in Hume's view it should not have this effect. Ancient orators "hurried away with such a torrent of sublime and pathetic, that they left their hearers no leisure to perceive the artifice, by which they were deceived." He continues, "Of all human productions, the orations of Demosthenes present to us the models, which approach the nearest to perfection." Some people claim that the disorders of antiquity gave ampler matter for eloquence, to which Hume replies, "It would be easy to find a Philip in modern times; but where shall we find a Demosthenes?" These reasons thus rejected, the only conclusion is that modern speakers simply do not make the effort or lack the genius and judgment of the past: "A few successful attempts of this nature might rouse the genius of the nation, excite the emulation of the youth, and accustom our ears to a more sublime and more pathetic elocution, than what we have been hitherto entertained with." As it is, "We are satisfied with our mediocrity, because we have had no experience of anything better." Hume concludes with a specific observation about modern orators: "Their great affectation of extemporary discourses has made them reject all order and method, which seems so requisite to argument, and without which it is scarcely possible to produce an entire conviction on the mind."

Hume's essay, though not so cogently argued as many of his writings, is an interesting medley of themes of classical and eighteenth-century rhetoric: the achievements of Greek and Latin compared with English (and the debate of the Ancients and Moderns was an important critical issue in this period); the sophistic strand of classical rhetoric, with its great admiration for the achievement of the orator; the effect of the new logic on rhetoric; interest in the sublime and the equation of genius with the grand style; the appeal of elocution.

Edmund Burke

The history of prose style is largely the history of a series of reactions. Renaissance Ciceronianism had been followed by the crisper baroque style, imitating Seneca and Tacitus. Reactions against baroque obscurity produced the Atticism of the early eighteenth century, best seen in Joseph Addison's writings.[24] During the course of the eighteenth century, sometimes encouraged by the theory of the sublime, there was some movement back toward the grand style: Johnson is more florid and complex than Addison, and among orators efforts were made to rival the eloquence of the ancients. In 1789 in his prosecution of Warren Hastings, governor of India, Edmund Burke, the author of the treatise on the sublime and the beautiful mentioned earlier in this chapter, seemed intent on surpassing Cicero's prosecution of Verres, the corrupt governor of Sicily. His fifteen published speeches, to Cicero's six, contain passages in the grand style and seek to move the passions of the House of Lords, sitting in judgment, by appeal to the Law of Nations which Burke vigorously claimed Hastings had transgressed. In his much-admired description of the descent of Hyder Ali to ravage the plain of the Carnotic as the result of Hastings's actions, Burke imitated Demosthenes' simile comparing Philip to a cloud; "Longinus" (39.4) had much praised it. The peroration of Burke's final speech against Hastings attempts an invocation analogous to the oath of Demosthenes in high seriousness, a quality which Hume had longed for in English:

My lords, at this awful close, in the name of the Commons, and surrounded by them, I attest the retiring, I attest the advancing generations, between which, as a link in the great chain of eternal order, we stand. We call this nation, we call the world to witness, that the Commons have shrunk from no labor; that we have been guilty of no prevarication; that we have made no compromise with crime; that we have not feared any odium whatsoever, in the long warfare which we have carried on with the crimes—with the vices— with the exorbitant wealth—with the enormous and overpowering influence of Eastern corruption. . . . My lords, it has pleased Providence to place us in such a state, that we appear every moment to be upon the verge of some great mutations. There is one thing, and one thing only, which defies all mutation; that which existed before the world, and will survive the fabric of the world itself; I mean justice; that justice, which, emanating from the Divinity, has a place in the breast of every one of us, given us for our guide with regard to ourselves and with regard to others, and which will stand after this globe is burned to ashes, our advocate or our accuser before the great Judge, when he comes to call upon us for the tenor of a well-spent life.

This is an exceedingly finely-worked piece of discourse, with its many tropes, figures of thought, and figures of diction as taught in the handbooks of classical rhetoric. But Cicero won the prosecution of Verres and did not even have to deliver all the speeches; the Lords acquitted Hastings on all counts.

George Campbell

The fourth approach to rhetoric in eighteenth-century Britain is the most studied in recent times: the systematic effort to think out a new theory of rhetoric on the basis of the work of the British Empiricist philosophers, and especially the work of David Hume. Locke had thought of the mind as an empty page on which experience (Greek *empeiria*) writes; knowledge comes partly from experience, partly from reflection on experience. Hume and others added to this the principle of association: the mind draws its conclusions from the association of resemblances, contiguities, or causes and effects. Passions arise in the mind either from direct affections (joy and sorrow, desire and aversion, hope and fear) or from indirect affections associated with objects and their causes. These concepts and others related to them constitute a theory of human nature and human knowledge which has implications for rhetoric. In *Elements of Criticism* (1762) Henry Home, Lord Kames, applied the new learning to rhetorical style. More significant were the studies of George Campbell, professor of divinity and principal of Marischal College at the University of Aberdeen, who attempted "to explore human nature and find herein the principles which underlie and explain the art of rhetoric."[25] The result was *The Philosophy of Rhetoric*, published in 1776. Book 1 is entitled "The Nature and Foundations of Eloquence," Book 2 "The Foundations and Essential Properties of Elocution," by which Campbell means style, and Book 3 "The Discriminating Properties of Elocution," which develops Campbell's theory of "vivacity," or liveliness of ideas, which he thought the quality primarily responsible for attention and belief.

Analysis of Campbell's innovative and challenging work is not appropriate here.[26] One feature of it, however, is relevant. Campbell departs radically from the traditional structure and terminology and many of the ideas of classical rhetoric, though others, like the roles of speaker and hearers and the stylistic virtues of purity and perspicuity, are discussed. He occasionally cites examples from classical literature or classical rhetoricians, including Aristotle, Cicero, and Quintilian, but at least as often he refers to modern writers. Nevertheless, he thinks of his work as directly linked to the classical tradition in rhetoric. In his introduction he traces the development of rhetoric as an art. The first step, he says, is Nature, as all neoclassicists would believe. The second is observation, the beginnings of the critical science of discovering modes of arguing or forms of speech. The third is to compare the various effects, favorable or unfavorable, of those attempts at speech, "to discover to what particular purpose each attempt is adapted, and in which circumstances only to be used. The fourth and last is to canvass those principles in our nature to which the various attempts are adapted, and by which, in any instance, their success or want of success may be accounted for." He continues:

Considerable progress had been made by the ancient Greeks and Romans, in devising the proper rules of composition, not only the two sorts of poesy, epic and dramatic, but also in the three sorts of orations which were in most frequent use among them, the deliberate, the judiciary, and the demonstrative. And I must acknowledge that, as far as I have been able to discover, there has been little or no improvement in this respect made by the moderns. The observations and rules transmitted to us from these distinguished names in the learned world, Aristotle, Cicero, and Quintilian, have been for the most part only translated by later critics, or put into a modish dress and new arrangement. And as to the fourth and last step, it may be said to bring us into a new country, of which, though there have been some successful incursions occasionally made upon its frontiers, we are not yet in full possession. (Introduction, p. li)

Campbell thus comes not to deny classical rhetoric, but to go beyond and fulfill understanding of it. When he gives his definition of eloquence in the opening paragraph of Book 1, "that art or talent by which the discourse is adapted to its end," he immediately cites Quintilian's support in a note and goes on to say that he chose this definition for two reasons: "it exactly corresponds to Tully's [Cicero's] idea of a perfect orator; and it is best adapted to the subject" of his own work.

Campbell's work was very widely studied, not the least in America, where over thirty editions were printed and where it was frequently used as a college text. Its long-term effect was to supply a modern rhetoric which satisfied many students of the subject and reduced their dependence on classical sources, not necessarily on classical statements of rules such as those in Quintilian, but on the more speculative discussions of rhetoric by Plato and Aristotle and by Cicero in *De Oratore*. It was widely believed in the eighteenth century, even by defenders of the Ancients, that modern philosophy had made remarkable strides beyond that of the past. The reputation of both Plato and Aristotle suffered generally at this time, and Campbell seemed to be providing a basic theory of rhetoric built on the best of modern thought.

Hugh Blair

Other aspects of classical rhetoric remained strong, however, and achieved their most definitive eighteenth-century statement in the work of Hugh Blair (1718–1800). Blair, like Campbell and Hume, was a member of the Scotch Enlightenment, one of a small band of intellectuals who brought a note of dispassionate common sense and reason to philosophy and literature in the middle and later eighteenth century, and a note of liberal imagination to the dour Calvinism of the North. Blair was a minister in Edinburgh who also served as Regius Professor of Rhetoric and Belles Lettres at the University of Edinburgh. The *Lectures on Rhetoric and Belles Lettres*, which he published in 1783, had been given over the previous twenty years or more and had largely been written in the late 1750s or early 1760s.[27] They thus took little account of the ideas of Campbell, though he is mentioned in one note.

Blair is the British Quintilian. He was a man of amiable disposition, peaceful sentiments, scholarly instincts, interested in teaching. Like Quintilian he held a chair funded by the head of state, the first such position in each country. Like Quintilian he was not a great original thinker but stood at the end of a complex tradition which was encountering new conditions. Both rhetoricians restated that tradition in intelligent, but essentially conservative ways, and produced an authoritative work which was very influential on the direction of future development. In Quintilian's case the restatement took the form of integrating rhetoric into a total educational system, which remained standard throughout Roman times and survived in the seven liberal arts of the Middle Ages. This restatement emphasized the concept of the orator as an ideal and gave special importance to the role, the theories, and the prose style of Cicero. Quintilian was aware of the limited opportunities for public address under the empire, in contrast to Greek times or the Roman republic, but glossed them over and optimistically hoped for still greater achievements in eloquence. In the case of Blair the restatement took the form of integration into the new concept of belles lettres; the achievements and opportunities of spoken discourse are discussed, but viewed somewhat pessimistically; and the field open to eloquence is presented as primarily in written forms. Appropriately, the major authority for rhetoric in Blair's view is Quintilian.

Blair's emphasis can be clearly seen from the structure of his course of lectures. Though his title was professor of "rhetoric and belles lettres" and the title of his published lectures follows that order, "belles lettres and rhetoric" would be a better description. He begins with a series of lectures on literary concepts important to his contemporaries: taste, criticism, genius, sublimity, and beauty. He then turns to the history of language, with special attention to the development and possibilities of English, culminating in a discussion of style along the lines of classical tropes and figures. He focuses on a rather small number of devices, discussed in depth, and avoids the pedantry of meaningless lists. He cites examples from Greek, Latin, and English poetry and concludes the first half of his course with four lectures on the style of Addison, analyzing specific *Spectator* papers, and one lecture on a passage in Jonathan Swift.

The second volume of the original publication of the lectures then turns to primary rhetoric—its history, its kinds, the oratory of senate, of bar, and of pulpit, the parts of an oration and its argumentation, and delivery. These topics are disposed of in nine lectures out of the total of forty-seven. Selections from Demosthenes, part of Cicero's speech for Cluentius, and a sermon by Bishop Atterbury are singled out for analysis. Blair has clearly profited from discussions of rhetoric in the previous century; he strongly emphasizes the importance of truth: "true eloquence," he says "is the art of placing truth in the most advantageous light for conviction and persuasion" (vol. II, p. 104).[28] Moreover, he dismisses the doctrine of topics as of little practical help to a modern student (II, p. 180).

This rather brief discussion of rhetorical theory is then followed by a lecture (number 34) entitled "Means of Improving in Eloquence":

To be an Eloquent Speaker, in the proper sense of the word, is far from being either a common or an easy attainment. Indeed, to compose a florid harangue on some popular topic, and to deliver it so as to amuse an Audience, is a matter not very difficult. But though some praise be due to this, yet the idea, which I have endeavored to give of Eloquence, is much higher. It is a great exertion of the human powers. It is the Art of being persuasive and commanding; the Art, not of pleasing the fancy merely, but of speaking both to the understanding and to the heart; of interesting the hearers in such a degree, as to seize and carry them along with us; and to leave them with a deep and strong impression of what they have heard. How many talents, natural and acquired, must concur for carrying this to perfection? A strong, lively, and warm imagination; quick sensibility of heart, joined with solid judgment, good sense, and presence of mind; all improved by great and long attention to Style and Composition; and supported also by the exterior, yet important qualifications, of a graceful manner, a presence not ungainly, and a full and tuneable voice. How little reason to wonder, that a perfect and accomplished Orator, should be one of the characters that is most rarely to be found? Let us not despair however. Between mediocrity and perfection, there is a very wide interval. (II, pp. 226–27)

This is the hymn to the orator from Gorgias, Isocrates, Cicero, and especially Quintilian, as sung by High Blair. He follows it with an adaptation of the last book of Quintilian. How does one improve in oratory? Nature must bestow talent; art must cultivate it. Personal character and disposition is most important; only a good man can be a good orator. Next most important is a fund of knowledge, to which should be added acquaintance with the general circle of "polite literature"—poetry, history, and the like. Then follows imitation of good models and exercise in composing and speaking. Last is put study of criticism. For this, he says,

It is to the original Antient Writers that we must chiefly have recourse; and it is a reproach to anyone, whose profession calls him to speak in public, to be unacquainted with them. In all the Antient Rhetorical Writers, there is, indeed, this defect, that they are too systematical, as I formerly showed; they aim at doing too much; at reducing Rhetoric to a complete and perfect Art, which may even supply invention with materials on every subject; insomuch, that one would imagine they expected to form an Orator by rule, in as mechanical a manner as one would form a Carpenter. Whereas, all that can, in truth, be done, is to give openings for assisting and enlightening Taste, and for pointing out to Genius the course it ought to hold. (II, p. 243)

There is in this just the slightest suggestion of pessimism about the study of classical rhetoric. It is unlikely to achieve, at least for the modern age, all it promises. Blair then mentions with approval Aristotle, who "investigated the principles of rhetoric with great penetration" and "who first took rhetoric out of the hands of the sophists and introduced reasoning and good sense into the art." Demetrius of Phaleron, Dionysius of Halicarnassus, and Cicero are "worthy of attention," but the latter's rules and observations may be thought "too vague and general." And "of all the antient writers on the subject of oratory, the most instructive and most useful" is Quintilian:

I know few books which abound more with good sense, and discover a greater degree of just and accurate taste, than Quinctilian's Institutions. Almost all the principles of good Criticism are to be found in them. He has digested into excellent order all the antient ideas concerning Rhetoric, and is, at the same time, himself an eloquent Writer. Though some parts of his work contain too much of the technical and artificial system then in vogue. . . . (II, p. 244–45)

With the next lecture Blair turns from oratory back to belles lettres to discuss the comparative merit of the Ancients and the Moderns—he takes the view that the Ancients are the superiors or equals of the Moderns in genius, or creative imagination, but that there have been remarkable developments in modern times in science and reasoning— and to take up, as the third and final part of his course, the major forms of modern literature, with critical examination of ancient and modern models: in other words, belles lettres. The total result, therefore, is to imbed the discussion of primary rhetoric into the middle of a framework of language and literature in written form, or to integrate rhetoric into belles lettres. This approach significantly contributed to the *letteraturizzazione* of rhetoric in the following century, when Blair's lectures were widely studied on both sides of the Atlantic. More than fifty editions of the full text are known to have been published, and as many more of abridgments.[29]

Blair discusses the history of oratory in his lectures on rhetoric, starting with lecture 25. His discussion takes account of Hume's remarks and is of considerable importance in understanding the later history of classical rhetoric. In one passage he compares Demosthenes with Cicero and concludes that though Cicero can be read with more ease and pleasure,

were the state in danger, or some great public interest at stake, which drew the serious attention of men, an Oration in the spirit and strain of Demosthenes, would have more weight, and produce greater effects than one in the Ciceronian manner. Were Demosthenes's Philippics spoken in a British Assembly, in a similar conjuncture of affairs, they would convince and persuade at this day. The rapid Style, the vehement reasoning, the disdain, anger, boldness, freedom, which perpetually animate them, would render their success infallible over any modern Assembly. I question whether the same can be said of Cicero's Orations; whose Eloquence, however beautiful, and however well suited to the Roman taste, yet borders oftener on declamation, and is more remote from the manner in which we now expect to hear real business and causes of importance treated. (II, lecture 26, pp. 31–32)

Although Blair notes the purity of style of Lactantius and Minutius Felix, and the "sprightliness and strength" of Augustine, he concludes that "none of the Fathers afford any just models of eloquence. . . . They are, in general, infected with the taste of that age, a love of swollen and strained thoughts, and of the play of words" (pp. 36–37). The lecture then turns to the state of oratory in modern times in France and in Britain.

In neither of those countries, has the talent of Public Speaking risen near to the degree of antient splendor. While, in other productions of genius, both in prose and in poetry, they have contended for the prize with Greece and Rome; nay, in some compositions, may be thought to have surpassed them: the names of Demosthenes and Cicero stand, at this day, unrivalled in fame; and it would be held presumptuous and absurd, to pretend to place any modern whatever on the same, or even on a nearly equal, rank. (II, p. 38)

Blair acknowledges that it is surprising that oratory had not reached greater heights in Britain, "when we consider that, of all the polite nations, it alone possesses a popular government or admits into the legislature, such numerous assemblies as can be supposed to lie under the dominion of eloquence." He notes Hume's observations on this subject but believes the causes can be identified. The French have adopted higher ideas of persuading and pleading than the British, but their composition tends to be too diffuse and deficient in strength and cogency. Hence the pulpit is the principal field of their eloquence, and their academicians, laboring under the misfortune of having no subject to discourse upon, run commonly into flattery and panegyric, the most barren and insipid of all topics. Lecture 29, "Eloquence of the Pulpit," compares the two nations in somewhat greater detail and more fairly, but here Blair is anxious to leave aside the matter of preaching and examine the state of civil oratory:

> The Greeks and Romans aspired to a more sublime species of Eloquence, than is aimed at by the Moderns. . . . Modern eloquence is much more cool and temperate; and in Great Britain especially, has confined itself almost wholly to the argumentative and rational. . . . Several reasons may be given why modern Eloquence has been so limited. . . . In many efforts of mere genius, the antient Greeks and Romans excelled us; but, on the other hand . . . in accuracy and closeness of reasoning on many subjects, we have some advantage. . . . Philosophy has made great progress. . . . A certain strictness of good sense has, in this island particularly, been cultivated. . . . Hence we are on our guard against the flowers of Elocution. . . . Our Public Speakers are obliged to be more reserved than the antients . . . owing, in great measure, to our phlegm and natural coldness. [The effect of climate on mankind and his arts was a popular subject at the time.]
>
> Though the Parliament of Great Britain be the noblest field which Europe, at this day, affords to a Public Speaker, yet Eloquence has never been so powerful an instrument there, as it was in the popular assemblies of Greece and Rome. Under some former reigns, the high hand of arbitrary power bore a violent sway; and in later times, ministerial influence has generally prevailed. . . . At the Bar, our disadvantage, in comparison to the antients, is great. . . . The system of law has become much more complicated. . . . With regard to the Pulpit, it has certainly been a great disadvantage, that the practice of reading Sermons, instead of repeating them from memory, has prevailed so universally . . . [and] the sectarians and fanatics before the Restoration, adopted a warm, zealous, and popular manner of preaching. . . . The odium of these sects drove the established church from that warmth which they were judged to have carried too far, into the opposite extreme of a studied coolness, and composure of manner. (II, pp. 41–44)

Blair in conclusion claims that oratory admits of great scope and is a field where much honor is to be reaped, but we must have regard to what modern taste and modern manners will bear. The result of this is of course the admission that oratory, as a fine art, is probably not possible in the modern world in anything like the way it was in antiquity; thus the emphasis, throughout the lectures, on cultivation of fine writing is complemented by an essentially pessimistic view about the eloquence of the spoken word in English.

The Decline of Neoclassical Rhetoric

The eroding of the authority of ancient writers on philosophical rhetoric by Campbell and his followers, and Blair's conclusion that oratory as a fine art was foreign to modern circumstances, with a resulting turn to literary composition and belles lettres in its place, are among the factors which led to a relative decline of the influence of classical rhetoric in the nineteenth century. That decline was encouraged by the weakening position of the classical languages in school and college curricula during the nineteenth century. In America, neoclassical rhetoric was still taught in the universities at the end of the eighteenth century, for example by Blair's classmate John Witherspoon at Princeton and by Timothy Dwight at Yale. Among American teachers of rhetoric, the strongest classical influence is that seen in the lectures given in 1806 by John Quincy Adams, the first holder of the Boylston Professorship of Rhetoric and Oratory at Harvard. "A subject which has exhausted the genius of Aristotle, Cicero, and Quintilian," said the future president in the opening lecture, "can neither require nor admit much additional illustration. To select, combine, and apply their precepts, is the only duty left for their followers of all succeeding times, and to obtain a perfect familiarity with their instructions is to arrive at the mastery of the art."[30] In the following lectures Adams turns more often to Quintilian; Plato he dismisses in lecture 3 as "intellectual chaos." Although he is familiar with Blair and other moderns, his presentation is one of the most classical to be found in modern times and even expounds the theory of the topics (lecture 9). In contrast, later nineteenth-century reference to classical authority is often window dressing. As Professor John McVikar at Columbia complained in 1833, the study of classics and the study of rhetoric drifted apart. "The present junior class knows nothing of Cicero's *De Oratore*," he lamented.[31] The Elocutionary Movement drew student and public attention, and rhetorical theory became an aspect of belles lettres and English composition. In the course of the century the Boylston Professorship, despite the founder's intention, was converted first into a chair in belles lettres and ultimately into a professorship of poetry.

In Britain, the last major treatment of rhetoric as a discipline in the classical tradition was the work of Richard Whately, entitled *Elements of Rhetoric, Comprising an Analysis of the Laws of Moral Evidence and of Persuasion, with Rules for Argumentative Composition and Elocution,* published in 1828 and revised and enlarged until the seventh edition of 1846. Although Whately's work continued long thereafter to be used as a textbook in America, rhetoric ceased to be a separate discipline in Britain and was studied, if at all, as a part of English composition. During these same years, however, classical philology advanced rapidly on an international basis and with it an understanding of Greek and Latin texts and of the circumstances of ancient life. Important landmarks in rhetorical scholarship on the continent were the *Rhetores Graeci* of Christian Walz (1832–1836) and the earliest version (1865) of what became Richard Volkman's *Die Rhetorik der Griechen und Römer in Systematischer Übersicht.* In Britain E. M. Cope of Cambridge published in 1867 *An Introduction to Aristotle's Rhetoric,* followed by a commentary on the Greek text edited by J. M. Sandys after Cope's death. In the preface to his *Introduction* Cope is at pains to explain the surprising fact that Aristotle was interested in rhetoric at all and to describe the place of that art in ancient Greece. Neither he nor Sandys gives any indication that the *Rhetoric* might be read for purposes other than philological and antiquarian, and this is the common view of nineteenth-century editors of classical texts.

In the twentieth century, however, not only Aristotle, but Plato and the sophists, and to a lesser extent other classical writers on rhetoric, have again been studied for what they have to say about speech, and at Cornell University and The University of Chicago and in the work of such critics as Kenneth Burke and Chaim Perelman the classical tradition in rhetoric seems to have entered a new phase in its long and distinguished history.

Conclusion:
A Dialogue of Orators

I went down yesterday to the Piraeus with Glaucon, the son of Phaedrus, in order to take the hydrofoil to Poros. He had persuaded me to seek out the sanctuary of Poseidon on Calauria and to visit the spot where Demosthenes, exactly twenty-three hundred years ago, drank the poison in his pen rather than surrender to Archias and the Macedonians. From the quay at Poros we set out on the long walk back into history, uphill through pine woods, and eventually found ourselves on a plateau, looking out over the Saronic Gulf. A few remains marked the temple and the *heroon*, which may well have contained the orator's tomb. Glaucon propped himself against a pine in that graceful way he has and took up his shorthand notebook as I nostalgically reminisced about the history of rhetoric and oratory. He reminded me of its birth in the freedom of the Greek democracies and we considered together its survival in ages of despotism and ignorance.

"But if rhetoric is really a product of democracy," asked Glaucon, "why is it that interest in rhetoric in modern times seems to have declined almost in proportion to the rise of democracy?" In partial reply I told him a true story that I had heard from my grandfather about a discussion many years ago and many miles away.

It was the first Fourth of July of the twentieth century, and the small New England town where my grandfather was a minor official, and where I later grew up, had outdone itself in celebrating the occasion with parades and speeches. An illustrious statesman, native to the region, had given an emotional and patriotic address which was the centerpiece of the program. Now in the twilight of a distinguished career, even by his political opponents he was regarded worthy of the highest office, which he never attained. Late in the day, waiting for the fireworks display to begin, he sat on the village green talking easily with his old friend the bishop of the Episcopal diocese, a man widely known for the beauty of his diction and the sincerity, if not the profundity, of his sermons.

"That was a fine speech, Senator," said the bishop, "a speech in the spirit of Pericles or Cicero."

"And an equally fine invocation, Bishop," said the senator. "But you know we were trained on rhetoric and you on elocution as well. When we entered the university the Boylston Professor still lectured on rhetoric and oratory and we still declaimed theses in the classical style. Speakers today have learned chiefly by trial and error and not by the system of Blair and Whately, not to say Aristotle and Quintilian. The finer points of the art escape them, and few can name the figures or identify the places. The whole thing is less of a disciplined art; spontaneity is everything. In the halls of Congress I know no one I would call truly eloquent, though there are many good enough debaters. I suppose the general decline of classical studies has much to do with it. A speaker who has never read Demosthenes or Cicero remains content with the eloquence of his own age."

"I'm not sure," replied the bishop. "I must admit I enjoyed reading Cicero and feel some nostalgia for the old eloquence, but I also know in my heart that it can disguise much that is deceitful. You will forgive an old friend saying that even your ringing words today about the Founding Fathers glossed over realities which gave birth to America and some of the flaws which remain in it. You only told one side of the story. Would we not be better off to admit that truth is the only satisfactory basis of oratory? And perhaps the world has been working toward that goal in its halting way. You remember what Blair says about Lactantius: essentially—I don't remember Blair's words—that he sold his birthright to the corrupted rhetoric of his age. Rhetoric is one of our inheritances from papism. It was only with the Reformation that the value of truth began to reassert itself. Ramus was the first step toward weakening the stranglehold of the old rhetoric. Bacon and Locke carried on the good work. The modern democracies and churches have completed it."

"I suppose that many would agree with you," said the senator, thoughtfully, "but more out of ignorance than out of acquaintance with the history of rhetoric. Would you seriously claim that the music of Bach or Mozart, the rhetoric of classical music, is lacking in truth compared with that uncontrolled self-expression which passes for musical style today?"

"You certainly know your man, Senator. But the arts tend to go too far, too fast. I was really thinking of something much simpler. What is the greatest modern speech? Surely the Gettysburg Address?"

"Look at it this way, my friend," continued the senator. "The Church took up rhetoric because she needed it. She was no longer preaching to simple men. She had come out of hiding and had to find a means to move the hearts of the powerful, the complacent, and the sophisticated. They listened to Chrysostom and Ambrose. What do you think converted Augustine himself?" The bishop shook his head at this but did not interrupt.

"And I think you are wrong about the later evidence you cite. Ramism was just a device for teaching schoolboys. It did not undermine classical rhetoric; it just appealed to different classical authorities. Much the same is true of Bacon and Locke. I don't see that what they demanded of rhetoric is essentially different from what Plato demanded in the *Phaedrus*. Plato's ideal rhetoric has never really been worked out in all its implications. Aristotle made a start. Fénelon took it up, but the next generation abandoned the cause. The moral and logical objections to classical rhetoric have been answered a thousand times: Wisdom and Eloquence need each other. Truth, yes. But what can Truth do alone? It seems to me more immoral to abandon Truth naked to her enemies than to practice some form of defense. As you might put it, Bishop, 'Those that have ears, let them hear.' But people have lost faith in systems and demand freedom from rules. I have heard it said that it was the Lisbon earthquake of 1755 that destroyed men's confidence in reason and the old arts."

"You do believe then that there has been a falling off in eloquence," said the bishop. "Won't you also agree that there is a new, if different, eloquence today? Perhaps a better one?"

"There is an Englishman named Jebb," said the senator. "I met him recently when he was lecturing in America, and we discussed British and American eloquence and how it compares with the ancients'. I thought his views well taken: that there have been some splendid moments in speech in both countries in modern times, but these have been single lines, short passages, happy phrases, and not the large-scale works of sustained art. Modern oratory is essentially romantic. What do we remember of the oratory of our own revolution, since you would tie eloquence and freedom? Patrick Henry the most, perhaps. 'I know not what course others may take, but as for me, give me liberty or give me death.' Is that the line? Who knows the argument of his speech? Indeed, there is considerable doubt that he even gave it as we read it now. Somebody wrote it up from memory, years later, and the famous phrase is an adaptation of something in Addison's tragedy of Cato. I grant you that the Gettysburg Address is moving, and it is certainly admired, so much so that I hesitate to say what I really feel about it. That it is not oratory at all, but poetry or a prayer. Its success, and the relative failure of Edward Everett on the same occasion, is the best sign that we do not know what oratory is or what it can be."

"Do you think anything like the old eloquence could ever come back, Senator?" inquired the bishop. "Has the decline of Greek and Latin removed the rich substance on which it fed and the models which showed the world what could be done?"

"Realistically I don't suppose it will come back in the same way," said the senator. "But there is no reason to despair. You remember that even Hume thought that if a few great speakers could ever be found, a new tradition would spring up in English. I think the native genius is there. When I was in England last I visited the House of Commons and heard a speech by the young son of Randolph Churchill. I was much impressed by the power of his thought and the vigor of his expression. Give him a cause and he could move the world. Another interesting change will occur if modern science can really create new opportunities for oral communication. Plato thought the introduction of writing did much harm to the arts; the introduction of printing has done more. Rhetoric has always had a tendency to turn its attention from public address to literature. It is safer, easier, more remote from audience reaction. Printing has created a vast industry for literature and it has also replaced oral narrative with documents. In the Congress we are furnished with great heaps of paper, but we rarely hear someone expound a subject simply and clearly. Printing has lost control. Nobody can possibly read or take in all that is printed. We are beginning to discover new possibilities of oral communication, and speech, more than Latin, is the training ground of rhetoric. First we had the telegraph and now Mr. Bell's telephone wires are beginning to be stretched across the country. We can hear a voice in a distant city. There is an Italian with a name something like Macaroni who has found a way to send electric impulses through waves in the air. What would be next but to send a visual image as well?"

"Ah, Senator, what castles in the air you build! And speaking of impulses through the air, there is the first roman candle of the evening. If we cannot have the thunder and lightning of Demosthenes, we can have little pyrotechnics of our own to enjoy." And the two turned their thoughts to other things. But my grandfather thought the senator had shown the greater understanding.

"And do you?" asked Glaucon. "Me?" said I. "It is enough for me to show what rhetoric has been and to try to preserve a feeling for its triumphs, as when you lured me to this delightful spot so that you could recline in the shade rather than pursue your rigorous studies of the Greeks with Professor Immerwahr at the American School of Classical Studies at Athens. It is time we moved on."

Notes

Chapter 1

1. I adopt the term from Vasile Florescu, *La Retorica nel suo sviluppo storico*, p. 43 and passim.
2. See Anne Salmond, "Mana Makes the Man: A Look at Maori Oratory and Politics," in *Political Language and Oratory in Traditional Society*, ed. Maurice Bloch, pp. 45–63, esp. pp. 55–63.
3. See Raymond Firth, "Speech-Making and Authority in Tikopia," ibid., pp. 29–43.
4. See Mark Hobart, "Orators and Patrons: Two Types of Political Leader in Balinese Village Society," ibid., pp. 65–92, esp. p. 75.
5. See Robert T. Oliver, *Communication and Culture in Ancient India and China*, pp. 61–83, and Sushil Kumar De, *History of Sanskrit Poetics* (Calcutta: K. L. Mukhopadhyay, 1966).
6. See Oliver, *Communication and Culture*, pp. 100–144, and *The Complete Works of Han Fei Tzu*, translated with an Introduction by W. L. Liao (London: A. Probsthain, 1959), pp. 106–12.
7. See Oliver, *Communication and Culture*, pp. 94–96.
8. The idea is inherent in Plato, *Gorgias* 462c, where Socrates describes rhetoric as an empirical knack, but it is more clearly stated by Quintilian (3.2.3).
9. See Albert Bates Lord, *The Singer of Tales* (Cambridge: Harvard Univ. Pr., 1960).
10. See Julian Jaynes, *The Origin of Consciousness in the Breakdown of the Bicameral Mind* (Boston: Houghton-Mifflin, 1976), pp 252–92.
11. Quotations from the *Iliad* are in the version of Richmond Lattimore, *The Iliad of Homer* (Chicago: Univ. of Chicago Pr., 1951).
12. See Dieter Lohmann, *Die Komposition der Reden in der Ilias*.
13. For an interesting discussion of these elements see M. H. Abrams, *The Mirror and the Lamp*, pp. 3–29.

Chapter 2

1. For a more detailed discussion of these and subsequent developments in the history of Greek rhetoric and of the evidence on which our knowledge is based, see George Kennedy, *The Art of Persuasion in Greece*, esp. pp. 52–124.
2. The best collection of the evidence is Ludwig Radermacher, "Artium Scriptores."
3. There is a translation by H. Rackham in the Loeb Classical Library volume of Aristotle, *Problems*, II, pp. 258–449.

Chapter 3

1. There are translations by K. J. Maidment in the Loeb Classical Library volume of the *Minor Attic Orators*, I, pp. 2–309, and by J. S. Morrison in *The Older Sophists*, ed. Rosamond Kent Sprague, pp. 106–240.
2. There are translations of Gorgias by George Kennedy in Sprague, *The Older Sophists*, pp. 30–67.
3. The figures expressly attributed to Gorgias (see Diodorus Siculus 12.53.4) are antithesis, isocolon, parison, and homoeoteleuton. Figures discussed in the *Rhetoric to Alexander* (26–28) are antithesis, parisosis (= isocolon), and paromoeosis (= homoeoteleuton and other similarities of sound).
4. See Jacqueline de Romilly, *Magic and Rhetoric in Ancient Greece*, pp. 3–22.
5. See Mario Untersteiner, *The Sophists*, trans. Kathleen Freeman, pp. 194–205, and Richard Leo Enos, "The Epistemology of Gorgias' Rhetoric: A Re-examination," *Southern Speech Communication Journal* 42 (1979): 35–51.
6. See Enos, ibid., p. 49.
7. See Werner Jaeger, *Paideia: The Ideals of Greek Culture*, III, pp. 46–155, and Kennedy, *Art of Persuasion*, pp. 174–206.
8. There are translations of Isocrates by George Norlin and LaRue Van Hook in the Loeb Classical Library.
9. See Harry Mortimer Hubbell, *The Influence of Isocrates on Cicero, Dionysius, and Aristides*.
10. There is a translation of Philostratus by Wilmer Cave Wright in the Loeb Classical Library.
11. There is a translation of Aristides' *Panathenaic Oration* and *To Plato in Defense of Oratory* by C. A. Behr in the Loeb Classical Library. The few surviving speeches of Herodes Atticus are not available in English.
12. See de Romilly, *Magic and Rhetoric*, pp. 75–88.
13. A translation of Menander by D. A. Russell and Nigel G. Wilson is forthcoming. The most extensive discussion of sophistic forms is Theodore C. Burgess, "Epideictic Literature."

Chapter 4

1. See W. K. C. Guthrie, *A History of Greek Philosophy, III: The Fifth-Century Enlightenment*, pp. 349–55.
2. Many good translations of the *Apology* are available, among them that by Hugh Tredennick in the Penguin volume entitled *The Last Days of Socrates*.
3. See W. K. C. Guthrie, *A History of Greek Philosophy, IV: Plato: The Man and His Dialogues, Earlier Period*, pp. 71–72.
4. See Guthrie, IV: *Plato*, pp. 284–85. A good translation of the *Gorgias* is that by W. C. Helmbold in the Bobbs-Merrill Library of the Liberal Arts.
5. In Latin *rhetor* is regularly used to mean a teacher of rhetoric, as, for example, in the title of the work on declamation by Seneca the Elder: *Oratorum Rhetorum Sententiae Divisiones Colores*.
6. See Guthrie, IV: *Plato*, pp. 396–97. A good translation of the *Phaedrus* is that by W. C. Helmbold and W. G. Rabinowitz in the Bobbs-Merrill Library of the Liberal Arts.
7. The structure of the second half of the dialogue thus consists of

   A. Discussion of writing (257c–258e); digression (258e–259d)
      B. The orator's need for knowledge (259d–261a)
         C. Is rhetoric an art? (261a–272c)
      B'. The orator's need for knowledge (272d–274b)
   A'. Discussion of writing (274b–278b); conclusion (278b–279c)

   For a slightly different symmetrical arrangement, see Paul Friedlander, *Plato, III: The Dialogues, Second and Third Periods*, pp. 230–42.
8. See the biography in Diogenes Laertius, Book 5. There is a translation by R. D. Hicks in the Loeb Classical Library.
9. See Anton-Hermann Chroust, "Aristotle's First Literary Effort: *The Gryllus*, a Lost Dialogue on the Nature of Rhetoric," *Revue des études grecques* 78 (1965): 576–91, reprinted in *Aristotle: The Classical Heritage of Rhetoric*, ed. Keith V. Erickson, pp. 37–51.
10. See Anton-Hermann Chroust, "Aristotle's Earliest Course of Lectures on Rhetoric," *L'Antiquité classique* 33 (1964): 58–72, reprinted in Erickson, *Aristotle: The Classical Heritage of Rhetoric*, pp. 22–36.
11. See Anfinn Stigen, *The Structure of Aristotle's Thought*.
12. The best translations of Aristotle's *Rhetoric* are those by J. H. Freese in the Loeb Classical Library, by W. Rhys Roberts in the Modern Library, ed. Friedrich Solmsen, and by Lane Cooper (New York: Prentice-Hall, 1960).
13. See Ernst Kapp, *Greek Foundations of Traditional Logic*, pp. 60–74.
14. The nineteenth-century British rhetorician Richard Whately criticized Aristotle's distinction as "strangely unphilosophical," since "all data we argue from must be something already existing"; see his *Elements of*

Rhetoric, note, pp. 39–40. It is likely that Aristotle's distinction is unnecessarily sharp because of the Greeks' distrust of direct evidence and preference for reasoning from probability.

15. See Gerard A. Hauser, "The Example in Aristotle's *Rhetoric*: Bifurcation or Contradiction?" *Philosophy and Rhetoric* 1 (1968): 78–90, reprinted in Erickson, *Aristotle: The Classical Heritage of Rhetoric*, pp. 156–68.

16. Zeno the Stoic compared dialectic to a closed fist, rhetoric to an open hand; see Cicero, *Orator* 113. The relationship of the orator to his audience probably has something to do with the difference; see Lloyd F. Bitzer, "Aristotle's Enthymeme Revisited," *Quarterly Journal of Speech* 45 (1959): 399–408, reprinted in Erickson, *Aristotle: The Classical Heritage of Rhetoric*, pp. 141–55.

17. See Chaim Perelman and L. Olbrechts-Tyteca, *The New Rhetoric: A Treatise on Argumentation*, pp. 47–57.

18. See Walter H. Beale, "Rhetorical Performative Discourse: A New Theory of Epideictic." *Philosophy and Rhetoric* 11 (1978): 221–46.

19. See Walter Burkert, "Aristoteles im Theater: zur Datierung des 3. Buchs der *Rhetorik* and der *Poetik*," *Museum Helveticum* 32 (1975): 67–72.

20. See Marsh McCall, *Ancient Rhetorical Theories of Simile and Comparison*, pp. 24–53.

21. See Kennedy, *Art of Persuasion*, pp. 273–78.

22. See Kennedy, *Art of Rhetoric*, pp. 349 and 360–62.

23. That is, a long syllable followed by three short syllables or three short syllables followed by a long syllable. Aristotle regards the former as a good opening rhythm, the latter as a good closing rhythm. These rhythms occur in Greek prose, but are not especially common.

24. See George A. Kennedy, "Aristotle on the Period," *Harvard Studies in Classical Philology* 63 (1958): 283–88.

25. See Kennedy, *Art of Persuasion*, pp. 278–82.

26. See Wilhelm Kroll, "Das Epicheirema."

27. Friedrich Solmsen, "The Aristotelian Tradition in Ancient Rhetoric," *American Journal of Philology* 62 (1941) 35–50; 169–90, reprinted in Erickson, *Aristotle: The Classical Heritage of Rhetoric*, pp. 278–309.

28. See Kennedy, *Art of Persuasion*, pp. 321–30, and Samuel Ijsseling, *Rhetoric and Philosophy in Conflict: A Historical Survey*. On the *De Inv.* prologue see Gabriel Nuchelmans, "Philologie et son mariage avec Mercure jusqu' à la fin du xiie siècle," *Latomus* 16 (1957): 94–107.

29. See Eleanore Stump, *Boethius's De Topicis Differentiis*, pp. 159–236.

30. There is a translation of the *Topics* of Aristotle by E. S. Forster in the Loeb Classical Library volume which contains the *Posterior Analytics*. For discussion of the history of topics see Stump, *Boethius's De Topicis Differentiis*, pp. 159–236.

31. There is a translation of the *Topica* of Cicero by H. M. Hubbell in the Loeb Classical Library volume which contains *De Inventione*.

32. See James J. Murphy, *Rhetoric in the Middle Ages: A History of Rhetorical Theory from Saint .Augustine to the Renaissance*, pp. 67–71; Michael C. Leff, "Boethius' *De Differentiis Topicis*, Book IV," in *Me-*

dieval Eloquence: Studies in the Theory and Practice of Medieval Rhetoric, ed. James J. Murphy, pp. 3–24; and Stump, *Boethius's De Topicis Differentiis*.

Chapter 5

1. See Cecil Wooten, "Le développement du style asiatique pendant l'époque hellénistique," *Revue des études grecques* 88 (1975): 94–104.
2. See George Kennedy, *The Art of Persuasion in Greece*, pp. 273–84.
3. Ibid., pp. 290–301.
4. Ibid., pp. 303–21. The fundamental work on Hermagoras is Dieter Matthes, "Hermagoras von Temnos, 1904–1955," *Lustrum* 3 (1958): 58–214.
5. Ibid., pp. 321–30.
6. See George Kennedy, *The Art of Rhetoric in the Roman World*, pp. 205–30, and Hans K. Schulte, *Orator: Untersuchungen über das Ciceronische Bildungsideal*, Frankfurter Studien zur Religion und Kultur der Antiken, 2 (Frankfurt: Klostermann, 1935).
7. See Richard Volkmann, *Die Rhetorik der Griechen und Römer in systematischer Übersicht*; Heinrich Lausberg, *Handbuch der literarischen Rhetorik: eine Grundlegung der Literaturwissenschaft*; and Josef Martin, *Antike Rhetorik: Technik und Methode*.
8. The *Rhetores Latini Minores* will be discussed later in this chapter. The *Rhetores Graeci* include Hermogenes, to be discussed in this chapter, and Aphthonius and a variety of commentators to be discussed in chapter 8.
9. See Kennedy, *Art of Rhetoric*, pp. 149–282.
10. There is a translation of *De Inventione* by H. M. Hubbell in the Loeb Classical Library. The Latin text of Victorinus is in Halm, *Rhetores Latini Minores*, pp. 153–310. "Victorinus" is probably Marius Victorinus, a fourth-century translator and commentator; see Pierre Hadot, *Marius Victorinus: recherches sur sa vie et ses oeuvres*. See also John O. Ward, "From Antiquity to the Renaissance: Glosses and Commentaries on Cicero's Rhetorica," in *Medieval Eloquence: Studies in the Theory and Practice of Medieval Rhetoric*, ed. James J. Murphy, pp. 25–67.
11. The general sentiment is Stoic; the praise of speech, however, is based on a similar passage in Isocrates' *Nicocles* (5). See Friedrich Solmsen, "Drei Rekonstruktionen zur antiken Rhetorik und Poetik," *Hermes* 67 (1932): 151–54. On influence see the work of Nuchelmans cited above, ch. 4, n. 28.
12. There is a fine edition with translation and notes by Harry Caplan in the Loeb Classical Library. See also Gualtiero Calboli, *Cornifici Rhetorica ad C. Herennium: Introduzione, testo critico, commento*.
13. See Kennedy, *Art of Rhetoric*, pp. 338–42.
14. See Frances A. Yates, *The Art of Memory*, and Herwig Blum, *Die antike Mnemotechnik*.

15. There is a translation by H. Rackham in the Loeb Classical Library. Book 1 is translated by E. N. P. Moor in *The Basic Works of Cicero*, ed. Moses Hadas (New York: The Modern Library, 1951), pp. 171–258.
16. There is a translation of *Orator* by H. M. Hubbell in the Loeb Classical Library volume containing Cicero's *Brutus*, trans. G. L. Hendrickson.
17. See George Kennedy, *Quintilian*. There is a translation by H. E. Butler in the Loeb Classical Library. Books 1–2.10 of the older and excellent translation by John Selby Watson are reprinted in *The Education of the Citizen Orator*, ed. James J. Murphy, in the Bobbs-Merrill Library of the Liberal Arts. See also the excellent French translation with extensive notes by Jean Cousin in the Budé series.
18. There is a translation of Seneca the Elder by Michael Winterbottom in the Loeb Classical Library.
19. See Chapter 3, note 13.
20. See Kennedy, *Art of Rhetoric*, pp. 619–33. A translation of the *Progymnasmata* can be found in Charles Sears Baldwin, *Medieval Rhetoric and Poetic*, pp. 23–38. *On Staseis* is translated by Raymond E. Nadeau, *Speech Monographs* 31 (1964): 361–424. A partial translation of *On Ideas* is included in *Ancient Literary Criticism: The Principal Texts in New Translations*, ed. Donald Andrew Russell and Michael Winterbottom, pp. 561–79.
21. See W. Schmid, "Zur antiken Stillehre aus Anlass von Proklos' *Chrestomathie*," *Rheinisches Museum* 49 (1894): 133–61.
22. See George L. Kustas, "Hermogenes, Aphthonius, and the Neoplatonists," in *Studies in Byzantine Rhetoric*, pp. 5–26.
23. The Latin text of these writers can be found in Halm, *Rhetores Latini Minores*. Translation of part of Fortunatianus is included in *Readings in Medieval Rhetoric*, ed. Joseph M. Miller, Michael H. Prosser, and Thomas W. Benson, pp. 25–32.
24. See John Monfasani, *George of Trebizond: A Biography and a Study of His Rhetoric and Logic*, pp. 280–81.
25. See John O. Ward, "From Antiquity to the Renaissance: Glosses and Commentaries on Cicero's *Rhetorica*," in *Medieval Eloquence: Studies in the Theory and Practice of Medieval Rhetoric*, ed. James J. Murphy, pp. 25–67.
26. Book 3 was often known in the Middle Ages as *Barbarismus*. For the text see *Grammatici Latini*, ed. Heinrich Keil (Leipzig: Teubner, 1864), IV, pp. 367–402.

Chapter 6

1. Demosthenes' *On the False Embassy* or Cicero's *Pro Murena* are examples of the former; Edmund Burke, the "dinner bell" of the House of Commons, may illustrate the latter.
2. See George Kennedy, *The Art of Persuasion in Greece*, pp. 172–73.

3. See George Kennedy, *The Art of Rhetoric in the Roman World*, pp. 446–64.
4. For translations of "Longinus," see note 6 below. There are translations of the *Dialogue on the Orators* by William Peterson in the Loeb Classical Library, by Alfred John Church and William Jackson Brodribb in the Modern Library volume *The Complete Works of Tacitus*, pp. 735–69, and by Herbert Benario in the Bobbs-Merrill Library of the Liberal Arts.
5. There is a translation, long out of print, by W. Rhys Roberts in *Dionysius of Halicarnassus, On Literary Composition*. A new translation is expected in the Loeb Classical Library.
6. Translations of "Longinus" include those by W. Hamilton Fyfe in the Loeb Classical Library volume of Aristotle, *Poetics*; G. M. A. Grube, *Longinus, On Great Writing*, in the Bobbs-Merrill Library of the Liberal Arts; D. A. Russell, *"Longinus," On Sublimity* (Oxford: Clarendon Pr., 1965); and T. S. Dorsch in *Classical Literary Criticism* in the Penguin series.
7. See Henry Guy, *L'Ecole des rhétoriqueurs*; Warner Forrest Patterson, *Three Centuries of Poetic Theory*, pp. 129–75; and Reinder P. Meijer, *Literature of the Low Countries*, pp. 47–71.
8. According to Vitruvius 1.1.3 the architect must know literature, drawing, geometry, history, philosophy, music, medicine, law, and astronomy.
9. See Richard McKeon, "Literary Criticism and the Concept of Imitation in Antiquity," *Modern Philology* 34 (1936): 1–35, reprinted in *Critics and Criticism*, ed. Ronald Salmon Crane, pp. 117–45; H. Koller, *Mimesis in der Antike*; and Gerald F. Else, "Imitation in the Fifth Century," *Classical Philology* 53 (1958): 73–90.
10. Cited by Syrianus on Hermogenes 2.23.6 and attributed to Aristophanes of Byzantium, the Hellenistic grammarian.
11. There is a translation by Harold North Fowler in the Loeb Classical Library volume of Plutarch, *Moralia* 10.
12. See Kennedy, *Art of Rhetoric*, pp. 342–63.
13. See ibid., pp. 29–37.
14. See Elaine Fantham, "Imitation and Decline: Rhetorical Theory and Practice in the First Century after Christ," *Classical Philology* 73 (1978): 102–16.

Chapter 7

1. There is no major study of Judeo-Christian rhetoric. Some basic philosophical or cultural issues are discussed by Eduard Norden in *Die antike Kunstprosa*, II, pp. 451–79. There are many studies of the rhetorical qualities of individual Christian writers, some of which are noted in the notes below. Important works on the attitude of Christianity to classical culture include Charles Norris Cochrane, *Christianity and Classical Culture: A Study of Thought and Action from Augustus to Augustine*; E. R.

Dodds, *Pagan and Christian in an Age of Anxiety: Some Aspects of Religious Experience from Marcus Aurelius to Constantine*; Edgar J. Goodspeed and Robert M. Grant, *A History of Early Christian Literature*; Werner Jaeger, *Early Christianity and Greek Paideia*; and Eduard Norden, *Agnostos Theos: Untersuchungen zur Formgeschichte religiöser Rede*.

Quotations from the Bible in this chapter are from the Revised Standard Version of the Bible, copyrighted 1946, 1952 © 1971, 1973, as printed in the *Oxford Annotated Bible* (New York: Oxford Univ. Pr., 1962), with permission of the publisher and the Division of Christian Education of the National Council of Churches.

2. See *Old Testament Form Criticism*, ed. John H. Hayes.
3. See Julian Jaynes, *The Origin of Consciousness in the Breakdown of the Bicameral Mind* (Boston: Houghton-Mifflin, 1976), pp. 293–313.
4. See W. Eugene March, "Prophecy," in Hayes, *Old Testament Form Criticism*, pp. 157–75.
5. Ibid., pp. 165–68.
6. In the later Hellenistic and Roman period there is some influence of classical ideas on Jewish concepts of wisdom; see *Aspects of Wisdom in Judaism and Early Christianity*, ed. Robert L. Wilken.
7. There is no comprehensive study of allegory. For an introduction see the article "Allegory" in *The Princeton Encyclopedia of Poetry and Poetics*, ed. Alex Preminger.
8. See Hartwig Thyen, *Der Stil der jüdisch-hellenistische Homilie*. A basic work on classical influences on Judaism is Saul Lieberman, *Hellenism in Jewish Palestine: Studies in the Literary Transmission, Beliefs, and Manners of Palestine in the Ist Cent. BCE–IVth Cent. CE*.
9. Page 43.
10. Ibid., pp. 126–31.
11. See Martin Dibelius, *A Fresh Approach to the New Testament and Early Christian Literature*, p. 262.
12. See Thyen, *Stil der Homilie*, pp. 19–20.
13. The bibliography is extensive. Among works in English see Frederick F. Bruce, *The Speeches in the Acts of the Apostles*; Ned B. Stonehouse, *The Areopagus Address*; and Bertil Gärtner, *The Areopagus Speech and Natural Revelation*.
14. See Johannes Weiss, *Beiträge zur paulinische Rhetorik*, and Rudolf Bultmann, *Der Stil der paulinischen Predigt und die kynisch-stoische Diatribe*.
15. See Hans Dieter Betz, "The Literary Composition and Function of Paul's Letter to the Galatians," *New Testament Studies* 21 (1975): 353–79; K. P. Donfried, "False Presuppositions in the Study of *Romans*," *Catholic Biblical Quarterly* 36 (1974): 332–55; Wilhelm Wuellner, "Paul's Rhetoric of Argumentation in *Romans*," *Catholic Biblical Quarterly* 38 (1976): 330–51; and F. Forrester Church, "Rhetorical Structure and Design in Paul's Letter to Philemon," *Harvard Theological Review*, in press.
16. A translation of the letter by Kirsopp Lake can be found in the Loeb Classical Library volume entitled *The Apostolic Fathers*, II, pp. 348–75.

17. See Robert Dick Sider, *Ancient Rhetoric and the Art of Tertullian*, and Timothy David Barnes, *Tertullian: A Historical and Literary Study*, pp. 186–232.

18. See William R. Schoedal, "Philosophy and Rhetoric in the *Adversus Haereses* of Irenaeus," *Vigiliae Christianae* 13 (1959): 22–32.

19. A translation by Kirsopp Lake can be found in the Loeb Classical Library volume entitled *The Apostolic Fathers*, I, pp. 125–63.

20. See Campbell Bonner, *The Homily on the Passion by Melito, Bishop of Sardis*, and A. Wifstrand, "The Homily of Melito on the Passion," *Vigiliae Christianae* 2 (1948): 201–23.

21. See John S. Chamberlin, *Increase and Multiply: Arts of Discourse Procedure in the Preaching of Donne*, p. 28.

22. On Origen as a rhetorician see Robert W. Smith, *The Art of Rhetoric in Alexandria*, pp. 92–94; on Origen as a preacher Jean Danielou, "Great Preachers, I: Origen," *Theology* 54 (1951): 10–15; on allegory C. W. Macleod, "Allegory and Mysticism in Origen and Gregory of Nyssa," *Journal of Theological Studies* 22 (1971): 362–79.

23. For a translation of *De Principiis* see *The Ante-Nicene Fathers*, ed. Alexander Roberts and James Donaldson (New York: Charles Scribner's, 1907), pp. 239–382.

24. See August Brinkmann, "Gregors des Thaumaturgen Panegyricus auf Origenes," *Rheinisches Museum* 56 (1901): 55–76, esp. 59–60.

25. See Henri Crouzel, *Grégoire le Thaumaturge: remerciement à Origène suivi de la lettre d'Origène à Grégoire*, pp. 79–92 and 186–94.

26. There is a translation by J. E. L. Oulton and H. J. Lawlor in the Loeb Classical Library volume of Eusebius, *The Ecclesiastical History*, II, pp. 398–445.

27. See Harold Allen Drake, *In Praise of Constantine: A Historical Study and New Translation of Eusebius' Tricennial Oration*.

28. See George Kennedy, "Athenian Sophists of the Fourth Century of the Christian Era: Julian of Cappadocia, Prohaeresius, Himerius, and Eunapius," *Yale Classical Studies* 27 (1979), in press.

29. See Rosemary Radford Ruether, *Gregory of Nazianzus: Rhetor and Philosopher*.

30. Based on the translation by Leo P. McCauley in *Funeral Orations by Saint Gregory Nazianzen and Saint Ambrose*, pp. 37–38.

31. See Leo V. Jacks, "Saint Basil and Greek Literature," *Catholic University of America Patristic Studies* 1 (1922), and James M. Campbell, "The Influence of the Second Sophistic on the Style of the Sermons of Saint Basil the Great," *Catholic University of America Patristic Studies* 2 (1922).

32. See *Saint Basile, Aux jeunes gens sur la manière de tirer profit des lettres helléniques*, ed. Fernand Boulenger.

33. See Thomas E. Ameringer, "The Stylistic Influence of the Second Sophistic on the Panegyrical Sermons of Saint John Chrysostom," *Catholic University of America Patristic Studies* 5 (1921); Harry M. Hubbell, "Chrysostom and Rhetoric," *Classical Philology* 19 (1924): 261–76; and Mary Albania Burns, "Saint John Chrysostom's Homilies *On the Statues*: A

study of Their Rhetorical Form," *Catholic University of America Patristic Studies* 22 (1930).

34. As translated by Ameringer, "Sermons of Saint John Chrysostom," p. 28.

35. See Henri-Irénée Marrou, "Synesius of Cyrene and Alexandrian Neoplatonism," in *The Conflict between Paganism and Christianity in the Fourth Century*, ed. Arnaldo Momigliano, pp. 126–50.

36. See Gerald L. Ellspermann, "The Attitude of the Early Christian Latin Writers toward Pagan Literature and Learning," *Catholic University of America Patristic Studies* 82 (1949): 23–42.

37. There is a translation of the whole letter by F. A. Wright in the Loeb Classical Library volume of Jerome, *Select Letters*, pp. 52–129. See also Arthur Stanley Pease, "The Attitude of Jerome toward Pagan Literature," *Transactions of the American Philological Association* 50 (1919): 150–67.

38. For a translation see Mary Francis McDonald, *Lactantius, The Divine Institutes, Books I–VIII* (Washington: Catholic University of America Press, 1964).

39. On Augustine's life see Peter Brown, *Augustine of Hippo: A Biography*. Works on Augustine and rhetoric, in addition to those cited in notes below, include Wilfrid Parsons, "A Study of the Vocabulary and Rhetoric of the Letters of Saint Augustine," *Catholic University of America Patristic Studies* 3 (1923); Mary Inez Bogan, "The Vocabulary and Style of the Soliloquies and Dialogues of Saint Augustine," *Catholic University of America Patristic Studies* 42 (1935); and Joseph Finaert, *Saint Augustin rhéteur* (Paris: "Les Belles Lettres," 1939).

40. For translation and discussion see Otto A. L. Dieter and William C. Kurth, "The *De Rhetorica* of Aurelius Augustinus," *Speech Monographs* 35 (1968): 90–108.

41. The best general discussion of *De Doctrina Christiana* is Henri-Irénée Marrou, *Saint Augustin et la fin de la culture antique*. For details see Sister Therese Sullivan, "S. Aureli Augustini Hipponiensis Episcopi *De Doctrina Christiana Liber Quartus*: A Commentary with a Revised Text, Introduction, and Translation," *Catholic University of America Patristic Studies* 23 (1930). On Augustine's practice see George Wright Doyle, "Saint Augustine's Tractates on the Gospel of John Compared with the Rhetorical Theory of *De Doctrina Christiana*."

42. Quotations from *De Doctrina Christiana* are given with the permission of the publisher in the translation of D. W. Robertson, Jr., *Saint Augustine, On Christian Doctrine*, Library of Liberal Arts (Indianapolis and New York: Bobbs-Merrill Company, 1958).

43. See Chamberlin, *Increase and Multiply*, pp. 34–43.

44. See W. R. Johnson, "Isocrates Flowering: The Rhetoric of Augustine," *Philosophy and Rhetoric* 9 (1976): 217–31.

45. See Brown, *Augustine of Hippo*, pp. 259–60.

46. Ibid., p. 266.

47. For example, by Charles Sears Baldwin, *Medieval Rhetoric and Poetic (to 1400)*, p. 51.

Chapter 8

1. The major accounts of Byzantine rhetoric are Herbert Hunger, *Die hochsprachliche profane Literatur der Byzantiner*, I: *Philosophie, Rhetorik, Epistolographie, Geschichtsschreibung, Geographie*, and Hans-Georg Beck, *Kirche und theologische Literatur im byzantinischen Reich*. Other important works include Karl Krumbacher, *Geschichte der byzantinische Literatur (527–1453)*, pp. 450–97; Georg L. Kustas, "The Function and Evolution of Byzantine Rhetoric," *Viator: Medieval and Renaissance Studies* 1 (1970): 55–73; idem, *Studies in Byzantine Rhetoric*. Texts of Byzantine rhetoricians are to be found in Christian Walz, *Rhetores Graeci*. Some additional editions are cited below. Very little material is available in English translation.

2. See Gregory Ostrogorsky, *History of the Byzantine State*, and the *Cambridge Medieval History*, IV: *The Byzantine Empire*, ed. J. M. Hussey.

3. For a picture of Greek rhetorical schools in late antiquity see Eunapius, *Lives of the Philosophers*, trans. Wilmer Cave Wright, in the Loeb Classical Library volume of Philostratus, *Lives of the Sophists*. For a survey of Byzantine education see Georgina Buckler, "Byzantine Education," in *Byzantium: An Introduction to East Roman Civilization*, ed. Norman H. Baynes and H. St. L. B. Moss, pp. 200–220; and Robert Browning, *Studies in Byzantine History, Literature, and Education*.

4. See M. L. Clarke, *Higher Education in the Ancient World*, p. 133.

5. See Ray Nadeau, "The *Progymnasmata* of Aphthonius in Translation," *Speech Monographs* 19 (1952): 264–85.

6. See Hunger, *Literatur der Byzantiner*, pp. 92–120 and 170–88.

7. See the discussion in Kustas, *Studies in Byzantine Rhetoric*, p. 22.

8. See Kustas, "Function and Evolution," p. 60.

9. See Marcella Gigante, ed., *Theodorus Metochites, Saggio critico su Demostene e Aristide*. A selection in Greek with English notes is included by Nigel G. Wilson in *An Anthology of Byzantine Prose*, pp. 130–34.

10. See Kustas, "Function and Evolution," p. 59; Gustav Karlsson, *Idéologie et cérémonial dans l'épistolographie byzantine*; and A. R. Littlewood, "An 'Ikon of the Soul': The Byzantine Letter," *Visible Language* 10 (1976): 197–226.

11. There is a translation by H. B. Dewing and Glanville Downey in the Loeb Classical Library volume of Procopius, VII.

12. This subject will be discussed in chapter 10

13. See the discussion for each period in Beck, *Kirche und theologische Literatur*.

14. See Cyril Mango, ed. and trans., *The Homilies of Photius, Patriarch of Constantinople*.

15. For the texts see Walz, *Rhetores Graeci*, IV–VII, and Hugo Rabe, *Syriani in Hermogenem Commentaria* (Leipzig: Teubner, 1892).

16. See Kustas, *Studies in Byzantine Rhetoric*, pp. 20–22.

17. For the texts and their relationship to each other see *Prolegomenon Syllagoge*, ed. Hugo Rabe.
18. On the theory see James A. Coulter, *The Literary Microcosm: Theories of Interpretation of the Later Neoplatonists*.
19. See Hermias, *In Platonis Phaedrum Scholia*, ed. P. Couvreur (Paris: E. Bouillon, 1901; reprinted New York: G. Olms, 1971), and Olympiodorus, *In Platonis Gorgiam Commentaria*, ed. L. G. Westerink (Leipzig: Teubner, 1970).
20. See J. M. Hussey, *Church and Learning in the Byzantine Empire, 867–1185*, pp. 73–88.
21. See Glanville Downey, "The Christian Schools of Palestine," *Harvard Library Bulletin* 12 (1951): 297–319.
22. See Louis Bréhier, "Notes sur l'histoire de l'enseignement supérieur à Constantinople," *Byzantion* 3 (1926): 73–94 and 4 (1927): 13–28; idem, "L'Enseignement classique et l'enseignement réligieux à Byzance," *Revue d'histoire et de philosophie réligieuse* 21 (1941): 34–69; F. Fuchs, *Die höheren Schulen von Konstantinopel im Mittelalter*, Byzantinisches Archiv, 8 (Stuttgart: Teubner, 1926); and Hussey, *Church and Learning*, pp. 51–72.
23. See Paul Speck, *Die kaiserliche Universität von Konstantinopel*.
24. See Wanda Wolska-Conus, "Les Ecoles de Psellos et de Xiphilin sous Constantin IX Monomaque," Centre de recherche d'histoire et civilisation Byzantine, *Travaux et Mémoires* 6 (1976): 223–43.
25. For the text see Walz, *Rhetores Graeci*, III, pp. 687–703.
26. See A. Meyer, "Psellos' Rede über den rhetorischen Charackter des Gregorius von Nazianzus," *Byzantinische Zeitschrift* 20 (1911): 27–100.
27. See Kustas, "Function and Evolution," p. 69.
28. See Robert Browning, "The Patriarchal School of Constantinople in the Twelfth Century," *Byzantion* 32 (1962): 167–202 and 33 (1963): 11–40.
29. See Gertrud Lindberg, *Studies in Hermogenes and Eustathios: the Theory of Ideas and Its Application in the Commentaries of Eustathios on the Epics of Homer*. For Eustathius' adaptation of Theophrastus' theory of delivery see J. Kaspar, "Theophrastus und Eustathius' *Peri Hypokriseos*," *Philologus* 69 (1910): 327–58. See also Peter Wirth, "Untersuchungen zur byzantinischen Rhetorik des zwölf Jahrhunderts mit besonderer Berucksichtigung der Schriften des Erzbischofs Eustathios von Thessalonike."
30. See R. M. Dawkins, "The Greek Language in the Byzantine Period," in Baynes and Moss, *Byzantium*, pp. 252–67.
31. Ibid., p. 257.
32. See Herbert Hunger, "Aspekte der griechischen Rhetorik von Gorgias bis zum Untergang von Byzanz," *Akademie der Wissenschaften, Wien, philosophisch-historische Klasse, Sitzungsberichte* 277, no. 3 (1977): 3–27.
33. See Kustas, *Studies in Byzantine Rhetoric*, pp. 63–100.
34. See Beck, *Kirche und theologische Literatur*, p. 546. Beck discusses panegyrical sermons and homilies by period.
35. See Hunger, *Literatur der Byzantiner*, pp. 120–45.
36. Ibid., pp. 145–57.

37. Ibid., pp. 157–70.
38. See John Monfasani, *George of Trebizond: A Biography and a Study of His Rhetoric and Logic.*

Chapter 9

1. On figures of speech and rhetorical ornamentation in the Middle Ages see Morris W. Croll, *Style, Rhetoric, and Rhythm,* pp. 255–67.
2. See Henri-Irénée Marrou, "Autour de la bibliothèque du Pape Agapit," *Ecole française de Rome, Mélanges d'archéologie et d'histoire* 48 (1931): 157–65 and Pierre Riché, *Education and Culture in the Barbarian West, Sixth through Eighth Centuries,* pp. 26–31.
3. See Theodore Haarhoff, *Schools of Gaul: A Study of Pagan and Christian Education in the Last Century of the Western Empire.*
4. Important works for the study of western medieval rhetoric include Charles Sears Baldwin, *Medieval Rhetoric and Poetic (to 1400) Interpreted from Representative Works;* R. R. Bolgar, *The Classical Heritage and Its Beneficiaries;* Ernst Robert Curtius, *European Literature and the Latin Middle Ages;* Max Manitius, *Geschichte der lateinischen Literatur des Mittelalters;* Richard McKeon, "Rhetoric in the Middle Ages," *Speculum* 17 (1942): 1–32; Joseph M. Miller, Michael H. Prosser, and Thomas W. Benson, *Readings in Medieval Rhetoric;* James J. Murphy, *Medieval Rhetoric: A Select Bibliography;* idem, ed., *Three Medieval Rhetorical Arts;* idem, *Rhetoric in the Middle Ages: A History of Rhetorical Theory from Saint Augustine to the Renaissance;* idem, ed., *Medieval Eloquence: Studies in the Theory and Practice of Medieval Rhetoric;* Louis J. Paetow, "The Arts Course at Medieval Universities with Special Reference to Grammar and Rhetoric"; Edward Kennard Rand, *Founders of the Middle Ages;* and Henry Osborn Taylor, *The Medieval Mind.*
5. See William H. Stahl, Richard Johnson, and E. L. Burge, *Martianus Capella and the Seven Liberal Arts,* I: *The Quadrivium of Martianus Capella with a Study of the Allegory and the Verbal Disciplines;* II: *The Marriage of Philology and Mercury* (translation).
6. See Leslie Webber Jones, ed. and trans., *An Introduction to Divine and Human Readings by Cassiodorus Senator.* The following quotation is from Jones, p. 127.
7. See Eleanore Stump, *Boethius's De Topicis Differentiis, Translated with Notes and Essays on the Text,* p. 80.
8. See Murphy, *Rhetoric in the Middle Ages,* p. 91. The *Speculatio de Cognatione Rhetoricae* is a short summary of rhetoric by Boethius, showing his strongly dialectical approach; there is a translation in Miller, Prosser, and Benson, *Readings in Medieval Rhetoric,* pp. 69–76. On Boethius' *Topica* see Michael C. Leff, "Boethius' *De Differentiis Topicis,* Book IV," in Murphy, *Medieval Eloquence,* pp. 3–24, with extensive bibliography, and Stump, *Boethius's De Topicis.*

9. See *New Catholic Encyclopedia*, XI, s.v. "Preaching," p. 686.
10. See Murphy, *Rhetoric in the Middle Ages*, pp. 292–97.
11. See Taylor, *The Medieval Mind*, I, p. 99.
12. For a translation of the section on rhetoric see Miller, Prosser, and Benson, *Readings in Medieval Rhetoric*, pp. 79–95.
13. See Jacques Fontaine, *Isidore de Séville et la culture classique dans l'Espagne wisigothique*, I, p. 332.
14. There is a translation of selections by Ernest Brehaut, *History of the Franks by Gregory Bishop of Tours* (New York: W. W. Norton, 1969).
15. There is a translation in Miller, Prosser, and Benson, *Readings in Medieval Rhetoric*, pp. 96–122.
16. The standard edition, with translation, is *Bede's Ecclesiastical History of the English People*, ed. Bertram Colgrave and R. A. B. Mynors (Oxford: Clarendon Press, 1969).
17. See Luke M. Reinsma, "Rhetoric in England: The Age of Aelfric, 970–1021," *Communication Monographs* 44 (1977): 388–403.
18. See Luitpold Wallach, "Charlemagne's *De Litteris Colendis* and Alcuin: A Diplomatic-Historical Study," *Speculum* 26 (1951): 288–305.
19. See Wilbur Samuel Howell, *The Rhetoric of Alcuin and Charlemagne: A Translation with an Introduction, the Latin Text, and Notes.*
20. See Luitpold Wallach, *Alcuin and Charlemagne: Studies in Carolingian History and Literature*, pp. 73–82.
21. There is a translation of 3.19 in Miller, Prosser, and Benson, *Readings in Medieval Rhetoric*, pp. 125–27. For discussion see Murphy, *Rhetoric in the Middle Ages*, pp. 82–87. Among other works by Hrabanus is an encomium of the Holy Cross in the tradition of Latin panegyrics.
22. There is no English translation. For the Latin text and some discussion see Karl Manitius, *Gunzo, Epistola ad Augienses und Anselm von Besate, Rhetorimachia*, Monumenta Germaniae Historica, Quellen zur Geistesgeschichte des Mittelalters, 2 (Weimar: Hermann Böhlaus, 1958), esp. pp. 75–86 and 102–3.
23. See Bolgar, *Classical Heritage*, p. 142.
24. See Baldwin, *Medieval Rhetoric*, pp. 206–7; Murphy, *Rhetoric in the Middle Ages*, pp. 194–268; and Helene Wieruszowski, *Politics and Culture in Medieval Spain and Italy*. An old standard study is Ludwig Rockinger, *Briefsteller und Formelbücher des eilften bis vierzehnten Jahrhunderts.*
25. For a translation of Alberic's *Flowers of Rhetoric* see Miller, Prosser, and Benson, *Readings in Medieval Rhetoric*, pp. 131–61.
26. See Paetow, "Arts Course," pp. 80–87.
27. See Maurice W. Croll, "The Cadence of English Oratorical Prose," *Studies in Philology* 16 (1919): 1–55, reprinted in *Style, Rhetoric, and Rhythm*, 303–59, from which the examples are taken, pp. 304–5. See also A. C. Clark, *The Cursus in Medieval and Vulgar Latin*, and Tore Janson, *Prose Rhythm in Medieval Latin from the 9th to the 13th Century.*
28. See Charles B. Faulhaber, "The *Summa Dictaminis* of Guido Faba," in Murphy, *Medieval Eloquence*, pp. 85–111.
29. The *Oculus Pastoralis* was printed by L. M. Muratori in *Antiquitates*

Italiae Medii Aevi (Milan: Societas Palatina, 1738–1742), IV, pp. 95ff. On the instructions to city officials see F. Hertter, *Die Podestaliteratur Italiens im 12. und 13. Jahrhundert.* See also N. Rubenstein, "Political Rhetoric in the Imperial Chancery," *Medium Aevum* 14 (1945): 21–43, and Paul Oskar Kristeller, *Renaissace Thought: The Classic, Scholastic, and Humanistic Strains*, pp. 105 and 155–56.

30. The *Rhetorica Novissima* was edited by A. Gaudenzi in 1892 (reprinted Turin: Bottega d'Erasmo, 1962). On Boncompagno see Murphy, *Rhetoric in the Middle Ages*, pp. 253–55.

31. See André Wilmart, "*L'Ars arengandi* de Jacques de Dinant avec un appendice sur ses ouvrages *De dictamine*," *Studi e Testi* 59 (1933): 113–51, and Emil J. Polak, *A Textual Study of Jacques de Dinant's Summa Dictaminis* (Geneva: Droz, 1975).

32. For a translation of 3.60–65 (on refutation) see Miller, Prosser, and Benson, *Readings in Medieval Rhetoric*, pp. 253–64.

33. See F. Maggini, *Brunetto Latini, La Rettorica* (Florence: Le Monnier, 1968).

34. See Taylor, *Medieval Mind*, I, pp. 298–307.

35. See John Bliese, "The Study of Rhetoric in the Twelfth Century," *Quarterly Journal of Speech* 63 (1977): 364–83, and Daniel D. McGarry, ed. and trans., *The Metalogicon of John of Salisbury: A Twelfth-Century Defense of the Verbal and Logical Arts of the Trivium.*

36. See Murphy, *Rhetoric in the Middle Ages*, p. 117.

37. See John O. Ward, "From Antiquity to the Renaissance: Glosses and Commentaries on Cicero's *Rhetorica*," in Murphy, *Medieval Eloquence*, pp. 25–67.

38. See Baldwin, *Medieval Rhetoric*, pp. 169–72, and A. Mollard, "La Diffusion de l'*Institution oratoire* au XIIᵉ siècle," *Moyen Age* 44 (1934): 161–75 and 45 (1935): 1–9.

39. For a translation of 3.2–3 and 7.6.270–295 see Miller, Prosser, and Benson, *Readings in Medieval Rhetoric*, pp. 222–27.

40. See Charles B. Faulhaber, *Latin Rhetorical Theory in Thirteenth and Fourteenth Century Castile.*

41. See Charles Homer Haskins, *The Renaissance of the Twelfth Century.*

42. See Edmond Faral, *Les Arts poétiques du XIIe et du XIIIe siècle: recherches et documents sur la technique littéraire du Moyen Age;* Baldwin, *Medieval Rhetoric*, pp. 183–205; Murphy, *Rhetoric in the Middle Ages*, pp. 135–93; and Ernest Gallo, "The *Poetria nova* of Geoffrey of Vinsauf," in Murphy, *Medieval Eloquence*, pp. 68–84. For translations see Ernest Gallo, "Matthew of Vendome: Introductory Treatise on the Art of Poetry," *Proceedings of the American Philosophical Society* 118 (1974): 51–92, and Jane B. Kopp, "Poetria nova," in Murphy, *Three Medieval Rhetorical Arts*, pp. 32–108.

43. See Franz Quadlbauer, "Die antike Theorie der *Genera Dicendi* im lateinischen Millelalter," *Akademie der Wissenschaften, Wien, philosophisch-historische Klasse, Sitzungsberichte* 241, no. 2 (1962), and Douglas Kelly,

"Topical Invention in French Literature," in Murphy, *Medieval Eloquence*, pp. 236–40.
44. See Paetow, "Arts Course," p. 60.
45. The statute has often been misinterpreted; but see John Bliese, "Rhetoric in the Twelfth Century," *Quarterly Journal of Speech* 63 (1977): 364–83, esp. pp. 370–72.
46. See Murphy, *Rhetoric in the Middle Ages*, pp. 97–101.
47. See Frances A. Yates, *The Art of Memory*, pp. 50–81.
48. See Baldwin, *Medieval Rhetoric*, pp. 228–57, and Murphy, *Rhetoric in the Middle Ages*, pp. 269–355.
49. A version of the sermon was written down by Archbishop Baldric and can be found in Johann Matthias Watterich, *Pontificum Romanorum Vitae* (Leipzig, 1862; reprinted Aalen: Scientia, 1966), II, pp. 599–603.
50. See Harry Caplan, "A Late Mediaeval Tractate on Preaching," *Of Eloquence*, p. 42.
51. For a translation see Miller, Prosser, and Benson, *Readings in Medieval Rhetoric*, pp. 162–81.
52. See Harry Caplan, "The Four Senses of Scriptural Interpretation and the Mediaeval Theory of Preaching," *Speculum* 4 (1929): 282–90, reprinted in *Of Eloquence*, pp. 93–104, esp. p. 98.
53. For a partial translation of *De Arte Praedicatoria*, see ibid., pp. 228–39.
54. See Murphy, *Rhetoric in the Middle Ages*, pp. 310–26.
55. See M. M. Davy, *Les Sermons universitaires parisiens de 1230–31: contribution à l'histoire de la prédication médiévale.*
56. For an abridged translation see Murphy, *Rhetoric in the Middle Ages*, pp. 344–55.
57. See also Eduard Norden, *Die antike Kunstprosa*, pp. 659–763.
58. See J. M. Manly, "Chaucer and the Rhetoricians," *Proceedings of the British Academy* 12 (1926): 95–113, and Robert O. Payne, "Chaucer's Realization of Himself as Rhetor," in Murphy, *Medieval Eloquence*, pp. 270–87 with additional bibliography.
59. See Caplan, *Of Eloquence*, pp. 288–90.
60. See G. E. von Gunebaum, *A Tenth-Century Document of Arabic Literary Theory and Criticism*; S. A. Bornebakker, "Aspects of the History of Literary Rhetoric and Politics in Arabic Literature," *Viator* 1 (1970): 75–95; and Vasile Florescu, *La Retorica nel suo sviluppo storico*, p. 22, n. 2.

Chapter 10

1. There is no comprehensive work on renaissance rhetoric. Charles Sears Baldwin, *Renaissance Literary Theory and Practice*, ed. Donald L. Clark, gives an introductory picture from a literary point of view. Other very useful works include R. R. Bolgar, *The Classical Heritage and Its Beneficiaries*; Walter J. Ong, *Ramus, Method, and the Decay of Dialogue*; Aldo Scaglione, *The Classical Theory of Composition from Its Origins to the Present*; Lee A. Sonnino, *A Handbook to Sixteenth-Century Rhetoric*;

and Brian Vickers, *Classical Rhetoric in English Poetry*. I have found useful the article "Retorica" by Fausto Ghisalberti in the *Enciclopedia Italiana*. Much renaissance writing on rhetoric has not been reedited in modern times, especially the handbooks. Some of the more literary works are to be found in Bernard Weinberg, *Tratti di poetica e retorica del cinquecento*. A number of sixteenth-century works are available on microfilm in *British and Continental Rhetoric and Elocution*.

2. See Paul Oskar Kristeller, *Renaissance Thought: The Classic, Scholastic, and Humanist Strains*, p. 9. On individual humanists see Rudolph Pfeiffer, *History of Classical Scholarship: From 1300 to 1850*, with bibliography.

3. On French antecedents of humanism see Kristeller, ibid., p. 94. On eloquence see Hannah H. Gray, "Renaissance Humanism: The Pursuit of Eloquence," *Journal of the History of Ideas* 24 (1963): 497–514.

4. See Osborne Bennett Hardison, Jr., *The Enduring Monument: A Study of the Idea of Praise in Renaissance Literary Theory and Practice*, and John M. McManamon, "The Ideal Renaissance Pope: Funeral Oratory from the Papal Court," *Archivum Historiae Pontificiae* 14 (1976): 9–70.

5. On oratory for practical political purposes see Hans Baron, *The Crisis of the Early Italian Renaissance: Civic Humanism and Republican Liberty in an Age of Classicism and Tyranny*. On classical rhetoric in the Church see John W. O'Malley, *Praise and Blame in Renaissance Rome: Rhetoric, Doctrine, and Reform in the Sacred Orators of the Papal Court, c. 1450–1521*.

6. See Jerrold E. Seigel, *Rhetoric and Philosophy in Renaissance Humanism: The Union of Eloquence and Wisdom, Petrarch to Valla*; Scaglione, *Theory of Composition*, pp. 143–44; and Ronald G. Witt, *Coluccio Salutati and His Public Letters*.

7. On the recovery of texts, see Pfeiffer, *History of Classical Scholarship From 1300 to 1850*, pp. 3–66.

8. For Poggio's description of his discovery of the Quintilian see Phyllis Walter Goodhart Gordan, *Two Renaissance Book Hunters: The Letters of Poggius Bracciolini to Nicolaus de Niccolis*, pp. 193–96.

9. See F. H. Colson, "Knowledge and Use of Quintilian after 1416," in his edition of *M. Fabii Quintiliani Institutionis Oratoriae Liber I* (Cambridge: The University Press, 1924), pp. lxiv–lxxviii.

10. For a partial list, see Weinberg, *Tratti di poetica e retorica*, I, pp. 566–81.

11. The account here is based on the work of John Monfasani, *George of Trebizond: A Biography and a Study of His Rhetoric and Logic*.

12. Text in ibid., pp. 365–69.

13. See ibid., pp. 259–60 and 289.

14. See ibid., pp. 265–66, and Scaglione, *Theory of Composition*, pp. 134–35.

15. See ibid., pp. 370–72. Monfasani prints the preface and has announced plans to edit the whole. My knowledge of the text is based on his discussion and on the 1547 edition (Lugduni apud Gryphium) in the Princeton University Library.

16. See Wilbur Samuel Howell, *Logic and Rhetoric in England, 1500–1700*,

pp. 66–115. On Fichet see Paul Oskar Kristeller, "An Unknown Sermon on Saint Stephen by Guillaume Fichet," *Studi e Testi* 236 (1964): 459–97, esp. 472–73. On Traversagni see James J. Murphy, "Caxton's Two Choices: Modern and Medieval Rhetoric in Traversagni's *Nova Rhetorica* and the Anonymous *Court of Sapience,*" *Medievalia et Humanistica*, n.s. 3 (1972): 241–55.

17. See Ong, *Ramus*, pp. 106 and 276.

18. See Monfasani, *George of Trebizond*, p. 332.

19. The closest to it is perhaps the *De Natura Logicae* of Jacopo Zabarella (1533–1589); see William F. Edwards, "Jacopo Zabarella: A Renaissance Aristotelian's View of Rhetoric and Poetry and Their Relation to Philosophy," in *Arts libéraux et philosophie au Moyen Age*, pp. 843–54.

20. See Eugenio Garin, "Note su alcuni aspetti delle retoriche rinascimentali e sulla *Retorica* del Patrizi," *Testi umanistici su la retorica: archivo di filosofia* 3 (1953): 7–53. The article includes some discussion of Speroni as well.

21. See Bernard Weinberg, *A History of Literary Criticism in the Italian Renaissance*. Weinberg neglects rhetoric.

22. For a translation see Izora Scott, *Controversies over the Imitation of Cicero*, part 2, pp. 19–130.

23. For a translation see Craig R. Thompson, *Collected Works of Erasmus, Literary and Educational Writings*, II, pp. 284–659.

24. See T. W. Baldwin, *William Shakespere's Small Latine and Lesse Greeke*, II, pp. 138–75, and Joseph X. Brennan, "Joannes Susenbrotus: A Forgotten Humanist," *Publications of the Modern Language Association* 75, no. 5 (December, 1960): 485–96.

25. See Monfasani, *George of Trebizond*, p. 38.

26. See Pfeiffer, *History of Classical Scholarship*, pp. 35–41.

27. The translation is that of Monfasani, *George of Trebizond*, pp. 304–5. See further James Richard McNally, "*Rector et Dux Populi:* Italian Humanists and the Relationship between Rhetoric and Logic," *Modern Philology* 67 (1969): 168–76.

28. See Ong, *Ramus*, pp. 92–130, and James Richard McNally, "*Dux illa Directrixque Artium:* Rudolph Agricola's Dialectical System," *Quarterly Journal of Speech* 52 (1966): 337–47.

29. See Donald Leman Clark, "The Rise and Fall of Progymnasmata in Sixteenth and Seventeenth Century Grammar Schools," *Speech Monographs* 19 (1952): 259–63.

30. There is a facsimile reprint of the 1539 edition of Agricola's *De Inventione Dialectica*, Monumenta Humanistica Belgica 2 (Nieuwkoop: de Graff, 1967); the text is also available on microfilm in *British and Continental Rhetoric and Elocution*, reel 8, item 92.

31. Melanchthon's *Elementorum Rhetorices Libri II* can be found in *Corpus Reformatorum* 13, ed. C. G. Bretschneider (Halle: C. A. Schwetscke, 1834–1860), pp. 413ff., and in *British and Continental Rhetoric and Elocution*, reel 14, item 126. Other rhetorical writings of Melanchthon are apparently not available in modern editions except for the *Dispositiones Rhetoricae*

of 1553, to be found in Hans Zwicker, *Philologische Schriften Philipp Melanchthons*, Supplementa Melanchthoniana 2, no. 1 (Leipzig, 1911; reprinted Frankfurt: Minerva, 1968). See also Leonard Cox, *The Arte or Crafte of Rhethoryke*, ed. Frederick Ives Carpenter, p. 91. Melanchthon is Cox's source, and Carpenter's edition prints some excerpts from Melanchthon. See also James Richard McNally, "Melanchthon's Earliest Rhetoric," in *Rhetoric: A Tradition in Transition*, ed. W. R. Fisher.

32. See Foster Watson, *Vives on Education: A Translation of the De Tradendis Disciplinis of Juan Luis Vives, Together with an Introduction*, pp. 180–200.

33. My discussion is based on the book by Fr. Walter J. Ong, *Ramus, Method, and the Decay of Dialogue: From the Art of Discourse to the Art of Reason*.

34. On the rhetorical works of Talon and Ramus see ibid., pp. 270–92.

35. Talon's rhetoric is available in *British and Continental Rhetoric and Elocution*, reel 15, item 140.

36. The text of the *Rhetor* is in *British and Continental Rhetoric and Elocution*, reel 4, item 39. For a translation of the *Ciceronianus* see Harold S. Wilson and Clarence A. Forbes, *Gabriel Harvey's Ciceronianus*.

37. For the text see *British and Continental Rhetoric and Elocution*, reel 2, item 17 (Butler) and Reel 4, item 33 (Fraunce). See also William B. Sanford, "English Rhetoric Reverts to Classicism, 1600–1650," *Quarterly Journal of Speech* 15 (1929): 503–75, and Howell, *Logic and Rhetoric*, pp. 247–81 and 318–41.

38. Some of the works mentioned in this paragraph are available in *British and Continental Rhetoric and Elocution*: Vossius, reel 7, item 77; Butler, reel 2, item 18; Farnaby, reel 3, item 31; Prideaux, reel 6, item 61.

39. See Vickers, *Classical Rhetoric in English Poetry*; Donald L. Clark, *Rhetoric and Poetry in the Renaissance*; and William G. Crane, *Wit and Rhetoric in the Renaissance: The Formal Basis of Elizabethan Prose Style*.

40. Shakespeare had apparently studied *Rhetorica ad Herennium*, Cicero's *Topica*, Susenbrotus' textbook on figures, Erasmus' *De Copia*, and perhaps Quintilian; see Baldwin, *William Shakespere's Small Latine and Lesse Greeke*, II, pp. 69–238.

41. See Morris William Croll, "The Sources of the Euphuistic Rhetoric," in Croll and Harry Clemons, *Euphues: The Anatomy of Wit; Euphues and His England* (London: Routledge and Sons, 1916), pp. xv–lxiv, reprinted in Croll, *Style, Rhetoric, and Rhythm*, pp. 255–85.

42. See Scott, *Controversies over the Imitation of Cicero*, part 1, and M. L. Clarke, "Non Hominis Nomen, Sed Eloquentiae," in *Cicero*, ed. T. A. Dorey, pp. 89–95.

43. See Croll, *Style, Rhetoric, and Rhythm*, pp. 167–202.

44. See Claude Palisca, "Ut Oratoria Musica: The Rhetorical Basis of Musical Mannerism," in *The Meaning of Mannerism*, ed. Franklin W. Robinson and Stephen G. Nichols, Jr., (Hanover, N.H.: The University Press of New England, 1972), pp. 37–65; and George J. Buelow, "Music, Rhetoric,

and the Concept of the Affections: A Selective Bibliography," *Music Library Notes* 31 (1973): 250–59.

45. See Karl R. Wallace, *Francis Bacon on Communication and Rhetoric*.
46. Quoted by Wallace, ibid., p. 4.
47. There are many editions of *The Advancement of Learning*. *De Dignitate et Augmentis* can be found in translation in *The Philosophical Works of Francis Bacon*, ed. John M. Robertson (London: George Routledge and Sons, 1905), pp. 413–638.
48. In the Latin text: "munus rhetoricae non aliud quam ut rationis dictamina phantasiae applicet et commendet ad exercitandum appetitum et voluntatem."
49. See Wallace, *Francis Bacon*, pp. 205–18.
50. See ibid., pp. 219–27.

Chapter 11

1. Io. Christ. Theoph. Ernesti, *Lexicon Technologiae Graecorum Rhetoricae* (Leipzig, 1795) and *Lexicon Technologiae Latinorum Rhetoricae* (Leipzig, 1797), both reprinted Hildesheim: Georg Olms, 1962.
2. My account is largely based on Hugh M. Davidson, *Audience, Words, and Art: Studies in Seventeenth-Century French Rhetoric*.
3. On Rapin and other French writers of the time, see Wilbur Samuel Howell, *Eighteenth-Century British Logic and Rhetoric*, pp. 503–35. Howell discusses the introduction of the term *belles lettres* into English, pp. 531–35.
4. See Wilbur Samuel Howell, *Logic and Rhetoric in England, 1500–1700*, pp. 342–63, and Davidson, *Audience, Words, and Art*, pp. 57–108.
5. See Davidson, ibid., pp. 109–40, and Kathleen M. Jamieson, "Pascal vs. Descartes: A Clash over Rhetoric in the Seventeenth Century," *Communication Monographs* 43 (1976): 44–50.
6. See *Fénelon's Dialogues on Eloquence*, ed. and trans. Wilbur Samuel Howell.
7. Bossuet discusses his theory of preaching in his *Panégyrique de Saint Paul*; see *Oeuvres oratoires de Bossuet*, ed. J. Lebarq (Lille and Paris: Desclée, de Brouwen and Cie., 1891), pp. 302–4.
8. The two characters in Cicero's *Tusculan Disputations* are M and A.
9. See Howell, *Eighteenth-Century British Logic and Rhetoric*, pp. 518–19.
10. See Irène Simon, *Neo-Classical Criticism 1660–1800*, pp. 7–35.
11. See Samuel H. Monk, *The Sublime: A Study of Critical Theories in 18th Century England*, chapter 1.
12. See Richard Foster Jones, "Ancients and Moderns: A Study of the Background of the Battle of the Books," *Washington University Studies*, n.s. 6 (1936).
13. See Edmund Burke, *A Philosophical Enquiry into the Origin of Our Ideas of the Sublime and Beautiful*, ed. J. T. Boulton.
14. See Howell, *Eighteenth-Century British Logic and Rhetoric*, pp. 448–502.

15. See Book 3, chapter 10, section 34: "Figurative speech also an abuse of language."
16. See Book 3, chapter 10, section 3: "The ends of language."
17. A popular Ciceronian rhetoric of the mid–eighteenth century was John Holmes, *The Art of Rhetoric Made Easy* (1755), which appended a summary of "Longinus"; see Howell, *Eighteenth-Century British Logic and Rhetoric*, pp. 125–41. On rhetorical texts used in eighteenth-century America see Warren Guthrie, "Rhetorical Theory in Colonial America," in *History of Speech Education in America: Background Studies*, ed. Karl R. Wallace.
18. Examples of textbooks include Nicolas Burton, *Figurae Grammaticae et Rhetoricae Latina Carmina Donatae* (1702), available in *British and Continental Rhetoric and Elocution*, Reel 2, item 15, and Anthony Blackwell, *Introduction to the Classics* (1718), ibid., Reel 1, item 7.
19. John Ward, *A System of Oratory Delivered in a Course of Lectures Publicly Read at Gresham College.*
20. See Frederick W. Haberman, "English Sources of American Elocution," in Wallace, *History of Speech Education in America*, pp. 105–26; and Howell, *Eighteenth-Century British Logic and Rhetoric*, pp. 145–256.
21. Reprinted New York: Benjamin Blom, 1968.
22. See Howell, *Eighteenth-Century British Logic and Rhetoric*, pp. 616–31.
23. David Hume, "Of Eloquence," in *Philosophical Works*, III: *Essays, Moral, Political, and Literary*, ed. T. H. Green and T. H. Grose, pp. 163–74.
24. See Jan Lannering, *Studies in the Prose Style of Joseph Addison* (Uppsala: Lundquist, and Cambridge: Harvard University Press, 1951).
25. See Lloyd F. Bitzer, Editor's Introduction to George Campbell, *The Philosophy of Rhetoric*, p. xxviii.
26. See Howell, *Eighteenth-Century British Logic and Rhetoric*, pp. 577–612.
27. See James L. Golden and Edward P. J. Corbett, *The Rhetoric of Blair, Campbell, and Whately*, p. 25. Howell discusses Blair in *Eighteenth-Century British Logic and Rhetoric*, pp. 648–71.
28. Page numbers in the text are to the original edition of 1783. There is a reproduction with introduction by Harold F. Harding, ed., *Lectures on Rhetoric and Belles Lettres by Hugh Blair* (Carbondale and Edwardsville: Southern Illinois University Press, 1965).
29. See Robert Morell Schmitz, *Hugh Blair*, pp. 144–45.
30. John Quincy Adams, *Lectures on Rhetoric and Oratory*, ed. J. Jeffrey Auer and Jerald L. Banninga, I, pp. 28–29.
31. Quoted by Marie Hochmuth and Richard Murphy in "Rhetorical and Elocutionary Training in Nineteenth-Century Colleges," in Wallace, *History of Speech Education in America*, p. 164.

Bibliography

This Bibliography contains, first, general works with which the student of the history of rhetoric should be familiar, many of which are also cited in the Notes; second, all books cited in the Notes except a small number cited in passing, for which full bibliographical information is supplied in the note itself; third, a small number of important works published as articles.

Abrams, M. H. *The Mirror and the Lamp.* New York: Oxford Univ. Pr., 1953.

Adams, John Quincy. *Lectures on Rhetoric and Oratory.* Edited with a New Introduction by J. Jeffrey Auer and Jerald L. Banninga. 2 vols. New York: Russell and Russell, 1962.

Arts libéraux et philosophie au Moyen Age: actes du Congrès international de philosophie médiévale, Montreal, 1967. Paris: J. Vrin, 1969.

Baldwin, Charles Sears. *Ancient Rhetoric and Poetic.* New York: Macmillan, 1924.

———. *Medieval Rhetoric and Poetic (to 1400) Interpreted from Representative Works.* New York: Macmillan, 1928.

———. *Renaissance Literary Theory and Practice.* Edited by Donald L. Clark. New York: Macmillan, 1939.

Baldwin, T. W. *William Shakespere's Small Latine and Lesse Greeke.* 2 vols. Urbana: Univ. of Illinois Pr., 1944.

Barnes, Timothy David. *Tertullian: A Historical and Literary Study.* Oxford: Clarendon Pr., 1971.

Baron, Hans. *The Crisis of the Early Italian Renaissance: Civic Humanism and Republican Liberty in an Age of Classicism and Tyranny.* Princeton: Princeton Univ. Pr., 1966.

Baynes, Norman H., and Moss, H. St. L. B. *Byzantium: An Introduction to East Roman Civilization.* Oxford: Clarendon Pr., 1948.

Beck, Hans-Georg. *Kirche und theologische Literatur im byzantinischen Reich.* Handbuch der Altertumswissenschaft 12, no. 2, part 1. Munich: Beck, 1959.

Blair, Hugh. *Lectures on Rhetoric and Belles Lettres.* Edited with a Critical

Bibliography

Introduction by Harold F. Harding. 2 vols. Carbondale and Edwardsville: Southern Illinois Univ. Pr., 1965.

Bloch, Maurice, ed. *Political Language and Oratory in Traditional Society*. New York: Academic Pr., 1975.

Blum, Herwig. *Die antike Mnemotechnik*. Spudasmata, 15. Hildesheim: G. Olms, 1969.

Bolgar, R. R. *The Classical Heritage and Its Beneficiaries*. Cambridge: Cambridge Univ. Pr., 1954.

————, ed. *Classical Influences on European Culture, A.D. 500–1500: Proceedings of an International Conference Held at King's College, Cambridge, April 1969*. Cambridge: Cambridge Univ. Pr., 1971.

Bonner, Campbell. *The Homily on the Passion by Melito, Bishop of Sardis*. London: Christophers, 1940.

Bonner, S. F. *Roman Declamation in the Late Republic and Early Empire*. Berkeley and Los Angeles: Univ. of California Pr., 1949.

Boulenger, Fernand, ed. *Saint Basile, Aux jeunes gens sur la manière de tirer profit des lettres helléniques*. Paris: Les Belles Lettres, 1952.

British and Continental Rhetoric and Elocution. Sixteen microfilm reels containing 143 items. Ann Arbor: University Microfilms, 1953.

Brown, Peter. *Augustine of Hippo: A Biography*. Berkeley and Los Angeles: Univ. of California Pr., 1969.

Browning, Robert. *Studies in Byzantine History, Literature, and Education*. London: Variorum Reprints, 1977.

Bruce, Frederick F. *The Speeches in the Acts of the Apostles*. London: Tyndale Pr., 1942.

Bultmann, Rudolf. *Der Stil der Paulinischen Predigt und die kynisch-stoische Diatribe*. Göttingen: Vandenhoeck und Ruprecht, 1910.

Burgess, Theodore C. "Epideictic Literature," *University of Chicago Studies in Classical Philology* 3 (1902): 89–261.

Burke, Edmund. *A Philosophical Enquiry into the Origin of Our Ideas of the Sublime and Beautiful*. Edited with an Introduction and Notes by J. T. Boulton. London: Routledge and Kegan Paul, 1958.

Calboli, Gualtiero, ed. *Cornifici Rhetorica ad C. Herennium: Introduzione, testo critico, commento*. Bologna: Ricardo Patron, 1969.

Campbell, George. *The Philosophy of Rhetoric*. Edited with a Critical Introduction by Lloyd F. Bitzer. Carbondale and Edwardsville: Southern Illinois Univ. Pr., 1963.

Caplan, Harry. *Of Eloquence: Studies in Ancient and Medieval Rhetoric*. Edited with an Introduction by Anne King and Helen North. Ithaca: Cornell Univ. Pr., 1970.

————, ed. *[Cicero] Ad Herennium De Ratione Dicendi*. Loeb Classical Library. Cambridge: Harvard Univ. Pr., 1954.

Chamberlin, John S. *Increase and Multiply: Arts of Discourse Procedure in the Preaching of Donne*. Chapel Hill: Univ. of North Carolina Pr., 1976.

Clark, A. C. *The Cursus in Medieval and Vulgar Latin*. Oxford: Clarendon Pr., 1910.

Bibliography

Clark, Donald L. *Rhetoric and Poetry in the Renaissance*. New York: Columbia Univ. Pr., 1922.

Clarke, M. L. *Higher Education in the Ancient World*. London: Routledge and Kegan Paul, 1971.

————. *Rhetoric at Rome: A Historical Survey*. London: Cohen and West, 1953.

Cochrane, Charles Norris. *Christianity and Classical Culture: A Study of Thought and Action from Augustus to Augustine*. London: Oxford Univ. Pr., 1957.

Cope, E. M. *An Introduction to Aristotle's Rhetoric with Analysis, Notes, and Appendices*. London and Cambridge: Macmillan, 1867; reprinted New York: G. Olms, 1970.

Corbett, Edward P. J. *Classical Rhetoric for the Modern Reader*. New York: Oxford Univ. Pr., 1965.

Coulter, James A. *The Literary Microcosm: Theories of Interpretation of the Later Neoplatonists*. Columbia Studies in the Classical Tradition, 2. Leiden: Brill, 1976.

Cox, Leonard. *The Arte or Crafte of Rhetoryke*. Edited by Frederick Ives Carpenter. Chicago: Univ. of Chicago Pr., 1899.

Crane, Ronald Salmon, ed. *Critics and Criticism*. Chicago: Univ. of Chicago Pr., 1952.

Crane, William G. *Wit and Rhetoric in the Renaissance: The Formal Basis of Elizabethan Prose Style*. New York: Columbia Univ. Pr., 1937.

Croll, Morris W. *Style, Rhetoric, and Rhythm: Essays by Morris W. Croll*. Edited by J. Max Patrick and Robert O. Evans. Princeton: Princeton Univ. Pr., 1966.

Crouzel, Henri, ed. *Grégoire le Thaumaturge: Remerciement à Origène suivi de la lettre d'Origène à Grégoire*. Paris: Editions du Cerf, 1969.

Curtius, Ernst Robert. *European Literature and the Latin Middle Ages*. Princeton: Princeton Univ. Pr., 1953.

Davidson, Hugh M. *Audience, Words, and Art: Studies in Seventeenth-Century French Rhetoric*. Columbus: Ohio State Univ. Pr., 1965.

Davy, M. M. *Les Sermons universitaires parisiens de 1230–31: contribution à l'histoire de prédication médiévale*. Paris: J. Vrin, 1931.

Dibelius, Martin. *A Fresh Approach to the New Testament and Early Christian Literature*. New York: Scribner's, 1936.

Dodds, E. R. *Pagan and Christian in an Age of Anxiety: Some Aspects of Religious Experience from Marcus Aurelius to Constantine*. Cambridge: Cambridge Univ. Pr., 1965.

Dorey, T. A., ed. *Cicero*. London: Routledge and Kegan Paul, 1964.

Doyle, George Wright. "Saint Augustine's Tractates on the Gospel of John Compared with the Rhetorical Theory of *De Doctrina Christiana*." Ph.D. dissertation, Univ. of North Carolina at Chapel Hill, 1975.

Drake, Harold Allen. *In Praise of Constantine: A Historical Study and New Translation of Eusebius' Tricennial Oration*. Berkeley and Los Angeles: Univ. of California Pr., 1976.

Bibliography

Erickson, Keith, ed. *Aristotle: The Classical Heritage of Rhetoric.* Metuchen, N. J.: Scarecrow Pr., 1974.

————, ed. *Aristotle's Rhetoric: Five Centuries of Philological Research.* Metuchen, N. J.: Scarecrow Pr., 1975.

Faral, Edmond. *Les Arts poétiques du XIIe et du XIIIe siècle: recherches et documents sur la technique littéraire du Moyen Age.* Bibliothèque de l'école des hautes études, 238. Paris: Honoré Champion, 1924.

Faulhaber, Charles B. *Latin Rhetorical Theory in Thirteenth and Fourteenth Century Castile.* Berkeley and Los Angeles: Univ. of California Pr., 1972.

Finaert, Joseph. *Saint Augustin rhéteur.* Paris: Les Belles Lettres, 1939.

Fisher, Walter R., ed. *Rhetoric: A Tradition in Transition.* East Lansing: Michigan State Univ. Pr., 1975.

Florescu, Vasile. *La Retorica nel suo sviluppo storico.* Bologna: Il Mulino, 1971.

Fontaine, Jacques. *Isidore de Séville et la culture classique dans l'Espagne wisigothique.* 2 vols. Paris: Etudes Augustiniennes, 1959.

Friedlander, Paul. *Plato, III: The Dialogues, Second and Third Periods.* Bollingen Series, 59. Princeton: Princeton Univ. Pr., 1969.

Gärtner, Bertil. *The Areopagus Speech and Natural Revelation.* Translated by Carolyn Hannay King. Uppsala: C. W. K. Gleerup, 1955.

Gigante, Marcella, ed. *Theodorus Metochites, Saggio critico su Demostene et Aristide.* Milan: Istituto editoriale cisalpino, 1969.

Golden, James L., and Corbett, Edward P. J. *The Rhetoric of Blair, Campbell, and Whately.* New York: Holt, Rinehart, and Winston, 1968.

Goodspeed, Edgar Johnson. *A History of Early Christian Literature.* Revised and enlarged by Robert M. Grant. Chicago: Univ. of Chicago Pr., 1966.

Gordan, Phyllis Walter Goodhart, ed. and trans. *Two Renaissance Book Hunters: The Letters of Poggius Bracciolini to Nicolaus de Niccolis.* Records of Civilization: Sources and Studies, 91. New York: Columbia Univ. Pr., 1966.

Grube, G. M. A. *The Greek and Roman Critics.* London: Methuen, 1965.

Gunebaum, G. E. von. *A Tenth-Century Document of Arabic Literary Theory and Criticism.* Chicago: Univ. of Chicago Pr., 1950.

Guthrie, W. K. C. *A History of Greek Philosophy.* 5 vols. to date. Cambridge: Cambridge Univ. Pr., 1969–1978.

Guy, Henry. *L'Ecole des rhétoriqueurs.* Bibliothèque littéraire de la renaissance, n.s. 4. Paris: Honoré Champion, 1910.

Haarhoff, Theodore. *Schools of Gaul: A Study of Pagan and Christian Education in the Last Century of the Western Empire.* London: Oxford Univ. Pr., 1920.

Hadot, Pierre. *Marius Victorinus: recherches sur sa vie et ses oeuvres.* Paris: Etudes Augustiniennes, 1971.

Halm, Karl, ed. *Rhetores Latini Minores.* Leipzig, 1863; reprinted Frankfurt: Minerva, 1964.

Hardison, Osborne Bennett, Jr. *The Enduring Monument: A Study of the Idea of Praise in Renaissance Literary Theory and Practice.* Chapel Hill: Univ. of North Carolina Pr., 1962.

Bibliography

Haskins, Charles Homer. *The Renaissance of the Twelfth Century*. Cambridge: Harvard Univ. Pr., 1927.

Havelock, Eric A., and Hershbell, Jackson. *Communication Arts in the Ancient World*. New York: Hastings House, 1978.

Hayes, John H., ed. *Old Testament Form Criticism*. San Antonio: Trinity Univ. Pr., 1974.

Hellwig, Antje. *Untersuchungen zur Theorie der Rhetorik bei Platon und Aristoteles*. Hypomnemata, 38. Göttingen: Vandenhoeck und Ruprecht, 1973.

Hertter, F. *Die Podestaliteratur Italiens im 12. und 13. Jahrhundert*. Leipzig and Berlin: Teubner, 1910.

Howell, Wilbur Samuel. *Eighteenth-Century British Logic and Rhetoric*. Princeton: Princeton Univ. Pr., 1971.

————. *Logic and Rhetoric in England, 1500–1700*. Princeton: Princeton Univ. Pr., 1956.

————, ed. and trans. *Fénelon's Dialogue on Eloquence*. Princeton: Princeton Univ. Pr., 1951.

————, ed. and trans. *The Rhetoric of Alcuin and Charlemagne*. With Latin text. Princeton: Princeton Univ. Pr., 1941.

Hubbell, Harry Mortimer. *The Influence of Isocrates on Cicero, Dionysius, and Aristides*. New Haven: Yale Univ. Pr., 1913.

Hume, David. *Philosophical Works, III: Essays, Moral, Political, and Literary*. Edited by T. H. Green and T. H. Grose. Aalen: Scientia Verlag, 1964.

Hunger, Herbert. *Die hochsprachliche profane Literatur der Byzantiner*, I: *Philosophie, Rhetorik, Epistolographie, Geschichtsschreibung, Geographie*. Handbuch der Altertumswissenschaft 12, no. 5, part 1. Munich: Beck, 1978.

Hussey, J. M. *Church and Learning in the Byzantine Empire, 867–1185*. London: Oxford Univ. Pr., 1937.

————, ed. *The Cambridge Medieval History, IV: The Byzantine Empire*. Cambridge: Cambridge Univ. Pr., 1966.

Ijsseling, Samuel. *Rhetoric and Philosophy in Conflict: An Historical Survey*. The Hague: Nijhoff, 1976.

Jaeger, Werner. *Paideia: The Ideals of Greek Culture*. Translated by Gilbert Highet. 3 vols. New York: Oxford Univ. Pr., 1939–1944.

————. *Early Christianity and Greek Paideia*. Cambridge: Harvard Univ. Pr., 1961.

Janson, Tore. *Prose Rhythm in Medieval Latin from the 9th to the 13th Century*. Stockholm: Almqvist and Wiksell International, 1975.

Jebb, R. C. *The Attic Orators from Antiphon to Isaeos*. 2 vols. London: Macmillan, 1893.

Jones, Leslie Webber, ed. and trans. *An Introduction to Divine and Human Readings by Cassiodorus Senator*. Records of Civilization: Sources and Studies, 40. New York: Columbia Univ. Pr., 1946.

Kapp, Ernst. *Greek Foundations of Traditional Logic*. New York: Columbia Univ. Pr., 1946.

Bibliography

Karlsson, Gustav. *Idéologie et cérémonial dans l'épistolographie byzantine.* Upsala: Studia Graeca Upsaliensia, 1962.

Kennedy, George. *The Art of Persuasion in Greece.* Princeton: Princeton Univ. Pr., 1963.

———. *The Art of Rhetoric in the Roman World.* Princeton: Princeton Univ. Pr., 1972.

———. *Quintilian.* Twayne World Authors Series. New York: Twayne Publishers, 1969.

King, Donald D., and Rix, H. David, trans. *Desiderius Erasmus of Rotterdam, On Copia of Words and Ideas.* Medieval Philosophical Texts in Translation, 12. Milwaukee: Marquette Univ. Pr., 1967.

Koller, H. *Die Mimesis in der Antike: Nachahmung, Darstellung, Ausdruck.* Berne: Francke, 1954.

Kristeller, Paul Oskar. *Renaissance Thought: The Classic, Scholastic, and Humanist Strains.* New York: Harper Torchbooks, 1961.

Kroll, Wilhelm. "Das Epicheirema." Akademie der Wissenschaften, Wien, philosophische-historische Klasse, *Sitzungsberichte* 216, no. 3. Vienna: Holder-Pichler-Tempsky, 1936.

———. "Rhetorik." *Paulys Real-Encyclopädie der classischen Altertumswissenschaft,* Supplementband 7, cols. 1039–1138. Stuttgart: Metzler, 1940.

Krumbacher, Karl. *Geschichte der byzantinische Literatur.* Munich: Beck, 1897; reprinted New York: B. Franklin, 1970.

Kustas, George L. *Studies in Byzantine Rhetoric.* Analecta Vlatadon, 17. Thessaloniki: Patriarchal Institute for Patristic Studies, 1973.

Laistner, M. L. W. *Thought and Letters in Western Europe, A.D. 500 to 900.* Ithaca: Cornell Univ. Pr., 1957.

Lausberg, Heinrich. *Handbuch der literarischen Rhetorik: eine Grundlegung der Literaturwissenschaft.* 2 vols. Munich: Max Hueber, 1960.

Lieberman, Saul. *Hellenism in Jewish Palestine: Studies in the Literary Transmission, Beliefs, and Manners of Palestine in the Ist Century BCE–IVth Century CE.* New York: Jewish Theological Seminary of America, 1962.

Lindberg, Gertrud. *Studies in Hermogenes and Eustathios: The Theory of Ideas and Its Application in the Commentaries of Eustathios on the Epics of Homer.* Lund: J. Lindell, 1977.

The Loeb Classical Library. Cambridge: Harvard Univ. Pr.; London: William Heinemann.

Lohmann, Dieter. *Die Komposition der Reden in der Ilias.* Berlin: De Gruyter, 1970.

McCall, Marsh. *Ancient Rhetorical Theories of Simile and Comparison.* Cambridge: Harvard Univ. Pr., 1969.

McCauley, Leo P., ed. and trans. *Funeral Orations by Saint Gregory Nazianzen and Saint Ambrose.* Washington, D.C.: Catholic Univ. of America Pr., 1953.

McGarry, Daniel D., ed. and trans. *The Metalogicon of John of Salisbury: A Twelfth Century Defense of the Verbal and Logical Arts of the Trivium.* Berkeley and Los Angeles: Univ. of California Pr., 1955.

Bibliography

Mango, Cyril, ed. and trans. *The Homilies of Photius, Patriarch of Constantinople.* Cambridge: Harvard Univ. Pr., 1958.

Manitius, Max. *Geschichte der lateinischen Literatur des Mittelalters.* Handbuch der Altertumswissenschaft, 9, no. 2. 3 vols. Munich: Beck, 1911–1931.

Marrou, Henri-Irénée. *A History of Education in Antiquity.* Translated by George Lamb. New York: Sheed and Ward, 1956.

————. *Saint Augustin et la fin de la culture antique.* Paris: E. de Boccard, 1938; reissued with "Retractatio," 1949.

Martin, Josef. *Antike Rhetorik: Technik und Methode.* Handbuch der Altertumswissenschaft 2, no. 3. Munich: Beck, 1974.

Meijer, Reinder P. *Literature of the Low Countries: A Short History of Dutch Literature in the Netherlands and Belgium.* Assen: Van Gorcum, 1971.

Miller, Joseph M.; Prosser, Michael H.; and Benson, Thomas W., eds. *Readings in Medieval Rhetoric.* Bloomington: Indiana Univ. Pr., 1973.

Momigliano, Arnaldo, ed. *The Conflict between Paganism and Christianity in the Fourth Century.* Oxford: Clarendon Pr., 1963.

Monfasani, John. *George of Trebizond: A Biography and a Study of His Rhetoric and Logic.* Columbia Studies in the Classical Tradition, 1. Leiden: Brill, 1976.

Monk, Samuel H. *The Sublime: A Study of Critical Theories in 18th Century England.* New York: Modern Language Association of America, 1935.

Murphy, James J. *Medieval Rhetoric: A Select Bibliography.* Toronto Medieval Bibliographies, 3. Toronto: Center for Medieval Studies, 1971.

————. *Rhetoric in the Middle Ages: A History of Rhetorical Theory From Saint Augustine to the Renaissance.* Berkeley and Los Angeles: Univ. of California Pr., 1974.

————, ed. *Medieval Eloquence: Studies in the Theory and Practice of Medieval Rhetoric.* Berkeley and Los Angeles: Univ. of California Pr., 1978.

————, ed. *Three Medieval Rhetorical Arts.* Berkeley and Los Angeles: Univ. of California Pr., 1971.

Norden, Eduard. *Agnostos Theos: Untersuchungen zur Formgeschichte religiöser Rede.* Stuttgart: Teubner, 1956.

————. *Die antike Kunstprose vom VI. Jahrhunderts vor Christus bis in die Zeit der Renaissance.* Leipzig: Teubner, 1909.

Oliver, Robert T. *Communication and Culture in Ancient India and China.* Syracuse: Syracuse Univ. Pr., 1971.

O'Malley, John W. *Praise and Blame in Renaissance Rome: Rhetoric, Doctrine, and Reform in the Sacred Orators of the Papal Court, c. 1450–1521.* Durham, N.C.: Duke Univ. Pr., 1979.

Ong, Walter J. *Ramus, Method, and the Decay of Dialogue: From the Art of Discourse to the Art of Reason.* Cambridge: Harvard Univ. Pr., 1958.

Ostrogorsky, Gregory. *History of the Byzantine State.* Edited and translated by J. M. Hussey. New Brunswick, N.J.: Rutgers Univ. Pr., 1969.

Paetow, Louis J. "The Arts Course at Medieval Universities with Special

Reference to Grammar and Rhetoric." *University of Illinois Studies* 3 (1910): 491–624.

Patterson, Annabel M. *Hermogenes and the Renaissance: Seven Ideas of Style.* Princeton: Princeton Univ. Pr., 1970.

Patterson, Warner Forrest. *Three Centuries of Poetic Theory.* Ann Arbor: Univ. of Michigan Pr., 1935.

Perelman, Chaim, and Olbrechts-Tyteca, L. *The New Rhetoric: A Treatise on Argumentation.* Translated by John Wilkinson and Purcell Weaver. Notre Dame, Ind.: Notre Dame Univ. Pr., 1969.

Pfeiffer, Rudolph. *History of Classical Scholarship: From the Beginnings to the End of the Hellenistic Age.* Oxford: Clarendon Pr., 1968.

————. *History of Classical Scholarship: From 1300 to 1850.* Oxford: Clarendon Pr., 1976.

Polak, Emil J. *A Textual Study of Jacques de Dinant's Summa Dictaminis.* Geneva: Droz, 1975.

Preminger, Alex, ed. *The Princeton Encyclopedia of Poetry and Poetics.* Princeton: Princeton Univ. Pr., 1965.

Rabe, Hugo, ed. *Prolegomenon Syllagoge.* Leipzig: Teubner, 1931.

Radermacher, Ludwig. "Artium Scriptores (Reste der voraristotelischen Rhetorik)." Akademie der Wissenschaften, Wien, philosophisch-historische Klasse, *Sitzungsberichte*, 217, no. 3. Vienna: Rudolf M. Rohrer, 1951.

Rand, Edward Kennard. *Founders of the Middle Ages.* Cambridge: Harvard Univ. Pr., 1928.

Riché, Pierre. *Education and Culture in the Barbarian West, Sixth through Eighth Centuries.* Translated by John J. Contreni. Columbia: Univ. of South Carolina Pr., 1976.

Roberts, W. Rhys, trans. *Dionysius of Halicarnassus, On Literary Composition.* London: Macmillan, 1910.

Rockinger, Ludwig. *Briefsteller und Formelbücher des eilften bis vierzehnten Jahrhunderts.* New York: B. Franklin, 1961.

Romilly, Jacqueline de. *Magic and Rhetoric in Ancient Greece.* Cambridge: Harvard Univ. Pr., 1975.

Ruether, Rosemary Radford. *Gregory of Nazianzus: Rhetor and Philosopher.* Oxford: Clarendon Pr., 1969.

Russell, Donald Andrew, and Winterbottom, Michael, eds. *Ancient Literary Criticism: The Principal Texts in New Translations.* Oxford: Clarendon Pr., 1972.

Scaglione, Aldo. *The Classical Theory of Composition from Its Origins to the Present: A Historical Survey.* Univ. of North Carolina Studies in Comparative Literature, 53. Chapel Hill: Univ. of North Carolina Pr., 1972.

Schmitz, Robert Morell. *Hugh Blair.* New York: King's Crown Pr., 1948.

Schwartz, Joseph, and Rycenga, John A. *The Province of Rhetoric.* New York: Ronald Pr., 1965.

Scott, Izora. *Controversies over the Imitation of Cicero as a Model for Style and Some Phases of Their Influence on the Schools of the Renaissance.* New York: Teachers College, Columbia Univ., 1910.

Seigel, Jerrold E. *Rhetoric and Philosophy in Renaissance Humanism: The*

Bibliography

Union of Eloquence and Wisdom, Petrarch to Valla. Princeton: Princeton Univ. Pr., 1968.

Sider, Robert Dick. *Ancient Rhetoric and the Art of Tertullian*. London: Oxford Univ. Pr., 1971.

Simon, Irène. *Neo-Classical Criticism, 1660–1800*. London: Edward Arnold, 1971.

Smith, Robert W. *The Art of Rhetoric in Alexandria*. The Hague: Mouton, 1974.

Sonnino, Lee A. *A Handbook to Sixteenth-Century Rhetoric*. London: Routledge and Kegan Paul, 1968.

Speck, Paul. *Die kaiserliche Universität von Konstantinopel*. Munich: Beck, 1974.

Sprague, Rosamond, ed. *The Older Sophists*. Columbia: Univ. of South Carolina Pr., 1972.

Stahl, William H.; Johnson, Richard; and Burge, E. L. *Martianus Capella and the Seven Liberal Arts*, I: *The Quadrivium of Martianus Capella with a Study of the Allegory and the Verbal Disciplines*; II: *The Marriage of Philology and Mercury*. Records of Civilization: Sources and Studies, 84. New York: Columbia Univ. Pr., 1971, 1977.

Stigen, Anfinn. *The Structure of Aristotle's Thought*. Oslo: Universitetsforlaget, 1966.

Stonehouse, Ned B. *The Areopagus Address*. London: Tyndale Pr., 1950.

Stump, Eleanore, ed. and trans. *Boethius's De Topicis Differentiis*. With Essays on the Text. Ithaca: Cornell Univ. Pr., 1978.

Taylor, Henry Osborn. *The Medieval Mind*. 2 vols. Cambridge: Harvard Univ. Pr., 1925.

Thompson, Craig R., ed. and trans. *Collected Works of Erasmus. Literary and Educational Writings* II: *De Copia, De Ratione Studii*. Toronto, Univ. of Toronto Pr., 1978.

Thyen, Hartwig. *Der Stil der Judisch-hellenistische Homilie*. Göttingen: Vandenhoeck und Ruprecht, 1955.

Untersteiner, Mario. *The Sophists*. Translated by Kathleen Freeman. Oxford: Basil Blackwell, 1953.

Vickers, Brian. *Classical Rhetoric in English Poetry*. London: Macmillan, 1970.

Volkmann, Richard. *Die Rhetorik der Griechen und Römer in systematischer Übersicht*. Leipzig: Teubner, 1885.

Wallace, Karl R. *Francis Bacon on Communication and Rhetoric*. Chapel Hill: Univ. of North Carolina Pr., 1943.

————, ed. *History of Speech Education in America: Background Studies*. New York: Appleton-Century-Crofts, 1954.

Wallach, Luitpold. *Alcuin and Charlemagne: Studies in Carolingian History and Literature*. Cornell Studies in Classical Philology, 32. Ithaca: Cornell Univ. Pr., 1959.

Walz, Christian, ed. *Rhetores Graeci*. 9 vols. London, 1832–1836; reprinted Osnabruck: Otto Zeller, 1968.

Ward, John. *A System of Oratory Delivered in a Course of Lectures Publicly*

Read at Gresham College. 2 vols. London, 1759; reprinted Hildesheim: G. Olms, 1969.

Watson, Foster, ed. and trans. *Vives on Education: A Translation of the De Tradendis Disciplinis*. Cambridge: Cambridge Univ. Pr., 1913.

Weinberg, Bernard. *A History of Literary Criticism in the Italian Renaissance*. Chicago: Univ. of Chicago Pr., 1961.

————, ed. *Trattati di poetica e retorica del cinquecento*. 4 vols. Bari: Giuseppe Laterza e Figli, 1970–1974.

Weiss, Johannes. *Beiträge zur paulinischen Rhetorik*. Göttingen: Vandenhoeck und Ruprecht, 1897.

Whately, Richard. *Elements of Rhetoric*. Edited with a Critical Introduction by Douglas Ehninger. Carbondale and Edwardsville: Southern Illinois Univ. Pr., 1963.

Wieruszowski, Helene. *Politics and Culture in Medieval Spain and Italy*. Rome: Edizione di Storia e Letteratura, 1971.

Wilder, Amos N. *The Language of the Gospel: Early Christian Rhetoric*. New York: Harper and Row, 1964.

Wilken, Robert L., ed. *Aspects of Wisdom in Judaism and Early Christianity*. South Bend, Ind.: Notre Dame Univ. Pr., 1975.

Wilson, Harold S., and Forbes, Clarence A., eds. *Gabriel Harvey's Ciceronianus*. University of Nebraska Studies in Humanities, 4. Lincoln: Univ. of Nebraska Pr., 1945.

Wilson, Nigel G., ed. *An Anthology of Byzantine Prose*. Berlin: de Gruyter, 1971.

Wilson, Thomas. *Arte of Rhetorique*. Edited by G. H. Mair. Oxford: Clarendon Pr., 1909.

Wirth, Peter. "Untersuchungen zur byzantinischen Rhetorik des zwölf Jahrhunderts mit besonderer Berucksichtgung der Schriften des Erzbischofs Eustathios von Thessalonike." Inaugural dissertation, Munich, 1960.

Witt, Ronald G. *Coluccio Salutati and His Public Letters*. Travaux d'humanisme et Renaissance, 15. Geneva: Droz, 1976.

Yates, Frances A. *The Art of Memory*. London: Routledge and Kegan Paul, 1966.

Index

Architecture, 6, 115
Areopagus, 28, 130
Argumentation, 25, 30, 31, 41, 62,
68–72, 93–95, 97, 126, 218, *See also*
Dialectic; Enthymeme; Proof;
Topics
Aristarchus, 117
Aristides, Aelius, 38, 39, 104, 164,
169, 171
Aristophanes of Byzantium, 116, 117
Aristotelian tradition in rhetoric, 37,
81–82, 92, 95, 189–90, 201
Aristotle, 60–85, 86, 96, 149, 166;
Categories, 83; esoteric works, 61;
Gryllus, 60–61; life of, 60; *Meta-
physics*, 62; *Nicomachean Ethics*,
62, 66, 77; *Organon*, 84, 166; *Poetics*, 56, 63, 66, 78, 115, 116, 205;
Politics, 65, 77; *Posterior Analytics*,
63; *Prior Analytics*, 63, 70, 207; in
Renaissance, 201, 217, 223, 229,
233, 234, 237, 240, 243; *Rhetoric*,
17, 19, 52, 57, 61–79, 82, 84, 111,
189 (influence of, 80–85, 189–90,
201, 204; Latin translations of,
174, 198, 201, 204); *Sophistical
Refutations*, 28, 83; *Synagoge
Technon*, 19, 61; teaches rhetoric,
52, 61; theory of causes, 62; theory
of knowledge, 216; *Topics*, 63, 65,
67, 68, 70, 76, 82–83, 178–79, 209;
in western Middle Ages, 189–90,
193
Arnauld, Antoine, 222
Arnobius, 146–47
Arrangement, 14, 72, 76, 77, 79, 88,
92, 97, 100, 112, 179, 192, 202, 206,
209, 210, 225
Ars arengandi, 187
Ars dictaminis. See *Dictamen*
Ars poetriae, 114, 188–89
Arts and sciences, 33, 62–63, 81–82,
115. *See also* Knowledge; Liberal
arts
Asianism, 86, 118, 136
Asinius Pollio, 111
Assos, 60

Athenagoras, 133
Attic Greek, 29, 34, 86, 118, 169
Atticism, 118–19, 140, 169, 231
Attic Orators, 117
Audience, 17, 72–75, 92, 109, 111,
145, 156, 218. *See also* Speaker,
speech, audience
Auerbach, Eric, 116
Augustine of Canterbury, 181
Augustine of Hippo, 6, 132, 135, 146,
149–60, 170, 177, 178, 180, 192, 205,
238, 244; *Against Cresconius*, 152;
Confessions, 5, 50, 149–52; *De
Civitate Dei*, 82, 159; *De Doctrina
Christiana*, 100, 104, 120, 127, 153–
60, 176, 179, 182, 184, 190, 223,
224, 225; *De Magistro*, 151–52; *De
Ordine*, 151; life, 149–51; spurious
handbook of rhetoric, 151
Aurispa, Giovanni, 199
Ausonius, 132, 173
Authority, 10, 12, 21, 72, 121–25, 126,
129, 151, 181, 182, 192

Bacon, Francis, 17, 62, 82, 215–19,
221, 224, 229, 243, 244
Bali, 7
Barbarism, 106
Barbaro, Francesco, 199
Bartholomeo of Messina, 189
Bary, René, 221
Barzizza, Gasparino, 202
Basel, 197, 205
Basil the Great, 39, 132, 143–45, 200
Bec, monastery of, 183, 188
Bede, 106, 181–82
Beirut, 140
Belles lettres, 222, 235–41
Bembo, Pietro, 214
Benedictines, 182
Bernard of Chartres, 188
Bernard of Clairvaux, 192
Bessarion, Cardinal, 200, 201
Bible. *See* New Testament; Old
Testament
Blackwell, Anthony, 267 (n.18)
Blair, Hugh, 24, 85, 102, 234–45, 243

George A. Kennedy, Paddison Professor of Classics, The University of North Carolina at Chapel Hill, is author of *The Art of Persuasion in Greece, Quintilian,* and *The Art of Rhetoric in the Roman World.*